T0131166

# Get the eBook FREE!

(PDF, ePub, Kindle, and liveBook all included)

We believe that once you buy a book from us, you should be able to read it in any format we have available. To get electronic versions of this book at no additional cost to you, purchase and then register this book at the Manning website.

Go to https://www.manning.com/freebook and follow the instructions to complete your pBook registration.

That's it!
Thanks from Manning!

*MLOps Engineering at Scale*

# MLOps Engineering
# at Scale

CARL OSIPOV

MANNING
SHELTER ISLAND

For online information and ordering of this and other Manning books, please visit
www.manning.com. The publisher offers discounts on this book when ordered in quantity.
For more information, please contact

Special Sales Department
Manning Publications Co.
20 Baldwin Road
PO Box 761
Shelter Island, NY 11964
Email: orders@manning.com

Manning Publications Co.
20 Baldwin Road
PO Box 761
Shelter Island, NY 11964

| | |
|---|---|
| Development editor: | Marina Michaels |
| Technical development editor: | Frances Buontempo |
| Review editor: | Mihaela Batinić |
| Production editor: | Deirdre S. Hiam |
| Copy editor: | Michele Mitchell |
| Proofreader: | Keri Hales |
| Technical proofreader: | Karsten Strøbaek |
| Typesetter: | Dennis Dalinnik |
| Cover designer: | Marija Tudor |

ISBN: 9781617297762
Printed in the United States of America

# brief contents

PART 1  MASTERING THE DATA SET .................................................. 1

    1 ■ Introduction to serverless machine learning  3

    2 ■ Getting started with the data set  15

    3 ■ Exploring and preparing the data set  38

    4 ■ More exploratory data analysis and
        data preparation  81

PART 2  PyTorch for serverless machine learning ......... 101

    5 ■ Introducing PyTorch: Tensor basics  103

    6 ■ Core PyTorch: Autograd, optimizers, and utilities  120

    7 ■ Serverless machine learning at scale  143

    8 ■ Scaling out with distributed training  162

PART 3  SERVERLESS MACHINE LEARNING PIPELINE ................. 189

    9 ■ Feature selection  191

   10 ■ Adopting PyTorch Lightning  213

   11 ■ Hyperparameter optimization  228

   12 ■ Machine learning pipeline  245

# contents

*preface xiii*
*acknowledgments xv*
*about this book xvii*
*about the author xxi*
*about the cover illustration xxii*

PART 1 MASTERING THE DATA SET ...................................1

1 **Introduction to serverless machine learning 3**

1.1 What is a machine learning platform? 5

1.2 Challenges when designing a machine learning platform 5

1.3 Public clouds for machine learning platforms 7

1.4 What is serverless machine learning? 8

1.5 Why serverless machine learning? 8

*Serverless vs. IaaS and PaaS 10 ▪ Serverless machine learning life cycle 11*

1.6 Who is this book for? 11

*What you can get out of this book 11*

1.7 How does this book teach? 12

1.8 When is this book not for you? 13

1.9 Conclusions 14

2   **Getting started with the data set   15**

2.1   Introducing the Washington, DC, taxi rides data set   16

*What is the business use case?   16 ▪ What are the business
rules?   16 ▪ What is the schema for the business service?   17
What are the options for implementing the business service?   18
What data assets are available for the business service?   19
Downloading and unzipping the data set   19*

2.2   Starting with object storage for the data set   20

*Understanding object storage vs. filesystems   21 ▪ Authenticating
with Amazon Web Services   22 ▪ Creating a serverless object
storage bucket   23*

2.3   Discovering the schema for the data set   26

*Introducing AWS Glue   26 ▪ Authorizing the crawler to
access your objects   27 ▪ Using a crawler to discover the
data schema   28*

2.4   Migrating to columnar storage for more efficient
analytics   31

*Introducing column-oriented data formats for analytics   31
Migrating to a column-oriented data format   33*

3   **Exploring and preparing the data set   38**

3.1   Getting started with interactive querying   39

*Choosing the right use case for interactive querying   39
Introducing AWS Athena   40 ▪ Preparing a sample data set   42
Interactive querying using Athena from a browser   43 ▪ Interactive
querying using a sample data set   44 ▪ Querying the DC taxi
data set   49*

3.2   Getting started with data quality   49

*From "garbage in, garbage out" to data quality   50 ▪ Before
starting with data quality   51 ▪ Normative principles for data
quality   52*

3.3   Applying VACUUM to the DC taxi data   58

*Enforcing the schema to ensure valid values   59 ▪ Cleaning up
invalid fare amounts   63 ▪ Improving the accuracy   66*

3.4   Implementing VACUUM in a PySpark job   74

*4* *More exploratory data analysis and data preparation* **81**

    4.1   Getting started with data sampling  82

        *Exploring the summary statistics of the cleaned-up data set*  *82*
        *Choosing the right sample size for the test data set*  *86* ▪ *Exploring*
        *the statistics of alternative sample sizes*  *88* ▪ *Using a PySpark job*
        *to sample the test set*  *92*

PART 2   PYTORCH FOR SERVERLESS MACHINE
           LEARNING ....................................................................101

*5* *Introducing PyTorch: Tensor basics*  **103**

    5.1   Getting started with tensors  104
    5.2   Getting started with PyTorch tensor creation
         operations  108
    5.3   Creating PyTorch tensors of pseudorandom
         and interval values  110
    5.4   PyTorch tensor operations and broadcasting  112
    5.5   PyTorch tensors vs. native Python lists  116

*6* *Core PyTorch: Autograd, optimizers, and utilities*  **120**

    6.1   Understanding the basics of autodiff  121
    6.2   Linear regression using PyTorch automatic
         differentiation  129
    6.3   Transitioning to PyTorch optimizers for gradient
         descent  132
    6.4   Getting started with data set batches for gradient
         descent  135
    6.5   Data set batches with PyTorch Dataset and
         DataLoader  136
    6.6   Dataset and DataLoader classes for gradient descent
         with batches  140

*7* *Serverless machine learning at scale*  **143**

    7.1   What if a single node is enough for my machine learning
         model?  144
    7.2   Using IterableDataset and ObjectStorageDataset  145
    7.3   Gradient descent with out-of-memory data sets  149

7.4   Faster PyTorch tensor operations with GPUs   154

7.5   Scaling up to use GPU cores   159

## 8  Scaling out with distributed training   162

8.1   What if the training data set does not fit in memory?   163

*Illustrating gradient accumulation   163   ▪   Preparing a sample model and data set   164   ▪   Understanding gradient descent using out-of-memory data shards   166*

8.2   Parameter server approach to gradient accumulation   169

8.3   Introducing logical ring-based gradient descent   170

8.4   Understanding ring-based distributed gradient descent   174

8.5   Phase 1: Reduce-scatter   176

8.6   Phase 2: All-gather   181

## PART 3   SERVERLESS MACHINE LEARNING PIPELINE .......189

## 9  Feature selection   191

9.1   Guiding principles for feature selection   192

*Related to the label   192   ▪   Recorded before inference time   194 Supported by abundant examples   196   ▪   Expressed as a number with a meaningful scale   197   ▪   Based on expert insights about the project   198*

9.2   Feature selection case studies   198

9.3   Feature selection using guiding principles   199

*Related to the label   199   ▪   Recorded before inference time   203 Supported by abundant examples   205   ▪   Numeric with meaningful magnitude   207   ▪   Bring expert insight to the problem   208*

9.4   Selecting features for the DC taxi data set   210

## 10  Adopting PyTorch Lightning   213

10.1   Understanding PyTorch Lightning   213

*Converting PyTorch model training to PyTorch Lightning   214 Enabling test and reporting for a trained model   221   ▪   Enabling validation during model training   223*

**11** *Hyperparameter optimization* 228

11.1 Hyperparameter optimization with Optuna 229

*Understanding loguniform hyperparameters 230 • Using categorical and log-uniform hyperparameters 231*

11.2 Neural network layers configuration as a hyperparameter 233

11.3 Experimenting with the batch normalization hyperparameter 235

*Using Optuna study for hyperparameter optimization 240 Visualizing an HPO study in Optuna 242*

**12** *Machine learning pipeline* 245

12.1 Describing the machine learning pipeline 246

12.2 Enabling PyTorch-distributed training support with Kaen 249

*Understanding PyTorch-distributed training settings 255*

12.3 Unit testing model training in a local Kaen container 257

12.4 Hyperparameter optimization with Optuna 259

*Enabling MLFlow support 264 • Using HPO for DcTaxiModel in a local Kaen provider 265 • Training with the Kaen AWS provider 269*

appendix A *Introduction to machine learning 273*
appendix B *Getting started with Docker 300*

*index 311*

# *preface*

A useful piece of feedback that I got from a reviewer of this book was that it became a "cheat code" for them to scale the steep MLOps learning curve. I hope that the content of this book will help you become a better informed practitioner of machine learning engineering and data science, as well as a more productive contributor to your projects, your team, and your organization.

In 2021, major technology companies are vocal about their efforts to "democratize" artificial intelligence (AI) by making technologies like deep learning more accessible to a broader population of scientists and engineers. Regrettably, the democratization approach taken by the corporations focuses too much on core technologies and not enough on the practice of delivering AI systems to end users. As a result, machine learning (ML) engineers and data scientists are well prepared to create experimental, proof-of-concept AI prototypes but fall short in successfully delivering these prototypes to production. This is evident from a wide spectrum of issues: from unacceptably high failure rates of AI projects to ethical controversies about AI systems that make it to end users. I believe that, to become successful, the effort to democratize AI must progress beyond the myopic focus on core, enabling technologies like Keras, PyTorch, and TensorFlow. *MLOps* emerged as a unifying term for the practice of taking experimental ML code and running it effectively in production. Serverless ML is the leading cloud-native software development model for ML and MLOps, abstracting away infrastructure and improving productivity of the practitioners.

I also encourage you to make use of the Jupyter notebooks that accompany this book. The DC taxi fare project used in the notebook code is designed to give you the practice you need to grow as a practitioner. Happy reading and happy coding!

# acknowledgments

I am forever grateful to my daughter, Sophia. You are my eternal source of happiness and inspiration. My wife, Alla, was boundlessly patient with me while I wrote my first book. You were always there to support me and to cheer me along. To my father, Mikhael, I wouldn't be who I am without you.

I also want to thank the people at Manning who made this book possible: Marina Michaels, my development editor; Frances Buontempo, my technical development editor; Karsten Strøbaek, my technical proofreader; Deirdre Hiam, my project editor; Michele Mitchell, my copyeditor; and Keri Hales, my proofreader.

Many thanks go to the technical peer reviewers: Conor Redmond, Daniela Zapata, Dianshuang Wu, Dimitris Papadopoulos, Dinesh Ghanta, Dr. Irfan Ullah, Girish Ahankari, Jeff Hajewski, Jesús A. Juárez-Guerrero, Trichy Venkataraman Krishnamurthy, Lucian-Paul Torje, Manish Jain, Mario Solomou, Mathijs Affourtit, Michael Jensen, Michael Wright, Pethuru Raj Chelliah, Philip Kirkbride, Rahul Jain, Richard Vaughan, Sayak Paul, Sergio Govoni, Srinivas Aluvala, Tiklu Ganguly, and Todd Cook. Your suggestions helped make this a better book.

# *about this book*

Thank you for purchasing *MLOps Engineering at Scale.*

## Who should read this book

To get the most value from this book, you'll want to have existing skills in data analysis with Python and SQL, as well as have some experience with machine learning. I expect that if you are reading this book, you are interested in developing your expertise as a machine learning engineer, and you are planning to deploy your machine learning–based prototypes to production.

This book is for information technology professionals or those in academia who have had some exposure to machine learning and are working on or are interested in launching a machine learning system in production. There is a refresher on machine learning prerequisites for this book in appendix A. Keep in mind that if you are brand new to machine learning you may find that studying both machine learning and cloud-based infrastructure for machine learning at the same time can be overwhelming.

If you are a software or a data engineer, and you are planning on starting a machine learning project, this book can help you gain a deeper understanding of the machine learning project life cycle. You will see that although the practice of machine learning depends on traditional information technologies (i.e., computing, storage, and networking), it is different from the traditional information technology in practice. The former is significantly more experimental and more iterative than you may have experienced as a software or a data professional, and you should be prepared for the outcomes to be less known in advance. When working with data, the machine learning practice is more like the scientific process, including forming hypotheses about data, testing alternative models to answer questions about the hypothesis, and ranking and choosing the best performing models to launch atop your machine learning platform.

If you are a machine learning engineer or practitioner, or a data scientist, keep in mind that this book is not about making you a better researcher. The book is not written to educate you about the frontiers of science in machine learning. This book also will not attempt to reteach you the machine learning basics, although you may find the material in appendix A, targeted at information technology professionals, a useful reference. Instead, you should expect to use this book to become a more valuable collaborator on your machine learning team. The book will help you do more with what you already know about data science and machine learning so that you can deliver ready-to-use contributions to your project or your organization. For example, you will learn how to implement your insights about improving machine learning model accuracy and turn them into production-ready capabilities.

## *How this book is organized: A road map*

This book is composed of three parts. In part 1, I chart out the landscape of what it takes to put a machine learning system in production, describe an engineering gap between experimental machine learning code and production machine learning systems, and explain how serverless machine learning can help bridge the gap. By the end of part 1, I'll have taught you how to use serverless features of a public cloud (Amazon Web Services) to get started with a real-world machine learning use case, prepare a working machine learning data set for the use case, and ensure that you are prepared to apply machine learning to the use case.

- Chapter 1 presents a broad view on the field on machine learning systems engineering and what it takes to put the systems in production.
- Chapter 2 introduces you to the taxi trips data set for the Washington, DC, municipality and teaches you how to start using the data set for machine learning in the Amazon Web Services (AWS) public cloud.
- Chapter 3 applies the AWS Athena interactive query service to dig deeper into the data set, uncover data quality issues, and then address them through a rigorous and principled data quality assurance process.
- Chapter 4 demonstrates how to use statistical measures to summarize data set samples and to quantify their similarity to the entire data set. The chapter also covers how to pick the right size for your test, training, and validation data sets and use distributed processing in the cloud to prepare the data set samples for machine learning.

In part 2, I teach you to use the PyTorch deep learning framework to develop models for a structured data set, explain how to distribute and scale up machine learning model training in the cloud, and show how to deploy trained machine learning models to scale with user demand. In the process, you'll learn to evaluate and assess the performance of alternative machine learning model implementations and how to pick the right one for the use case.

- Chapter 5 covers the PyTorch fundamentals by introducing the core tensor application programming interface (API) and helping you gain a level of fluency with using the API.
- Chapter 6 focuses on the deep learning aspects of PyTorch, including support for automatic differentiation, alternative gradient descent algorithms, and supporting utilities.
- Chapter 7 explains how to scale up your PyTorch programs by teaching about the graphical processing unit (GPU) features and how to take advantage of them to accelerate your deep learning code.
- Chapter 8 teaches about data parallel approaches for distributed PyTorch training and covers, in-depth, the distinction between traditional, parameter, server-based approaches and the ring-based distributed training (e.g., Horovod).

In part 3, I introduce you to the battle-tested techniques of machine learning practitioners and cover feature engineering, hyperparameter tuning, and machine learning pipeline assembly. By the conclusion of this book, you will have set up a machine learning platform that ingests raw data, prepares it for machine learning, applies feature engineering, and trains high-performance, hyperparameter-tuned machine learning models.

- Chapter 9 explores the use cases around feature selection and feature engineering, using case studies to build intuition about the features that can be selected or engineered for the DC taxi data set.
- Chapter 10 teaches how to eliminate boilerplate engineering code in your DC taxi PyTorch model implementation by adopting a framework called PyTorch Lightning. Also, the chapter navigates through the steps required to train, validate, and test your enhanced deep learning model.
- Chapter 11 integrates your deep learning model with an open-source hyperparameter optimization framework called Optuna, helping you train multiple models based on alternative hyperparameter values, and then ranking the trained models according to their loss and metric performance.
- Chapter 12 packages your deep learning model implementation into a Docker container in order to run it through the various stages of the entire machine learning pipeline, starting from the development data set all the way to a trained model ready for production deployment.

## About the code

You can access the code for this book from my Github repository: github.com/osipov/smlbook. The code in this repository is packaged as Jupyter notebooks and is designed to be used in a Linux-based Jupyter notebook environment. This means that you have options when it comes to how you can execute the code. If you have your own, local

Jupyter environment, for example, with the Jupyter native client (JupyterApp: https://github.com/jupyterlab/jupyterlab_app) or a Conda distribution (https://jupyter.org/install), that's great! If you do not use a local Jupyter distribution, you can run the code from the notebooks using a cloud-based service such as Google Colab or Binder. My Github repository README.md file includes badges and hyperlinks to help you launch chapter-specific notebooks in Google Colab.

I strongly urge you to use a local Jupyter installation as opposed to a cloud service, especially if you are worried about the security of your AWS account credentials. Some steps of the code will require you to use your AWS credentials for tasks like creating storage buckets, launching AWS Glue extract-transform-load (ETL) jobs, and more. The code for chapter 12 must be executed on node with Docker installed, so I recommend planning to use a local Jupyter installation on a laptop or a desktop where you have sufficient capacity to install Docker. You can find out more about Docker installation requirements in appendix B.

## liveBook discussion forum

Purchase of *MLOps for Engineering at Scale* includes free access to liveBook, Manning's online reading platform. Using liveBook's exclusive discussion features, you can attach comments to the book globally or to specific sections or paragraphs. It's a snap to make notes for yourself, ask and answer technical questions, and receive help from the author and other users.

To access the forum, go to https://livebook.manning.com/#!/book/mlops-engineering-at-scale/discussion. Be sure to join the forum and say hi! You can also learn more about Manning's forums and the rules of conduct at https://livebook.manning.com/#!/discussion.

Manning's commitment to our readers is to provide a venue where a meaningful dialogue between individual readers and between readers and the author can take place. It is not a commitment to any specific amount of participation on the part of the author, whose contribution to the forum remains voluntary (and unpaid). We suggest you try asking the author some challenging questions lest his interest stray! The forum and the archives of previous discussions will be accessible from the publisher's website as long as the book is in print.

# *about the author*

**CARL OSIPOV** has been working in the information technology industry since 2001, with a focus on projects in big data analytics and machine learning in multi-core, distributed systems, such as service-oriented architecture and cloud computing platforms. While at IBM, Carl helped IBM Software Group to shape its strategy around the use of Docker and other container-based technologies for serverless cloud computing using IBM Cloud and Amazon Web Services. At Google, Carl learned from the world's foremost experts in machine learning and helped manage the company's efforts to democratize artificial intelligence with Google Cloud and TensorFlow. Carl is an author of over 20 articles in professional, trade, and academic journals; an inventor with six patents at USPTO; and the holder of three corporate technology awards from IBM.

# about the cover illustration

The figure on the cover of *MLOps Engineering at Scale* is captioned "Femme du Thibet," or a woman of Tibet. The illustration is taken from a collection of dress costumes from various countries by Jacques Grasset de Saint-Sauveur (1757–1810), titled *Costumes de Différents Pays*, published in France in 1797. Each illustration is finely drawn and colored by hand. The rich variety of Grasset de Saint-Sauveur's collection reminds us vividly of how culturally apart the world's towns and regions were just 200 years ago. Isolated from each other, people spoke different dialects and languages. In the streets or in the countryside, it was easy to identify where they lived and what their trade or station in life was just by their dress.

The way we dress has changed since then and the diversity by region, so rich at the time, has faded away. It is now hard to tell apart the inhabitants of different continents, let alone different towns, regions, or countries. Perhaps we have traded cultural diversity for a more varied personal life—certainly for a more varied and fast-paced technological life.

At a time when it is hard to tell one computer book from another, Manning celebrates the inventiveness and initiative of the computer business with book covers based on the rich diversity of regional life of two centuries ago, brought back to life by Grasset de Saint-Sauveur's pictures.

# Part 1

# *Mastering the data set*

Engineering an effective machine learning system depends on a thorough understanding of the project data set. If you have prior experience building machine learning models, you might be tempted to skip this step. After all, shouldn't the machine learning algorithms automate the learning of the patterns from the data? However, as you are going to observe throughout this book, machine learning systems that succeed in production depend on a practitioner who understands the project data set and then applies human insights about the data in ways that modern algorithms can't.

# Introduction to serverless
# machine learning

*1*

## This chapter covers

- What serverless machine learning is and why you should care
- The difference between machine learning code and a machine learning platform
- How this book teaches about serverless machine learning
- The target audience for this book
- What you can learn from this book

A Grand Canyon–like gulf separates experimental machine learning code and production machine learning systems. The scenic view across the "canyon" is magical: when a machine learning system is running successfully in production it can seem prescient. The first time I started typing a query into a machine learning–powered autocomplete search bar and saw the system anticipate my words, I was hooked. I must have tried dozens of different queries to see how well the system worked. So, what does it take to trek across the "canyon?"

It is surprisingly easy to get started. Given the right data and less than an hour of coding time, it is possible to write the experimental machine learning code and re-create the remarkable experience I have had using the search bar that predicted my words. In my conversations with information technology professionals, I find that many have started to experiment with machine learning. Online classes in machine learning, such as the one from Coursera and Andrew Ng, have a wealth of information about how to get started with machine learning basics. Increasingly, companies that hire for information technology jobs expect entry-level experience with machine learning.[1]

While it is relatively easy to experiment with machine learning, building on the results of the experiments to deliver products, services, or features has proven to be difficult. Some companies have even started to use the word *unicorn* to describe the unreasonably hard-to-find machine learning practitioners with the skills needed to launch production machine learning systems. Practitioners with successful launch experience often have skills that span machine learning, software engineering, and many information technology specialties.

This book is for those who are interested in trekking the journey from experimental machine learning code to a production machine learning system. In this book, I will teach you how to assemble the components for a machine learning platform and use them as a foundation for your production machine learning system. In the process, you will learn:

- How to use and integrate public cloud services, including the ones from Amazon Web Services (AWS), for machine learning, including data ingest, storage, and processing
- How to assess and achieve data quality standards for machine learning from structured data
- How to engineer synthetic features to improve machine learning effectiveness
- How to reproducibly sample structured data into experimental subsets for exploration and analysis
- How to implement machine learning models using PyTorch and Python in a Jupyter notebook environment
- How to implement data processing and machine learning pipelines to achieve both high throughput and low latency
- How to train and deploy machine learning models that depend on data processing pipelines
- How to monitor and manage the life cycle of your machine learning system once it is put in production

Why should you invest the time to learn these skills? They will not make you a renowned machine learning researcher or help you discover the next ground-breaking machine learning algorithm. However, if you learn from this book, you can prepare yourself to deliver the results of your machine learning efforts sooner and more productively, and grow to be a more valuable contributor to your machine learning project, team, or organization.

---

[1]  If you need or would like a refresher on machine learning basics, there is a section about the topic in appendix A.

## 1.1    What is a machine learning platform?

If you have never heard of the phrase "yak shaving" as it is used in the information technology industry,[2] here's a hypothetical example of how it may show up during a day in a life of a machine learning practitioner:

> *My company wants our machine learning system to launch in a month . . . but it is taking us too long to train our machine learning models . . . so I should speed things up by enabling graphical processing units (GPUs) for training . . . but our GPU device drivers are incompatible with our machine learning framework . . . so I need to upgrade to the latest Linux device drivers for compatibility . . . which means that I need to be on the new version of the Linux distribution.*

There are many more similar possibilities in which you need to "shave a yak" to speed up machine learning. The contemporary practice of launching machine learning–based systems in production and keeping them running has too much in common with the yak-shaving story. Instead of focusing on the features needed to make the product a resounding success, too much engineering time is spent on apparently unrelated activities like re-installing Linux device drivers or searching the web for the right cluster settings to configure the data processing middleware.

Why is that? Even if you have the expertise of machine learning PhDs on your project, you still need the support of many information technology services and resources to launch the system. "Hidden Technical Debt in Machine Learning Systems," a peer-reviewed article published in 2015 and based on insights from dozens of machine learning practitioners at Google, advises that mature machine learning systems "end up being (at most) 5% machine learning code" (http://mng.bz/01jl).

This book uses the phrase "machine learning platform" to describe the 95% that play a supporting yet critical role in the entire system. Having the right machine learning platform can make or break your product.

If you take a closer look at figure 1.1, you should be able to describe some of the capabilities you need from a machine learning platform. Obviously, the platform needs to ingest and store data, process data (which includes applying machine learning and other computations to data), and serve the insights discovered by machine learning to the users of the platform. The less obvious observation is that the platform should be able to handle multiple, concurrent machine learning projects and enable multiple users to run the projects in isolation from each other. Otherwise, replacing only the machine learning code translates to reworking 95% of the system.

## 1.2    Challenges when designing a machine learning platform

How much data should the platform be able to store and process? AcademicTorrents .com is a website dedicated to helping machine learning practitioners get access to public data sets suitable for machine learning. The website lists over 50 TB of data

---

[2]  The phrase is thought to have originated at the MIT AI Lab in the 1990s (see http://mng.bz/m1Pn).

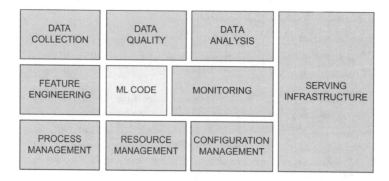

**Figure 1.1**  Although machine learning code is what makes your machine learning system stand out, it amounts to only about 5% of the system code according to the experiences described in "Hidden Technical Debt in Machine Learning Systems" by Google's Sculley et al. Serverless machine learning helps you assemble the other 95% using cloud-based infrastructure.

sets, of which the largest are 1–5 TB in size. Kaggle, a website popular for hosting data science competitions, includes data sets as large as 3 TB. You might be tempted to ignore the largest data sets as outliers and focus on more common data sets that are at the scale of gigabytes. However, you should keep in mind that successes in machine learning are often due to reliance on larger data sets. "The Unreasonable Effectiveness of Data," by Peter Norvig et al. (http://mng.bz/5Zz4), argues in favor of the machine learning systems that can take advantage of larger data sets: "simple models and a lot of data trump more elaborate models based on less data."

A machine learning platform that is expected to operate on a scale of terabytes to petabytes of data for storage and processing must be built as a distributed computing system using multiple inter-networked servers in a cluster, each processing a part of the data set. Otherwise, a data set with hundreds of gigabytes to terabytes will cause out-of-memory problems when processed by a single server with a typical hardware configuration. Having a cluster of servers as part of a machine learning platform also addresses the input/output bandwidth limitations of individual servers. Most servers can supply a CPU with just a few gigabytes of data per second. This means that most types of data processing performed by a machine learning platform can be sped up by splitting up the data sets in chunks (sometimes called *shards*) that are processed in parallel by the servers in the cluster. The distributed systems design for a machine learning platform as described is commonly known as *scaling out*.

A significant portion of figure 1.1 is the serving part of the infrastructure used in the platform. This is the part that exposes the data insights produced by the machine learning code to the users of the platform. If you have ever had your email provider classify your emails as spam or not spam, or if you have ever used a product recommendation feature of your favorite e-commerce website, you have interacted as a user with the serving infrastructure part of a machine learning platform. The serving infrastructure for a major email or an e-commerce provider needs to be capable of making the decisions for millions of users around the globe, millions of times a second. Of course, not every machine learning platform needs to operate at this scale. However, if you are planning to deliver a product based on machine learning, you need to keep in mind that it is within the realm of possibility for digital products and services to reach hundreds of millions of users in months. For example, Pokemon Go, a machine learning–powered video game from Niantic, reached half a billion users in less than two months.

Is it prohibitively expensive to launch and operate a machine learning platform at scale? As recently as the 2000s, running a scalable machine learning platform would have required a significant upfront investment in servers, storage, networking as well as software and the expertise needed to build one. The first machine learning platform I worked on for a customer back in 2009 cost over $100,000 USD and was built using on-premises hardware and open source Apache Hadoop (and Mahout) middleware. In addition to upfront costs, machine learning platforms can be expensive to operate due to waste of resources: most machine learning code underutilizes the capacity of the platform. As you know, the training phase of machine learning is resource-intensive, leading to high utilization of computing, storage, and networking. However, trainings are intermittent and are relatively rare for a machine learning system in production, translating to low average utilization. Serving infrastructure utilization varies based on the specific use case for a machine learning system and fluctuates based on factors like time of day, seasonality, marketing events, and more.

## 1.3    *Public clouds for machine learning platforms*

The good news is that public cloud-computing infrastructure can help you create a machine learning platform and address the challenges described in the previous section. In particular, the approach described in this book will take advantage of public clouds from vendors like Amazon Web Services, Microsoft Azure, or Google Cloud to provide your machine learning platform with:

1   Secure isolation so that multiple users of your platform can work in parallel with different machine learning projects and code
2   Access to information technologies like data storage, computing, and networking when your projects need them and for as long as they are needed
3   Metering based on consumption so that your machine learning projects are billed just for the resources you used

This book will teach you how to create a machine learning platform from public cloud infrastructure using Amazon Web Services as the primary example. In particular, I will teach you:

- How to use public cloud services to cost effectively store data sets regardless of whether they are made of kilobytes of terabytes of data
- How to optimize the utilization and cost of your machine learning platform computing infrastructure so that you are using just the servers you need
- How to elastically scale your serving infrastructure to reduce the operational costs of your machine learning platform

## 1.4   What is serverless machine learning?

**Serverless machine learning** is a model for the software development of machine learning code written to run on a machine learning platform hosted in a cloud-computing infrastructure with consumption-based metering and billing.

If a machine learning system runs on a server-based cloud-computing infrastructure, why is this book about *serverless* machine learning? The idea of using servers from a public cloud for a machine learning platform clearly contradicts the premise of server*less*. Machine learning without servers? How is that even possible?

Before you object to the use of the word *serverless* in the definition, keep in mind that information technology professionals working with cloud-computing platforms have adopted serverless as a moniker to describe an approach to using cloud computing, including computing, storage, and networking, as well as other cloud resources and services, in a way that helps them spend their time more effectively, improve their productivity, and optimize costs. Serverless does not mean without servers; it means that when using a serverless approach a developer can ignore the existence of servers in a cloud provider and focus on writing code.

Serverless, as it is used in this book, describes an approach for building machine learning systems that enables the machine learning practitioners to spend as much of their time as possible on writing machine learning code and to spend as little of their time as possible on managing and maintaining the computing, storage, networking, and operating systems; middleware; or any other parts of the underlying information technology needed to host and run the machine learning platform. Serverless machine learning also delivers on a key idea for cost optimization in cloud-computing: consumptive billing. This means that with serverless machine learning, you are billed just for the resources and services that you use.

*Machine learning*, as used in academia as well as in the information technology industry, covers a broad spectrum of algorithms and systems, including those that defeated top human players at the ancient board game of Go, won on the TV show *Jeopardy*, and generated deep-fake images of the world's celebrities and leaders. This book focuses on a specific subfield of machine learning known as supervised learning with structured (tables of rows and columns) data. If you are worried that this subfield is too narrow, note that over 80% of production machine learning systems implemented and used at various stages of maturity at Google, arguably the leader in adopting machine learning, are built using supervised learning from structured data sets.

## 1.5   Why serverless machine learning?

Prior to serverless machine learning, developers involved in getting machine learning code to run in production had to either work in concert with team members from an operations organization or take on the operations role themselves (this is known in the industry as DevOps). The responsibility of the development role included writing the machine learning code, for example, the code to perform inference, such as estimating a house sales price from real estate property records. Once the code was ready, the developers packaged it, typically as part of a machine learning framework such as PyTorch (more about PyTorch in part 2) or along with external code libraries so that it could be executed as an application (or a microservice) on a server, as shown in figure 1.2.

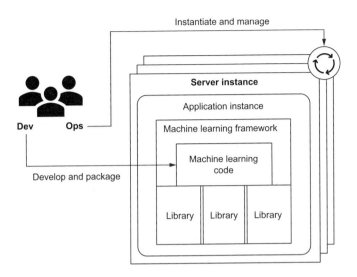

**Figure 1.2   Before serverless platforms, most cloud-based machine learning platforms relied on infrastructure-as-a-service (IaaS) or platform-as-a-service (PaaS) service models, illustrated in the figure. Both IaaS and PaaS require an operations role responsible for instantiating infrastructure: server-based, in the case of IaaS, or application-based, in the case of PaaS. Operations are also responsible for managing the life cycle of the infrastructure once it is running.**

The operations role involved instantiating the infrastructure required to run the code while ensuring the infrastructure had the appropriate capacity (memory, storage, bandwidth). The role also was responsible for configuring the server infrastructure with the operating system, middleware, updates, security patches, and other prerequisites. Next, operations started the execution of the developer's code as one or more application instances. After the code was up and running, operations managed the execution of the code, ensuring that requests were serviced with high availability (i.e., reliably) and low latency (i.e., responsively). Operations were also called to help reduce costs by optimizing infrastructure utilization. This meant continuously monitoring the levels of CPU, storage, network bandwidth, and service latency in order to change the infrastructure capacity (e.g., de-provision servers) and achieve target utilization goals.

Cloud-computing service models such as IaaS replaced physical servers with virtual servers and thus made operations more productive: it took significantly less time and effort to provision and de-provision virtual servers than physical ones. The operations were further automated in the cloud with features such as auto-scaling, which automatically provisioned and de-provisioned virtual servers depending on near-real-time measurements of CPU, memory, and other server-level metrics. PaaS, a more abstract cloud service model, further reduced the operation overhead with virtual servers pre-configured for code execution runtimes, along with pre-installed middleware and operating systems.

While cloud-computing service models like IaaS and PaaS worked well for the serving infrastructure part of machine learning platforms, they fell short elsewhere. While performing exploratory data analysis as preparation for training, a machine learning engineer may execute dozens of different queries against data before settling on the right one. In IaaS and PaaS models, this means that the infrastructure handling data analysis queries needs to be provisioned (sometimes by the operations team) even before the first query can execute. To make matters worse, the utilization of the provisioned infrastructure is entirely at a whim of the user. In an extreme example, if the machine learning engineer runs just one data analysis query a day and it takes 1 hour to execute, the data analysis infrastructure can end up idle while still incurring costs for the other 23 hours of the day.

### 1.5.1   *Serverless vs. IaaS and PaaS*

In contrast, the serverless approach illustrated in figure 1.3 helps further optimize the utilization and costs of the machine learning platform. Serverless platforms eliminate the need for performing traditional operations tasks. With serverless machine learning, the machine learning platform takes over the entire life cycle of the machine learning code, instantiating and managing it. This is accomplished by the platform hosting a dedicated runtime for different programming languages and functions. For example, a service runtime exists to execute Python code for running machine learning model training, another to execute SQL code for structured data queries, and more.

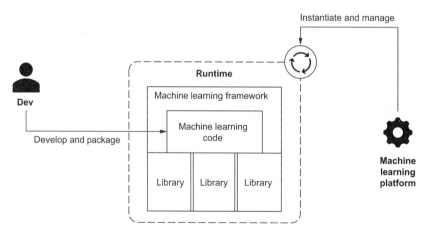

**Figure 1.3   Serverless platforms eliminate the need for operations to manage the life cycle of the code infrastructure. The cloud-based platform is responsible for instantiating the code in runtime to service requests and for managing the infrastructure to ensure high availability, low latency, and other performance characteristics.**

The most impactful consequence of using serverless as opposed to IaaS or PaaS models is cost. With both IaaS and PaaS models, public cloud vendors bill based on provisioned capacity. In contrast, with serverless models, it is possible to optimize machine learning platform costs based on whether the code is actually executed on the platform.

Serverless and machine learning exist at the intersection of two information technologies. On one hand, machine learning opens the potential for new products, new features, or even re-invented industries based on capabilities that previously didn't exist in the marketplace. On the other hand, serverless models strike the balance between productivity and customization, enabling developers to focus on building differentiating capabilities while reusing existing components from cloud-computing platforms. The serverless approach is more than a re-use of black box components. It is about rapidly assembling project-specific machine learning platforms that can be customized with code to enable the development of new products and services.

### 1.5.2 Serverless machine learning life cycle

Machine learning–based systems become more valuable when they can operate at scale, making frequent and repetitive decisions about data while supporting a large quantity of users. To get a sense of machine learning operating at this scale, think about your email provider classifying emails as spam or not spam for millions of emails every second and for millions of concurrent users around the globe. Alternatively, consider product recommendations ("If you bought this, you may also like that") from a major e-commerce website.

While machine learning–based systems grow more valuable at larger scales, just like with any software project, they should still work efficiently when they are small, and if successful, scale for growth. Yet most software projects don't become overnight successes and don't grow to reach billions of users. Although this can sound expensive from a cost perspective, the serverless part in serverless machine learning, in this book, is about ensuring your project can benefit from the original promise of public cloud computing: paying only for what you use, no more and no less.

## 1.6 Who is this book for?

The serverless machine learning approach described in this book is targeted at teams and individuals who are interested in building and implementing a machine learning system that may need to be scaled up to a potentially large number of users and large quantity of requests and data volumes, but that also needs to scale down when necessary to stay cost efficient. Even if you decide against using machine learning algorithms in a project, you can still use this book to learn about how serverless and cloud computing can help you manage, process, and analyze data.

### 1.6.1 What you can get out of this book

If you are planning to put a machine learning system in production, at some point you have to decide whether to buy or to build the supporting 95%, in other words, the components of a machine learning platform. The examples, such as the ones from

"Hidden Technical Debt in Machine Learning Systems," include the serving infrastructure, data collection, verification, storage, monitoring, and more.

If you plan to build most or all of your machine learning platform, you can approach this book as a series of design use cases or inspirational examples from a sample machine learning project. The book demonstrates how the platform capabilities are implemented in cloud-computing platforms from various public cloud vendors, including AWS, Google Cloud, and Microsoft Azure. The book will also teach you about the features you will need for the machine learning platform, including object storage, data warehousing, interactive querying, and more. Whenever possible, the book will highlight the open source projects you can use in your platform buildout. While this book will not give you the step-by-step instructions for how to build your machine learning platform, you can use it as a case study and a guide for the components of the architecture that you should be building.

If you are planning to acquire most of the machine learning platform capabilities, the book gives you the instructions and walks you through the process for how to build a sample machine learning project and then put it into production using Amazon Web Services. The book will also walk you through the implementation steps for a machine learning platform, including the source code needed for the project. Whenever possible, the approach in this book relies on portable open source technologies such as Docker (more about Docker in appendix B) and PyTorch (more about PyTorch in part 2) that will ease the process of porting the project to other cloud providers such as Google Cloud and Microsoft Azure.

## 1.7    *How does this book teach?*

The field of machine learning exists at the intersection of computer science and statistics. So, it should come as no surprise that there are alternative routes for introducing a reader to the applications of machine learning. Many information technology professionals began their studies of machine learning with the well-known Coursera class by Andrew Ng (https://www.coursera.org/learn/machine-learning). Those with a statistical or academic background often cite *An Introduction to Statistical Learning* by James et al. (Springer, 2013), as their first textbook on machine learning.

This book takes a software engineering approach to machine learning. This means that for the purposes of this book, *machine learning* is the practice of building software-based systems with the defining ability to automatically derive answers from data in order to augment, and often replace, the need for humans in repetitive data-driven decision making. The focus on software engineering also means that the details of the machine learning algorithms, techniques, and statistical foundations will be covered with less rigor compared to how they are treated by the other sources mentioned. Instead, this book will focus on describing how to engineer production-ready systems that have machine learning–based features at their core.

## 1.8    *When is this book not for you?*

Based on everything you've read so far, you may develop a mistaken impression that serverless machine learning is suitable to every application of machine learning. So, when does it make sense to use serverless machine learning? I will be the first to admit that it does not apply in every circumstance. If you are working on an experimental, one-of-a-kind project, one that is limited in scope, size, or duration, or if your entire working data set is and always will be small enough to fit in memory of a virtual server, you should reconsider using serverless machine learning. You are probably better off with an approach with a dedicated single virtual server (single node) and a Jupyter notebook in an Anaconda installation, Google Colaboratory, or a similar Jupyter notebook hosting environment.

The serverless approach does help optimize the costs related to running a machine learning project on a public cloud; however, this does not mean that re-implementing the project from this book is free of charge. To get the most from this book, you will want to use your AWS account to reproduce the examples described in the upcoming chapters. To do so you will need to spend about $45 USD to re-create the project by following the steps described in the book. However, to benefit from the book, you don't need to stick to AWS. Whenever possible, this book will make references to alternative capabilities from other vendors such as Google Cloud and Microsoft Azure. The good news is that this book's entire project can be completed within the free credit allowances available from the three major public cloud vendors. Alternatively, if you choose not to implement code examples or the project from this book in a public cloud, you can also rely on the descriptions to get a conceptual understanding of what it takes to launch a machine learning system at scale.

Keep in mind that you should not use the approach in this book if you are not prepared to maintain your system after it is put into production. The reality is that the serverless approach integrates with the capabilities of the public cloud platforms, such as AWS, and those capabilities, specifically their APIs and endpoints, change over time. While the public cloud vendors have an approach for providing you with some stability for those endpoints (e.g., managed phaseout plans), you should be prepared for vendors to introduce new features and changes that, in turn, mean you should be prepared to invest time and effort in maintaining your features over time. If you need to minimize and control the extent of maintainability, the serverless approach is not for you.

Privacy concerns could give rise to another host of reasons to avoid using a public cloud-based infrastructure for your project. Although most public cloud providers offer sophisticated encryption key-based data security mechanisms, and have features to help meet data privacy needs, in a public cloud you can achieve a high degree of certainty in data privacy but not necessarily a complete guarantee that your data and processes will be secure. With that said, this book does not teach you how to ensure 100% security for your data in the cloud, how to provide authentication and authorization, nor how handle other types of security concerns for the machine learning systems described in the book. Whenever possible, I provide references that can help you with security, but it is outside the scope of this book to teach you the security aspects of data and privacy.

From a portability standpoint, the approach described in this book tries to strike the balance between ideal code portability and the need to minimize the amount of effort needed to deploy a machine learning project. If portability is the overriding concern for you, you will be better off attempting a different approach. For example, you can rely on complex infrastructure management stacks, such as Kubernetes or Terraform, for infrastructure deployment and runtime management. You should also not use the serverless machine learning approach if you are determined to use a proprietary framework or technology that is incompatible with the stack used in this book. The book will attempt to use nonproprietary, portable, and open source tools whenever possible.

## 1.9    Conclusions

What problems can this book solve for the reader, and what value can the reader get out of it? The contemporary practice of machine learning sucks too much productivity out of a machine learning practitioner. This book teaches the reader to work efficiently though a sample machine learning project. Instead of navigating the maze of alternatives for a machine learning platform, risking mistakes or failure, this book teleports the reader right to the well-trodden path of experienced machine learning practitioners. Instead of having to rediscover the practices of machine learning yourself, you can use this book to take advantage of the capabilities that work well for the requirements of the vast majority of machine learning projects.

This book is for someone who already has some experience with machine learning because it does not teach machine learning from scratch. The book focuses on practical, pragmatic understanding of machine learning and provides you with just enough knowledge to understand and complete the sample project. By the end of the book, you will have completed your machine learning project, deployed it to a machine learning platform on a public cloud, made your system available as a highly available web service accessible to anyone on the internet, and prepared for the next steps of ensuring the system's long-term success.

### Summary

- Successful machine learning systems consist of about 5% machine learning code. The rest is the machine learning platform.
- Public cloud-computing infrastructure enables cost-effective scalability for a machine learning platform.
- Serverless machine learning is a model for the software development of machine learning code that is written to run on a machine learning platform hosted in a cloud-computing infrastructure.
- Serverless machine learning can help you develop new products and services by rapidly assembling a machine learning system.
- This book will help you navigate the path from experimental machine learning code to a production machine learning system running in a public cloud.

# *Getting started with the data set*

**This chapter covers**

- Introducing a use case for machine learning
- Starting with object storage for serverless machine learning
- Using crawlers to automatically discover structured data schemas
- Migrating to column-oriented data storage for more efficient analytics
- Experimenting with PySpark extract-transform-load (ETL) jobs

In the previous chapter, you learned about serverless machine learning platforms and some of the reasons they can help you build a successful machine learning system. In this chapter, you will get started with a pragmatic, real-world use case for a serverless machine learning platform. Next, you are asked to download a data set of a few years' worth of taxi rides from Washington, DC, to build a machine learning model for the use case. As you get familiar with the data set and learn about the steps for using it to build a machine learning model, you are introduced to the key technologies that are a part of a serverless machine learning platform, including object storage, data crawlers, metadata catalogs, and distributed data processing (extract-transform-load) services. By the conclusion of the chapter, you will also see examples with code and shell commands that illustrate how these technologies can be used with Amazon Web Services (AWS) so that you can apply what you learned in your own AWS account.

## 2.1 Introducing the Washington, DC, taxi rides data set

This section dives into the details of the business domain and the business rules for the taxicab industry in Washington, DC. You might be tempted to skip these details; after all, they are probably irrelevant to the data sets you are planning to use in your machine learning projects. However, I encourage you to treat this section as a case study illustrating the kinds of questions you should ask about any business domain where you are planning to apply machine learning. As you explore the business use case in this section, you can learn more about the factors behind the DC taxi trips data and better prepare for building a machine learning model.

### 2.1.1 What is the business use case?

Imagine that you are a machine learning engineer working for a plucky startup planning to launch an autonomous, driverless car to take over the ride-sharing industry and outmaneuver companies like Waymo, Uber, and Lyft. Your business leadership decided that the first market your service will launch in is Washington, DC. Since your startup wants to offer prices that are competitive with regular taxis, you have been asked to write some code to estimate how much it costs a passenger to take a regular taxi from one location to another within the boundaries of Washington, DC, and the nearby areas of Virginia and Maryland.

### 2.1.2 What are the business rules?

The business rules for calculating the Washington, DC, taxi fares are available on the web from dc.gov.[1] The rules are as follows:

- The charge for the first 1/8 of a mile is $3.50.
- Each additional 1/8 of a mile is charged at $0.27, which adds up to $2.16 per mile.
- A special duration-based charge is $25 per hour and is accrued in 1-minute increments.

The duration-based charge applies to situations when the cab is in a traffic jam so that the fare amount continues to increase over time. The dc.gov website also lists additional special charges (e.g., for snow emergency days), but let's ignore them for now.

---

[1]  January 2018 archive.org snapshot of the taxi fares: http://mng.bz/6m0G.

### 2.1.3    What is the schema for the business service?

For a more concrete specification of the taxi fare estimation service interface, a software engineer could define the data types for the input and output values as shown in table 2.1. The interface expects an input consisting of pickup and drop-off locations (each in terms of a pair of latitude and longitude coordinates), as well as a timestamp with an expected start time of the trip. The output of the service is just the dollar amount of the estimated taxi fare. The values provided in table 2.1 as examples apply to a short, half-mile taxi trip, which costs about $6.12. Due to the fixed charge of $3.50 for the first 1/8 of the mile, and $0.81 for the remaining 3/8 distance ($0.27 * 3), the remaining $1.81 is likely due to the taxi spending time in midday heavy traffic on a Monday in a busy area of downtown DC.

**Table 2.1    Schema and example values for a taxi fare estimation service interface**

| Input | | |
|---|---|---|
| **Name** | **Data Type** | **Example Value** |
| Pickup location latitude | FLOAT[a] | 38.907243 |
| Pickup location longitude | FLOAT | –77.042754 |
| Drop-off location latitude | FLOAT | 38.90451 |
| Drop-off location longitude | FLOAT | –77.048813 |
| Expected start time of the trip | TIMESTAMP[b] | 01/12/2015 12:42 |

| Output | | |
|---|---|---|
| **Name** | **Data Type** | **Example Value** |
| Estimated fare (dollars) | FLOAT | 6.12 |

a.  The schema data types are illustrated using the ANSI SQL format.
b.  The timestamp is stored as a string using the month/day/year hour:minute format.

The latitude and longitude coordinates of the trip from table 2.1 correspond to a pickup address of 1814 N St. NW and a drop-off address of 1100 New Hampshire Ave. NW in Washington, DC. Note that the service does not perform any geocoding; in other words, the service expects pickup and drop-off locations as latitude and longitude coordinates instead of human-readable addresses like 1100 New Hampshire Ave. NW. Of course, a user of your service is not expected to type in the latitude and longitude values of the coordinates. Instead, the user can be prompted to visually drop pins for pickup and drop-off locations on a map in your mobile application. The latitude and longitude of the dropped pins can then be used directly with the service. Alternatively, there are geocoding features available from Google Maps and similar services, but they are outside the scope of this book.

### 2.1.4   *What are the options for implementing the business service?*

The trip from the example in table 2.1 is based on just one of many possible taxi routes in the DC area. For the purposes of the taxi fare estimation service, a taxi trip can take place across any pickup and drop-off location, as long as both are within the diamond-shaped boundary, which includes the entirety of Washington, DC, as well as the nearby areas of Maryland and Virginia. The area on the interactive map (https://osm.org/go/ZZcaT9__–) includes all possible pickup and drop-off locations for the DC taxi trips in this book. A user of your startup's mobile application could place pickup and drop-off pins within the area boundary to get back an estimated price for the trip.

Before diving into the implementation of a machine learning project for estimating the taxi fare, consider the traditional software engineering approach for building the fare estimation service. A software engineer (assume they are unfamiliar with machine learning) may start by developing code to use business rules for calculating the fare and by integrating the code with a route planning application programming interface (API) from a service such as Google Maps or Bing Maps. Both APIs can calculate the shortest driving route from one location to another and estimate the distance as well as the duration for the route. The actual route the taxi driver takes and the duration of the trip can vary based on traffic, road closures, weather, and other factors, but this approach provides a reasonable estimate of the distance. Next, the distance returned by the API can be combined with the business rules to calculate the estimated taxi fare.

The traditional software engineering approach to building the taxi fare estimation service has several advantages. The service is straightforward to implement, even for a junior software engineer. There is a large pool of engineers worldwide with the skills to deliver the implementation. Once implemented, the service should produce accurate estimates, except in the extreme cases where the taxi rides are impacted by unusual traffic, weather, or emergency events.

However, for a startup, relying on a route-planning service can be expensive. Services like Google Maps charge per API request to perform route planning and calculate distances, and to choose a route based on traffic. The costs of these services can quickly add up. Also, keep in mind the additional costs of the users of your service, who will estimate the price of a trip without actually taking the ride. While a larger company could explore the option of developing an on-premises, internal deployment of a route-planning service by building on open source data software or by purchasing a license from a vendor, the cost of doing so is prohibitive for a startup.

Instead of relying on traditional software engineering to build the taxi fare estimation service, in this book you are introduced to a machine learning approach implemented using the serverless capabilities of AWS.

### 2.1.5    *What data assets are available for the business service?*

The Office of the Chief Technology Officer for Washington, DC, maintains a website that hosts data from taxi rides that took place within the DC-area boundaries.[2] In this book, you will use this historical data set of the taxi rides from 2015 through 2019 to build machine learning models to estimate how much it costs to travel by taxi around DC. The key advantage of the machine learning approach is that it will not depend on an expensive external service for route planning and distance calculations. The model will learn from the taxi rides data to estimate the fares based on taxi trips taken across different locations in DC.

Later in the book, you will also deploy the models to AWS as a web service with an internet-accessible API for taxi fare predictions. The service will process HTTP (hyper-Text transfer protocol) requests containing geographic coordinates of the pickup and drop-off locations and will return the estimated taxi fare. The service's API will also take into account the start time of the trip so that the model can correctly adjust the predicted fare. For example, fares for multiple trips across the same pickup and drop-off locations will vary depending on the time of the day (rush hour versus middle of the night), day of the week (weekday versus weekend), and even day of the year (holi-day versus workday).

You are also going to observe that the machine learning approach can be adapted with minimal changes as your service expands to support other geographi-cal areas. Instead of hardcoding city-specific business rules for every city where your startup wants to launch, you can simply extend the data set with data about taxi trips in other cities.

### 2.1.6    *Downloading and unzipping the data set*

Start with the data set by downloading and unzipping the files from opendata.dc.gov.[3] Once the files are downloaded, you should be able to confirm that you have the data for years 2015 through 2019, with a separate zip file for each year. Note that the data set for 2019 is limited to the data from January through June. After you unzip the files, the entire data set should take up to 12 GiB of disk space.

> **NOTE**    After unzipping the files, the contents of the data set get placed into separate subdirectories. Before proceeding, move all the files from the data set to a single directory. Don't worry about overwriting the README_DC_ Taxicab_trip.txt file; there is an identical copy of this file for every year of the data set.

The instructions in this book assume that you are using the bash (or similar) shell in Linux or MacOS as your shell environment. Once you have downloaded and unzipped

---

[2]  Catalog of DC taxi rides from 2015 through 2019: http://mng.bz/o8nN.
[3]  Catalog of DC taxi rides from 2015 through 2019: http://mng.bz/o8nN.

the files, you should be able to confirm that the data set occupies roughly 12 GiB on your disk using the du command from your shell:

```
du -cha --block-size=1MB
```

resulting in the output that starts with the following.

<br/>

**Listing 2.1   Unzipped files of the DC taxi trips data set from 2015 to 2019**

```
8.0K     ./README_DC_Taxicab_trip.txt
176K     ./taxi_2015_01.txt
 60M     ./taxi_2015_02.txt
151M     ./taxi_2015_03.txt
190M     ./taxi_2015_04.txt
302M     ./taxi_2015_05.txt
317M     ./taxi_2015_06.txt

...

11986    total
```

For brevity, the output of the du command in listing 2.1 omits most of the files in the data set, replacing them with the ellipsis. The entire listing is available as a Github Gist (http://mng.bz/nrov).

Inside the zip files, the data is packaged as a collection of text files (with a ".txt" extension) that use the | (pipe) character to separate columns within each row. It is common for machine learning practitioners to refer to such files as *pipe-delimited comma-separated values* (CSVs). Although this industry terminology is confusing, I will keep with the practice of using the acronym CSV for this data format throughout the book.

The CSV files for the DC taxi data set contain a header row, meaning that the first row of every file has string labels for every column, for example MILEAGE, FAREAMOUNT, and others. The remaining rows in the files are the records of the taxi trips, one trip per row. Every zip file also contains an identical copy of the README_DC_Taxicab_trip.txt file, which provides some additional documentation for the data asset. The key parts of the documentation are covered later in this chapter.

## 2.2    *Starting with object storage for the data set*

This section introduces you to the first serverless capability from the machine learning project in this book. You are going to build on what you know about traditional filesystems to start learning about serverless object storage. Next, you are going to use a command line interface for AWS to create a serverless object storage location for the DC taxi data set and start to copy your CSV files to the location. You are going to become acquainted with using public cloud object storage for your machine learning data sets and complete the transfer of the DC taxi data set to object storage for further processing.

This section and the rest of the book will use examples based on Simple Storage Service (S3) from AWS to explain how serverless object storage can help you with machine learning projects. However, you should know that other public cloud vendors, such as Google Cloud and Microsoft Azure, offer similar capabilities.

### 2.2.1 Understanding object storage vs. filesystems

There are many similarities between filesystems and object storage, so you will find it easier to understand object storage if you start by focusing on the differences (table 2.2). Recall that filesystems are designed to store mutable, or changeable, data in a named location. This means that with a filesystem you can open a file, navigate to any line or a byte location in the file, change as many or as few bytes as you would like, and then save the changes back to the filesystem. Since files in a filesystem are mutable, after you make the change the original data is gone and is replaced on the storage medium (for example, on a solid-state drive) with your changes.

Table 2.2 While both filesystems and object storage services have similar features such as hierarchies of folders and support common operations such as copy, delete, and move, there are some important differences, as highlighted in this table.

| File system/Files | Serverless object storage/Objects |
|---|---|
| Mutable | Immutable |
| Lack globally unique names | Can be globally identified using a URL |
| Data redundancy across multiple storage devices | Data redundancy across multiple availability zones (data centers) and multiple storage devices |

In contrast, objects in object storage are immutable. Once you have created an object in object storage, it stores exactly the data that was placed in the object when it was created. You can create a new version of an object with your changes, but as far as the object storage service is concerned, the new version is an additional object occupying additional storage space. Of course, you can also delete an entire object, freeing up the storage space.

Unlike files, objects in serverless object storage services like AWS S3 are designed to be accessible on the internet using the HTTP protocol. By default, public internet access to objects is disabled. However, any object in serverless object storage can be made available via a public URL. To support this capability, object storage services organize objects into *buckets* (known as *containers* in Azure), which are named locations with globally unique identifiers. Every object in object storage must exist within a bucket, either directly or under some hierarchical, folder-like name structure. For example, if <guid> is a globally unique identifier name for an S3 bucket, an object named dataset could be accessible via a URL directly from the S3 bucket using https://<guid>.us-east-2.amazonaws.com/dataset or under a folder named "2015" within the bucket using https://<guid>.us-east-2.amazonaws.com/2015/dataset.

The "us-east-2" portion of the object URL from the example is due to another difference between traditional filesystems and object storage. Unlike filesystems that rely on multiple storage devices within the same physical server for data redundancy,[4] object storage providers like AWS replicate data across both multiple storage devices and multiple physical data centers called *availability zones*. A redundant cluster of availability zones within a metropolitan area, interconnected by a high bandwidth and a low latency network, is called a *region*. The "us-east-2" part of the object URL specifies an AWS-specific code name for a region storing the object.

Why should you use serverless object storage for the DC taxi rides data set and for the taxi fare estimation service? For the purposes of your machine learning project, with serverless object storage you will not have to worry about running out of storage space. Services like S3 can help you scale from gigabyte- to petabyte-sized data sets. As you recall from the definition of serverless in chapter 1, using serverless object storage ensures that you won't have any storage infrastructure to manage, and you will be charged based on the amount of data you keep in your storage bucket. Also, since object storage can provide an HTTP-based interface to the stored objects, it takes less effort to access and to integrate with the data that you have stored.

## 2.2.2 *Authenticating with Amazon Web Services*

The remaining examples in this chapter depend on AWS services. If you are planning to run the code from the examples, you should have the AWS Software Development Kit (SDK) installed, and you should know your AWS account's access and secret keys. The details of the SDK installation are available from the AWS documentation (https://docs.aws.amazon.com/cli).

If you don't have your AWS access and secret keys available, you can generate a new pair by navigating to the AWS management console (https://console.aws.amazon .com/), clicking on your user name in the upper right-hand corner drop-down menu, and choosing "My Security Credentials." To create a new pair of keys, click on the "Create access key" button.

The instructions in this book assume that you have your shell configured with AWS environment variables using

```
export AWS_ACCESS_KEY_ID=███████████████████████████
export AWS_SECRET_ACCESS_KEY=███████████████████████████
```

before running any of the commands that depend on the AWS SDK.

> **NOTE**   In this book, all of the listings replace sensitive account-specific information with a sequence of ■ characters. Take care to use your account-specific values for AWS access and secret keys.

---

[4]  A redundant array of independent disks is used to ensure data redundancy in server hardware: http://mng.bz/v4ax.

To verify that you have specified valid values for the environment variables `AWS_ACCESS_KEY_ID` and `AWS_SECRET_ACCESS_KEY` you can run

```
aws sts get-caller-identity
```

which, in the case of a successful authentication with AWS, should return your `UserId`, `Account`, and `Arn`[5] values:

```
{
    "UserId": "█████████████████████████",
    "Account": "███████████████",
    "Arn": "arn:aws:iam::██████████████████:user/█████████████"
}
```

### 2.2.3 *Creating a serverless object storage bucket*

This section walks you through the steps for creating an S3 bucket and uploading your DC taxi data files as objects to the bucket (figure 2.1). The steps in this section are completed using the command line interface (CLI) for AWS, but if you prefer, you can complete the same sequence of steps using the graphical user interface of the AWS management console (https://console.aws.amazon.com). This book focuses on the CLI-based approach because it allows for the steps to be easily explained, tested, and re-used as part of a script-based automation.

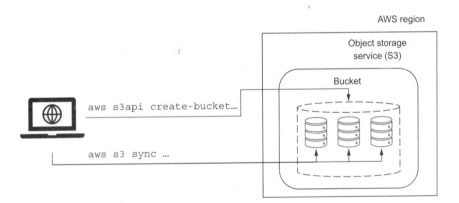

Figure 2.1 **To transfer the DC taxi data set to object storage in AWS, you are going to create an S3 bucket using the** `aws s3api create-bucket` **command specifying the region and a globally unique identifier for the bucket. Next, you are going to use** `aws s3 sync` **to upload the data set files to a folder named "csv" in the bucket.**

The selection of the region (and as a consequence of the location) for the bucket is important for low latency access to the data stored in the bucket. Going forward, you

---

[5] Amazon Resource Name (ARN) is an AWS-specific, globally unique identifier for resources, including user IDs and accounts in AWS. You can learn more about ARNs from http://mng.bz/4KGB.

should remember to run any of the code that processes your data from the same region you placed your S3 bucket. This section assumes that you will be using the us-east-2 region to store the data set.

To export the setting for the AWS_DEFAULT_REGION variable, which is going to be used to specify the default region of the bucket, run

```
export AWS_DEFAULT_REGION=us-east-2
echo $AWS_DEFAULT_REGION
```

which should print back your chosen value for the bucket region.

Since bucket names are supposed to be globally unique, it makes no sense for this book to publish a fixed and identical bucket name in the code listing. Instead, listing 2.2 uses the $RANDOM environment variable, which always returns a pseudorandom value. The value is then hashed using the MD5 hash function to a unique identifier consisting of a sequence of numbers and characters. The BUCKET_ID variable is then set to the value of the first 32 characters of the hash string, as returned by the output of the cut command.

Listing 2.2   **Using a pseudorandom generator for a likely unique value of the bucket ID**

```
export BUCKET_ID=$(echo $RANDOM | md5sum
  | cut -c -32)        ⊲── Use the first 32 characters of an MD5
                            hash of the Linux pseudorandom
echo $BUCKET_ID             number generator.
```

**NOTE**  If you are running the commands in listing 2.2 using Mac OSX or BSD, you may need to use md5 instead of md5sum.

At this point, you should have exported the environment variables specifying the globally unique identifier (in BUCKET_ID) and the region (in AWS_DEFAULT_REGION) for the bucket.

Before creating the bucket, run

```
aws sts get-caller-identity
```

to ensure that your shell is still configured with valid values for the environment variables, AWS_ACCESS_KEY_ID and AWS_SECRET_ACCESS_KEY, required to authenticate with AWS.

Notice that the following command, which creates the bucket, uses the aws s3api instead of the aws s3 you may have expected. This is for compatibility with the legacy, fine-grained AWS CLI features that were made available prior to the introduction of aws s3 commands.

**NOTE**  If you would like to use us-east-1 (the Northern Virginia region) instead of us-east-2, you need to drop the LocationConstraint argument to the aws s3api create-bucket command.

Create the bucket

```
aws s3api create-bucket --bucket dc-taxi-$BUCKET_ID-$AWS_DEFAULT_REGION \
--create-bucket-configuration LocationConstraint=$AWS_DEFAULT_REGION
```

and confirm that the command returns a result similar to the following JavaScript object notation (JSON) response, using your values for the BUCKET_ID and AWS_ DEFAULT_REGION environment variables in place of the ■ characters:

```
{
"Location": "http:/dc-taxi-
████████████████████████████████████-████████████.s3
➥ .amazonaws.com/"
}
```

Although the response to the aws s3api create-bucket command returns an HTTP URL for the bucket, you will usually refer to the bucket by an AWS specific naming scheme that starts with the s3:// prefix. If you lose track of the name you can recreate it using

```
echo s3://dc-taxi-$BUCKET_ID-$AWS_DEFAULT_REGION.
```

You can also use the AWS CLI list-buckets command to print out all the buckets that exist in your AWS account; however, the printed names will not use the s3:// prefix:

```
aws s3api list-buckets
```

The list-buckets command can provide you with a second confirmation that the bucket was created successfully. Once you know that the bucket was created, change the present working directory of your shell to the directory containing the data set files from listing 2.1.

Next, use the aws s3 sync command to replicate the data set files to the bucket. The command recursively transfers new and modified files to or from a location in an S3 bucket. While running, the command relies on multiple threads to speed up the transfer.

Transfer the CSV files from your local working directory to a csv folder in your bucket using

```
aws s3 sync . s3://dc-taxi-$BUCKET_ID-$AWS_DEFAULT_REGION/csv/
```

The time that it takes to transfer the data depends on the bandwidth you have available. In most cases, you should expect that it will take over 10 minutes, so this is a good point to take a break and resume once the transfer is over.

After the sync command completes, you can confirm that the data set files are stored under the csv folder in the bucket using the aws s3 ls command. Just as with

Unix-like operating systems, the `ls` command in S3 lists the contents of a folder. Try running the following:

```
aws s3 ls --recursive --summarize \
--human-readable s3://dc-taxi-$BUCKET_ID-$AWS_DEFAULT_REGION/csv/
```

Notice that you have transferred 11.2 GiB of CSV files to your object storage bucket. This quantity of data transferred to the bucket should match the size of the data set contents from listing 2.1.

After the files have been uploaded to the object storage, they are available for download and processing; however, the data is not yet distinguishable from unstructured binary large objects (BLOBs). To catalog the data structure in the CSV files, you are going to have to crawl the files and discover the data schema.

## 2.3    Discovering the schema for the data set

At this point, you have created a csv folder in your object storage bucket and have transferred the DC taxi data set consisting of 11.2 GiB worth of CSV files to the folder. Before starting with the analysis of the files, it is important to identify and understand the data set's schema. While it is possible to discover the data set schema manually, for example, by searching the opendata.dc.gov website for the schema specification or by exploring the contents of the CSV files directly, an automated approach can simplify and accelerate the process of schema discovery. In this section, you will learn about a data crawler service that can help you automate schema discovery for your data sets so you can better keep up with schema changes in your data. You are also going to crawl the CSV files of the DC taxi data set and persist the schema of the data set in a data catalog.

### 2.3.1    Introducing AWS Glue

Glue is as an umbrella name for a toolkit of different AWS services that you can use to prepare your data set for analysis. In this book, you will learn about the Glue data catalog, Glue extract-transform-load (data processing) jobs, and the Glue library for distributed data processing.

The Glue data catalog is a metadata repository designed to store information about data assets, data schemas, and data provenance. The data catalog consists of one or more databases, which exist to organize a collection of tables together. Since Glue databases and tables are designed to store metadata, your project data must exist in storage outside of Glue. For example, Glue tables can store schema for data stored in object storage, relational (for example MySQL or PostgreSQL), or NoSQL databases.

In addition to data schemas, Glue tables maintain information about the time when the schema was inferred from the data, as well as some basic statistics about the data, such as the number of objects from object storage used to store the data, the number of rows in the data, and the average amount of space occupied by a row in object storage.

While it is possible to manually create a table in the Glue database, in this section you will learn about using a Glue crawler to create a table automatically. If you are familiar with the term *crawler* in the context of web search engines, keep in mind that Glue crawlers are different. They are designed to process and analyze structured data formats rather than web pages. A Glue crawler is a process that

1  Establishes a connection to a storage location with structured data (e.g., to an object storage bucket)
2  Identifies the format used by the data (e.g., CSV)
3  Analyzes the data to infer the data schema, including the various column data types, such as integers, floating point numbers, and strings

Crawlers can be scheduled to periodically recrawl the data, so if the schema of your data changes over time, a crawler will be able to detect that change the next time it runs and update the schema in a table.

To create a crawler, you need to provide a crawler configuration that specifies one or more targets, in other words, the unique identifiers specifying storage locations with the data that should be processed by the crawler. In addition, a crawler in AWS must assume a security role to access the data in the crawler configuration target. The cloud providers like AWS require you to create a security identity, known as a *role*, whenever an application, service, or a process (e.g., an AWS Glue crawler) is accessing cloud resources on your behalf.

### 2.3.2  *Authorizing the crawler to access your objects*

Prior to creating a crawler for the DC taxi data, you should complete the steps in listing 2.3 to create a role called `AWSGlueServiceRole-dc-taxi`. The `aws iam create-role` command (listing 2.3 ❶), creates the role with a policy document that permits the Glue service (glue.amazonaws.com) to assume the `AWSGlueServiceRole-dc-taxi` security role as specified by the `sts:AssumeRole` permission. In short, the policy document specifies that the Glue crawler should use the `AWSGlueServiceRole-dc-taxi` role.

> **Listing 2.3  Allowing AWS Glue crawler to access the files in your object storage bucket**

```
aws iam create-role \
  --path "/service-role/" \
  --role-name AWSGlueServiceRole-dc-taxi          ◁──┐  Create a security role named
  --assume-role-policy-document '{                  ❶  AWSGlueServiceRole-dc-taxi.
  "Version": "2012-10-17",
  "Statement": [
    {
      "Effect": "Allow",
      "Principal": {
        "Service": "glue.amazonaws.com"
      },
```

```
      "Action": "sts:AssumeRole"
    }
  ]
}'
aws iam attach-role-policy \                          ② Attach the AWS Glue policy
  --role-name AWSGlueServiceRole-dc-taxi \               to the AWSGlueServiceRole-
  --policy-arn arn:aws:iam::aws:policy/service-role/AWSGlueServiceRole   dc-taxi role.

aws iam put-role-policy \
  --role-name AWSGlueServiceRole-dc-taxi \            Assign a policy document
  --policy-name GlueBucketPolicy \                     to AWSGlueServiceRole-
  --policy-document '{                                 dc-taxi to enable crawling
    "Version": "2012-10-17",                        ③ of the data set S3 bucket.
    "Statement": [
      {
        "Effect": "Allow",
        "Action": [
          "s3:*"
        ],
        "Resource": [
          "arn:aws:s3:::dc-taxi-'$BUCKET_ID'-'$AWS_DEFAULT_REGION'/*"
        ]
      }
    ]
}'
```

The aws iam attach-role-policy command (listing 2.3 ②) attaches an existing service role defined by AWS Glue (AWSGlueServiceRole) to the AWSGlueServiceRole-dc-taxi role. Attaching the role ensures that the AWSGlueServiceRole-dc-taxi role can access Glue databases and tables and perform other required operations with AWS resources. The details of the AWSGlueServiceRole specification are available from the AWS documentation (http://mng.bz/XrmY).

The aws iam put-role-policy command (listing 2.3 ③) specifies that the AWSGlueServiceRole-dc-taxi role is allowed to access the contents of the object storage bucket you created and populated with the DC taxi CSV files earlier in this chapter.

### 2.3.3  *Using a crawler to discover the data schema*

In this section you will create a database and a crawler in Glue, configure the crawler to process the DC taxi data, and run the crawler to populate the database with a table containing the data schema. You have the option of using a browser interface to AWS[6] to complete these steps. However, listing 2.4 and upcoming listings in this chapter will explain the CLI-based commands to create a Glue database and a crawler, and to start the crawler to discover the DC taxi data schema.

---

[6] AWS Glue user interface is available from https://console.aws.amazon.com/glue.

In listing 2.4 **❶**, the aws glue create-database command creates the Glue metadata database named dc_taxi_db, which is going to be used to store a schema for the DC taxi data set along with a table based on the schema.

**Listing 2.4  Creating a database and confirming the database exists**

```
aws glue create-database --database-input '{
  "Name": "dc_taxi_db"
}'

aws glue get-database --name 'dc_taxi_db'
```

◁── **Create the database ❶ named dc_taxi_db.**

◁── **Confirm the database named ❷ dc_taxi_db was created.**

Since it is a process, a Glue crawler cycles through a sequence of states. Once a crawler is created successfully, it begins its existence in a READY state. After is it started, the crawler transitions to a RUNNING state. While in a RUNNING state, it establishes a connection to a storage location specified in the crawler configuration. Based on the crawler configuration, the crawler identifies what locations in storage are included or excluded from processing and uses the data in the locations to infer the data schema. The RUNNING state often takes the longest period of time for the crawler to complete because it is the state in which the crawler is doing most of the work. Next, the crawler transitions to a STOPPING state to populate a Glue data catalog table with the schema and other metadata discovered during the process. Assuming that the process completes successfully, the crawler returns to a READY state.

**Listing 2.5  Creating and starting a Glue crawler**

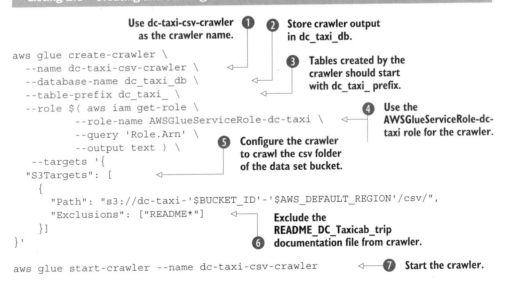

**Use dc-taxi-csv-crawler ❶ as the crawler name.**

**❷ Store crawler output in dc_taxi_db.**

**❸ Tables created by the crawler should start with dc_taxi_ prefix.**

```
aws glue create-crawler \
  --name dc-taxi-csv-crawler \
  --database-name dc_taxi_db \
  --table-prefix dc_taxi_ \
  --role $( aws iam get-role \
        --role-name AWSGlueServiceRole-dc-taxi \
        --query 'Role.Arn' \
        --output text ) \
  --targets '{
  "S3Targets": [
    {
      "Path": "s3://dc-taxi-'$BUCKET_ID'-'$AWS_DEFAULT_REGION'/csv/",
      "Exclusions": ["README*"]
    }]
}'

aws glue start-crawler --name dc-taxi-csv-crawler
```

**❹ Use the AWSGlueServiceRole-dc-taxi role for the crawler.**

**❺ Configure the crawler to crawl the csv folder of the data set bucket.**

**Exclude the README_DC_Taxicab_trip ❻ documentation file from crawler.**

◁──❼ **Start the crawler.**

In listing 2.5, the crawler is created using dc-taxi-csv-crawler ❶ and is configured to store the metadata discovered during the crawling process in the dc_taxi_db database. The crawler is also configured to use a table prefix of dc_taxi_ for any tables created by the crawler in the database.

Notice that the command specified by listing 2.5 ❹, is more complex than other shell commands you have encountered in this chapter. In bash, a command enclosed in $( ) characters are evaluated first, and the output of the evaluation is used in the original command. So, the aws iam get-role command nested in $( ) is used to find out the Amazon resource name (Arn) for the role you created in listing 2.3.

In listing 2.5 ❺, the crawler is configured to crawl the csv folder in the object storage bucket where you uploaded the DC taxi data files, taking care to ignore objects with a README prefix ❻.

Finally, dc-taxi-csv-crawler is started using the aws glue start-crawler command per listing 2.5 ❼.

In case of the DC taxi data set, the crawling process should take just over a minute. To monitor the state of the crawler, you can use the AWS management console from your browser, or run the following command to print out the state of the crawler:

```
aws glue get-crawler --name dc-taxi-csv-crawler --query 'Crawler.State' \
--output text
```

While the crawler is running, the state should be running. As soon as the crawler is done it should change to ready.

**NOTE** To print a refreshed state of the crawler every two seconds, you can type in "watch" before the aws glue get-crawler command.

Once the crawler returns to the READY state, you can find out whether the crawl succeeded using

```
aws glue get-crawler --name dc-taxi-csv-crawler --query 'Crawler.LastCrawl'
```

The last crawl details requested by the --query 'Crawler.LastCrawl' argument include a status message indicating whether the last run of the crawler succeeded or failed.

Assuming the crawler completed successfully, you can list the column names and the column data types of the schema discovered by the crawler using

```
aws glue get-table --database-name dc_taxi_db --name dc_taxi_csv.
```

Notice that the table name "dc_taxi_csv" was automatically assigned by the crawler based on the combination of the crawler table prefix from listing 2.5 ❷, and the csv folder name in the crawled bucket, as specified by ❸ in listing 2.5.

Keep in mind that you can also view the schema printed by the aws glue get-table command using your browser by navigating to the Glue service in AWS,[7]

---

[7] AWS Glue user interface is available from https://console.aws.amazon.com/glue.

choosing "Data Catalog > Databases > Tables" on the left sidebar, and clicking on the dc_taxi_csv table on the right.

At this point, your project has progressed beyond treating the DC taxi data as a collection of BLOBs and created a more detailed specification for the structure of the data, enumerating the data columns and their data types. However, the CSV data format you have been using so far is poorly suited for efficient and scalable analysis. In the upcoming sections of this chapter, you will learn how you can modify your data format to reduce latency for your analytical data queries.

## 2.4 *Migrating to columnar storage for more efficient analytics*

In the next chapter of this book, you will learn about an interactive query service that can help you query the DC taxi data set using the table and data schema you discovered with the Glue crawler. However, as explained in this section, analytical queries against row-oriented data storage formats such as CSV are inefficient when working with large data sets. Although you could dive into the analysis of the DC data set right away, this section is going to first introduce you to the benefits of using column-oriented (columnar) data storage formats like Apache Parquet instead of CSV for analytics. After explaining the advantages and disadvantages of column-oriented formats, the remainder of the section will cover another serverless capability of AWS for distributed data processing using PySpark (Apache Spark). By the conclusion of the section, you will learn an example of a typical PySpark job that can help you re-encode your CSV files into the Parquet format so that in the upcoming chapters you can analyze the data set faster and more efficiently.

### 2.4.1 *Introducing column-oriented data formats for analytics*

The CSV data format used by the DC taxi data set is an example of a row-oriented format. With CSV files, every line in a file stores a single row of data from the structured data set. Row-oriented data formats (illustrated on the left side of figure 2.2) are commonly used by traditional relational databases to store sequences of data records. The row-oriented format works well for transactional workloads that are typical for relational databases. Transactional workloads operate on individual rows of data and often just on a single row at a time. For example, consider a transactional database that stores a record of a taxi trip. If a passenger decides to change the destination of the trip halfway there, a transactional database can easily handle identifying the row of data about the trip, updating the latitude and the longitude coordinates for the destination, and then saving the changes back to the database.

Analytical workloads are significantly different from transactional ones. While performing an analytical query on a data set, it is typical to process all of the rows in a data set, for example to identify rows with taxi trips during specific hours of a day or to exclude rows with trips where the fare is more than $20. Analytical queries often include aggregation functions that process a set of values across matching rows and

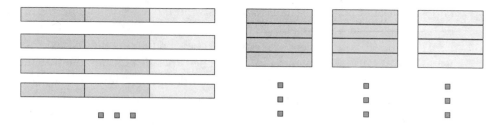

Figure 2.2   **Row-oriented storage (left) used by CSV files and traditional relational databases, is designed for transactional processing, enabling changes to a row of data at a time. Column-oriented storage (right) used by Apache Parquet and many modern data warehouses, works best with analytical queries over immutable datasets.**

compute a single value based on the set. Examples of aggregation functions include sum, average (arithmetic mean), minimum, and maximum.

To perform an analytical query on data in a row-oriented storage format, a processing node needs to fetch and operate on a block of rows at a time. For example, consider a query that computes the average taxi trip duration for the trips started between the hours of 11:00 a.m. and 1:00 p.m. To filter the rows with matching trip times, it is necessary to transfer blocks of rows from storage to the processing node, despite the fact that most of the data in the block will consist of information unrelated to the query, such as the pickup and drop-off coordinates, drop-off time, and more.

In addition to the unnecessarily long transfer times for the data moved between the storage and the node, row-oriented formats waste precious, high-speed cache memory in the processor. Since most of the data per row is unusable for performing the query, the contents of the caches need to be evicted frequently and unnecessarily to replace one block of rows with another.

In contrast, column-oriented data formats (right side of figure 2.2) store data in columns instead of rows. Most modern data warehouse systems use columnar storage, and the format was also adopted by open source projects like Apache Parquet[8] to improve efficiency of analytical workloads.

Consider how the analytical query to find the average taxi trip duration for a midday trip would work in the column-oriented format. To filter the matching trip times, only the data for the trip start time column needs to be transferred to the processing node. Once the trips with matching start times are found, only the corresponding entries from the trip duration column need to be fetched to compute the average.

In both steps there are significant savings with the amount of data that needs to be transferred to the processing node and to its cache. In addition, columnar formats

---

[8]   Apache Parquet is an open source columnar data storage format developed as a collaboration between Twitter and Cloudera and maintained by the Apache Software Foundation project. You can learn more about the format from https://github.com/apache/parquet-mr.

support various encoding and compression schemes to convert text data to binary to further reduce the amount of storage space occupied by data.[9]

Keep in mind that columnar formats are not designed for transactional workloads. The compression and encoding schemes used by formats such as Parquet add latency to write operations compared to simple file appends or row-specific changes that are possible with row-oriented formats in CSV files or traditional databases. If you are planning to adopt Parquet or another columnar format, you need to remember that these formats are best suited for immutable data sets. For example, the records of DC taxi trip data are not expected to change, making Parquet a great format to adopt for more efficient storage and for lower latency analytical queries.

### 2.4.2 *Migrating to a column-oriented data format*

As you learned earlier in this chapter, AWS Glue includes the capability to create and run data-processing jobs, including jobs that extract-transform-load (ETL) data into destination storage for analysis. In this section, you will create and use ETL jobs in Glue to transform the original, row-oriented, CSV-based DC taxi data set to a column-oriented Parquet format and load the resulting Parquet objects to a location in your S3 bucket.

Glue data-processing jobs can be implemented using the Python programming language. Since Glue is serverless, as a machine learning practitioner you will simply need to implement the job and submit the job code to the Glue service. The service will be responsible for validating your code, ensuring that it can execute, provisioning the distributed infrastructure, completing the job using the infrastructure, and tearing down the infrastructure once the job is finished.

An example of a Python-based job to convert the CSV data set to the Parquet format and store the converted data as objects in S3 is shown in listing 2.6.

The code in the listing, starting from the beginning of the file until ❶, consists of standard library imports for the objects and functions needed by the code. Code between ❶ and ❷ is the boilerplate heading for an instantiation of a Glue job and amounts to initialization of the job based on the runtime arguments passed to the job instance.

The key steps in the code are annotated with ❸ and ❹. The createOrReplace-TempView method used at ❸ modifies the state of the Spark session to declare a temporary (nonmaterialized) view named dc_taxi_csv that can be queried using a SQL statement.

The method at ❹ executes a SQL query against the dc_taxi_csv view so that the job can process the contents of the CSV files from the data set and output a selection of columns, while casting the content of the columns into both DOUBLE and STRING data types.

---

[9] Examples of encoding and compression schemes used by Apache Parquet columnar storage format are available from http://mng.bz/yJpJ.

The job commit operation at ❺ simply instructs the job to persist the output of the transformation to storage.

**Listing 2.6   Saving the code in the listing to a file named "dctaxi_csv_to_parquet.py"**

```
import sys
from awsglue.transforms import *
from awsglue.utils import getResolvedOptions
from pyspark.context import SparkContext
from awsglue.context import GlueContext
from awsglue.job import Job

args = getResolvedOptions(sys.argv, ['JOB_NAME',
                                      'BUCKET_SRC_PATH',
                                      'BUCKET_DST_PATH',
                                      'DST_VIEW_NAME'])

BUCKET_SRC_PATH = args['BUCKET_SRC_PATH']
BUCKET_DST_PATH = args['BUCKET_DST_PATH']
DST_VIEW_NAME = args['DST_VIEW_NAME']

sc = SparkContext()
glueContext = GlueContext(sc)
logger = glueContext.get_logger()
spark = glueContext.spark_session

job = Job(glueContext)
job.init(args['JOB_NAME'], args)

df = ( spark.read.format("csv")
        .option("header", True)
        .option("inferSchema", True)
        .option("delimiter", "|")
        .load("{}".format(BUCKET_SRC_PATH)) )

df.createOrReplaceTempView("{}".format(DST_VIEW_NAME))

query_df = spark.sql("""

 SELECT
    origindatetime_tr,

    CAST(fareamount AS DOUBLE) AS fareamount_double,
    CAST(fareamount AS STRING) AS fareamount_string,

    origin_block_latitude,
    CAST(origin_block_latitude AS STRING) AS origin_block_latitude_string,

    origin_block_longitude,
    CAST(origin_block_longitude AS STRING) AS origin_block_longitude_string,

    destination_block_latitude,
    CAST(destination_block_latitude AS STRING)
      AS destination_block_latitude_string,
```

❶ Import AWS Glue Job to later manage the job life cycle.

❷ Retrieve the **JOB_NAME** parameter passed to the job.

❸ Read the CSV files located at **BUCKET_SRC_PATH** into a Spark DataFrame.

```
      destination_block_longitude,
      CAST(destination_block_longitude AS STRING)
        AS destination_block_longitude_string,

      CAST(mileage AS DOUBLE) AS mileage_double,
      CAST(mileage AS STRING) AS mileage_string
```

```
  FROM dc_taxi_csv
```
**④** **Eliminate the new lines in the Python multiline string of the SQL query for Spark SQL compatibility.**

```
""".replace('\n', ''))
```

```
query_df.write.parquet("{}".format(BUCKET_DST_PATH), mode="overwrite")
```

**Save using Parquet format to the object storage location specified by BUCKET_DST_PATH.** **⑤**

```
job.commit()
```

Note that you need to save the contents of listing 2.6 to a file named dctaxi_csv_to_parquet.py. As shown in listing 2.7, you need to upload the job source code file to a location in your S3 bucket to ensure that the Glue service can access it to start a job.

**Listing 2.7  Uploading to `glue/dctaxi_csv_to_parquet.py` in your project's bucket**

```
aws s3 cp dctaxi_csv_to_parquet.py \
s3://dc-taxi-$BUCKET_ID-$AWS_DEFAULT_REGION/glue/
```
**Copy the PySpark job file to the Glue folder of the S3 bucket.**

**Confirm that the file uploaded as expected.**
```
aws s3 ls \
s3://dc-taxi-$BUCKET_ID-$AWS_DEFAULT_REGION/glue/dctaxi_csv_to_parquet.py
```

You should expect an output similar to the following, with a different timestamp in the first column:

```
upload: ./dctaxi_csv_to_parquet.py to
⮕ s3://dc-taxi-███████████████████████-
      ███████████████/glue/
⮕ dctaxi_csv_to_parquet.py
2020-04-20 14:58:22       1736 dctaxi_csv_to_parquet.py
```

After the job file is uploaded, you should create and start the job as shown in listing 2.8.

**Listing 2.8  Creating and starting the `dc-taxi-csv-to-parquet-job` Glue job**

```
aws glue create-job \
  --name dc-taxi-csv-to-parquet-job \
  --role `aws iam get-role \
  --role-name AWSGlueServiceRole-dc-taxi \
  --query 'Role.Arn' \
  --output text` \
  --default-arguments \
  '{"--TempDir":"s3://dc-taxi-'$BUCKET_ID'-'$AWS_DEFAULT_REGION'/glue/"}' \
```

```
  --command '{
    "ScriptLocation": "s3://dc-taxi-'$BUCKET_ID'-'$AWS_DEFAULT_REGION'
        /glue/dctaxi_csv_to_parquet.py",
    "Name": "glueetl",
    "PythonVersion": "3"
}'

aws glue start-job-run \
  --job-name dc-taxi-csv-to-parquet-job \
  --arguments='--BUCKET_SRC_PATH="'$(
      echo s3://dc-taxi-$BUCKET_ID-$AWS_DEFAULT_REGION/csv/
    )'",
  --BUCKET_DST_PATH="'$(
      echo s3://dc-taxi-$BUCKET_ID-$AWS_DEFAULT_REGION/parquet/
    )'",
  --DST_VIEW_NAME="dc_taxi_csv"'
```

To monitor the execution of the job you can use the following command directly, or prefix it with a `watch` command:

```
aws glue get-job-runs --job-name dc-taxi-csv-to-parquet-job \
--query 'JobRuns[0].JobRunState'
```

After the job succeeds, you can list the contents of the `parquet` folder in the bucket using

```
aws s3 ls --recursive --summarize --human-readable \
s3://dc-taxi-$BUCKET_ID-$AWS_DEFAULT_REGION/parquet/


...
Total Objects: 99
   Total Size: 940.7 MiB
```

and confirm that the compression caused by the conversion to the Parquet format reduced the data size to 940.7 MiB from 11.2 GiB of CSV data stored in the row-oriented format.

Then, you can create a new table in the Glue data catalog and have the table describe the newly created data stored in the Apache Parquet format. Use the approach from listing 2.5, with a few changes, including the following:

1 Renaming the crawler to dc-taxi-parquet-crawler ❶, ❸, ❹
2 Changing the bucket location to use the `parquet` folder ❷
3 Dropping the `Exclusions` option, since the Parquet-formatted data does not include a `README` file ❷

```
aws glue create-crawler \                      Create an instance of the
--name dc-taxi-parquet-crawler \               dc-taxi-parquet-crawler
--database-name dc_taxi_db \               ❶  crawler.
--table-prefix dc_taxi_ \
--role `aws iam get-role --role-name AWSGlueServiceRole-dc-taxi
    --query 'Role.Arn' --output text` --targets '{
```

```
  "S3Targets": [
    {
      "Path": "s3://dc-taxi-'$BUCKET_ID'-'$AWS_DEFAULT_REGION'/parquet/"
    }]
}'
```

**Crawl the parquet subfolder of the S3 bucket containing the converted data set.** ❷

```
aws glue start-crawler \
--name dc-taxi-parquet-crawler
```

**Start the crawler.** ❸

```
aws glue get-crawler --name dc-taxi-parquet-crawler --query 'Crawler.State'\
--output text
```

**Get the current crawler state.** ❹

You can confirm that the transformation of the data from CSV to Parquet resulted in a new Glue table. If you execute

```
aws glue get-table --database-name dc_taxi_db --name dc_taxi_parquet
```

then the output should be similar to the one from when you ran the `aws glue get-table` command against the `dc_taxi_csv` table, with the exception of the change in the value for the `Parameters.classification` key. The value should change from `csv` to `parquet`.

## Summary

- A machine learning approach to building a taxi fare estimation service can help you reduce operational costs and avoid hardcoding city-specific business rules.
- You will use a publicly available data set of taxi trips in DC to learn how to build a taxi fare estimation API using serverless machine learning.
- Serverless object storage services (such as S3) help you take what you already know about managing data as files on filesystems and apply that to storing and managing large data sets (gigabytes to petabytes of data) as objects in object storage.
- AWS Glue data crawlers help you discover the schema of your data regardless of whether your data is in filesystems, object storage, or relational databases.
- AWS Glue extract-transform-load job services help you move data across various storage locations, transforming the data in the process to prepare it for analysis.
- The column-oriented data format improves data-processing efficiency for analytical queries.

# Exploring and preparing the data set

3

**This chapter covers**

- Getting started with AWS Athena for interactive querying
- Choosing between manually specified and discovered data schemas
- Approaching data quality with VACUUM normative principles
- Analyzing DC taxi data quality through interactive querying
- Implementing data quality processing in PySpark

In the previous chapter, you imported the DC taxi data set into AWS and stored it in your project's S3 object storage bucket. You created, configured, and ran an AWS Glue data catalog crawler that analyzed the data set and discovered its data schema. You also learned about the column-based data storage formats (e.g., Apache Parquet) and their advantages over row-based formats for analytical workloads. At the conclusion of the chapter, you used a PySpark job running on AWS Glue to convert the original, row-based, comma-separated values (CSV) format of the DC taxi data set to Parquet and stored it in your S3 bucket.

In this chapter, you will learn about Athena, another serverless feature of AWS that is going to prove valuable for the analysis of the DC taxi rides data set using Standard Query Language (SQL). You will use Athena to start with exploratory data analysis (EDA) and identify some of the data quality issues that exist in the data set. Next, you will learn about VACUUM, an acronym for a set of normative principles about data cleaning and data quality for effective machine learning. Following the VACUUM principles, you will explore the data quality issues that exist in the DC taxi data set and learn about using Athena to repeatably and reliably sample subsets of the entire DC taxi data set for analysis. Finally, you will implement a PySpark job to create a clean, analysis-ready version of the data set.

In addition, you will learn about and practice the basics of data quality for tabular data sets,[1] an important aspect of an effective machine learning project. While working on data quality, you will learn about the principles behind data quality for machine learning and how to apply them using SQL and PySpark on your machine learning platform.

## 3.1 Getting started with interactive querying

This section starts by providing you with an overview of the use cases for data queries as opposed to the data-processing jobs used to transform CSV to Parquet in chapter 2. Then, as you are introduced to Athena, an interactive query service from AWS, you will learn about the advantages and disadvantages of using a *schema-on-read approach* to structured data querying, prepare to experiment with a sample taxi data set, and apply alternative schemas to that data set. By the conclusion of the section, the objective is to get you ready to use a browser-based interface to AWS Athena and to explore data quality issues in the DC taxi fare data set. As you are working on the implementation in this section, you are going to start picking up the skills needed for exploratory data analysis of the DC taxi fare data set and start practicing the kinds of queries that will become useful when working on improving its data quality.

### 3.1.1 Choosing the right use case for interactive querying

This section clarifies the distinction between I/O-intensive and compute-intensive workloads as well as how to choose from technologies like AWS Glue, AWS Athena, Google Cloud DataProc, or Google Cloud BigQuery for these two categories of workloads.

To develop an intuition about when to use interactive query services, it is valuable to first introduce a distinction between high throughput versus low latency in data processing. Recall that both row-oriented formats (like CSV) and column-oriented formats (like Parquet) can be used to store a structured data set organized into tables of rows and columns. This book uses the term *record* to describe a single row of data from a structured data set. Describing data sets in terms of records as opposed to rows

---

[1] While a 2016 survey (http://mng.bz/Mvr2) claimed that 60% of the data scientists' time is spent addressing data quality issues, a more recent and larger survey brought the estimate down to 15% (http://mng.bz/g1KR). For more insights about these oft-cited statistics, check out http://mng.bz/ePzJ.

helps to avoid confusion about whether the data is stored in a row- or a column-oriented format. In other words, a record is independent of the underlying data storage format.

In chapter 2, you used a PySpark job hosted on AWS Glue to execute a high-throughput workload to migrate data records from CSV to Parquet. A distinguishing characteristic of high-throughput workloads is a *one-to-many* (sometimes *one-to-any*) relationship between input and output records: a single record used as an input to the workload can produce zero, one, or many output records. For example, a simple SQL statement that begins with SELECT * returns an output record for every input record in the data storage, a SELECT paired with a WHERE clause can filter a portion of records, while a more complex SQL statement involving a SELF JOIN can square the total number of records returned from a table. In practice, the one-to-many relationship means that the number of the output records is of the same order of magnitude and is not substantially different from the number of the input records. Such workloads can also be described as input/output intensive because the underlying IT infrastructure executing the workload spends more time reading from and writing to storage compared to the amount of time spent computing.

As you observed when starting a PySpark job in chapter 2, the CSV-to-Parquet re-encoding workload took on the order of minutes for completion. The high latency of the workload (here, latency describes the duration from the start to the finish of the Glue job) was caused by writing a record of Parquet output for every record of CSV input. The high throughput of the workload describes the total quantity of records processed in terms of the sum of the quantities of the input and output records. Since time spent processing the input and output records is a sizable majority of the total duration of this category of the workloads, they are also described as input/output (I/O) intensive.

In contrast to AWS Glue, which is designed for high-throughput workloads, interactive query services like Athena from AWS and BigQuery from Google are designed for low-latency, many-to-one (or many-to-few) workloads where many input records (think majority of all the records in a table) are aggregated to a few (or often to just one) output record. Examples of many-to-one workloads include SQL statements that use functions like COUNT, SUM, or AVG and other aggregation functions used with SQL GROUP BY clauses. Many-to-few workloads are common when identifying sets of unique values for a column using SQL operations like SELECT DISTINCT. The many-to-one and many-to-few workloads can also be described as compute intensive, because the underlying IT infrastructure spends more time performing compute (e.g., computing an arithmetic mean) than input/output operations (e.g., reading or writing data).

### 3.1.2   *Introducing AWS Athena*

This section provides a high-level overview of the AWS Athena interactive query service and describes how Athena applies a schema-on-read approach for data processing and analysis.

Athena is a serverless query service from AWS, designed primarily for interactive analysis of structured and semi-structured data using ANSI SQL and SQL extensions.

Interactive analysis means that Athena is designed to execute compute-intensive SQL workloads with low latency and return results within a matter of seconds. This also means that while it is possible to use Athena to extract, transform, and load (ETL) data, you should plan on using PySpark instead of Athena for your ETL code to support high-throughput rather than low-latency data processing. If you have ever used an interactive query interface for a relational database, such as MySQL or PostgreSQL, you know that Athena provides similar functionality. Although Athena is targeted at interactive analysis by end users through a browser-based interface, there is also support for API-based access. As a query service, Athena differs from traditional relational databases and data warehouses in the following important ways:

- Athena relies on AWS services for data storage and does not store source data or metadata for queries. For example, Athena can query data sets from S3, as well as from MySQL, DynamoDB, or other data sources that provide Athena data source connectors (http://mng.bz/p9vP). When data is produced as a result of a query, Athena stores the data to a pre-configured S3 bucket.
- Athena software is based on an open source PrestoDB distributed query engine (https://prestodb.io) developed in part by Facebook engineers. The implementation was demonstrated to scale to Facebook's internal workloads involving queries over hundreds of petabytes of data.
- Athena does not use the schema-on-write approach of traditional, relational, data warehouses. This means that Athena can interpret the same data according to mutually exclusive schema definitions; for example, Athena can query a column of identical data values as a string or as a number. This approach is often described as *schema-on-read*.

In chapter 2, you learned about using crawlers to discover data schemas from data as well as how to create databases and tables in the data catalog based on the discovered schemas. Athena requires that a table be defined in the data catalog before the service can query the data described by the table. As illustrated by the dashed lines on figure 3.1, Athena can be used to define schemas for data stored in a data storage service such as S3. Alternatively, Athena can query tables defined based on the metadata discovered by a crawler.

Relying on Athena to define schemas for a table in the data catalog has both advantages and disadvantages. Since many real-world data sets stored in data warehouses and used for machine learning are wide (consisting of many columns), defining a table schema using Athena translates to the effort required to explicitly specify SQL data types for each column in the schema. Although it may seem that the effort is limited in scope, keep in mind that the schema definition needs to be maintained and updated whenever there is a change in the underlying data set. However, if you need to be able to query the same data using data schemas containing mutually exclusive data types, then using Athena to define schemas is the right option.

In contrast, if you use the crawler-based schema definition approach, you don't need to explicitly specify the data types as they are automatically discovered by the

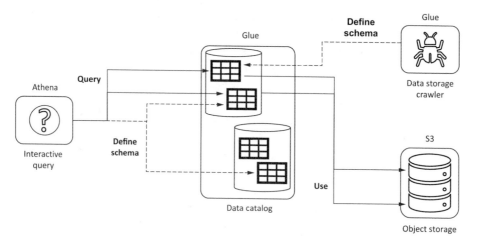

**Figure 3.1   The Athena query service can both define a schema and use one defined by a Glue crawler to analyze the data using alternative schema definitions for the same data set. Alternative and mutually exclusive schemas can help you apply the right schema for your specific use case.**

crawler. The crawler can also be scheduled to run periodically, updating the schema definition based on changes in the data. The downside of using the crawler is relevant when you need to query data using an alternative data schema with differences from the automatically discovered one. In the crawler-based approach, this translates to either using Athena to define the alternative schema or implementing a PySpark job that applies the alternative schema to the data set. Recall that the PySpark job that you implemented at the conclusion of chapter 2 re-encoded STRING data types (for example, for fare amount) to DOUBLE.

### 3.1.3   *Preparing a sample data set*

In this section, you will start working with a tiny CSV data set to better understand the advantages and disadvantages of relying on Athena to define the schema for it. In the data set, the rows contain values representing a taxi trip fare amount as well as the latitude and longitude coordinates of the trip pickup and drop-off locations.

To begin querying this tiny data set using Athena, you need to first upload the corresponding CSV file, consisting of just five rows of data to a folder of your S3 bucket.

Create a CSV file named trips_sample.csv on your local filesystem and preview it by executing the following bash commands:

```
wget -q https://gist.githubusercontent.com/osipov/
⮕ 1fc0265f8f829d9d9eee8393657423a9/
⮕ raw/9957c1f09cdfa64f8b8d89cfec532a0e150d5178/trips_sample.csv

ls -ltr trips_sample.csv

cat trips_sample.csv
```

Assuming the bash commands executed successfully, the output of cat should have produced an output resembling table 3.1.

**Table 3.1  The type interpretation of data values in this data set[a] depends on your choice of a schema.**

| Fare amount | Origin | | Destination | |
|---|---|---|---|---|
| | Latitude | Longitude | Latitude | Longitude |
| 8.11 | 38.900769 | −77.033644 | 38.912239 | −77.036514 |
| 5.95 | 38.912609 | −77.030788 | 38.906445 | −77.023978 |
| 7.57 | 38.900773 | −77.03655 | 38.896131 | −77.024975 |
| 11.61 | 38.892101 | −77.044208 | 38.905969 | −77.0656439 |
| 4.87 | 38.899615 | −76.980387 | 38.900638 | −76.97023 |

a. The CSV file for the sample data set of five DC taxi rides is available from http://mng.bz/OQrP.

Next, copy the contents of the file to the samples folder in your S3 object storage bucket and confirm that it copied successfully by running the following:

```
aws s3 cp trips_sample.csv s3://dc-taxi-$BUCKET_ID-$AWS_DEFAULT_REGION
➥ /samples/trips_sample.csv

aws s3 ls s3://dc-taxi-$BUCKET_ID-$AWS_DEFAULT_REGION/samples/
➥ trips_sample.csv
```

If you correctly uploaded the sample file, the output of the aws s3 ls command should report that it is 378 bytes in size.

### 3.1.4  *Interactive querying using Athena from a browser*

This section introduces the browser-based graphical user interface (GUI) for AWS Athena. Although it is possible to use the Athena GUI to perform the queries used throughout this chapter, data analysis automation and reproducibility is more straightforward to demonstrate with a command line interface (CLI)–based access to the Athena API rather than with the browser. So, while this section covers how to use the browser-based interface, later sections focus on scripting CLI-based queries.

To access the Athena interface from your browser, navigate to the Athena service using the AWS Services dropdown menu in the AWS Console top menu. You should be able to click through to a screen that resembles the one shown in figure 3.2.

Note that on the Athena interface screen you need to make sure you are accessing Athena from the region that matches the value of your $AWS_DEFAULT_REGION environment variable, the one where you have uploaded your CSV file. As with other AWS services, you can change the region using the dropdown menu in the upper right-hand corner of the AWS console top menu.

**Figure 3.2   Screen capture of the Athena's browser-based interface illustrating the key components you need to know for interactive querying**

The selection highlighted as 1 in figure 3.2 specifies the data catalog database you created in chapter 2. Make sure you have dc_taxi_db selected as the database. Once the database is selected, confirm that in the selection highlighted as 2 you can see the tables you created using the crawler in the dc_taxi_db database. The tables should be named dc_taxi_csv and dc_taxi_parquet.

SQL queries for Athena are specified using a tabbed SQL editor highlighted as 3 in figure 3.2. If this is your first time using Athena, before running a query you will need to specify a query result location for the service. By default, the output of every query executed by Athena is saved to the query result location in S3. Execute the following bash shell command and copy the output to your clipboard:

```
echo s3://dc-taxi-$BUCKET_ID-$AWS_DEFAULT_REGION/athena/
```

Notice from the output of the shell command that Athena will store the query locations results to the athena folder in your bucket.

Before you run your first query, you should configure the S3 query result location by first clicking on the "set a query result location" hyperlink shown in the upper part of the screenshot in figure 3.2, then pasting the value you just copied to the clipboard into the result location text field in the dialog, and finally clicking Save.

### 3.1.5   *Interactive querying using a sample data set*

This section explains how to apply schema-on-read in Athena using the few records from the trips_sample.csv file. In later sections, you are going to be able to apply the same technique to larger data sets.

Since the upcoming Athena examples rely on using a scripted, CLI-based access to Athena API, start by configuring Athena to use the athena folder in your S3 bucket as the location to store results of Athena queries. This means that you should execute the following from your shell:

```
aws athena create-work-group --name dc_taxi_athena_workgroup \
--configuration "ResultConfiguration={OutputLocation=
    s3://dc-taxi-$BUCKET_ID-$AWS_DEFAULT_REGION/athena},
    EnforceWorkGroupConfiguration=false,PublishCloudWatchMetricsEnabled=false"
```

Once the dc_taxi_athena_workgroup is created, you can start using Athena via the CLI.

Since Athena is integrated with the Glue data catalog, the database and the schema definitions from a data catalog table can be applied at data read time (i.e., when querying data) as opposed to data write time. However, to illustrate the schema-on-read capability of Athena, instead of using a crawler to discover a table schema for the five sample trips, you will first pre-populate the data catalog using tables with manually defined schemas. The first table you will create treats all of the data values in trips_sample.csv as STRING data type, as shown in listing 3.1. Later, you will create a second table that treats the same values as DOUBLE.

Listing 3.1 Defining a schema for the five DC trips data set using STRING types

```
CREATE EXTERNAL TABLE IF NOT EXISTS dc_taxi_db.dc_taxi_csv_sample_strings(
        fareamount STRING,
        origin_block_latitude STRING,
        origin_block_longitude STRING,
        destination_block_latitude STRING,
        destination_block_longitude STRING
)
ROW FORMAT DELIMITED FIELDS TERMINATED BY ','
LOCATION 's3://dc-taxi-$BUCKET_ID-$AWS_DEFAULT_REGION/samples/'
TBLPROPERTIES ('skip.header.line.count'='1');
```

To define the schema for the dc_taxi_db.dc_taxi_csv_sample_strings table using the SQL statement from listing 3.1, execute the following sequence of commands from your bash shell.

Listing 3.2 Shell-based query of AWS Athena using AWS CLI

```
SQL="                                                       ◁─────
CREATE EXTERNAL TABLE IF NOT EXISTS dc_taxi_db.dc_taxi_csv_sample_strings(
        fareamount STRING,
        origin_block_latitude STRING,          Save the string-based
        origin_block_longitude STRING,         schema definition to the
        destination_block_latitude STRING,     SQL shell variable.
        destination_block_longitude STRING
)
```

```
ROW FORMAT DELIMITED FIELDS TERMINATED BY ','
LOCATION 's3://dc-taxi-$BUCKET_ID-$AWS_DEFAULT_REGION/samples/'
TBLPROPERTIES ('skip.header.line.count'='1');"

ATHENA_QUERY_ID=$(aws athena start-query-execution \
--work-group dc_taxi_athena_workgroup \
--query 'QueryExecutionId' \               Start the Athena query
--output text \                            based on the contents
--query-string "$SQL")                     of the SQL variable.

echo $SQL
                                           Repeatedly check and
echo $ATHENA_QUERY_ID                      report on whether the
until aws athena get-query-execution \     Athena query is finished.
  --query 'QueryExecution.Status.State' \
  --output text \
  --query-execution-id $ATHENA_QUERY_ID | grep -v "RUNNING";
do
  printf '.'
  sleep 1;
done
```

At this point, based on your experience with using SQL to query relational databases, you might be tempted to query the dc_taxi_csv_sample_strings table using a SQL statement that starts with SELECT *. However, when working with columnar data stores, it is better to avoid SELECT * whenever possible. As you learned in chapter 2, columnar stores maintain individual columns of data across multiple files as well as across different parts of files. By specifying just the names of the columns that you need for your query, you direct a column-aware query engine like Athena to process just the parts of the data you need, reducing the overall quantity of data processed. With Athena, as well as with serverless query services from other public cloud vendors,[2] lower amounts of data processed translate to lower costs. Since Athena is serverless, you are billed by AWS based on the amount of data processed by your Athena queries.

Also, the script in listing 3.2 is quite verbose. To keep query examples in this chapter concise, proceed by downloading a utils.sh script:

```
wget -q https://raw.githubusercontent.com/osipov/smlbook/master/utils.sh
ls -l utils.sh
```

Once downloaded, the script should take up 4,776 bytes on your filesystem. This script is loaded in the upcoming examples using the source utils.sh command and is invoked by passing a SQL query for Athena to the athena_query_to_table function.

When Athena is querying data using the schema from the dc_taxi_csv_sample_strings table you just created, the data is processed by interpreting the latitude and longitude coordinates as a STRING data type. Treating the coordinate values as strings

---

[2]  Examples include Google BigQuery: https://cloud.google.com/bigquery.

can be useful when passing a pair of the coordinates to a web page script in order to display a pin on an interactive map in a browser. Notice that the following query does not involve any data type casting since the data is read by Athena from the source CSV data as a STRING. Hence, it is possible to use the ANSI SQL || (double vertical bar) operation directly on the data values to perform the concatenation operation.

**Listing 3.3  Using STRING data type for coordinates to simplify browser-based use cases**

```
source utils.sh
SQL="
SELECT

origin_block_latitude || ' , ' || origin_block_longitude
    AS origin,

destination_block_latitude || ' , ' || destination_block_longitude
    AS destination

FROM
    dc_taxi_db.dc_taxi_csv_sample_strings
"
athena_query_to_table "$SQL" \
"ResultSet.Rows[*].[Data[0].VarCharValue,Data[1].VarCharValue]"
```

This results in an output resembling the following, where each row contains string data types, concatenating the latitude and longitude values:

| origin | destination |
|---|---|
| 38.900769, –77.033644 | 38.912239, –77.036514 |
| 38.912609, –77.030788 | 38.906445, –77.023978 |
| 38.900773, –77.03655 | 38.896131, –77.024975 |
| 38.892101000000004, –77.044208 | 38.905969, –77.06564399999999 |
| 38.899615000000004, –76.980387 | 38.900638, –76.97023 |

Alternatively, Athena can use a different schema, treating the same coordinate values as a floating point data type to compute the differences between the largest and smallest fare amounts in the data set. Execute the following Athena operation from your shell to create the dc_taxi_csv_sample_double table where every value in the trips_sample.csv file is interpreted as an SQL DOUBLE:

```
%%bash
source utils.sh ; athena_query "
CREATE EXTERNAL TABLE IF NOT EXISTS dc_taxi_db.dc_taxi_csv_sample_double(
    fareamount DOUBLE,
```

```
          origin_block_latitude DOUBLE,
          origin_block_longitude DOUBLE,
          destination_block_latitude DOUBLE,
          destination_block_longitude DOUBLE
)
ROW FORMAT DELIMITED FIELDS TERMINATED BY ','
LOCATION 's3://dc-taxi-$BUCKET_ID-$AWS_DEFAULT_REGION/samples/'
TBLPROPERTIES ('skip.header.line.count'='1');
"
```

After the `dc_taxi_csv_sample_double` table becomes available for a query, you can try processing the values in the source data file as doubles, for example, by trying to find the difference between the largest and the smallest amounts for the taxi fare in the five-row data set:

```
source utils.sh ; athena_query_to_pandas "
SELECT ROUND(MAX(fareamount) - MIN(fareamount), 2)
FROM dc_taxi_db.dc_taxi_csv_sample_double
"
```

The `athena_query_to_pandas` function in the listing saves the output of the Athena query to a temporary /tmp/awscli.json file on your filesystem. First, define the Python utility function as shown in the following listing.

**Listing 3.4   Reporting Athena results as a pandas `DataFrame`**

```
import pandas as pd
def awscli_to_df():
  json_df = pd.read_json('/tmp/awscli.json')
  df = pd.DataFrame(json_df[0].tolist(), index = json_df.index, \
    columns = json_df[0].tolist()[0]).drop(0, axis = 0)

  return df
```

Then, you can conveniently preview the contents of the tmp/awscli.json file as a pandas `DataFrame`, so that calling `awscli_to_df()` outputs the following:

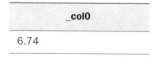

| _col0 |
|-------|
| 6.74  |

The output shows that there was a $6.74 difference between the maximum and the minimum values for the taxi fare in the data set. Also, since the last query did not use the `AS` keyword to assign a name for the sole column in the result, Athena used an automatically generated column name of `_col0`.

### 3.1.6  *Querying the DC taxi data set*

This section gets you started with using AWS Athena to query the DC taxi data set so that in the upcoming sections you are prepared to analyze DC taxi data quality.

As you recall from chapter 2, the Parquet-formatted version of the DC taxi data was stored as the dc_taxi_parquet table in the dc_taxi_db database. Let's attempt a query of 10 rows of this table using the Athena CLI:

```
source utils.sh ; athena_query_to_pandas "
SELECT fareamount_double,
       origindatetime_tr,
       origin_block_latitude_double,
       origin_block_longitude_double,
       destination_block_latitude_double,
       destination_block_longitude_double
FROM dc_taxi_db.dc_taxi_parquet
LIMIT 10
"
```

Don't forget to use the awscli_to_df() function to output the result using pandas.

Due to the parallel and distributed nature of data processing performed by Athena, the order of rows in the dc_taxi_parquet table will be different for every execution of the last query. Hence, the 10 rows you will see as the output of the query will be different from mine. However, even with just 10 rows of the results you should be able to find rows with missing values. The missing values will appear as empty cells or None values in one or more columns.

For example, you may find that your output has missing values for the origin but not for the destination coordinates. In some cases, all but the fare amount and the trip origin date/time values will be missing in the results. The imported DC taxi trip data set has data quality issues.

While the transformation of the DC taxi data to the Parquet format in chapter 2 helped you optimize query and analytics performance for working with the data, you have not yet performed any quality checks against the data set. In short, you don't know if the data available to you can be trusted. What does it mean to address these quality issues? What problems should or should not be fixed? How much effort should you put into cleaning the data? When does the cleaned-up data set achieve sufficiently good quality for data analysis and machine learning?

## 3.2  *Getting started with data quality*

This part of the chapter is written differently from other sections. Whereas most of the chapter focuses on the technical knowledge and detailed instruction in a form of specific steps for working with serverless machine learning technologies, this part is normative rather than prescriptive. In other words, you should first understand what data quality for machine learning should be like, and then learn the steps involved in applying data quality to your machine learning data set. My goal for this part is to teach you the data quality criteria you should use across any machine learning project, regardless of the data set, so this section deals primarily with concepts rather than code.

Let's face it: data cleanup is an important but not the most exciting topic in machine learning, so to make the data quality principles more concrete, easier to remember, and hopefully more interesting, this section relies heavily on real-world case studies and data cleanup examples you can apply to your next machine learning project. If you prefer to proceed directly to the practical steps of cleaning up the DC taxi data, feel free to jump ahead to section 3.3.

### 3.2.1   *From "garbage in, garbage out" to data quality*

This subsection illustrates a rationale for addressing data quality issues and describes the data quality questions that are answered in the later parts of this chapter.

"Garbage in, garbage out" is a well-known cliché in the information technology industry. In the context of this book, it means that if the input into your machine learning system is garbage, then the machine learning algorithms will train on garbage, and the outputs of machine learning will be garbage as well. The cliché points to the importance of data quality for a machine learning project, but it does not give evidence that garbage in, garbage out is critical or relevant to real-world data analysis and machine learning.

In 2010, as the global economy was still recovering from the financial meltdown that took place a few years prior, two Harvard economists, Carmen M. Reinhart and Kenneth S. Rogoff, published a research paper deconstructing policies that could help countries get their economies growing again. In the paper, the economists argued that countries that incur debt of over 90% of their gross domestic product (GDP) face economic declines. In part based on the analysis from the economists, some European Union (EU) countries adopted harsh austerity measures, slashing salaries and eliminating thousands of jobs. As it turned out, the data used for the analysis was wrong.

The politicians who based their policies on the Reinhart-Rogoff results fell victim to the classic garbage in, garbage out problem. The Reinhart-Rogoff fiasco is just one instance of many where an analysis of poor quality data led to billions of dollars in negative consequences. Even prior to the digital transformation accelerated by the COVID-19 pandemic, the highly respected *Harvard Business Review* magazine published a notable claim that the total cost of bad data to the US economy should be measured in thousands of billions of US dollars.[3]

The issue of data quality is important, but as a machine learning practitioner, it may not be immediately obvious that you are working with a poor quality data set. How do you know if your data is garbage or if it is of sufficient quality to perform machine learning?

---

[3]  In 2016, an influential *Harvard Business Review* article cited another study, "Bad Data Costs the U.S. $3 Trillion Per Year": http://mng.bz/Yw47.

### 3.2.2 *Before starting with data quality*

This subsection helps you understand the questions that should be answered about any structured (tabular) data set before addressing the data quality issues in it.

Before you can begin to work on data quality, you need more than just a structured data set. You need to know answers to the kinds of questions you have already answered about the DC taxi data:

- *Can the data set be queried as one or more tables of rows and columns?* In other words, are you querying data stored using a structured data set format? Recall that in chapter 2 you looked at definitions of row- (e.g., CSV) and column-oriented (e.g., Apache Parquet) storage formats for structured data. Since VACUUM is a set of data quality principles for structured data sets, it does not apply to unstructured formats used for natural language text, images, audio, and video.

- *What questions do you need to answer based on which columns?* The DC taxi data set–based machine learning example in this book is built around the question "What is the value for the fare amount column, given that you know the start time of a DC taxi trip, as well as the latitude and longitude coordinates for the pickup and the drop-off locations of the trip?" Knowing the questions you wish to ask about the data also helps you understand the *essential data* in your data set—in other words, the data in scope for training of your machine learning system to answer the questions. In addition to the essential data, your data set may also contain *reference data* that is useful for ensuring the quality (specifically the accuracy) of your essential data but does not need to be cleaned up with the same degree of rigor. For example, the values in the `mileage` column of the DC taxi data set are not essential to answering the questions but are useful as a reference to compare against the values of the `fareamount` column and to ensure that the fare amount values have the right degree of data quality.

- *What is the schema for the essential data?* Before you can begin cleaning up the data set, you need to create a data schema in the catalog with changes that ensure the data values are specified using appropriate data types and constraints. The data schema specifies the data type for every column of a data set. Yet, while the data type specifications are necessary for the schema to help ensure data quality, they are not sufficient. For every data type, you should also be able to specify whether it is *nullable*. Here, data type nullability is equivalent to the DDL (data definition language) nullability and indicates whether a value is allowed to be missing. You should also specify any constraints that further limit the range of possible values: with string types, these can include regular expressions, while with integer types, these can be specified using interval ranges. The section on valid data illustrates the constraints using practical examples.

In the previous chapter, you used a crawler and a data catalog to discover and store the discovered data schema for the DC taxi data set. The schema in the catalog is similar to a DDL schema (part of the SQL standard) that describes data types such as integers, floats, timestamps, and more. Keep in mind that the discovered schema may or may not be the right schema to use.

So what does it mean to have the right schema? More precisely, what does it mean for a schema to consist of data types that are appropriate for the data set's values? Just as with DDL schemas, the choice of the appropriate data types is a tradeoff. On one hand, the schema should use data types that are sufficiently general to preserve the data values without loss of information. On the other hand, the data types should support (without type casting) expected operations on the data values while making efficient use of storage space. For example, the latitude and longitude coordinates from the DC taxi data set should be specified in the schema as floating point values (DOUBLE data type) instead of Unicode strings so that the coordinate values can be used for distance calculations.

### 3.2.3   *Normative principles for data quality*

This section is about the principles behind the *valid, accurate, consistent, uniform,* and *unified model* (VACUUM) for structured data quality, along with cautionary tales to serve as case studies. The principles are normative, meaning that they define what quality data ought to be like instead of prescribing the specific steps or code for the implementation of data quality processing. The value of the principles is in a comprehensive and rigorous definition behind the claim that the data that complies with VACUUM is sufficiently "clean" and ready for machine learning.

Think of the VACUUM principles as a checklist of guidelines, criteria, or metrics of data quality that you should explore as part of your machine learning project. Keep in mind that doctors and pilots (as well as many other professionals) use checklists, but having a checklist will not make you a pilot or a doctor. If you are planning to develop professional expertise in data quality, you will need to develop your data-cleaning skills. Once you have the right experience in place, a checklist can help jog your memory and ensure that you do not miss important data quality aspects.

#### VALID

On January 31, 2020, the United Kingdom left the EU. So, should an EU data warehouse store the string value United Kingdom as a valid value in a column with names of EU member countries?

You could argue that beginning February 1, 2020, United Kingdom should stop being a valid data value in any column mentioning EU member states. However, this approach is counterproductive: excluding United Kingdom from a set of valid values means that any historical data associated with the column (in other words, any records dated prior to February 1, 2020) are associated with a value that is not valid. If a value in a data set was valid at any point of the data set's existence, it should remain valid.

> **NOTE**   This definition does not specify whether a combination of multiple valid values across multiple columns is valid; this issue will be addressed in the upcoming section on accuracy.

More precisely, a data value in a column is *valid* if it:

- *Matches the column data type specified by the schema.* For a data value to be valid, it must match the data type specified by the schema. SQL-based data type definitions in a schema may include the following:
  - `INTEGER` (for example, in a column storing an elevator floor number)
  - `DOUBLE` (for example, a percentage of users who click a Subscribe button on a website)
  - `TIMESTAMP` (for example, the time an order was placed on a website)
  - `BOOLEAN` (for example, whether a taxi trip ended at an airport)
  - `STRING` (for example, the text of comments left in a comment box on a survey)
- *Matches one or more of the following constraints*:
  - *Nullability*—This constraint applies to any data type and specifies whether a value in a data column is allowed to have a `NULL` value. For example, a `TIMESTAMP` data value storing the date of birth in a driver's license database must be non-nullable (i.e., should not be permitted to have a `NULL` value), while a user's Twitter handle on a customer profile web page can be specified as nullable to handle the cases when the handle is unknown or not specified. Nullable data types can also include `INTEGER`s (e.g., a rating of a taxi ride by a passenger on a scale of 1–5, with a `NULL` value representing no rating), and other data types.
  - *Enumeration*—This constraint applies to any data type and specifies a validation set, a dictionary, or an enumeration of valid values for a data type. With `STRING` values, the enumerations may include names of US states, or major airports in the New York City area, such as `LGA`, `JFK`, `EWR`. The enumeration constraint for a schema may specify an `INTEGER` data type for a country code column in a data set of phone numbers using an enumeration of valid country phone codes. Recall from the example at the beginning of this section that the enumeration must include all values that have ever been valid for the column. So, in any data set older than February 1, 2020, in a data column that stores EU country names, `United Kingdom` is a valid value, regardless of the fact that the UK left the EU on January 31, 2020.
  - *Range*—This constraint is data type specific and can be one of the following types:
    - *Interval constraint* is used for numeric or date/time data types. As an example of valid integer data values, consider a data set with an activity log for a single elevator in a skyscraper. One of the data columns in the data set stores the floor number where the elevator stopped. Since not all floors in this hypothetical skyscraper are accessible by the elevator and the numbering systems skips the 13th floor due to superstition, the constraints on possible values include intervals from –3 to –1 for the parking garage, and 1 to 12 and 14 to 42. The typical notation for this interval is [[–3, –1] or (0, 12] or

[14,42]], where the square brackets indicate that the value is included in the interval while the parentheses indicate that the interval does not include the value neighboring the parenthesis. The or keyword in this case represents the set union operation (in other words, a logical or).

- A similar approach is used when working with DOUBLE and other floating point data types. For example, a probability value can be specified with an interval range constraint from 0.0 to 1.0, [0.0, 1.0]
- Intervals are also common with TIMESTAMP data types for a date/time range where they are used to describe periods such as workdays, weekends, or holidays (e.g., dates: [2020-01-01 00:00:00, 2021-01-01 00:00:00]).
- *Regular expression constraint* is used in the cases of the STRING data type to specify the space of the valid values. For example, in a database that stores Twitter handles of social media influencers, a regular expression can specify that any value that matches /^@[a-zA-Z0-9_]{1,15}$/ is valid. Keep in mind that regular expressions also apply to many data columns that appear numeric; for instance, IP addresses consist primarily of numbers but are commonly stored as a string.
  - *Rule*—This constraint applies to any data type and specifies computable conditions to decide whether a value is valid. For example, if you have ever used a "Save my payment for later" feature on a website to permit a PCI-DSS-compliant[4] vendor to store your credit card number, you should know that a rule constraint for a credit card number is based on Luhn algorithm,[5] which computes parity check bits that ensure a credit card number is valid.

At this point, you have seen the criteria specifying and examples illustrating what it means for a single value in a data set to be valid or invalid. However, it is straightforward to come up with an example of a record consisting entirely of valid values but with an obvious data quality problem. Here's a made-up record from a hypothetical data set that lists locations with a continent and country information:

| Continent | Country | Lat | Lon |
| --- | --- | --- | --- |
| South America | United States | 38.91 | −77.03 |

All the values, including South America, United States, as well as the latitude/longitude coordinates, have valid values for the respective columns. Recall that the valid principle from VACUUM focuses on data quality problems and validation checks

---

4   The Payment Card Industry Data Security Standard specifies, among other things, the requirements for storing cardholder data: https://www.pcicomplianceguide.org/faq/#1.
5   The Luhn algorithm is named after IBM scientist Hans Peter Luhn: https://spectrum.ieee.org/hans-peter-luhn-and-the-birth-of-the-hashing-algorithm.

within a single value. To address the data quality issue in this example, you need to learn about the accuracy principle.

**ACCURATE**

When you learned about valid data, you looked at an example of a data set of records about member states of the EU. As part of the example, you saw that `United Kingdom` is a valid value for the EU country column. Suppose you are working with a data record that has two columns: the first with a date/time of the membership and the second with the name of the country:

| Date of Record | Member State |
|---|---|
| 2020-01-31 | United Kingdom |
| 2020-02-01 | United Kingdom |

While all of the values in the example are valid, it is impossible to assert that the second row is garbage without using an external (to the data record) reference data source. The reference should be able to process the values from the entire record and indicate whether (or to what extent) the record is inaccurate.

More precisely, a data record is *accurate* if all the data values that are part of the record are valid and the combination of the values in the record are reconciled to a reference data source. By the way of an example, consider a database of college alumni, with the date of alumni college enrollment and the date of their college graduation. Checking the database for accuracy requires references to external sources of truth, such as an admissions database and a transcript database. In financial records, inaccuracy can be due to a mismatch between a credit card number and its PIN code. Sometimes accuracy problems arise when joining multiple tables incorrectly, for example, in a data record stating that the movie *Titanic* was produced by Guy Ritchie in 1920.

The accuracy assurance for values such as domain names are a particularly difficult category because the reference data source, domain registration, and DNS databases change over time. For example, if you try to create an email mailing list and check the domain name part of an email using a regular expression, the data in the list may be valid but not accurate in the sense that some of the emails do not map to valid domain names. You may attempt to send an email to the address from the mailing list to confirm that the domain name and the email resolve to an accurate address. Even prior to sending the email, you may attempt to perform a DNS lookup to verify the accuracy of the domain name.

In the UK leaving the EU example, improving the quality of the data in the data set means that the reference data source must exist with the master record of the timestamps for the start and the end dates of an EU state membership. However, for many organizations the challenge with reference data sources isn't that there are too few of them, but rather that there are too many. The next section on consistency will illustrate this problem with more examples.

### CONSISTENT

In January of 2005, an owner of a small house in Valparaiso, a town of about 30,000 residents in Porter County, Indiana, received a a notice that the annual tax assessment value of his house was set at $400 million. The notice, which also included a demand for a tax payment of $8 million, came as a surprise to the owner of the modest house since just the year prior the tax payment amounted to $1,500. Although the issue with data accuracy was soon resolved, the story did not end there.

The data systems of Valparaiso did not follow the data quality consistency principle, so the original data accuracy problem propagated into the budgeting system for the town. The small town's budget was drawn with an assumption of an $8 million tax payment, so the town had to claw back $3.1 million from schools, libraries, and other budget-funded units. That year, Porter County ended up with many unhappy students and parents as the schools had to cover a $200,000 budget shortfall.[6]

Consistency issues arise when different and conflicting validation and accuracy implementations are used across different data silos: databases, data stores, or data systems. While each individual silo can be valid and accurate according to a silo-specific set of definitions, achieving consistency means ensuring a common set of standards for valid and accurate data before integrating the data from systems across silos that span different technology and organizational boundaries.

For example, was the UK a member of the EU at 11:30 p.m. on January 31, 2020? If you are not mindful of data quality, the answer may depend on your data set. In a UK data set, you can expect a valid and accurate record showing that the UK was not an EU member country at 11:30 p.m. on January 31, 2020. Yet, in an EU data set, an identical combination of the date, time, and country name values is an accurate record for an EU country member. As you have probably guessed, the inconsistency is due to different assumptions about storing the date and time values across different data sets. The UK data set in this example uses the Greenwich Mean time zone, while the EU data set uses Central European time.

Even when joining tables within a single data set, or a single data silo, it is important to ensure consistency of validation and accuracy rules. Typical issues arise when using phone numbers and emails as unique identifiers for a user: since phone numbers and emails may change owners, joining tables based on this information might lead to problems. Another example might include different approaches for storing other identifiers such as phone numbers. Some might uniquely identify with a country code, and others may not. This might be as simple as using different primary keys with the same individual across different systems, maybe creating a new primary key to join

---

[6]  *Chesterton Tribune,* a daily newspaper in Indiana, published an article about the Valparaiso debacle: http://mng.bz/GOAN.

together or it might be more subtle. For example, some systems might use a 5+4 ZIP code; other systems might use a five-digit ZIP code per individual.

## UNIFORM

The Mars Climate Orbiter, a $125 million robotic space probe, was launched by NASA to Mars in 1998. Less than 12 months later, during an orbit change maneuver, it skidded off the atmosphere of Mars and was gone. The cause was simple: the designers of the orbiter integrated two independently developed systems where one was using US customary (imperial) units of measurement and another was based on the SI (metric) units. Thus, non-uniform tables were UNION-ed together (concatenating records) and data with non-uniform records appeared in the data set. Since the data measurement values used by the orbiter were not uniform across multiple data records, NASA wasted $125 million of its budget.

The distinction between consistency and uniformity is subtle but important. As illustrated by the Mars orbiter example, ensuring consistency of validation and accuracy rules across data silos is insufficient to address data quality. The *uniform* principle states that for every column in a data set, all records should use data that was recorded using the same (uniform) measurement system. Instead of continuing with the NASA example, consider a more down-to-earth scenario of a data set created to analyze customer satisfaction with different video streaming services.

Suppose some streaming services are prompting users to rate their satisfaction with content on a scale from 0–4 stars after each viewing. Other services may use a value of 0 to indicate no response on a scale of 1–4 stars. Although the rules around valid values for both are identical, to ensure data quality, it is insufficient to specify that customer satisfaction should be a DOUBLE value with valid interval of [0, 4] and then apply this interval consistently across video-streaming service data silos. For instance, if the average satisfaction scores for each service are recorded daily and joined to prepare an aggregated average score, the result is not uniform across rows in the data set. Specifically, the service that uses the value of 0 to indicate no response will be penalized in the analysis.

Uniformity issues often arise over the lifetime of a data set. Consider a grocery store chain that enforces a store aisle coding system where all stores have aisles numbered 1–8, with each aisle corresponding to a produce category, such as 1 for dairy, 2 for meats, 3 for frozen foods, and so on. As soon as a single store violates the aisle coding system, for instance by coding dairy as 2 instead of 1, uniformity is violated across the entire grocery chain.

## UNIFIED

In a 1912 book, influential logician and philosopher Bertrand Russell used a story to illustrate the problem with inductive reasoning, a fundamental principle behind machine learning. Paraphrasing Russell, here's the fable in a nutshell:

> *On December 1, a turkey was born in the United States. It was no ordinary turkey. Some say it was the most intelligent turkey that ever lived. The genius turkey soon figured out*

*the patterns of the night sky and the role of the sun in casting shadows, and realized that it was fed at 7:00 a.m. every day. Reasoning that food was critical to well-being, it proceeded to ask itself whether it would be worthwhile to plot an escape, risking hunger and death, or if it would be safer to remain a well-fed captive. Having re-invented statistics, the rational genius turkey gathered data, developing increasing confidence that it will be fed every day at 7:00 a.m. regardless of the position of the sun, the moon, the stars, temperature, precipitation, and other factors. Sadly, the morning of the Thanksgiving Day the food did not come, and the head of the genius turkey landed on a chopping block.*

The story (which is meant to be more facetious rather than tragic) is here to help you remember that the machine learning models that you create, no matter how complex, are little more than digital versions of Russell's turkey. Their success is based solely on their capacity to take advantage of the data available to them. In contrast, as a machine learning practitioner, you can make your machine learning project more successful through curiosity and causal and deductive reasoning: by discovering facts and data sets that are novel and relevant to the project's use case, unifying the discovered information with the data set on hand, and expanding the scope of the relevant training data available to train models. You can also help minimize the risks to the machine learning project's success by discovering and addressing potential sources of non-obvious systemic bias in the training data set, unifying and bringing into alignment the cultural values of the project's operating environment and the contents of the data set.

While you can rely on machine learning models to perform effective inductive reasoning, it is your responsibility to enforce the *unified* principle, meaning that your data set:

- Is a single place for the data relevant to your project's machine learning use case(s)
- Aligns the criteria used by your use case to achieve unbiased data-driven decision making, with the content of the data being used for machine learning model training
- Depends on a common data quality process for the data used for machine learning model training and for the data used with a trained machine learning model

The unified principle is a part of VACUUM to remind you that data quality is a journey and not a destination.

## 3.3    *Applying VACUUM to the DC taxi data*

Now that you know about the VACUUM data quality principles, it is time to apply the principles to the DC taxi data set. In this section, you are going to start with a single table of data and focus on how to implement the data quality queries that ensure that the data set is valid, accurate, and uniform.

### 3.3.1 *Enforcing the schema to ensure valid values*

This section introduces the SQL statements you can execute against the DC taxi data set to check for invalid values and eliminate them from further analysis.

The schema shown in table 3.2 matches the version you have first encountered in chapter 2. The schema specifies the required data types for the taxi fare estimation service interface using SQL types. In the upcoming chapters of the book, when you will start training machine learning models from the DC taxi data, NULL values in the training data set can create problems. (Consider asking a machine learning model to estimate taxi fare for a NULL pickup location!) So, the schema is designed to ensure that none of the data values are permitted to be NULL.

Table 3.2  Schema and example values for a taxi fare estimation service interface

| Input | | |
|---|---|---|
| **Name** | **Data Type** | **Example Value** |
| Pickup location latitude | FLOAT | 38.907243 |
| Pickup location longitude | FLOAT | –77.042754 |
| Dropoff location latitude | FLOAT | 38.90451 |
| Dropoff location longitude | FLOAT | –77.048813 |
| Expected start time of the trip | STRING[a] | 01/12/2015 12:42 |
| **Output** | | |
| **Name** | **Data Type** | **Example Value** |
| Estimated fare (dollars) | FLOAT | 6.12 |

a. The timestamp is stored as a string using the month/day/year hour:minute format.

Let's kick off the effort of cleaning up the data set for machine learning by finding out the number of the timestamps with NULL values in the origindatetime_tr column using the following query from your shell, assuming you executed the Python awscli_to_df() function from listing 3.4 to output the query result using pandas:

```
source utils.sh ; athena_query_to_pandas "
SELECT
    (SELECT COUNT(*) FROM dc_taxi_db.dc_taxi_parquet) AS total,
    COUNT(*) AS null_origindate_time_total
FROM
    dc_taxi_db.dc_taxi_parquet
WHERE
    origindatetime_tr IS NULL
"
```

This results in the following:

| total | null_origindate_time_total |
|---|---|
| 67435888 | 14262196 |

For brevity the upcoming code snippets will no longer remind you to run `source utils.sh ; athena_query_to_pandas` or `awscli_to_df()`.

Recall that the SQL `COUNT(*)` function[7] returns the count of both `NULL` and non-`NULL` values. However, since the `WHERE` clause of the SQL query restricts the output to the rows where `origindatetime_tr` is `NULL`, the output of the SQL query reports that 14,262,196 rows are `NULL` out of the total 67,435,888 rows in the entire data set.

Beyond ensuring that the `origindatetime_tr` values are non-`NULL`, it is also critical to confirm the values comply with the regular expression definition for valid timestamp values. In practice this means that it should be possible to parse the non-`NULL` values of the `origindatetime_tr` column into relevant elements of a timestamp, including year, month, day, hour, and minute.

Fortunately, you do not have to implement the regular expression parsing rules to process the date/times. The following SQL query takes the difference between the total number of the rows in the data set and the number of the `origindatetime_tr` values that are not `NULL` and can be correctly parsed using the SQL `DATE_PARSE` function which uses the `%m/%d/%Y %H:%i` format in the DC taxi data set:

```
SELECT
    (SELECT COUNT(*) FROM dc_taxi_db.dc_taxi_parquet)
    - COUNT(DATE_PARSE(origindatetime_tr, '%m/%d/%Y %H:%i'))
    AS origindatetime_not_parsed
FROM
    dc_taxi_db.dc_taxi_parquet
WHERE
    origindatetime_tr IS NOT NULL;
```

This results in the following:

| origindatetime_not_parsed |
|---|
| 14262196 |

Since the difference returned by the statement is also equal to 14,262,196, this means that all but the `NULL` values of the timestamp can be parsed. Also, notice that the SQL statement uses a SQL subquery to compute the total number of rows in the data set,

---

[7]  The warning about `SELECT *` that you read about in this chapter does not apply to `COUNT(*)` since the two are fundamentally different operations in SQL: the former returns the values from all columns for every row, while the latter returns just the row count.

including both NULL and non-NULL values because the subquery does not include a WHERE clause. The WHERE clause at the ending of the outer SQL query applies only to the calculation of the COUNT of the values that can be correctly parsed by the DATE_PARSE function.

Let's continue to apply the validation rules to the origin and destination locations. Since in the use case the latitude and longitude coordinates for the origin and destination locations are non-nullable, let's explore the impact of the validation rules on the coordinate values as shown next.

**Listing 3.5 How often parts of the pickup location coordinate are missing**

```
SELECT
    ROUND(100.0 * COUNT(*) / (SELECT COUNT(*)
                        FROM dc_taxi_db.dc_taxi_parquet), 2)

        AS percentage_null,

    (SELECT COUNT(*)
     FROM dc_taxi_db.dc_taxi_parquet
     WHERE origin_block_longitude_double IS NULL
     OR origin_block_latitude_double IS NULL)

        AS either_null,

    (SELECT COUNT(*)
     FROM dc_taxi_db.dc_taxi_parquet
     WHERE origin_block_longitude_double IS NULL
     AND origin_block_latitude_double IS NULL)

        AS both_null

FROM
    dc_taxi_db.dc_taxi_parquet
WHERE
    origin_block_longitude_double IS NULL
    OR origin_block_latitude_double IS NULL
```

This results in the following:

| percentage_null | either_null | both_null |
|---|---|---|
| 14.04 | 9469667 | 9469667 |

According to the results of the query, in the data set, origin_block_latitude and origin_block_latitude are missing in pairs (i.e., both are NULL values if either is NULL) in 9,469,667 rows, or roughly 14.04% of the data set.

A similar analysis of the destination coordinates uses the following SQL statement:

```
SELECT
    ROUND(100.0 * COUNT(*) / (SELECT COUNT(*)
                        FROM dc_taxi_db.dc_taxi_parquet), 2)

        AS percentage_null,

    (SELECT COUNT(*)
     FROM dc_taxi_db.dc_taxi_parquet
     WHERE destination_block_longitude_double IS NULL
     OR destination_block_latitude_double IS NULL)

        AS either_null,

    (SELECT COUNT(*)
     FROM dc_taxi_db.dc_taxi_parquet
     WHERE destination_block_longitude_double IS NULL
     AND destination_block_latitude_double IS NULL)

        AS both_null

FROM
    dc_taxi_db.dc_taxi_parquet
WHERE
    destination_block_longitude_double IS NULL
    OR destination_block_latitude_double IS NULL
```

This results in

| percentage_null | either_null | both_null |
|-----------------|-------------|-----------|
| 19.39 | 13074278 | 13074278 |

which shows that 13,074,278 rows have destination coordinates with NULL values, which is roughly 19.39% of the entire data set.

The fractions of the NULL values for the origin and destination coordinates are clearly significant. In the potential worst case of missing values, you could find that 42.4% (i.e., 24.59% + 17.81%) of the rows had either the origin or destination coordinates missing. However, in the data set, a large portion of the missing values overlap, meaning that if either origin or destination is NULL, the other coordinate is NULL as well. You can find the count and the fraction of the missing coordinates using the following:

```
SELECT
    COUNT(*)
      AS total,

    ROUND(100.0 * COUNT(*) / (SELECT COUNT(*)
                        FROM dc_taxi_db.dc_taxi_parquet), 2)
        AS percent
```

```
FROM
    dc_taxi_db.dc_taxi_parquet

WHERE
    origin_block_latitude_double IS NULL
    OR origin_block_longitude_double IS NULL
    OR destination_block_latitude_double IS NULL
    OR destination_block_longitude_double IS NULL
```

This results in

| total | percent |
|-------|---------|
| 16578716 | 24.58 |

which shows that 24.58%, or 16,578,716 rows, in the data set do not have a useful pair of origin and destination coordinates. Since the pickup and the drop-off locations are a required part of the taxi fare estimation service specification, let's focus the data quality efforts on the remaining 75.42% of the rows with usable pickup and drop-off coordinates.

### 3.3.2 *Cleaning up invalid fare amounts*

This section walks you though the SQL statements to analyze the `fare_amount` column and enforce validation rules for the column values.

The PySpark job that populated the `dc_taxi_parquet` table performed some validation processing on the original data set. If you query Athena for the schema of the table, notice that the values needed for the project exist as both string and double types. Having both types means that in the cases when a value cannot be converted to the desired `DOUBLE` type (e.g., when a value cannot be parsed as a double), the original value is preserved and available for troubleshooting of the data.

According to the schema specifications described in chapter 2, every taxi trip record must have non-`NULL` values in the fare amount, trip start timestamp, and origin and destination latitude/longitude coordinates. Let's start by investigating the instances where the `fareamount_double` column contains `NULL` values, which are not allowed according to the schema. Since the `fareamount_string` column is a source of information for fare amount values that failed the parsing from `STRING` to `DOUBLE`, you can learn more about the problem values using the following SQL statement.

**Listing 3.6  Values of the `fareamount_string` column that failed to parse as doubles**

```
SELECT
    fareamount_string,
    COUNT(fareamount_string) AS rows,
    ROUND(100.0 * COUNT(fareamount_string) /
        ( SELECT COUNT(*)
          FROM dc_taxi_db.dc_taxi_parquet), 2)
```

```
        AS percent
FROM
    dc_taxi_db.dc_taxi_parquet
WHERE
    fareamount_double IS NULL
    AND fareamount_string IS NOT NULL
GROUP BY
    fareamount_string;
```

This results in the following:

| fareamount_string | rows | percent |
|---|---|---|
| NULL | 334964 | 0.5 |

The SQL statement in listing 3.6 filters the set of the values of the fareamount_string to focus only on the cases where PySpark failed to parse the fare amount, or more precisely on the rows where fareamount_double (the column containing the outputs for the parsing algorithm) has a NULL value while the fareamount_string (the column containing the inputs to the parsing algorithm) is not a NULL value.

According to the output of the query, there are 334,964 such entries where the parse failed. All correspond to the case where fareamount_string is equal to a string value of 'NULL'. This is good news because only about 0.5% of the data set is impacted by this problem, and there is no additional work to be done: the 'NULL' values cannot be converted to DOUBLE. Had the output of listing 3.6 found cases where some of the DOUBLE values were not parsed because they contained extra characters, such as in strings '$7.86', it would have been necessary to implement additional code to correctly parse such values to DOUBLE.

To continue the search for invalid fareamount values, it is worthwhile to explore some of the summary statistics of the fareamount_double column. The following SQL query moves the summary statistics computation into a separate subquery using two WITH clauses. Note that the data-specific query is packaged as a subquery named src and with the stats subquery referencing the result from src.

**Listing 3.7  Reusable pattern for de-coupling the statistics query from the data query**

```
WITH
src AS (SELECT
            fareamount_double AS val
        FROM
            dc_taxi_db.dc_taxi_parquet),

stats AS
    (SELECT
        MIN(val) AS min,
        APPROX_PERCENTILE(val, 0.25) AS q1,
        APPROX_PERCENTILE(val ,0.5) AS q2,
```

```
        APPROX_PERCENTILE(val, 0.75) AS q3,
        AVG(val) AS mean,
        STDDEV(val) AS std,
        MAX(val) AS max
    FROM
        src)

SELECT
    DISTINCT min, q1, q2, q3, max

FROM
    dc_taxi_db.dc_taxi_parquet, stats
```

This results in the following:

| min | q1 | q2 | q3 | max |
|---|---|---|---|---|
| −2064.71 | 7.03 | 9.73 | 13.78 | 745557.28 |

Based on the minimum value in the data set reported by the output of the query in listing 3.7, it should be clear that the data set is impacted by a category of values that are not valid: the taxi fares should not be negative or less than \$3.25. Recall from the review of the DC taxi business rules in chapter 2 that the minimum charge for a taxi ride in DC is \$3.25. Let's find the percentage of the data set impacted:

```
WITH
src AS (SELECT
            COUNT(*) AS total
        FROM
            dc_taxi_db.dc_taxi_parquet
        WHERE
            fareamount_double IS NOT NULL)

SELECT
    ROUND(100.0 * COUNT(fareamount_double) / MIN(total), 2) AS percent
FROM
    dc_taxi_db.dc_taxi_parquet, src
WHERE
    fareamount_double < 3.25
    AND fareamount_double IS NOT NULL
```

This results in the following:

| percent |
|---|
| 0.49 |

The output indicates that only 0.49% of the rows are impacted by the fare amount values that are negative or below the minimum threshold, so they can be readily ignored by the analysis. From the validation standpoint this means that implementation of the validation rules should be modified to use the values greater than or equal to 3.25.

### 3.3.3    *Improving the accuracy*

In this section, let's take a closer look at the accuracy of the NULL values by comparing them against a reference data source of trip mileage values. As you learned in the previous section, the NULL values for taxi fare add up to just 0.5% of the DC taxi data set. Using reference data in the `mileage_double` column can help you better understand the cases when the mileage of the trip translates into NULL fare amounts.

---

**Listing 3.8    Summary statistics for the `mileage_double` values**

```
SELECT
    fareamount_string,
    ROUND( MIN(mileage_double), 2) AS min,
    ROUND( APPROX_PERCENTILE(mileage_double, 0.25), 2) AS q1,
    ROUND( APPROX_PERCENTILE(mileage_double ,0.5), 2) AS q2,
    ROUND( APPROX_PERCENTILE(mileage_double, 0.75), 2) AS q3,
    ROUND( MAX(mileage_double), 2) AS max
FROM
    dc_taxi_db.dc_taxi_parquet
WHERE
    fareamount_string LIKE 'NULL'
GROUP BY
    fareamount_string
```

This results in the following:

| fareamount_string | min | q1 | q2 | q3 | max |
|---|---|---|---|---|---|
| NULL | 0.0 | 0.0 | 1.49 | 4.79 | 2591.82 |

The SQL statement in listing 3.8 reports the summary statistics (including minimum, maximum, and quartile values) for the mileage column only for the cases where the `fareamount_string` failed to parse, or more specifically where it is equal to 'NULL'. The output of the query indicates that more than a quarter of the cases (the lower quartile, the range from the minimum value up to 25th percentile) correspond to trips of 0 miles. At least a quarter of the mileage values (between the middle and upper quartiles, the range that includes 50th and 75th percentiles) appear to be in a reasonable mileage range for DC taxis.

At this point, you may consider several data augmentation experiments to try to recover missing `fareamount_double` data values by computing an estimate of the fare from the mileage column. The experiments could replace the missing fare amount values using an estimate. For example, you could replace the NULL fare amounts in the cases where the mileage is in the middle quartile with the arithmetic mean (average) `fareamount` for the known fare amounts in the same range. More sophisticated estimators, including machine learning models, are also possible.

However, since the output in listing 3.8 indicates that it would help address roughly 0.12% (= 0.25 * 0.49%) of the data set, these experiments are unlikely to have a significant impact on the overall performance of the fare estimation model.

Based on the output of the query in listing 3.7, the maximum value for the fare amount appears to be a garbage data point. Yet from the standpoint of the data schema it is valid, as 745,557.28 is less than the maximum value of the SQL DOUBLE data type.

Addressing the issue with the upper bound for fare amount values requires an application of an accuracy rule. Recall that validation checks should be performed without a reference to an external data source.

In the case of the DC taxi data set, the maximum fare amount is not explicitly specified as a business rule. However, using some commonsense reasoning and reference data outside of the DC taxi data set, you can come up with some sensible upper bounds on the maximum fare amount:

- *Estimate 1.* The maximum fare amount depends on the miles driven per work shift of a taxi driver. A quick internet search tells us that a DC taxi driver is required to take at least 8 hours of a break from driving within every 24-hour period. So, hypothetically, a driver may drive a maximum of 16 hours. According to websites of DC, Maryland, and Virginia, the maximum speed limit across those areas are capped at 70 mph. Even in the absurd case where the driver is driving 16 hours at the maximum speed limit, the maximum distance travelled during that time is 1,120 miles.

  Clearly a 1,120-mile taxi ride with an estimated fare of **$2,422.45** (1,120 miles * $2.16/mile + $3.25 base fare) is a hypothetical upper boundary that will not translate to an accurate DC taxi fare amount. However, instead of throwing out this estimate, the right thing to do is to take it under advisement and refine it by aggregating it with more estimates.

- *Estimate 2.* Instead of focusing on the distance traveled, you can also estimate the maximum fare amount based on time. Consider that according to the DC taxi fare rules, a taxi can be hired at $35 per hour. Since the maximum amount of time a cabbie is permitted to work is 16 hours, you can calculate another, distance-independent, estimate for the upper bound of the fare amount at $560 = 16 hour * $35/hour.

- *Estimate 3.* An upper bound on the taxi fare can also be based on the distance of a trip between the two furthest corners of the locations in the data set. The DC taxi data set boundary described in chapter 2 is roughly a square with downtown DC in the middle. You can find the locations of the lower-left and the upper-right points on the square using the following query:

```
SELECT
  MIN(lat) AS lower_left_latitude,
  MIN(lon) AS lower_left_longitude,
  MAX(lat) AS upper_right_latitude,
  MAX(lon) AS upper_right_longitude

FROM (
  SELECT
    MIN(origin_block_latitude_double) AS lat,
    MIN(origin_block_longitude_double) AS lon
  FROM "dc_taxi_db"."dc_taxi_parquet"

  UNION

  SELECT
    MIN(destination_block_latitude_double) AS lat,
    MIN(destination_block_longitude_double) AS lon
  FROM "dc_taxi_db"."dc_taxi_parquet"

  UNION

  SELECT
    MAX(origin_block_latitude_double) AS lat,
    MAX(origin_block_longitude_double) AS lon
  FROM "dc_taxi_db"."dc_taxi_parquet"

  UNION

  SELECT
    MAX(destination_block_latitude_double) AS lat,
    MAX(destination_block_longitude_double) AS lon
  FROM "dc_taxi_db"."dc_taxi_parquet"

)
```

This results in the following:

| lower_left_latitude | lower_left_longitude | upper_right_latitude | upper_right_longitude |
|---------------------|----------------------|----------------------|------------------------|
| 38.81138            | –77.113633           | 38.994909            | –76.910012             |

Plugging the latitude and longitude coordinates reported by the query into OpenStreetMap (http://mng.bz/zEOZ) yields 21.13 miles, or an estimate of **$48.89** (21.13 * $2.16/mile + $3.25).

- *Estimate 4.* For yet another estimation technique, recall that according to the central limit theorem (CLT) of statistics, the sum (and consequently the average) of arithmetic means of random samples[8] of fare amount values is distributed

---

[8] The sample size is expected to consist of at least a few tens of records, and the records should be independent and sampled with replacement.

according to the Gaussian (bell-shaped) distribution. You can generate a thousand random samples of arithmetic means of taxi mileages from the data (so you can later compute their mean) using an SQL statement.

> **Listing 3.9  Unzipped files of the DC taxi trips data set from 2015 to 2019**

```
WITH dc_taxi AS
(SELECT *,
    origindatetime_tr
    || fareamount_string
    || origin_block_latitude_string
    || origin_block_longitude_string
    || destination_block_latitude_string
    || destination_block_longitude_string
    || mileage_string AS objectid

    FROM "dc_taxi_db"."dc_taxi_parquet"

    WHERE fareamount_double >= 3.25
            AND fareamount_double IS NOT NULL
            AND mileage_double > 0 )

SELECT AVG(mileage_double) AS average_mileage
FROM dc_taxi
WHERE objectid IS NOT NULL
GROUP BY
➥ MOD( ABS( from_big_endian_64( xxhash64( to_utf8( objectid ) ) ) ), 1000)
```

Note the complex logic in the `GROUP BY` portion of the statement. The `objectid` column in the data set contains a unique identifier for every row of data represented with sequentially ordered integer values. You could use a `GROUP BY MOD(CAST(objectid AS INTEGER), 1000)` clause instead of the version in listing 3.9. However, if the `objectid` values are based on the original order of the taxi trips in the data set, each resulting sample would be made of mileage values that are exactly 1,000 rows apart from each other in the data set. Such an ordered, interval-structured sampling may introduce unintended bias in the calculations. For example, if there are roughly 1,000 taxi rides in DC per hour, and trains from DC to New York City leave the train station at the top of every hour, then some samples will contain primarily taxi rides terminating at the train station. Other regularly spaced samples may consist of too many end-of-day taxi rides.

Random sampling (based on pseudorandom values used in computing) can address the bias problem of sampling over regular intervals. However, using a pseudorandom number generator to group values as in the following `GROUP BY` clause has several disadvantages:

```
GROUP BY MOD(ABS(RAND()), 1000)
```

First, it is impossible to exactly reproduce the results of the sampling since the random number generator does not guarantee deterministic behavior: there is no way to specify a random number seed that will guarantee a sequence of identical pseudo-random values across multiple executions of the SQL statement.

Second, even if you attempted to pre-compute pseudo-random identifiers for every row in the data set and save the rows along with the identifiers to a separate table for future re-use, the table would soon become out of date. For example, if the DC taxi data set expanded to include 2020 taxi rides, a subsequent Glue crawler indexing of the data would invalidate the source data table and force re-creation of new pseudo-random identifiers.

In contrast, the approach used in listing 3.9 and shown here has the advantages of the pseudorandom shuffling of the data set, eliminating unintended bias, and pro-duces identical results across queries regardless of additions to the data set, as long as each row of data can be uniquely identified:

```
GROUP BY MOD(ABS(from_big_endian_64(xxhash64(to_utf8(objectid)))), 1000)
```

In the SQL statement, the application of the functions to `objectid` play the role of the unique identifier. The combination of the `xxhash64` hashing function and the `from_big_endian_64` produces what is effectively a pseudorandom but deterministic value from `objectid`.

As a visual confirmation that the averages of the fare amount samples generated in listing 3.9 approximate the Gaussian distribution, the following histogram in fig-ure 3.3 is a plot based on the listing with an arbitrary choice of the pseudorandom number seed value.

Recall that the original intention behind using 1,000 random samples of mean val-ues in the `average_mileage` column was to compute the mean of the samples. Since in a normal distribution roughly 99.99% of the values are within four standard devia-tions away from the mean, the following SQL statement yields another statistical esti-mate for the upper bound on the taxi ride mileage and consequently another estimate for the upper bound on the fare amount:

```
WITH dc_taxi AS
(SELECT *,
    origindatetime_tr
    || fareamount_string
    || origin_block_latitude_string
    || origin_block_longitude_string
    || destination_block_latitude_string
    || destination_block_longitude_string
    || mileage_string AS objectid

  FROM "dc_taxi_db"."dc_taxi_parquet"

  WHERE fareamount_double >= 3.25
        AND fareamount_double IS NOT NULL
        AND mileage_double > 0 ),
```

```
dc_taxi_samples AS (
    SELECT AVG(mileage_double) AS average_mileage
    FROM dc_taxi
    WHERE objectid IS NOT NULL
    GROUP BY
        MOD( ABS( from_big_endian_64( xxhash64( to_utf8( objectid ) ) ) ),
        1000)
)
SELECT AVG(average_mileage) + 4 * STDDEV(average_mileage)
FROM dc_taxi_samples
```

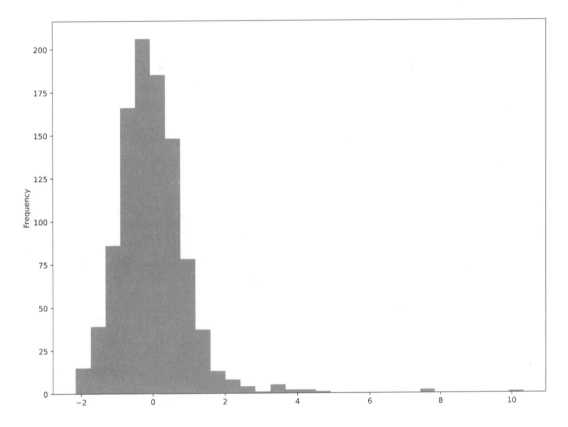

**Figure 3.3  Random sampling in listing 3.9 relies on the CLT for estimation.**

This execution yields approximately 12.138 miles, or roughly **$29.47** (12.01 * $2.16/mile + $3.25) as yet another upper-bound fare estimate. Of course, the advantage of the statistical approach explained in this section is that it can be used directly with the fareamount_double column, as in the following SQL statement:

```
WITH dc_taxi AS
(SELECT *,
    origindatetime_tr
    || fareamount_string
    || origin_block_latitude_string
    || origin_block_longitude_string
    || destination_block_latitude_string
    || destination_block_longitude_string
    || mileage_string AS objectid

    FROM "dc_taxi_db"."dc_taxi_parquet"

    WHERE fareamount_double >= 3.25
          AND fareamount_double IS NOT NULL
          AND mileage_double > 0 ),

dc_taxi_samples AS (
    SELECT AVG(fareamount_double) AS average_fareamount
    FROM dc_taxi
    WHERE objectid IS NOT NULL
    GROUP BY
        MOD( ABS( from_big_endian_64( xxhash64( to_utf8( objectid ) ) ) ), 1000)
)
SELECT AVG(average_fareamount) + 4 * STDDEV(average_fareamount)
FROM dc_taxi_samples
```

This yields an upper bound of $15.96.

While you can continue exploring alternative ideas for estimates, this is a good point to stop and evaluate the average upper bound for the fare amount so far.

Using a simple averaging implementation in Python

```
means = [15.96, 29.19, 48.89, 560, 2,422.45]
sum(means) / len(means)

179.748
```

shows that the estimated upper bound for taxi fare is $179.75

While it is certainly possible to continue working on ideas for a better upper bound, let's estimate how much data is left after using the upper bound of $179.75:

```
SELECT
    100.0 * COUNT(fareamount_double) /
      (SELECT COUNT(*)
      FROM dc_taxi_db.dc_taxi_parquet
      WHERE fareamount_double IS NOT NULL) AS percent
FROM
    dc_taxi_db.dc_taxi_parquet
WHERE (fareamount_double < 3.25 OR fareamount_double > 179.75)
      AND fareamount_double IS NOT NULL;
```

This results in the following:

| percent |
| --- |
| 0.48841 |

Note that only about 0.49% percent of the data was excluded based on the bounds.

However, rerunning the summary statistics on the `fareamount_double` column using the new bounds produces significantly more sensible summary statistics:

```
WITH src AS (SELECT fareamount_double AS val
             FROM dc_taxi_db.dc_taxi_parquet
             WHERE fareamount_double IS NOT NULL
             AND fareamount_double >= 3.25
             AND fareamount_double <= 180.0),
stats AS
     (SELECT
       ROUND(MIN(val), 2) AS min,
       ROUND(APPROX_PERCENTILE(val, 0.25), 2) AS q1,
       ROUND(APPROX_PERCENTILE(val, 0.5), 2) AS q2,
       ROUND(APPROX_PERCENTILE(val, 0.75), 2) AS q3,
       ROUND(AVG(val), 2) AS mean,
       ROUND(STDDEV(val), 2) AS std,
       ROUND(MAX(val), 2) AS max
     FROM src)
SELECT min, q1, q2, q3, max, mean, std
FROM stats;
```

This results in the following:

| min | q1 | q2 | q3 | max | mean | std |
| --- | --- | --- | --- | --- | --- | --- |
| 3.25 | 7.03 | 9.73 | 13.78 | 179.83 | 11.84 | 8.65 |

Now that the accuracy checks for the `fareamount` column are done, you should be ready to repeat the accuracy exercise with the pickup and drop-off coordinates. While it is possible to determine whether the latitude and longitude coordinates are valid based on their value alone, you need a reference data source to decide whether a value is accurate. The OpenStreetMap service used to generate the DC taxi map in chapter 2 can also be used to confirm the accuracy of the origin and destination coordinates in the data set.

Using the SQL statement and OpenStreetMap (http://mng.bz/01ez) to check the minimum and maximum coordinates for the origin latitude and longitude columns confirms that resulting pairs (38.81138, −77.113633) and (38.994217, −76.910012) are within DC boundaries:

```
SELECT
    MIN(origin_block_latitude_double) AS olat_min,
    MIN(origin_block_longitude_double) AS olon_min,
    MAX(origin_block_latitude_double) AS olat_max,
    MAX(origin_block_longitude_double) AS olon_max,
    MIN(destination_block_latitude_double) AS dlat_min,
    MIN(destination_block_longitude_double) AS dlon_min,
    MAX(destination_block_latitude_double) AS dlat_max,
    MAX(destination_block_longitude_double) AS dlon_max,
FROM
    dc_taxi_db.dc_taxi_parquet
```

This outputs the following:

| olat_min | olon_min | olat_max | olon_max | dlat_min | dlon_min | dlat_max | dlon_max |
|----------|----------|----------|----------|----------|----------|----------|----------|
| 38.81138 | –77.113633 | 38.994909 | –76.910012 | 38.81138 | –77.113633 | 38.994217 | –76.910012 |

## 3.4 Implementing VACUUM in a PySpark job

In this section, you will use what you learned about data quality in the DC taxi data set and apply your findings to implement a PySpark job. The purpose of the job is to perform high-throughput data cleanup of the dc_taxi_parquet table populated in chapter 2 using a distributed cluster of Apache Spark servers available from AWS Glue. The job should be implemented as a single Python file named dctaxi_parquet_vacuum.py; however, in this section, the file is split into separate code snippets, which are explained one by one in the upcoming paragraphs. The cleaned-up copy of the data set will be saved by the job to the parquet/vacuum subfolder in your S3 bucket.

The initial part of the code snippet for the PySpark job is in listing 3.10. Note that the lines of code up until ❶ are identical to the code from the PySpark job in chapter 2. This should not come as a surprise because this part of the code involves the import of prerequisite libraries and assignment of commonly used variables in PySpark jobs. The line of code annotated with ❶ is the first that's distinct from the chapter 2 PySpark job. Note that the line is reading the Parquet-formatted data set you created at the end of chapter 2 and have been querying using Athena in this chapter.

> **Listing 3.10 PySpark DataFrame reading code in dctaxi_parquet_vacuum.py**

```
import sys
from awsglue.transforms import *
from awsglue.utils import getResolvedOptions
from pyspark.context import SparkContext
from awsglue.context import GlueContext
from awsglue.job import Job

args = getResolvedOptions(sys.argv, ['JOB_NAME',
                                     'BUCKET_SRC_PATH',
                                     'BUCKET_DST_PATH',
                                     ])
```

```
BUCKET_SRC_PATH = args['BUCKET_SRC_PATH']
BUCKET_DST_PATH = args['BUCKET_DST_PATH']

sc = SparkContext()
glueContext = GlueContext(sc)
logger = glueContext.get_logger()
spark = glueContext.spark_session

job = Job(glueContext)
job.init(args['JOB_NAME'], args)

df = ( spark
       .read
       .parquet(f"{BUCKET_SRC_PATH}") )
```

**①** Read the source Parquet data set into a Spark DataFrame.

To select the subset of the data for cleanup, the Spark `DataFramecreateOrReplace-TempView` method is invoked from the line with **①** in listing 3.11. The method creates a temporary view named `dc_taxi_parquet` as part of the `SparkSession`, which is accessible via the `spark` variable. The view enables Spark to query the `DataFrame` created at **①** using the SQL query that starts on the line with **②** referencing the `dc_taxi_parquet` view **③**.

The content of the `WHERE` clause that begins at **④** should not come as a surprise. The checks for `NULL` values and the range bounds for the `fareamount_double` column are exactly the condition defined in section 3.3.

The call to the method `replace` at **⑤** replaces any instances of newline characters in the multiline string with an empty character. The `replace` method is needed to ensure that the multiline string used to specify the SQL query in the PySpark job is compatible with the SQL query parser used by Spark.

**Listing 3.11 PySpark data cleanup implementation saved to `dc_taxi_vacuum.py`**

```
df.createOrReplaceTempView("dc_taxi_parquet")

query_df = spark.sql("""
SELECT
    origindatetime_tr,
    fareamount_double,
    origin_block_latitude,
    origin_block_longitude,
    destination_block_latitude,
    destination_block_longitude
FROM
    dc_taxi_parquet

WHERE
    origindatetime_tr IS NOT NULL
    AND fareamount_double IS NOT NULL
    AND fareamount_double >= 3.25
    AND fareamount_double <= 180.0
    AND origin_block_latitude IS NOT NULL
```

**①** Alias the source data set in df as dc_taxi_parquet for Spark SQL API.

**②** Create a DataFrame query_df populated based on the SQL query in this snippet.

**③** Query dc_taxi_parquet to output the clean values for further analysis.

**④** Filter records according to the VACUUM analysis in section 3.3.

```
       AND origin_block_longitude IS NOT NULL
       AND destination_block_latitude IS NOT NULL
       AND destination_block_longitude IS NOT NULL


""".replace('\n', ''))    ◄──────┐    **Eliminate newline characters in**
                                  │    **the Python multiline string for**
                              ❺    **Spark SQL API compatibility.**
```

Since the original STRING-formatted column origindatetime_tr in the data set needs to be formatted as a numeric value for machine learning, the PySpark DataFrame API code in listing 3.12 first converts the column to a SQL TIMESTAMP ❶, eliminating any NULL values that may have been produced due to failed conversion from STRING to TIMESTAMP. The derived column is then further broken up into numeric, INTEGER columns, including year, month, day of the week (dow), and hour of the taxi trip. The last step following the conversion removes the temporary origindatetime_ts column, drops any records with missing data, and eliminates duplicate records.

**Listing 3.12   PySpark data cleanup implementation saved to dc_taxi_vacuum.py**

```
#parse to check for valid value of the original timestamp
from pyspark.sql.functions import col, to_timestamp, \
    dayofweek, year, month, hour
from pyspark.sql.types import IntegerType

#convert the source timestamp into numeric data needed for machine learning
query_df = (query_df
  .withColumn("origindatetime_ts", \
    to_timestamp("origindatetime_tr", "dd/MM/yyyy HH:mm"))    ◄──┐    **Parse the trip**
  .where(col("origindatetime_ts").isNotNull())                     **origindatetime_tr**
  .drop("origindatetime_tr")                                       **timestamp using the**
  .withColumn( 'year_integer',                        ◄──┐         **dd/MM/yyyy HH:mm**
    year('origindatetime_ts').cast(IntegerType()) )       ❶       **pattern.**
  .withColumn( 'month_integer',
    month('origindatetime_ts').cast(IntegerType()) )             **Construct numeric**
  .withColumn( 'dow_integer',                                     **columns based on year,**
    dayofweek('origindatetime_ts').cast(IntegerType()) )  ❷      **month, day of the week,**
  .withColumn( 'hour_integer',                                    **and hour of trip.**
    hour('origindatetime_ts').cast(IntegerType()) )
  .drop('origindatetime_ts') )

#drop missing data and duplicates    ❸    **Eliminate any records**
query_df = ( query_df                       **with missing or**
        .dropna()          ◄──┐             **duplicated data.**
        .drop_duplicates() )
```

The concluding part of the PySpark job, shown in listing 3.13, persists the resulting PySpark DataFrame as a Parquet-formatted data set in the AWS S3 location specified by the BUCKET_DST_PATH parameter. Note that the listing declares a save_stats_metadata function, which computes the summary statistics (using the PySpark describe function) of the cleaned-up data set, and saves the statistics as a single CSV file located in a

AWS S3 subfolder named .meta/stats under the S3 location from the BUCKET_DST_ PATH parameter.

**Listing 3.13 PySpark data cleanup implementation saved to dc_taxi_vacuum.py**

```
(query_df
 .write
 .parquet(f"{BUCKET_DST_PATH}", mode="overwrite"))
```
Persist the cleaned-up data set to BUCKET_DST_PATH in Parquet format.

```
def save_stats_metadata(df, dest, header = 'true', mode = 'overwrite'):
  return (df.describe()
    .coalesce(1)
    .write
    .option("header", header)
    .csv( dest, mode = mode ) )

save_stats_metadata(query_df,
    f"{BUCKET_DST_PATH}/.meta/stats")
```
Save the metadata about the cleaned-up data set as a separate CSV file.

```
job.commit()
```

For convenience, the entire PySpark job described is shown. Prior to executing this job, make sure you save the contents of the code listing to a file named dc_taxi_ vacuum.py.

**Listing 3.14 PySpark data clean-up code saved to dc_taxi_vacuum.py**

```
import sys
from awsglue.transforms import *
from awsglue.utils import getResolvedOptions
from pyspark.context import SparkContext
from awsglue.context import GlueContext
from awsglue.job import Job

args = getResolvedOptions(sys.argv, ['JOB_NAME',
                                     'BUCKET_SRC_PATH',
                                     'BUCKET_DST_PATH',
                                     ])

BUCKET_SRC_PATH = args['BUCKET_SRC_PATH']
BUCKET_DST_PATH = args['BUCKET_DST_PATH']

sc = SparkContext()
glueContext = GlueContext(sc)
logger = glueContext.get_logger()
spark = glueContext.spark_session

job = Job(glueContext)
job.init(args['JOB_NAME'], args)

df = ( spark
        .read
        .parquet(f"{BUCKET_SRC_PATH}") )
df.createOrReplaceTempView("dc_taxi_parquet")
```

```
query_df = spark.sql("""
SELECT
    fareamount_double,
    origindatetime_tr,
    origin_block_latitude_double,
    origin_block_longitude_double,
    destination_block_latitude_double,
    destination_block_longitude_double
FROM
  dc_taxi_parquet
WHERE
    origindatetime_tr IS NOT NULL
    AND fareamount_double IS NOT NULL
    AND fareamount_double >= 3.25
    AND fareamount_double <= 180.0
    AND origin_block_latitude_double IS NOT NULL
    AND origin_block_longitude_double IS NOT NULL
    AND destination_block_latitude_double IS NOT NULL
    AND destination_block_longitude_double IS NOT NULL
""".replace('\n', ''))


#parse to check for valid value of the original timestamp
from pyspark.sql.functions import col, to_timestamp, \
    dayofweek, year, month, hour
from pyspark.sql.types import IntegerType

#convert the source timestamp into numeric data needed for machine learning
query_df = (query_df
  .withColumn("origindatetime_ts",
    to_timestamp("origindatetime_tr", "dd/MM/yyyy HH:mm"))
  .where(col("origindatetime_ts").isNotNull())
  .drop("origindatetime_tr")
  .withColumn( 'year_integer',
    year('origindatetime_ts').cast(IntegerType()) )
  .withColumn( 'month_integer',
    month('origindatetime_ts').cast(IntegerType()) )
  .withColumn( 'dow_integer',
    dayofweek('origindatetime_ts').cast(IntegerType()) )
  .withColumn( 'hour_integer',
    hour('origindatetime_ts').cast(IntegerType()) )
  .drop('origindatetime_ts') )

#drop missing data and duplicates
query_df = ( query_df
            .dropna()
            .drop_duplicates() )

(query_df
 .write
 .parquet(f"{BUCKET_DST_PATH}", mode="overwrite"))

def save_stats_metadata(df, dest, header = 'true', mode = 'overwrite'):
  return (df.describe()
    .coalesce(1)
```

```
    .write
    .option("header", header)
    .csv(dest, mode = mode))

save_stats_metadata(query_df, f"{BUCKET_DST_PATH}/.meta/stats")

job.commit()
```

The `utils.sh` script file first introduced in section 3.3 includes bash functions to simplify execution of PySpark jobs in AWS Glue from your bash shell. Notice that in
listing 3.15 the PySpark job from listing 3.14 is referenced by the file name `dctaxi_`
`parquet_vacuum.py` and is used to start the AWS Glue job named `dc-taxi-parquet-`
`vacuum-job`. The job uses the Parquet-formatted DC taxi data set that you analyzed
earlier in this chapter to populate the `parquet/vacuum` subfolder of your AWS S3
bucket with a cleaned-up version of the data. The VACUUM-ed version is also persisted in the Parquet format.

> **Listing 3.15   Using bash to launch the PySpark job in `dctaxi_parquet_vacuum.py`**

```
%%bash
wget -q https://raw.githubusercontent.com/osipov/smlbook/master/utils.sh
source utils.sh

PYSPARK_SRC_NAME=dctaxi_parquet_vacuum.py \
PYSPARK_JOB_NAME=dc-taxi-parquet-vacuum-job \
BUCKET_SRC_PATH=s3://dc-taxi-$BUCKET_ID-$AWS_DEFAULT_REGION/parquet \
BUCKET_DST_PATH=s3://dc-taxi-$BUCKET_ID-$AWS_DEFAULT_REGION/parquet/vacuum \
run_job
```

Assuming that the PySpark job from listing 3.15 completes successfully, you should
observe an output resembling the following:

```
{
    "JobName": "dc-taxi-parquet-vacuum-job"
}
{
    "Name": "dc-taxi-parquet-vacuum-job"
}
{
    "JobRunId":
        "jr_8a157e870bb6915eef3b8c0c280d1d8596613f6ad79dd27e3699115b7a3eb55d"
}
Waiting for the job to finish.................SUCCEEDED
```

## Summary

- An interactive query service like AWS Athena can help with exploratory data analysis of structured data sets ranging from gigabytes to terabytes in size.
- The schema-on-read approach enables interactive query services to apply multiple, different data schemas to the same data set.
- VACUUM principles can help your machine learning project develop mature data quality practices compared to the garbage in, garbage out approach.
- An interactive query service, such as the PrestoDB-based AWS Athena and distributed data-processing platform Apache Spark-based AWS Glue, can be used to implement VACUUM principles for data sets stored in a public cloud.

# More exploratory data analysis and data preparation

4

**This chapter covers**

- Analyzing summary statistics of the DC taxi data set
- Evaluating alternative data set sizes for machine learning
- Using statistical measures to choose the right machine learning data set size
- Implementing data set sampling in a PySpark job

In the last chapter, you started with the analysis of the DC taxi fare data set. After the data set was converted to an analysis-friendly Apache Parquet format, you crawled the data schema and used the Athena interactive querying service to explore the data. These first steps of data exploration surfaced numerous data quality issues, motivating you to establish a rigorous approach to deal with the garbage in, garbage out problem in your machine learning project. Next, you learned about the VACUUM principles for data quality along with several case studies illustrating the real-world relevance of the principles. Finally, you applied VACUUM to the DC taxi data set to "clean" it and prepare a data set of sufficient quality to proceed with sampling from the data set for machine learning.

This chapter picks up with using the VACUUM-ed data set for a more in-depth data exploration. In this chapter, you will analyze the summary statistics (arithmetic means, standard deviations, and more) of the data set in order to make a better-informed decision about the sizes of the training, validation, and test data sets for machine learning. You'll compare common approaches for the selection of the data set sizes (e.g., using a 70/15/15% split) to an approach that takes the statistics of the data sets into account to pick the right size. You will learn about using statistical measures such as the standard error of the mean, z-scores, and p-values to help you evaluate alternative data set sizes and how to implement data-driven experiments for selecting the right size using PySpark.

## 4.1    *Getting started with data sampling*

This section introduces you to a more rigorous, data-driven, and reusable approach for choosing the right training, validation, and test data set split sizes for your data set. Using examples from the DC taxi data, you are going to explore the key statistical measures important for choosing the right data set size and then implement a PySpark job using a data set size-selection approach that can be re-used for other data sets.

One of the most common questions I hear from junior machine learning practitioners is about the selection of the data set size for training, validation, and test data sets. This should not come as a surprise since online courses, blogs, and machine learning tutorials often use numbers like 70/15/15%, meaning that 70% of the project data set should be allocated to training, 15% to validation, and 15% to held-out test data. Some courses argue for 80/10/10% splits or 98/1/1% for "big data" data sets. The well-known Netflix Prize used a roughly 97.3/1.35/1.35% split for a data set on the order of 100 million records, but with less than 1 GB in volume, should it qualify as "big data?"

### 4.1.1   *Exploring the summary statistics of the cleaned-up data set*

In this section, you are going to load the cleaned-up data set metadata as a pandas `DataFrame` and explore the summary statistics (including counts, arithmetic means, standard deviations, and more) of the data set.

At the conclusion of chapter 3, along with the cleaned-up version of the data set, the dctaxi_parquet_vacuum.py PySpark job used a `save_stats_metadata` function to save some metadata information with the statistical description for the data set, including the total number of rows, means, standard deviations, minimums, and maximums for every column of values. To read this information into a pandas `DataFrame` named df, execute the following code:

```
!pip install fsspec s3fs         ◁──────┐  Install the Python
                                         │  packages needed by
import s3fs                               │  pandas to read from S3.
import pandas as pd
```

```
df = pd.read_csv(f"s3://dc-taxi-{os.environ['BUCKET_ID']}-
➡ {os.environ['AWS_DEFAULT_REGION']}/parquet/
➡ vacuum/.meta/stats/*")        ◁────┐  Read the metadata into
                                     │  a pandas DataFrame.
print(df.info())
```

The code installs the s3fs library in your environment to access data from S3 using pandas read_csv API. The rest of the code lists the objects from the parquet/vacuum/.meta/stats/* subfolder of your S3 bucket and reads the contents of the CSV file from the folder into a pandas DataFrame.

The output of the info method of the data frame reports the schema of the data stored as well as the amount of memory consumed by the data.

**Listing 4.1  Output of `df.info()` for `dctaxi_parquet_vacuum.py` metadata**

```
<class 'pandas.core.frame.DataFrame'>
RangeIndex: 5 entries, 0 to 4
Data columns (total 10 columns):
 #   Column                             Non-Null Count   Dtype
---  ------                             --------------   -----
 0   summary                            5 non-null       object
 1   fareamount_double                  5 non-null       float64
 2   origin_block_latitude_double       5 non-null       float64
 3   origin_block_longitude_double      5 non-null       float64
 4   destination_block_latitude_double  5 non-null       float64
 5   destination_block_longitude_double 5 non-null       float64
 6   year_integer                       5 non-null       float64
 7   month_integer                      5 non-null       float64
 8   dow_integer                        5 non-null       float64
 9   hour_integer                       5 non-null       float64
dtypes: float64(9), object(1)
memory usage: 528.0+ bytes
None
```

Note that the schema in listing 4.1 aligns with the schema used by SQL queries from chapter 2, with a few minor changes: instead of DOUBLE, the data frame uses float64 and object instead of STRING. Also, there is a new summary column that did not exist in the DC taxi data set in S3. The summary column was created by the describe method of the dctaxi_parquet_vacuum.py PySpark job from chapter 3 and is used to store the name of the statistical functions, such as mean and count, for each row in the metadata table.

To get started, you can index the data frame using the summary column and look at the result

```
summary_df = df.set_index('summary')
summary_df
```

which produces

| summary | fareamount | origin_block_lattitude | origin_block_longitude | destination_block_lattitude | destination_block_longitude | year_integer | month_integer | dow_integer | h |
|---|---|---|---|---|---|---|---|---|---|
| count | 14,262,196.00 | 14,262,196.00 | 14,262,196.00 | 14,262,196.00 | 14,262,196.00 | 14,262,196.00 | 14,262,196.00 | 14,262,196.00 | 14,262,196.00 |
| mean | 9.74 | 38.90 | -77.03 | 38.91 | -77.03 | 2,016.62 | 6.57 | 3.99 | 14.00 |
| stddev | 4.54 | 0.01 | 0.02 | 0.02 | 0.02 | 1.28 | 3.45 | 2.01 | 6.15 |
| min | 3.25 | 38.81 | -77.11 | 38.81 | -77.11 | 2,015.00 | 1.00 | 1.00 | 0.00 |
| max | 179.56 | 38.99 | -76.91 | 38.99 | -76.91 | 2,019.00 | 12.00 | 7.00 | 23.00 |

Let's save the size of the data set (i.e., in terms of the number of the values per column) to a separate variable ds_size, which is going to be used later:

```
ds_size = summary_df.loc['count'].astype(int).max()
print(ds_size)
```

Once executed, this prints 14262196.

The code to obtain the size of the data set relies on the max method to find the largest count of values across all the columns in the data set. In the case of the cleaned-up DC taxi data set, all columns return an identical count because none contain NULL, None, or NaN values. Although for the DC taxi data set max is unnecessary, it is good practice to keep using the function to correctly count the largest number of rows needed to store the data.

Since the upcoming part of the chapter is focused on sampling from the data, create two separate series to gather the data set mean (mu)

```
mu = summary_df.loc['mean']
print(mu)
```

which should output

```
fareamount_double                        9.74
origin_block_latitude_double            38.90
origin_block_longitude_double          -77.03
destination_block_latitude_double       38.91
destination_block_longitude_double     -77.03
year_integer                         2,016.62
month_integer                            6.57
dow_integer                              3.99
hour_integer                            14.00
Name: mean, dtype: float64
```

and the standard deviation (sigma) statistics

```
sigma = summary_df.loc['stddev']
print(sigma)
```

which print the following:

```
fareamount_double                    4.539085
origin_block_latitude_double         0.014978
origin_block_longitude_double        0.019229
destination_block_latitude_double    0.017263
destination_block_longitude_double   0.022372
year_integer                         1.280343
month_integer                        3.454275
dow_integer                          2.005323
hour_integer                         6.145545
Name: stddev, dtype: float64
```

### 4.1.2   *Choosing the right sample size for the test data set*

In this section, you are going to explore the effectiveness of using machine learning "rules of thumb" for choosing data set sizes and decide the appropriate sizes for the DC taxi data set. Although this section uses the DC taxi data set as an example, you will learn about an approach for choosing the right sizes for the training, test, and validation data sets regardless of the actual data set you are using.

Now that you know about the average values of the numeric columns in the cleaned-up data set, you are prepared to tackle the question of how many records from the data set should be allocated to training your machine learning model and how many should be held out for the test and validation data sets. When preparing training, validation, and test data sets, many machine learning practitioners rely on rules of thumb or heuristics to decide on the sizes. Some argue for an 80/10/10% split across training, validation, and test, while others claim that the split should be 98/1/1% when the data set is large, without specifying what "large" means.

When approaching the issues of the number of records to allocate to training, validation, and test data sets, it is valuable to recall the basic rationale behind them. What makes the selection of the right percentage for the training versus test data set difficult is that they are fundamentally in opposition to one another. On one hand, the percentage of the data set used for the machine learning model training should be as large as possible. On the other hand, the percentage of the data set held out for the test should be large enough so that the performance of a trained machine learning model on the test data set is a meaningful estimate for how the model is expected to perform on unseen samples from the population data.

### Test and validation data sets

The test data set described in this book will not be used to check the model for overfitting. Although some machine learning literature uses test data sets to ensure that the model is generalizing, this book will use a separate validation data set for this purpose. The approach used in this book is illustrated in this figure.

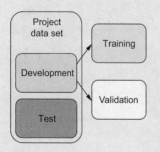

The cleaned-up project data set is split into development and test sets in this chapter. Upcoming chapters cover further splits of the development data set into training and validation data sets.

You can use some basic results from statistics to help you with the choice of the size. The idea is to ensure that the test data set is large enough so that it is statistically similar to the entire data set.

To start, consider the upper and the lower bounds for the fraction of the data set to use for test data. With respect to the upper bound, when using 70% for training, you can allocate 15% for validation and test. On the lower bound, you may consider allocating as little as 1% for test and validation. To better illustrate the idea of a lower bound, let's consider a more extreme case of allocating just 0.5% of data for testing.

You can obtain the number of records for various percentages (fractions) using

```
fractions = [.3, .15, .1, .01, .005]
print([ds_size * fraction for fraction in fractions])
```

which returns

```
[4278658.8, 2139329.4, 1426219.6, 142621.96, 71310.98]
```

When working with sample sizes, it helps to put the sizes in terms of powers of two. This is helpful for several reasons. When computing statistics from samples (e.g., standard error of the mean of samples), you are going to find that exponential changes in the size of the data set are needed to achieve linear changes to the values of the statistics. Also, in statistical formulas it is common to take square roots of the sample size, and starting with powers of two simplifies the calculations.

To find the power of two estimates for the fractions of the data set, you can use the following code:

```
from math import log, floor
ranges = [floor(log(ds_size * fraction, 2)) for fraction in fractions]
print(ranges)
```

Note that the code takes the base 2 logarithm of the actual number of records that correspond to the fractions from 30% to 0.5% of the data set. Since the value of the logarithm can be a non-integer value, the floor function returns the data set size at the power of two that can store up an approximated fraction of the data set.

Hence, the output of the code

```
[22, 21, 20, 17, 16]
```

corresponds to a range from $2^{22} = 4,194,304$ to $2^{16} = 65,536$.

Although data sets in this range can easily fit in the memory of a modern laptop, let's attempt an experiment to identify the smallest fraction of the data set that can be sampled and still be used to report an accurate performance metric for a machine learning model. The valuable part of the experiment isn't the finding, but rather the illustration of the process for finding the right sample size. The process is valuable because it can be repeated even with larger data sets.

For the experiment, let's continue using the upper part of the range as the largest sample size, $2^{22} = 4,194,304$, but start with a much smaller part of the range of $2^{15} = 32,768$:

```
sample_size_upper, sample_size_lower = max(ranges) + 1, min(ranges) - 1
print(sample_size_upper, sample_size_lower)
```

The maximum and the minimum values returned by the code are as follows:

```
(23, 15)
```

Given the range, you can figure out how well it approximates fractions of the data set by running

```
sizes = [2 ** i for i in range(sample_size_lower, sample_size_upper)]
original_sizes = sizes
fracs = [ size / ds_size for size in sizes]
print(*[(idx, sample_size_lower + idx, frac, size) \
  for idx, (frac, size) in enumerate(zip(fracs, sizes))], sep='\n')
```

which results in

```
(0, 15, 0.0022975423980991427, 32768)
(1, 16, 0.004595084796198285, 65536)
(2, 17, 0.00919016959239657, 131072)
(3, 18, 0.01838033918479314, 262144)
(4, 19, 0.03676067836958628, 524288)
(5, 20, 0.07352135673917257, 1048576)
(6, 21, 0.14704271347834513, 2097152)
(7, 22, 0.29408542695669027, 4194304)
```

which shows that a test data set size of $2^{15}$ covers only about 0.23% of the data set while a test data size of $2^{22}$ covers roughly 29.4%.

### 4.1.3   *Exploring the statistics of alternative sample sizes*

This section describes how to use a standard error of the mean statistic along with diminishing returns (a marginal) to produce candidate sizes (in terms of the number of records) for the test data set. In the following listing, the function sem_over_range from listing 4.2 computes a pandas DataFrame specifying the standard error of the mean (SEM) for every column in the data set and every sample size from sample_size_lower to sample_size_upper. In this example, the range corresponds to values from 32,768 to 4,194,304.

**Listing 4.2    SEM for every column across candidate sample sizes**

The sem_over_range function uses the sample ranges along with the data sets mu and sigma.

Convert the sample ranges to a pandas Series.

Create a pandas DataFrame by computing standard error of the mean for each sample size and column sigma.

```
import numpy as np
def sem_over_range(lower, upper, mu, sigma):
  sizes_series = pd.Series([2 ** i \
    for i in range(lower, upper + 1)])
  est_sem_df = \
```

```
        pd.DataFrame( np.outer( (1 / np.sqrt(sizes_series)), sigma.values ),
                        columns = sigma.index,
                        index = sizes_series.values)
    return est_sem_df


sem_df = sem_over_range(sample_size_lower, sample_size_upper, mu, sigma)
sem_df
```

The function sem_over_range from listing 4.2 computes a pandas DataFrame specifying the standard error of the mean (SEM) for every column in the data set and every sample size from sample_size_lower to sample_size_upper. In this example, the range corresponds to values from 32,768 to 4,194,304.

Recall that for any of the columns in the data set, given its population standard deviation ($\sigma$) and the number of records (observations) in the column ($n$), the SEM is defined as $\frac{\sigma}{\sqrt{n}}$.

Since the raw SEM values returned in the sem_df DataFrame from listing 4.2 are not easily interpretable, it is valuable to plot a graph to illustrate the overall trend of change in the SEM as the sample size grows. You can display this trend using the matplotlib library, plotting the average SEM values in the sem_df data frame across columns using

```
import matplotlib.pyplot as plt
%matplotlib inline

plt.figure(figsize = (12, 9))
plt.plot(sem_df.index, sem_df.mean(axis = 1))
plt.xticks(sem_df.index,
           labels = list(map(lambda i: f"2^{i}",
                             np.log2(sem_df.index.values).astype(int))),
           rotation = 90);
```

which results in figure 4.1.

The plot in figure 4.1 uses powers of two for the annotations on the horizontal axis to describe the sample sizes in the data frame. Notice that the plot captures the trend of diminishing returns on the increase in the sample size. Although the sample size grows exponentially, the slope (the instantaneous rate of change in the SEM given a sample size) of the average SEM flattens with every doubling.

Since it is valuable to allocate as much data as possible to the training data set, you can take advantage of the diminishing returns heuristic to discover a lower bound size for the test data set. The idea is to find a sample size such that if it were any larger, the improvements to the SEM would yield diminishing returns.

To identify the point of diminishing returns (also known as the *marginal*) on the doubling of the sample size, you can start by looking at the total reduction in the SEM for each increase in the sample size. This is computed using sem_df.cumsum() in the

90     CHAPTER 4   *More exploratory data analysis and data preparation*

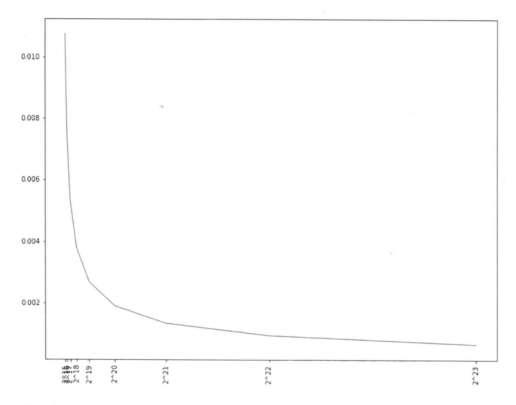

**Figure 4.1   Exponential increase in sample size is expensive: larger samples require exponentially more memory, disk space, and compute while yielding less improvement in terms of the reduction in the standard error of the mean.**

following code snippet. Then, to obtain a single aggregate measure for each sample size, the mean(axis = 1) computes the average of the total reduction in SEM across the columns in the data set:

```
agg_change = sem_df.cumsum().mean(axis = 1)
agg_change
```

which produces

```
32768      0.01
65536      0.02
131072     0.02
262144     0.03
524288     0.03
1048576    0.03
2097152    0.03
4194304    0.03
8388608    0.04
dtype: float64
```

The values of the agg_change pandas series are plotted in figure 4.2. Notice that the sample size highlighted with an arrow corresponds to the sample size of $2^{20}$ and is also the point where the SEM reduction due to increase in the sample size begins to yield diminishing returns.

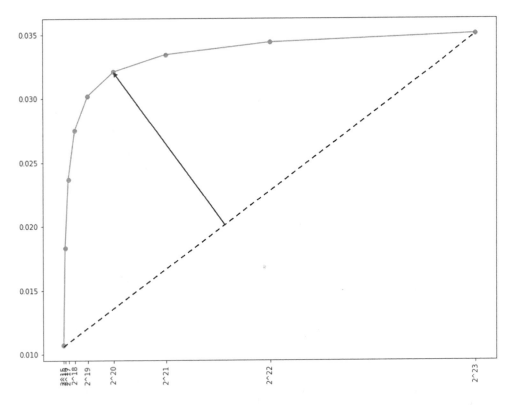

**Figure 4.2  The marginal sample size corresponds to the largest sample size before the point of diminishing returns.**

This point, the marginal, can be computed in Python using the following marginal function:

```python
import numpy as np

def marginal(x):
    coor = np.vstack([x.index.values,
            x.values]).transpose()

    return pd.Series(index = x.index,
        data = np.cross(coor[-1] - coor[0], coor[-1] - coor) \
            / np.linalg.norm(coor[-1] - coor[0])).idxmin()
```

**Create a NumPy array of data points with sample sizes on the x-axis and SEM values on the y-axis.**

**Compute the distances from the data points to an imaginary line connecting the largest and the smallest sample size data points.**

```
SAMPLE_SIZE = marginal(agg_change).astype(int)
SAMPLE_SIZE, SAMPLE_SIZE / ds_size
```

Here, the marginal is computed by looking at data points of sample sizes against cumulative reduction in SEM, drawing an imaginary line between the smallest and largest sample sizes (dashed line in figure 4.2) and identifying the data point with the furthest distance at the right angle to the imaginary line.

When applied to the DC taxi data set, the `marginal` function computes the following:

```
(1048576, 0.07352135673917257)
```

Here, the marginal test sample size chosen by the diminishing returns heuristic corresponds to 1,048,576 records, or roughly 7% of the data set.

If it were possible to use a sample of any 1,048,576 records as a test data set, it would be valuable for maximizing the amount of data available to machine learning model training. However, the SEM measure is designed to identify a *lower* bound for the sample size and does not indicate that an arbitrary data set of this size is the right one to use for the test data set.

You can use p-values of a sample of 1,048,576 records to establish confidence in the sample by answering the fundamental question of statistical hypothesis testing: what is the degree of certainty that the sample comes from the population?

### 4.1.4   *Using a PySpark job to sample the test set*

In this section, you are going to experiment by randomly sampling 1,048,576 records (the size identified in the previous section) using a PySpark job in order to create the test data set. Once the test set is sampled, the remaining records are persisted to a separate DC taxi development data set. Both development and test data sets are also analyzed to compute p-values as well as other summary statistics.

Since the implementation of the entire PySpark job is roughly 90 lines of code, in this section the job is introduced as a series of code snippets. The preamble to the job, shown in listing 4.3, resembles the PySpark jobs in chapters 2 and 3. As in the earlier chapters, this part of the job implementation imports the relevant libraries and resolves job arguments.

> **Listing 4.3   PySpark `DataFrame` reading code in `dctaxi_dev_test.py`**

```
import sys
from awsglue.transforms import *
from awsglue.utils import getResolvedOptions
from pyspark.context import SparkContext
from awsglue.context import GlueContext
from awsglue.job import Job

args = getResolvedOptions(sys.argv, ['JOB_NAME',
                                     'BUCKET_SRC_PATH',
```

```
                                       'BUCKET_DST_PATH',
                                       'SAMPLE_SIZE',
                                       'SAMPLE_COUNT',
                                       'SEED'
                                       ])

sc = SparkContext()
glueContext = GlueContext(sc)
logger = glueContext.get_logger()
spark = glueContext.spark_session

job = Job(glueContext)
job.init(args['JOB_NAME'], args)

BUCKET_SRC_PATH = args['BUCKET_SRC_PATH']
df = ( spark.read.format("parquet")
         .load( f"{BUCKET_SRC_PATH}" ))
```

> **Construct a pandas DataFrame df based on the BUCKET_SRC_PATH parameter.**

The implementation related to sampling of the test set from the cleaned-up DC taxi data set begins in listing 4.4 where the sample fraction of the entire data set size is computed and saved to the variable `sample_frac`. In order to compute the summary statistics of the cleaned-up data set in PySpark, the implementation relies on the Kaen library PySpark utility function `spark_df_to_stats_pandas_df`, which returns a pandas `DataFrame` from the PySpark `DataFrame` instance named df. The pandas `summary_df` in turn provides standard pandas `DataFrame` API access to data set averages (`mu`) and standard deviations (`sigma`) for each of the columns in the cleaned-up data set.

> **Listing 4.4  PySpark `DataFrame` reading code in `dctaxi_dev_test.py`**

```
SAMPLE_SIZE = float( args['SAMPLE_SIZE'] )
dataset_size = float( df.count() )
sample_frac = SAMPLE_SIZE / dataset_size

from kaen.spark import spark_df_to_stats_pandas_df, \
                 pandas_df_to_spark_df, \
                 spark_df_to_shards_df

summary_df = spark_df_to_stats_pandas_df(df)
mu = summary_df.loc['mean']
sigma = summary_df.loc['stddev']
```

> **The sample size in terms of a fraction as needed for Spark randomSplit method**

> **Import Spark and pandas utilities from the kaen package.**

> **Create the pandas DataFrame with statistics of the Spark DataFrame.**

> **Save the data set standard deviation as sigma.**

> **Save the data set mean as mu.**

The summary statistics along with the `sample_frac` values are used in listing 4.5 to perform random sampling. The PySpark `randomSplit` method partitions the cleaned-up DC taxi data set into the `test_df` consisting of a maximum of `SAMPLE_SIZE` rows and totaling roughly `sample_frac` of the entire data set from the df data frame.

**Listing 4.5   PySpark DataFrame reading code in `dctaxi_dev_test.py`**

```
                    Use the SEED to initialize
                    pseudorandom number
                          generators.                           Work around a poor choice
                                                                (p-value < 0.05) for a SEED
SEED = int(args['SEED'])           ◁───┐                        value using at most SAMPLE_
SAMPLE_COUNT = int(args['SAMPLE_COUNT'])      ◁──────────────   COUNT samples.
BUCKET_DST_PATH = args['BUCKET_DST_PATH']
                                                 Sample the test data set into
                                                 Spark test_df DataFrame, the
for idx in range(SAMPLE_COUNT):                  rest to dev_df.
  dev_df, test_df = ( df
                          .cache()               ◁──────
   Ensure that the test_df     .randomSplit([1.0 - sample_frac,         Use the sample_frac
   is limited to at most                    sample_frac],     ◁──────   fraction of the records
   SAMPLE_SIZE records.                   seed = SEED) )              in the df for the test
                                                                     data set.
  └─▷  test_df = test_df.limit( int(SAMPLE_SIZE) )

    test_stats_df = \                                      ◁──────────
      spark_df_to_stats_pandas_df(test_df, summary_df,
                               pvalues = True, zscores = True)

    pvalues_series = test_stats_df.loc['pvalues']              Create a pandas
    if pvalues_series.min() < 0.05:                            test_stats_df
      SEED = SEED + idx    ◁──────                             DataFrame with
    else:                          Sample again in case of a poor   summary statistics
      break                        sample (pvalue < 0.05), up to     of test_df.
                                   SAMPLE_COUNT times.
```

The part of the job implementation shown in listing 4.6 is responsible for saving the development (`dev_df`) and the test (`test_df`) data sets to S3. For each of the data sets, Spark saves the records in a CSV format to the `BUCKET_DST_PATH` with the header information. Also, for both development and test the implementation saves additional metadata (which is shown later in this section) to the `BUCKET_DST_PATH` subfolders: `.meta/stats` and `.meta/shards`.

The `stats` subfolder stores a CSV file with the summary statistics, including the count, mean, p-values, and others. The `shards` subfolder is stored to facilitate processing of the data set during training and store the metadata about the number of CSV part files and the number of records per part file used to save the data sets in S3.

**Listing 4.6   PySpark DataFrame reading code in `dctaxi_dev_test.py`**

```
for df, desc in [(dev_df, "dev"), (test_df, "test")]:
    ( df
    .write
    .option('header', 'true')
    .mode('overwrite')
    .csv(f"{BUCKET_DST_PATH}/{desc}") )

    stats_pandas_df = \
    spark_df_to_stats_pandas_df(df,
                              summary_df,
```

```
                                            pvalues = True,
                                            zscores = True)

    ( pandas_df_to_spark_df(spark,  stats_pandas_df)
    .coalesce(1)
    .write
    .option('header', 'true')
    .mode('overwrite')
    .csv(f"{BUCKET_DST_PATH}/{desc}/.meta/stats") )

    ( spark_df_to_shards_df(spark, df)
    .coalesce(1)
    .write
    .option('header', True)
    .mode('overwrite')
    .csv(f"{BUCKET_DST_PATH}/{desc}/.meta/shards") )

job.commit()
```

For convenience, the full implementation of the PySpark job as it should be persisted
in a file named dctaxi_dev_test.py is shown next.

Listing 4.7  PySpark `dctaxi_dev_test.py` job to sample dev and test data sets

```
import sys
from awsglue.transforms import *
from awsglue.utils import getResolvedOptions
from pyspark.context import SparkContext
from awsglue.context import GlueContext
from awsglue.job import Job

args = getResolvedOptions(sys.argv, ['JOB_NAME',
                                     'BUCKET_SRC_PATH',
                                     'BUCKET_DST_PATH',
                                     'SAMPLE_SIZE',
                                     'SAMPLE_COUNT',
                                     'SEED'
                                     ])

sc = SparkContext()
glueContext = GlueContext(sc)
logger = glueContext.get_logger()
spark = glueContext.spark_session

job = Job(glueContext)
job.init(args['JOB_NAME'], args)

BUCKET_SRC_PATH = args['BUCKET_SRC_PATH']
df = ( spark.read.format("parquet")
        .load( f"{BUCKET_SRC_PATH}" ))
```

```
SAMPLE_SIZE = float( args['SAMPLE_SIZE'] )
dataset_size = float( df.count() )
sample_frac = SAMPLE_SIZE / dataset_size

from kaen.spark import spark_df_to_stats_pandas_df, \
                        pandas_df_to_spark_df, \
                        spark_df_to_shards_df

summary_df = spark_df_to_stats_pandas_df(df)
mu = summary_df.loc['mean']
sigma = summary_df.loc['stddev']


SEED = int(args['SEED'])
SAMPLE_COUNT = int(args['SAMPLE_COUNT'])
BUCKET_DST_PATH = args['BUCKET_DST_PATH']

for idx in range(SAMPLE_COUNT):
  dev_df, test_df = ( df
                        .cache()
                        .randomSplit( [1.0 - sample_frac, sample_frac],
                                        seed = SEED) )
    test_df = test_df.limit( int(SAMPLE_SIZE) )

    test_stats_df = \
      spark_df_to_stats_pandas_df(test_df, summary_df,
                                    pvalues = True, zscores = True)

    pvalues_series = test_stats_df.loc['pvalues']
    if pvalues_series.min() < 0.05:
      SEED = SEED + idx
    else:
      break


for df, desc in [(dev_df, "dev"), (test_df, "test")]:
    ( df
    .write
    .option('header', 'true')
    .mode('overwrite')
    .csv(f"{BUCKET_DST_PATH}/{desc}") )

    stats_pandas_df = \
    spark_df_to_stats_pandas_df(df,
                                  summary_df,
                                  pvalues = True,
                                  zscores = True)

    ( pandas_df_to_spark_df(spark,  stats_pandas_df)
    .coalesce(1)
```

```
    .write
    .option('header', 'true')
    .mode('overwrite')
    .csv(f"{BUCKET_DST_PATH}/{desc}/.meta/stats") )

    ( spark_df_to_shards_df(spark, df)
    .coalesce(1)
    .write
    .option('header', True)
    .mode('overwrite')
    .csv(f"{BUCKET_DST_PATH}/{desc}/.meta/shards") )

job.commit()
```

Before the PySpark job in the `dctaxi_dev_test.py` file can be executed in AWS Glue, you need to configure several environment variables. The `SAMPLE_SIZE` and `SAMPLE_COUNT` operating system environment variables should be set using the values of the corresponding Python variables:

```
os.environ['SAMPLE_SIZE'] = str(SAMPLE_SIZE)
os.environ['SAMPLE_COUNT'] = str(1)
```

As in the previous chapter, the PySpark job is executed using the convenience functions from the `utils.sh` script. Start by downloading the script to your local environment using the following command in your bash shell:

```
wget -q --no-cache https://raw.githubusercontent.com/
➥ osipov/smlbook/master/utils.sh
```

Once the `utils.sh` script is downloaded, you can use it to launch and monitor the PySpark job implemented in the `dctaxi_dev_test.py` file. Launch the job by running the following in your shell environment:

```
source utils.sh

PYSPARK_SRC_NAME=dctaxi_dev_test.py \
PYSPARK_JOB_NAME=dc-taxi-dev-test-job \
ADDITIONAL_PYTHON_MODULES="kaen[spark]" \
BUCKET_SRC_PATH=s3://dc-taxi-$BUCKET_ID-$AWS_DEFAULT_REGION/parquet/vacuum \
BUCKET_DST_PATH=s3://dc-taxi-$BUCKET_ID-$AWS_DEFAULT_REGION/csv \
SAMPLE_SIZE=$SAMPLE_SIZE \
SAMPLE_COUNT=$SAMPLE_COUNT \
SEED=30 \
run_job
```

Note that the job is going to read the Parquet files saved in chapter 3 from the `parquet/vacuum` subfolder and save the development and test data set under the `csv/dev` and csv/test subfolders in your S3 bucket. This job should take about eight minutes to finish on AWS Glue. Assuming it completes successfully, it should produce an output resembling the following:

```
Attempting to run a job using:
  PYSPARK_SRC_NAME=dctaxi_dev_test.py
  PYSPARK_JOB_NAME=dc-taxi-dev-test-job
  AWS_DEFAULT_REGION=us-west-2
  BUCKET_ID=c6e91f06095c3d7c61bcc0af33d68382
  BUCKET_SRC_PATH=s3://dc-taxi-c6e91f06095c3d7c61bcc0af33d68382-
➡     us-west-2/parquet/vacuum
  BUCKET_DST_PATH=s3://dc-taxi-c6e91f06095c3d7c61bcc0af33d68382-
➡     us-west-2/csv
  SAMPLE_SIZE=1048576
  SAMPLE_COUNT=1
  BINS=
  SEED=30
upload: ./dctaxi_dev_test.py to s3://dc-taxi-
➡     c6e91f06095c3d7c61bcc0af33d68382-us-west-2/glue/dctaxi_dev_test.py
2021-08-15 17:19:37       2456 dctaxi_dev_test.py
{
    "JobName": "dc-taxi-dev-test-job"
}
{
    "Name": "dc-taxi-dev-test-job"
}
{
    "JobRunId": [CA
    "jr_05e395544e86b1534c824fa1559ac395683f3e7db35d1bb5d591590d237954f2"
}
Waiting for the job to finish.....................................SUCCEEDED
```

Since the PySpark job persists metadata about the data sets, you can use pandas to review the contents of the metadata. To preview the statistical summary of the test set, execute the following Python code:

```
pd.options.display.float_format = '{:,.2f}'.format

test_stats_df = pd.read_csv(f"s3://dc-taxi-{os.environ['BUCKET_ID']}-
➡   {os.environ['AWS_DEFAULT_REGION']}/csv/test/.meta/stats/*.csv")

test_stats_df = test_stats_df.set_index('summary')
test_stats_df
```

Assuming the PySpark job executed correctly, the printout of the test_stats_df for the test data set should resemble the following:

| summary | faremount_ double | origin_block_ latitude_ double | origin_block_ longitude_ double | destination_ block_latitude_ double | destination_ block_ longitude_ double | year_integer | month_integer | dow_integer | hour_integer |
|---|---|---|---|---|---|---|---|---|---|
| count | 1.04768e+06 | 1.04768e+06 | 1.04768e+06 | 1.04768e+06 | 1.04768e+06 | 1.04768e+06 | 1.04768e+06 | 1.04768e+06 | 1.04768e+06 |
| mean | 9.74142 | 38.9046 | −77.0303 | 38.9063 | −77.03 | 2016.63 | 6.57281 | 3.98396 | 14.0013 |
| stddev | 4.55633 | 0.0149956 | 0.0192404 | 0.0172897 | 0.0223437 | 1.28039 | 3.4563 | 2.00472 | 6.15162 |
| min | 3.25 | 38.8135 | −77.1136 | 38.8121 | −77.1136 | 2015 | 1 | 1 | 0 |
| max | 174.31 | 38.9936 | −76.9109 | 38.9942 | −76.9101 | 2019 | 12 | 7 | 23 |
| zscores | 0.0361973 | −1.08741 | 1.53739 | 0.104719 | 0.576018 | 1.48047 | 1.02444 | −1.51348 | 0.668207 |
| pvalues | 0.971125 | 0.276857 | 0.124197 | 0.916599 | 0.564603 | 0.138749 | 0.305626 | 0.130157 | 0.504001 |

The metadata about the CSV part files (shards) of the development data set should have been saved to the csv/dev/.meta/shards subfolder of your S3 bucket. If you preview this metadata in a pandas DataFrame using the following code

```
import pandas as pd
dev_shards_df = pd.read_csv(f"s3://dc-taxi-{os.environ['BUCKET_ID']}-
➥ {os.environ['AWS_DEFAULT_REGION']}/csv/dev/.meta/shards/*")

dev_shards_df.sort_values(by = 'id')
```

the output should consist of a three-column table, where the id column stores the ID of the CSV part file from the csv/dev subfolder in S3 and the corresponding entry in the count column specifies the number of the rows in the part file. The contents of the data frame should resemble the following:

|    | id | count |
|----|----|-------|
| 39 | 0 | 165669 |
| 3 | 1 | 165436 |
| 56 | 2 | 165754 |
| 53 | 3 | 165530 |
| 63 | 4 | 165365 |

...

|    |    |        |
|----|----|--------|
| 72 | 75 | 164569 |
| 59 | 76 | 164729 |
| 2 | 77 | 164315 |
| 11 | 78 | 164397 |
| 22 | 79 | 164406 |

## Summary

- Using a fixed percentage–based heuristic to pick the size of a held-out test data set can waste valuable machine learning model training data.
- Measuring diminishing results from increasing the size of a data set can help with choosing the lower bound for the size of the test and validation data sets.
- Ensuring that a test data set has sufficient z-score and p-values can prevent choosing a data set size that's too small for machine learning.
- Serverless PySpark jobs can be used to evaluate alternative test data sets and report on their statistical summaries.

# Part 2

# PyTorch for serverless machine learning

Before starting with PyTorch, I spent several years working with TensorFlow versions 1 and 2. Since I switched to PyTorch, I became more productive as a machine learning practitioner, and I found my experience learning and using PyTorch delightful. I wanted to share this experience with the readers of this book. In the process, I aim to help you pick up the core elements of PyTorch, guide you though the levels of abstraction available in the framework, and prepare you to transition from using PyTorch in isolation to using machine learning models implemented in PyTorch and integrated into a broader machine learning pipeline.

- In chapter 5, I cover the PyTorch fundamentals, introducing the core tensor application programming interface (API) and helping you gain a level of fluency with using the API to flatten the learning curve of the later chapters.
- In chapter 6, you will focus on learning the deep learning aspects of PyTorch, including support for automatic differentiation, alternative gradient descent algorithms, and supporting utilities.
- In chapter 7, you'll scale up your PyTorch programs by learning about the graphical processing unit (GPU) features and how to take advantage of GPUs to accelerate your machine learning code.
- In chapter 8, you will learn about data parallel approaches for distributed PyTorch training and cover in-depth the distinction between traditional, parameter server-based approaches and ring-based distributed training (e.g., Horovod).

# Introducing PyTorch: Tensor basics

5

**This chapter covers**

- Introducing PyTorch and PyTorch tensors
- Using PyTorch tensor creation methods
- Understanding tensor operations and broadcasting
- Exploring PyTorch tensor performance on CPUs

In the previous chapter, you started with a cleaned-up version of the DC taxi data set and applied a data-driven sampling procedure in order to identify the right fraction of the data set to allocate to a held-out, test data subset. You also analyzed the results of the sampling experiments and then launched a PySpark job to generate three separate subsets of data: training, validation, and test.

This chapter takes you on a temporary detour from the DC taxi data set to prepare you to write scalable machine learning code using PyTorch. Don't worry; chapter 7 returns to the DC taxi data set to benchmark a baseline PyTorch machine learning model. In this chapter, you will focus on learning about PyTorch, one of the top frameworks for deep learning and many other types of machine learning algorithms. I have used TensorFlow 2.0, Keras, and PyTorch for machine learning projects that required distributed training on a machine learning platform and found PyTorch to be the best one. PyTorch scales from mission-critical, production machine learning use cases at Tesla[1] to state-of-the-art research at OpenAI.[2]

Since you will need a practical understanding of core PyTorch concepts before you can start applying them to machine learning with the DC taxi data set, this chapter focuses on equipping you with an in-depth knowledge of the core PyTorch data structure: a tensor. Most software engineers and machine learning practitioners have not used tensors as a part of their mathematics, programming, or data structures curricula, so you should not be surprised if this is new.

In section 5.1, I introduce a comprehensive definition of a PyTorch tensor. For now, keep in mind that if you have ever implemented a matrix in a programming language using an array of arrays (i.e., an array containing other arrays), you are well on your way to understanding tensors. As a working definition, you can consider a *tensor* to be a generic data structure that can store and operate on variables, arrays, matrices, and their combinations. In this book, the most complex tensors you encounter are effectively arrays of matrices, or arrays of arrays of arrays, if you prefer a more recursive description.

## 5.1   *Getting started with tensors*

This section defines a tensor in the context of machine learning use cases, explains the attributes of tensors, including tensor dimension and shape, and finally introduces you to the basics of creating tensors using PyTorch as opposed to using native Python data types. By the conclusion of this section, you should be prepared to study the advantages of PyTorch tensors over native Python data types for machine learning use cases.

The term *tensor* has subtly different definitions depending on whether it is used in mathematics, physics, or computer science. While learning about a geometric interpretation of tensors from mathematics or a stress mechanics interpretation from physics can enrich your understanding of the abstract aspects of a tensor, this book uses a narrower definition that is more relevant for a practitioner applying tensors to machine learning. Throughout this book the term describes a data structure (i.e., a data container) for basic data types such as integers, floats, and Booleans.

Since tensors are closely related to arrays, it is worthwhile to spend a moment reviewing the key attributes of an array or a Python list. An *array* is just an ordered collection of data values. In most programming languages, an array index can take on a value from a finite set of integers, based on a range of values from zero to one less than the number of elements in the array.[3] For example, in Python, this range is

```
range(len(a_list))
```

---

[1]  Tesla machine learning use cases for PyTorch are presented by Andrej Karpathy, director of AI at Tesla: https://www.youtube.com/watch?v=oBklltKXtDE.

[2]  OpenAI is well known for creating state-of-the-art natural language processing GPT models, standardized on PyTorch: https://openai.com/blog/openai-pytorch/.

[3]  Of course in Python it is possible to use slicing notation, but that is not relevant to this explanation.

where a_list is the name of an instance of a Python list. Hence, different arrays have different valid index values. In contrast, all arrays consisting of basic data types, regardless of length, have a tensor dimension equal to one.

A *dimension* is defined here as the total number of indices (not the values of indices) needed to access a value in a data structure. This definition is convenient because it helps describe different data structures using a single number. For example, a matrix has a dimension of two because it takes two indices, a row index and a column index, to pinpoint a data value in a matrix. For example, using Python, a naive matrix implementation can use a list of lists:

```
mtx = [[3 * j + i for i in range(3)] for j in range(3)]
print(mtx[1][2])
```

where mtx evaluates to

```
[[0, 1, 2],
 [3, 4, 5],
 [6, 7, 8]]
```

and the value of mtx[1][2] is printed out as 5. Since the matrix has a dimension of two, two index values—1 for the row index and 2 for the column index—had to be specified to access the value of 5 in the matrix.

The dimension also specifies a measure of array nesting that is needed to implement a data structure. For example, mtx, with a dimension of 2, requires an array of arrays, while an array of matrices (dimension 3), requires an array of arrays of arrays. If you consider a data structure with a dimension of 0, in other words one that requires zero indices to access a value, you'll soon realize that this data structure is just a regular variable. For a visualization of tensors with dimensions (also known as *tensor rank*) 0, 1, 2, and 3, look at figure 5.1.

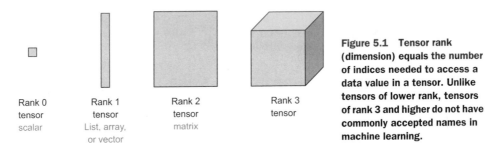

Rank 0 tensor
scalar

Rank 1 tensor
List, array, or vector

Rank 2 tensor
matrix

Rank 3 tensor

**Figure 5.1   Tensor rank (dimension) equals the number of indices needed to access a data value in a tensor. Unlike tensors of lower rank, tensors of rank 3 and higher do not have commonly accepted names in machine learning.**

A tensor is a data structure capable of storing arrays of an arbitrary number of dimensions, or more concisely, a tensor is an n-dimensional array. Based on this definition, a flat Python list, or any flattened array, is a one-dimensional tensor, sometimes also described as a rank 1 tensor. A Python variable is a zero-dimensional tensor, commonly described as a scalar, or less often as a rank 0 tensor. A two-dimensional tensor is usually called a matrix. For higher dimensional examples, consider a matrix used to represent grayscale images in terms of pixel values, where a value of 0 is black, 255 is white, and the numbers in between are gray colors of increasing brightness. Then, a three-dimensional tensor is a convenient data structure for an ordered collection of grayscale images, so the first of the three indices specifies an image and the remaining two specify the row and column location of a pixel in the image. A three-dimensional tensor also works well for a color image (but not a collection of color images), such that the first index specifies red, green, blue, or opacity (alpha) channels for the color, while the remaining indices specify a pixel location in the corresponding image. Continuing with this example, a four-dimensional tensor can be used for a sequential collection of color images.

With this foundational knowledge in place, you are ready to create your first tensor in PyTorch.

---

**Listing 5.1   A rank 0 tensor implemented using PyTorch**

```
import torch as pt
alpha = pt.tensor(42)
alpha
```

**1** Import PyTorch library and alias it as pt.

**2** Create a rank 0 tensor (scalar) with a value of 42.

Once this code is executed, it outputs

```
tensor(42)
```

After you have imported the PyTorch library and aliased it as pt **1**, the next line of the code **2** simply creates a scalar (rank 0) tensor and assigns it to a variable named alpha. When executed on 64-bit Python runtimes, where the value of 42 from listing 5.1 is represented as a 64-bit integer, the alpha tensor is instantiated using the PyTorch torch.LongTensor class.

For any PyTorch tensor, you can use the type method to discover the specific tensor class used to instantiate the tensor:

```
alpha.type()
```

This outputs

```
torch.LongTensor
```

The torch.LongTensor, as well as torch.FloatTensor and other tensor classes for various basic Python data types, are subclasses of the torch.Tensor class.[4] The subclasses of torch.Tensor include support for different processor architectures (devices); for

---

[4] Refer to the torch.Tensor documentation for the complete list of the subclasses in PyTorch: https://pytorch.org/docs/stable/tensors.html#torch-tensor.

example, `torch.LongTensor` is a class with a CPU-specific tensor implementation, while `torch.cuda.LongTensor` is a GPU-specific tensor implementation. PyTorch support for GPUs is described in more detail in chapter 7.

In your machine learning code, you should primarily rely on the tensor dtype attribute instead of the `type` method because dtype returns the tensor's type in a device-independent fashion, ensuring that your code can be easily ported across devices. The dtype for `alpha`,

```
alpha.dtype
```

outputs a device-independent description of the data type[5]

```
torch.int64
```

To access the value stored by the tensor, you can use the `item` method

```
alpha.item()
```

which in this case displays 42.

To confirm that `alpha` tensor is a scalar, you can access the tensor's shape attribute,

```
alpha.shape
```

which prints out `torch.Size([])`.

The PyTorch library uses the `torch.Size` class to specify the details of the size (also known as the shape) of a tensor. Here, the size consists of an empty, zero-length list since the `alpha` scalar is rank 0. In general, the length of the `torch.Size` list is equal to the dimension of the tensor. For example,

```
len(alpha.shape)
```

outputs 0. The shape of a tensor specifies the number of elements stored in a tensor along the tensor's dimensions. For example, a one-dimensional PyTorch tensor created from a Python list of the first five Fibonacci numbers,

```
arr = pt.tensor([1, 1, 2, 3, 5])
arr.shape
```

produces `torch.Size([5])` which confirms that there are five elements in the first and only dimension of the `arr` tensor.

If you create a PyTorch matrix (rank 2 tensor) from a Python list of lists,

```
mtx = pt.tensor([ [  2,   4,  16,  32,  64],
                  [  3,   9,  27,  81, 243]] )
```

---

[5] The comprehensive listing of the PyTorch supported `dtype` values is available at http://mng.bz/YwyB.

then `mtx.shape` returns the size of `torch.Size([2, 5])` since there are two rows and five columns in the `mtx` matrix.

Standard Python indexing and the `item` method continue to work as expected: to retrieve the value in the upper left-hand corner of the `mtx` tensor, you use `mtx[0][0].item()`, which returns 2.

When working with tensors of rank 2 or higher in PyTorch you need to know about an important default limitation: the number of elements in the trailing dimensions; in other words, second and higher dimensions must be consistent, such as if you attempt to create a matrix with four elements in the second (column) dimension while the other columns have five elements.

**Listing 5.2    PyTorch tensors with support variable**

```
pt.tensor([  [  2,   4,  16,  32,  64],
             [  3,   9,  27,  81, 243],
             [  4,  16,  64, 256]          ])
```

PyTorch reports an error:

```
ValueError: expected sequence of length 5 at dim 1 (got 4)
```

Since PyTorch uses zero-based indexing for the dimensions, the second dimension has an index of 1 as reported by the `ValueError`. Although the default PyTorch tensor implementation does not support "ragged" tensors, the `NestedTensor` package aims to provide support for this category of tensors.[6]

## 5.2    *Getting started with PyTorch tensor creation operations*

Previously, you saw that you can create a PyTorch scalar tensor from a value (e.g., a Python integer) and an array tensor from a collection of values (e.g., from a Python list); however, there are other factory methods that can help you create tensors. In this section, you will practice creating PyTorch tensors using factory methods from the PyTorch APIs. These methods are useful when creating tensors for mathematical operations common in machine learning code, and in general, when a tensor is based on non-data set values.

When instantiating a tensor using the factory methods, the shape of the desired tensor is explicitly specified unless the desired shape can be inferred by PyTorch from the method's arguments (as explained later in this section). For example, to create a two-row and three-column matrix of zeros using the `zeros` factory method, use

```
pt.zeros( [2, 3] )
```

---

[6]   The `NestedTensor` class is available as a PyTorch package here: https://github.com/pytorch/nestedtensor.

which produces

```
tensor([[0., 0., 0.],
        [0., 0., 0.]])
```

Given an instance of a tensor, you can confirm that the tensor has the desired shape by using the tensor's shape attribute,

```
pt.zeros( [2, 3] ).shape
```

which returns an instance of `torch.Size` for the shape, in this case, matching what you have passed to the zeros method:

```
torch.Size([2, 3])
```

PyTorch tensor factory methods let you specify the tensor shape by passing one or more integers to a method. For example, to create an array of 10 ones, you can use the ones method,

```
pt.ones(10)
```

which returns an array of length 10,

```
tensor([1., 1., 1., 1., 1., 1., 1., 1., 1., 1.])
```

while `pt.ones(2, 10)` returns a matrix of 2 rows and 10 columns:

```
tensor([[1., 1., 1., 1., 1., 1., 1., 1., 1., 1.],
        [1., 1., 1., 1., 1., 1., 1., 1., 1., 1.]])
```

When working with factory methods you can specify the data type for the values in a tensor. While methods like ones return tensors of float values by default, you can override the default data type using the `dtype` attribute. For example, to create an array of integer ones, you can invoke

```
pt.ones(10, dtype=pt.int64)
```

which returns

```
tensor([1, 1, 1, 1, 1, 1, 1, 1, 1, 1])
```

Other PyTorch-supported data types include 16- and 32-bit integers, 16-, 32-, and 64-bit floats, bytes (unsigned 8-bit integers), and Booleans.[7]

---

[7] Detailed information about the PyTorch tensor data types is available from https://pytorch.org/docs/stable/tensors.html.

## 5.3    Creating PyTorch tensors of pseudorandom and interval values

This section introduces you to the PyTorch APIs used to create tensors populated with data values sampled from commonly used probability distributions, including standard normal, normal (Gaussian), and uniform distribution. The section also describes how to create tensors consisting of interval (regularly spaced) values. Learning the APIs described in this section is going to help you generate synthetic data sets valuable for testing and troubleshooting machine learning algorithms.

Deep learning and many machine learning algorithms depend on the capability of generating pseudorandom numbers. Before using PyTorch random sampling factory methods, you want to invoke the `manual_seed` method to set the seed value used to sample the pseudorandom numbers. If you invoke the `manual_seed` using the same seed value as used in this book, you will be able to reproduce the results described in this section. Otherwise, your results look different. The following code snippets assume that you are using a seed value of 42 set:

```
pt.manual_seed(42)
```

After the seed is set, if you are using PyTorch v1.9.0, you should expect to obtain pseudorandom numbers identical to the ones in the following examples. The `randn` method samples from the standard normal distribution, so you can expect the values to have a mean of 0 and a standard deviation of 1. To create a $3 \times 3$ tensor of the sampled values, invoke

```
pt.randn(3,3)
```

which outputs

```
tensor([[ 0.3367,  0.1288,  0.2345],
        [ 0.2303, -1.1229, -0.1863],
        [ 2.2082, -0.6380,  0.4617]])
```

To sample values from a normal distribution having the mean and standard deviation different from 1 and 0, respectively, you can use the `normal` method, for example, specifying the mean of 100, standard deviation of 10, and a rank 2 tensor of 3 rows and 3 columns:

```
pt.normal(100, 10, [3, 3])
```

resulting in

```
tensor([[102.6735, 105.3490, 108.0936],
        [111.1029,  83.1020,  90.1104],
        [109.5797, 113.2214, 108.1719]])
```

For tensors of pseudorandom values sampled from a uniform distribution, you can use the randint method, for example, to sample uniformly from 0 (inclusive) to 10 (exclusive), and return a $3 \times 3$ matrix:

```
pt.randint(0, 10, [3, 3])
```

which produces

```
tensor([[9, 6, 2],
        [0, 6, 2],
        [7, 9, 7]])
```

The randint and normal methods are the ones most frequently used in this book. PyTorch provides a comprehensive library of pseudorandom tensor generators,[8] but covering them all is beyond the scope of this book.

As explained in more detail in section 5.5, there is significant memory overhead involved in creating a Python list of integer values. Instead, you can use the arange method to create PyTorch tensors with interval (regularly spaced) values in a specified range. PyTorch arange behaves similarly to the range operator in Python, so

```
pt.arange(10)
```

returns

```
tensor([0, 1, 2, 3, 4, 5, 6, 7, 8, 9])
```

As you would expect from your experience using Python, arange in PyTorch can be called with additional parameters for the range start, end, and step (sometimes called a stride), so to create a tensor of odd numbers from 1 to 11, you can use

```
pt.arange(1, 13, 2)
```

which outputs

```
tensor([ 1,  3,  5,  7,  9, 11])
```

Just as with the Python range, the resulting sequence excludes the end sequence parameter value (the second argument), while the step is specified as the third argument to the method.

Instead of having to calculate the value of the step size for the arange method, it can be more convenient to use the linspace method and specify the number of elements that should exist in the resulting tensor. For example, to create a tensor

---

[8] For detailed documentation of the PyTorch random sampling factory methods, visit http://mng.bz/GOqv.

of 5 elements with values in the range that starts with 0 and ends with and includes the value of 10, you can use the `linspace` method,

```
pt.linspace(0, 10, 5)
```

which results in

```
tensor([ 0.0000,  2.5000,  5.0000,  7.5000, 10.0000])
```

As a part of the implementation, the `linspace` method calculates the appropriate step size to use such that all elements in the resulting tensor are within an equal distance of each other. Also, by default, `linspace` creates a tensor of floating point values.

Now that you are familiar with functions that create tensors, you are prepared to move on to performing common tensor operations such as addition, multiplication, exponentiation, and others.

## 5.4   *PyTorch tensor operations and broadcasting*

This section introduces you to the PyTorch features for performing common mathematical operations on PyTorch tensors and clarifies the rules for applying operations to tensors of various shapes. Upon completion of this section, you should be prepared to use PyTorch tensors as part of mathematical expressions that are used in machine learning code.

Since PyTorch overloads standard Python mathematical operators, including +, -, *, /, and **, it is easy to get started with tensor operations. For example,

```
pt.arange(10) + 1
```

is equivalent to invoking `pt.arange(10).add(1)`, and both output

```
tensor([ 1,  2,  3,  4,  5,  6,  7,  8,  9, 10])
```

When adding a PyTorch tensor and a compatible Python basic data type (float, integer, or Boolean), PyTorch atomically converts the latter to a PyTorch scalar tensor (this is known as *type coercion*). Hence, the operations

```
pt.arange(10) + 1
```

and

```
pt.arange(10) + pt.tensor(1)
```

are equivalent.

The default implementations of the PyTorch APIs perform immutable operations on tensors. So, when developing PyTorch machine learning code, it is critical that you remember that the addition operation as well as the other standard Python math operations overloaded by PyTorch return a new tensor instance. You can easily confirm that by running

```
a = pt.arange(10)
id(a), id(a + 1)
```

which outputs a tuple of PyObject identifiers with two distinct values, one for each tensor. PyTorch also provides a collection of in-place operators that mutate (modify) a tensor. This means that PyTorch replaces the tensor's values directly in the memory of the tensor's device, without allocating a new PyObject instance for a tensor. For example, using the add_ method

```
a = pt.arange(10)
id(a), id(a.add_(1))
```

returns a tuple with two identical object identifiers.

> **NOTE** In PyTorch API design, all operations that mutate (change) a tensor in place use a _ postfix, for example, mul_ for in-place multiplication, pow_ for in-place exponentiation, abs_ for in-place absolute value function, and so on.[9]

When working on machine learning code you will surely find yourself having to perform common mathematical operations on nonscalar tensors. For example, if you are given two tensors a and b, what does it mean for PyTorch to find the value of a + b?

**Listing 5.3 Tensors added element-wise as they have identical shapes**

```
a = pt.arange(10)
b = pt.ones(10)
```

As you should expect, since a has the value of

```
tensor([0, 1, 2, 3, 4, 5, 6, 7, 8, 9])
```

and b has the value of

```
tensor([1., 1., 1., 1., 1., 1., 1., 1., 1., 1.])
```

their sum is equal to

```
tensor([ 1.,  2.,  3.,  4.,  5.,  6.,  7.,  8.,  9., 10.])
```

so here a + b is equivalent to incrementing each element of the tensor a by 1. This operation can be described as an element-wise addition of the tensors a and b since

---

[9] For a detailed reference on in-place tensor operations, visit https://pytorch.org/docs/stable/tensors.html and search for "in-place."

for each element of the tensor a PyTorch finds a value with a corresponding element index in the tensor b and adds them together to produce the output.

What if you try to add

```
a = pt.ones([2, 5])
b = pt.ones(5)
```

where the logic of element-wise addition does not make immediate sense: which elements of tensor a should be increased by one? Should the first, second, or both rows of tensor a be incremented by one?

To understand how addition works in this example and other situations where the shapes of the tensors in an operation are different, you need to become familiar with *broadcasting*,[10] which PyTorch performs behind the scenes to produce the following result for a + b:

```
tensor([[2., 2., 2., 2., 2.],
        [2., 2., 2., 2., 2.]])
```

PyTorch attempts tensor broadcasting whenever the shapes of the tensors used in an operation are not identical. When performing an operation on two tensors with different sizes, some dimensions might be re-used, or "broadcast," to complete the operation. If you are given two tensors, a and b, you can check whether an operation involving both can be performed using broadcasting by invoking can_broadcast.

---
**Listing 5.4   Broadcasting possible when can_broadcast returns true**

```
def can_broadcast(a, b):
  return all( [x == y or x == 1 or y == 1 \
    for x, y in zip( a.shape[::-1], b.shape[::-1] ) ] )
```

This broadcasting rule depends on the trailing dimensions of the tensors, or the dimensions of the tensors aligned in the reverse order. Even the simple example of adding a scalar to a tensor involves broadcasting: when a = pt.ones(5) and b = pt.tensor(42), the shapes are torch.Size([5]) and torch.Size([]), respectively. Hence, the scalar must be broadcast five times to tensor a as shown in figure 5.2.

Broadcasting does not require copying or duplicating tensor data in memory; instead, the contents of the tensor that result from broadcasting are created by directly computing from the values of the tensors used in the operation. Effective use and understanding of broadcasting can help you reduce the amount of memory needed for your tensors and increase the performance of your tensor operations.

---

[10] Broadcasting is a popular technique used by various computing libraries and packages such as NumPy, Octave, and others. For more information about PyTorch broadcasting, visit https://pytorch.org/docs/stable/notes/broadcasting.html.

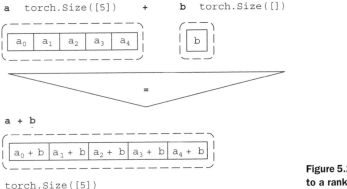

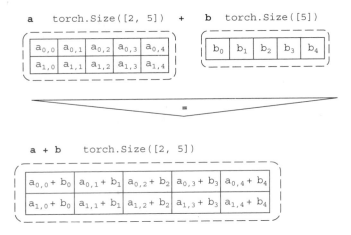

Figure 5.2   Broadcasting a scalar b
to a rank 1 tensor a

To illustrate broadcasting with a more complex example where a = pt.ones([2, 5]) and b = pt.ones(5), notice that the broadcasting re-uses the values from the tensor b (right side of figure 5.3) such that the indices along the trailing dimension are aligned in the resulting a + b tensor, while the leading dimension is preserved from tensor a.

Figure 5.3   Broadcasting a rank 1 tensor b to a rank 2 tensor a

Based on the broadcasting examples you have seen so far, you might come away with an incorrect impression that broadcasting happens only in one direction: from one of the tensors in an operation to another. This is false. Notice that according to the rule from listing 5.4, both tensors involved in an operation can broadcast data to each other. For instance, in figure 5.4, tensor a is broadcast to tensor b three times (based on the first dimension), and then contents of tensor b are broadcast in the opposite direction (along the second dimension) to produce the resulting tensor a+b of the size torch.Size([3, 2, 5]).

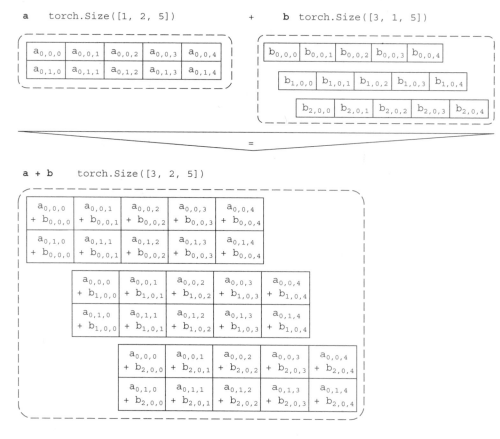

**Figure 5.4  Broadcasting is bidirectional with the first dimension of b broadcast to a and the second dimension of a broadcast to b.**

## 5.5    *PyTorch tensors vs. native Python lists*

In this section, you will dive into the details of how native Python data structures compare to PyTorch tensors with respect to memory use and into why PyTorch tensors can help you make more efficient use of memory for machine learning use cases.

Most modern-day laptops use central processing units (CPUs) that run at frequencies from 2 to 3 Ghz. To keep the calculations simple, let's ignore some of the advanced instruction for execution pipelining features of modern processors and interpret a 2-Ghz processor frequency to mean that it takes a processor roughly half a nanosecond (ns) to execute a single instruction, such as an instruction to add two numbers and store the result. While a processor can execute an instruction in less than 1 ns, the processor has to wait over 100 times as long, anywhere from 50 to 100 ns, to fetch a piece of data from the main computer memory (dynamic random access memory). Of course, some data a processor uses resides in a cache, which can be accessed within single-digit nanoseconds, but low-latency caches are limited in size, typically measured in single-digit MiB.[11]

Suppose you are writing a computer program where you need to perform some computations with a tensor of data, such as processing an array of 4,096 integers and incrementing each by 1. To achieve high performance for such a program, lower-level programming languages such as C or C++ can allocate the input data array within a single chunk in computer memory. For example, in the C programming language, an array of 4,096 integer values, each 64 bits in width, can be stored as a sequence of 64-bit values within some contiguous memory range, such as from address 0x8000f to address 0x9000f.[12]

Assuming all of the 4,096 integer values are in a contiguous memory range, the values can be transferred from the main memory to the processor cache as a single chunk, helping to reduce the total latency of the addition calculation for the values. As shown on the left side of figure 5.5, a C integer occupies just enough memory needed to store the integer's value so that an array of C integers can be stored as a sequence of addressable memory locations. Note that the number 4,096 is chosen deliberately: since 4,096 * 8 (bytes per 64-bit integer) = 32,768 bytes is a common L1 cache size for x86 processors in the year 2020. This means that the roughly 100-ns latency penalty is incurred every time the cache needs to be flushed and refilled with another 4,096 integers that need to be fetched from the computer memory.

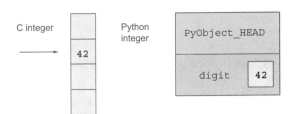

**Figure 5.5   Values of C integers (left) are stored directly as addressable memory locations. Python integers (right) are stored as address references to a generic `PyObject_HEAD` structure, which specifies the data type (integer) and the data value.**

This high-performance approach does not work with native Python integers or lists. In Python, all data types are stored in the computer memory as Python objects (PyObjects). This means that for any data value, Python allocates memory to store the value along with a metadata descriptor known as `PyObject_HEAD` (right side of figure 5.5), which keeps track of the data type (e.g., whether the data bits describe an integer or a floating point number) and supporting metadata, including a reference counter to keep track of whether the data value is in use.[13] For floating point and

---

[11] For a comprehensive breakdown of latency numbers that every computer programmer should know, visit https://gist.github.com/jboner/2841832.

[12] Of course, actual memory addresses for a program in a modern computer are unlikely to have values like 0x8000f or 0x9000f; these values are used here for illustration purposes.

[13] Python uses this reference counter to decide whether the data value is no longer in use so that the memory used for the data can be safely de-allocated and released for use by other data.

other primitive data values, the overhead of the PyObject metadata can more than triple the amount of memory required to store a data value.

To make matters worse from a performance standpoint, Python lists (e.g., a list PyObject as illustrated on the left side of figure 5.6) store the values by reference to their PyObject memory addresses (right side of figure 5.6) and rarely store all the values within a continuous chunk in memory. Since each PyObject stored by a Python list may be scattered across many dispersed locations in computer memory, in the worst case scenario, there is a potential for 100-ns latency penalty per value in a Python list, due to the need to flush out and refill the cache for each of the values.

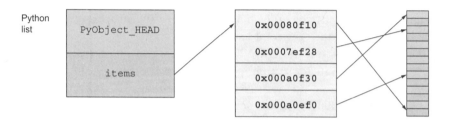

**Figure 5.6   Integers in a Python list (PyListObject) are accessed by reference (memory address) as `items` in the PyListObjects, requiring an additional memory access to find the PyObject for each integer. Depending on memory fragmentation, individual-integer PyObjects can be scattered across memory, leading to frequent cache misses.**

PyTorch tensors (as well as other libraries such as NumPy) implement high-performance data structures using low-level, C-based code to overcome the inefficiencies of the higher-level Python-native data structures. PyTorch, specifically, uses a C-based ATen tensor library[14] to ensure that PyTorch tensors store the underlying data using cache-friendly, contiguous memory chunks (called *blobs* in ATen) and provides bindings from Python to C++ to support access to the data via PyTorch Python APIs.

To illustrate the difference in performance, look at the following code snippet that uses the Python `timeit` library to measure the performance of processing lists of integer values ranging from 2 to roughly 268 million ($2^{28}$) in length and incrementing each value in a list by 1,

```
import timeit
sizes = [2 ** i for i in range(1, 28)]

pylist = [ timeit.timeit(lambda: [i + 1 for i in list(range(size))],
                         number = 10) for size in sizes ]
```

---

[14]  For ATen documentation, visit https://pytorch.org/cppdocs/#aten.

and using a similar approach to measure the time it takes to increment the values in a tensor array by 1:

```
pytorch = [ timeit.timeit(lambda: pt.tensor(list(range(size))) + 1,
                          number = 10) for size in sizes ]
```

As shown in figure 5.7, you can compare the performance of PyTorch tensors over native Python lists by plotting the sizes on the x-axis versus ratio on the y-axis, where the ratio is defined as:

```
ratio = [pylist[i] / pytorch[i] for i in range(len(pylist))]
```

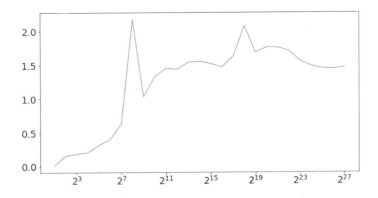

**Figure 5.7**  The ratio of Python to PyTorch performance shows consistently faster PyTorch performance for the increment operation benchmark, starting with lists of 10,000 elements and higher.

## Summary

- PyTorch is a deep learning–oriented framework with support for high-performance tensor-based machine learning algorithms.
- PyTorch tensors generalize scalars, arrays (lists), matrices, and higher-dimensional arrays into a single high-performance data structure.
- Operations that use multiple tensors, including tensor addition and multiplication, depend on broadcasting to align tensor shapes.
- C/C++-based tensors in PyTorch are more memory efficient and enable higher compute performance compared to Python-native data structures.

# Core PyTorch: Autograd, optimizers, and utilities

## This chapter covers

- Understanding automatic differentiation
- Using automatic differentiation with PyTorch tensors
- Getting started with PyTorch `SGD` and `Adam` optimizers
- Applying PyTorch to linear regression with gradient descent
- Using data set batches for gradient descent
- PyTorch `Dataset` and `DataLoader` utility classes for batches

In chapter 5, you learned about the tensor, a core PyTorch data structure for n-dimensional arrays. The chapter illustrated the significant performance advantages of PyTorch tensors over native Python data structures for arrays and introduced PyTorch APIs for creating tensors as well as performing common operations on one or more tensors.

This chapter teaches another key feature of the PyTorch tensors: support for calculation of gradients using *automatic differentiation* (autodiff). Described as one of the major advances in scientific computing since 1970, autodiff is suprisingly simple and was invented by Seppo Linnainmaa, a master's student at the University of Helsinki.[1] The first part of this chapter introduces you to the fundamentals of autodiff by showing how you can implement the core algorithm for a scalar tensor using basic Python.

The remainder of this chapter explains how to use the autodiff feature of the PyTorch tensor APIs to calculate machine learning model gradients in a simple example of applying gradient descent to a linear regression problem based on a tiny, synthetic data set. In the process, you will learn the PyTorch autodiff APIs and how to use them to implement the standard sequence of steps used in machine learning with gradient descent. The chapter concludes by demonstrating the `torch.optim` package with various gradient descent optimizers and showing you how to take advantage of the optimizers as part of your machine learning code.

## 6.1 Understanding the basics of autodiff

This section introduces the ideas behind autodiff and teaches its fundamentals by walking you through a simple example of implementing autodiff using only core Python programming language constructs, without PyTorch. In the process, you will gain a deeper understanding of the PyTorch autodiff functionality and develop the knowledge that will help you troubleshoot PyTorch autodiff in your projects. In this section, you will see that while autodiff is surprisingly straightforward, it is an algorithm that supports complex applications of the calculus chain rule. In later sections, you will apply what you learned and use autodiff features of PyTorch tensors.

The autodiff feature of PyTorch tensors is one of the core reasons the framework became popular for deep learning and for many machine learning algorithms that depend on gradient descent as well as related optimization techniques. While it is possible to use autodiff by treating it as a black box without fully understanding how it works, if you wish to develop the skills for troubleshooting autodiff in production scenarios, it is valuable to have at least a basic understanding of this critical PyTorch feature.

PyTorch implements an autodiff approach known as *reverse-mode accumulation automatic differentiation*, which is an efficient approach for computing gradients (defined in appendix A) of the kinds of loss functions that are commonly used in machine learning, including mean squared error and cross entropy. More precisely, PyTorch autodiff has $O(n)$ computational complexity, where n is the total number of operations (e.g., addition or multiplication operations) in the function, as long as the function has more input than output variables.

If you are already familiar with reverse-mode accumulation automatic differentiation, feel free to skip to section 6.2, which explains how to use PyTorch autodiff APIs

---

[1] The story of automatic differentiation and back propagation is described in detail here: http://people.idsia .ch/~juergen/who-invented-backpropagation.html.

for machine learning. Otherwise, this section will help you gain a deeper understanding of the PyTorch autodiff API design and its use.

If you are just starting to learn about autodiff, you need to know that it is distinct from other popular differentiation techniques such as numeric or symbolic differentiation. Numeric differentiation is commonly taught in undergraduate computer science courses and is based on an approximation of $\lim_{\epsilon \to 0} \frac{f(x + \epsilon) - f(x)}{\epsilon}$. Unlike numeric differentiation, autodiff is numerically stable, meaning that it provides accurate values of gradients even at the extreme values of the differentiated functions and is resilient to the accumulation of small errors introduced by floating point number approximations to real numbers.

Unlike symbolic differentiation, autodiff does not attempt to derive a symbolic expression of the differentiated function. As a result, autodiff typically requires less computation and memory. However, symbolic differentiation derives a differentiated function that can be applied across arbitrary input values, unlike autodiff, which differentiates a function for specific values of the function's input variables one at a time.

A great way to understand autodiff is to implement a toy example of it yourself. In this section, you will implement autodiff for a trivial tensor, a scalar, add support for computing gradients of functions that use addition as well as multiplication, and then explore how you can use your implementation to differentiate common functions.

To start, define a `Scalar` Python class, storing the value of the scalar (`val`) and its gradient (`grad`):[2]

```
class Scalar:
  def __init__(self, val):
    self.val = val
    self.grad = 0
```

In order to better track the contents of the `Scalar` instances and to support a nicer printout of the instance values, let's also add a `__repr__` method, returning a string representation of the instance:

```
def __repr__(self):
  return f"Value: {self.val}, Gradient: {self.grad}"
```

With this implementation in place, you can instantiate an object of the `Scalar` class, for example using `Scalar(3.14)`.

> **Listing 6.1    `grad` attribute to store the gradient of the `Scalar` tensor**

```
class Scalar:
  def __init__(self, val):
    self.val = val
    self.grad = 0.0
```

---

[2]  In dense mathematical papers about automated differentiation, the `Scalar` class is known as a dual number and the `grad` as the adjoint.

```
    def __repr__(self):
        return f"Value: {self.val}, Gradient: {self.grad}"

print(Scalar(3.14))
```

Once executed, this should return the output

```
Value: 3.14, Gradient: 0
```

which corresponds to the string returned by the \_\_repr\_\_ method.

Next, let's enable addition and multiplication of Scalar instances by overriding the corresponding Python methods. In reverse-mode autodiff, this is know as the implementation of the *forward pass* which simply computes the values from the Scalar operations:

```
def __add__(self, other):
    out = Scalar(self.val + other.val)
    return out

 def __mul__(self, other):
    out = Scalar(self.val * other.val)
    return out
```

At this point, you can perform basic arithmetic on Scalar instances, so that

```
class Scalar:
  def __init__(self, val):
    self.val = val
    self.grad = 0

  def __repr__(self):
    return f"Value: {self.val}, Gradient: {self.grad}"

  def __add__(self, other):
    out = Scalar(self.val + other.val)
    return out

  def __mul__(self, other):
    out = Scalar(self.val * other.val)
    return out

Scalar(3) + Scalar(4) * Scalar(5)
```

correctly evaluates to

```
Value: 23, Gradient: 0
```

and confirms that the implementation respects arithmetic precedence rules.

The entire implementation at this point amounts to exactly a dozen lines of code that should be easy to understand. You are already more than halfway done, because this implementation correctly computes the forward pass of autodiff.

To support the *backward pass* that calculates and accumulates the gradients, you need to make a few small changes to the implementation. First, the Scalar class needs to be initialized with a backward function that is set to be a no-op by default ❶.

Listing 6.2  backward method placeholder for backward pass support

```
class Scalar:
    def __init__(self, val):
        self.val = val
        self.grad = 0
        self.backward = lambda: None
    def __repr__(self):
        return f"Value: {self.val}, Gradient: {self.grad}"
    def __add__(self, other):
        out = Scalar(self.val + other.val)
        return out
    def __mul__(self, other):
        out = Scalar(self.val * other.val)
        return out
```

❶ Use lambda: None as the default implementation.

Surprisingly, this implementation is enough to start computing gradients of trivial linear functions. For instance, to find out the gradient of $\frac{\partial y}{\partial x}$ for a linear function $y = x$ at $x = 2.0$, you can start by evaluating

```
x = Scalar(2.0)
y = x
```

which initializes the x variable to have a value of a Scalar(2.0) and declares the function $y = x$. Also, since it is such a simple case, the forward pass of computing y is just a no-op and does nothing.

Next, prior to using the backward function you have to perform two prerequisite steps: first, zero out the gradient of the variable (I will explain why shortly), and second, specify the gradient of the output y. Since x is a single variable in your function, zeroing out its gradient amounts to running

```
x.grad = 0.0
```

If you find the step of setting x.grad = 0.0 unnecessary since grad is already set to zero as part of the __init__ method, keep in mind that this example is for a trivial function, and as you later extend the implementation to more complex functions, the need for setting gradients to zero is going to become more clear.

The second step is to specify the value of the gradient of the output, y.grad, with respect to itself, which can be expressed as $\frac{\partial y}{\partial y}$. Luckily, this value is trivial to figure out if you have ever divided a number by itself: y.grad is just 1.0.

So, to perform reverse-mode accumulating autodiff on this trivial linear function, you simply execute

```
x = Scalar(2.0)
y = x

x.grad = 0.0
y.grad = 1.0
y.backward()
```

and then discover the value of $\frac{\partial y}{\partial x}$ using

```
print(x.grad)
```

which correctly outputs `1.0`.

If you have been paying attention to the definition of y = x, you are well within your rights to protest that this entire sequence of calculations simply took the gradient from the `y.grad = 1.0` statement and printed it back. If that's your line of thinking, you are absolutely correct. Just as with the example of $\frac{\partial y}{\partial y}$, when computing the gradient for $\frac{\partial y}{\partial x}$, for a function y = x, the ratio of change to y, in terms of a change to x, is just `1.0`. However, this simple example illustrates an important sequence of autodiff operations that stay the same even with complex functions:

- Specifying the values of the variables
- Specifying the output in terms of the variables (forward pass)
- Ensuring the gradients of the variables are set to zero
- Calling `backward()` to compute the gradients (backward pass)

If you are comfortable with the reasoning about differentiation so far, you should be ready to move on to computing gradients of more complex functions. With autodiff, computation of the gradients happens within the functions that implement mathematical operations. Let's start with the easier one, addition:

```
def __add__(self, other):
  out = Scalar(self.val + other.val)

  def backward():
    self.grad += out.grad
    other.grad += out.grad
    self.backward()
    other.backward()
  out.backward = backward

  return out
```

Notice that the direct computation, accumulation, and recursive computations of the gradient happen in the body of the `backward` function assigned to the `Scalar` produced by the addition operation.

To understand the logic behind `self.grad += out.grad` and the similar `other.val += out.grad` instruction, you can either apply basic rules of calculus or some straightforward reasoning about change. The relevant fact from calculus informs you that for a function $y = x + c$, where c is some constant, then $\frac{\partial y}{\partial x} = 1.0$. This is nearly identical to the previous example with the computation of the gradient for $y = x$: despite adding a constant value to x, the ratio of change to y, in terms of a change to x, is still just `1.0`. With respect to the code, this means that the amount of change contributed by `self.grad` to `out.grad` is identical to the value of `out.grad`.

What about cases where the code is computing gradients for a function without a constant, in other words $y = x + z$, where both x and z are variables? In terms of the implementation, why should `out.grad` be treated as a constant when computing `self.grad`? The answer comes down to the definition of a gradient, or a partial derivative with respect to one variable at a time. Finding the gradient of `self.grad` is equivalent to answering the question "Assuming all variables, except for `self.grad`, stay constant, what is the ratio of a change in y to a change of `self.grad`?" Hence, when computing the gradient `self.grad`, other variables can be treated as constant values. This reasoning also applies when computing the gradient for `other.grad`, except in this case `self.grad` is treated as a constant.

Also, note that as part of the calculation of the gradient in the __add__ method, both `self.grad` and `other.grad` are accumulating gradients using the `+=` operator. Understanding this part of the autodiff is critical to understanding why the gradients need to be zeroed out before running the `backward` method. Simply put, if you invoke the `backward` method more than once, the values in the gradients will continue to accumulate, yielding undesirable results.

Last but not least, the lines of code `self.backward()` and `other.backward()` that invoke the `backward` method recursively ensure that the implementation of autodiff also handles function composition, such as `f(g(x))`. Recall that in the base case the `backward` method is just a no-op `lambda: None` function, which ensures that the recursive calls always terminate.

To try out the __add__ implementation with a backward pass support, let's look at a more complex example by redefining y as a sum of x values:

```
x = Scalar(2.0)
y = x + x
```

From calculus, you may recall that the derivative of $y = x + x = 2 * x$ is just 2.

Let's confirm this using your implementation of the `Scalar`. Again, you need ensure that the gradients of x are zeroed out, initialize $\frac{\partial y}{\partial y} = 1$, and execute the backward function:

```
x.grad = 0.0
y.grad = 1.0
y.backward()
```

At this point, if you print out

```
x.grad
```

it returns the correct value of

```
2.0
```

To get a better understanding of why $\frac{\partial y}{\partial x}$ evaluated to 2.0, recall the definition of the backward function implemented in the __add__ method. Since y is defined as y = x + x, both `self.grad` and `other.grad` reference the same instance of the x variable within the backward method. Hence, a change to x translates to twice the change to y, or the gradient, $\frac{\partial y}{\partial x}$ is 2.

Next, let's extend the implementation of the Scalar class to support gradient calculations when multiplying Scalars. The implementation is just six additional lines of code in the __mul__ function:

```
def __mul__(self, other):
  out = Scalar(self.val * other.val)

  def backward():
    self.grad += out.grad * other.val
    other.grad += out.grad * self.val
    self.backward()
    other.backward()
  out.backward = backward

  return out
```

With multiplication, the logic behind the gradient derivation is more complex than with addition, so it is worthwhile to review it in more detail. Just as with addition, suppose you are trying to derive the gradient with respect to `self.grad`, which means that for the calculation, `other.val` can be considered a constant c. When computing the gradient of $y = c * x$ with respect to x, the gradient is just c, meaning that for every change to x, y changes by c. When computing the gradient of the `self.grad`, c is just the value of `other.val`. Similarly, you can flip the calculation of the gradient for `other.grad` and treat `self` Scalar as a constant. This means that `other.grad` is a product of `self.val` and the `out.grad`

With this change in place, the entire implementation of the Scalar class is just the following 23 lines of code:

```
class Scalar:
  def __init__(self, val):
    self.val = val
    self.grad = 0
    self.backward = lambda: None
```

```
def __repr__(self):
  return f"Value: {self.val}, Gradient: {self.grad}"
def __add__(self, other):
  out = Scalar(self.val + other.val)
  def backward():
    self.grad += out.grad
    other.grad += out.grad
    self.backward(), other.backward()
  out.backward = backward
  return out
def __mul__(self, other):
  out = Scalar(self.val * other.val)
  def backward():
    self.grad += out.grad * other.val
    other.grad += out.grad * self.val
    self.backward(), other.backward()
  out.backward = backward
  return out
```

To gain more confidence that the implementation is working correctly, you can try running the following test case:

```
x = Scalar(3.0)
y = x * x
```

Repeat the earlier steps to zero out the gradients and specify the value of the output gradient as 1.0:

```
x.grad = 0.0
y.grad = 1.0
y.backward()
```

Using calculus rules, it is straightforward to figure out the expected result analytically: given $y = x^2$, the $\frac{\partial y}{\partial x} = 2 * x$. So for x = 3.0, your implementation of the Scalar should return the gradient value of 6.0.

You can confirm this by printing out

```
x.grad
```

which returns

```
6.0.
```

The Scalar implementation also scales to more complex functions. Using $y = x^3 + 4*x + 1$ as an example, where the gradient $\frac{\partial y}{\partial x} = 3 * x^2 + 4$ so $\frac{\partial y}{\partial x} = 31$ when $x = 3$, you can implement this function y using your Scalar class by specifying

```
x = Scalar(3.0)
y = (x * x * x) + (Scalar(4.0) * x) + Scalar(1.0)
```

and then running

```
x.grad = 0.0
y.grad = 1.0
y.backward()

x.grad
```

to confirm that the implementation correctly returns the value of `31.0`.

The implementation of autodiff for the `Scalar` is trivial compared to the features available with PyTorch tensors. However, it can give you a deeper understanding of the capabilities that PyTorch provides when you are computing gradients and shed light on when and why you need to use the seemingly magical `zero_grad` and `backward` functions of the PyTorch tensor autodiff APIs.

## 6.2 *Linear regression using PyTorch automatic differentiation*

This section builds on the explanation of the autodiff algorithm from section 6.1 and introduces you to autodiff support in PyTorch. As a motivating example, the section walks you through the process of solving a single variable linear regression problem using PyTorch autodiff and a basic implementation of gradient descent. In the process, you will learn about using PyTorch autodiff APIs, practice implementing the forward and backward passes for a differentiable model, and prepare for a deeper dive into applying PyTorch in the upcoming chapters.

To illustrate the autodiff feature in PyTorch, let's use it along with the gradient descent algorithm to solve the classic linear regression problem. To set up the problem, let's generate some sample data,

```
X = pt.linspace(-5, 5, 100)
```

so that the variable X holds 100 values, evenly spaced in the range from –5 to 5. In this example, suppose that $y = 2x + \varepsilon$, where $\varepsilon$ is a random number sampled from a standard normal distribution ($\epsilon \sim N(0,1)$) so that y can be implemented with PyTorch as:

```
y = 2.0 * X + pt.randn(len(X))
```

The purpose of adding `randn` noise to the y function is to illustrate the ability of the algorithm to correctly estimate the slope of the line, in other words, to recover the value of `2.0` using just the training data tensors y, X.

At this point, if you were to graph the values of X along the horizontal axis and y on the vertical axis, you should expect to see a plot resembling the one shown in figure 6.1. Of course, your specific values may vary if you have used a different random seed.

Next, to set up a differentiable model for the gradient descent algorithm you need to specify the model parameters along with an initial guess of the values of the parameters. For this simplified case of linear regression without a bias, the only model

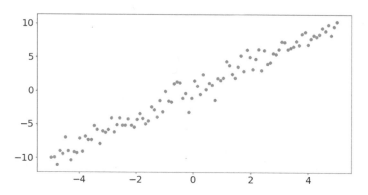

**Figure 6.1    A sample regression problem to explain the basics of PyTorch tensor APIs**

parameter you need to specify is the slope of the line. To initialize the parameter you can use the randn function sampling from the standard normal distribution:

```
w = pt.randn(1, requires_grad = True)
```

So far in this chapter you have not seen the requires_grad parameter used here by the randn tensor factory method to instantiate the value of w. In section 6.1, where I introduced the inner workings to the autodiff algorithm, you saw that calculation of the gradient requires additional memory and computation overhead for every data value in a tensor. For example, for every Scalar instance, autodiff required an additional grad attribute along with a definition of a recursive backward function.

For machine learning models, supporting autodiff can more than double the amount of memory a tensor needs. Hence, when instantiating a tensor using factory methods, PyTorch disables tensor autodiff by default, requiring you to use the requires_grad parameter to explicitly enable the support. However, if a tensor is derived from a tensor that has requires_grad enabled, then the derived tensor (known as *non-leaf* tensor) has requires_grad set to True automatically.

Once the model parameter w is initialized, the forward pass of the algorithm is ready to be implemented. In this case, the forward pass is to simply guess (predict) the y values using the value of the w parameter. The forward pass is implemented as a forward method that returns the value of the mean squared error of the predictions:

```
def forward(X):
  y_pred = X * w
  mse_loss = pt.mean((y_pred - y) ** 2)
  return mse_loss
```

Take a careful look at the body of the forward method to count all the tensors that get instantiated by PyTorch during the calculation of the mean squared error formula. The first tensor y_pred contains the predicted values for y based on a given value of w. The second tensor is y_pred - y and contains the individual errors of the predictions, while the third tensor contains the squared errors (y_pred - y) ** 2. Finally, the fourth tensor is computed using the `mean` function, which returns a scalar with the value of the mean squared error of the predictions.

None of the four tensors instantiated in the `forward` method needed a manual specification of `requires_grad = True` because PyTorch automatically deduced that in order for the framework to support the computation of the gradients for the `w` tensor, it also needed to enable `requires_grad` for the non-leaf tensors derived from `w`. In general, given an arbitrary PyTorch tensor, you can check the values of its `requires_grad` attribute to determine whether it can be used for gradient calculations. For example, within the body of the `forward` method, `y_pred.requires_grad` returns `True`.

In this chapter you have not yet worked with PyTorch tensor aggregation functions such as `mean`. In the `forward` method, the `mean` function simply computes an arithmetic mean of the tensor values (i.e., the mean of the squared errors) and returns the aggregated result as a scalar. In upcoming chapters you are going to learn more about `mean` and other PyTorch tensor aggregation functions.

With the code for the forward pass in place, there is enough groundwork to complete the implementation of gradient descent using PyTorch autodiff. Recall that the values of `y` and `X` in the code are based on the equation $y = 2x + \varepsilon$. The following code performs 25 iterations of gradient descent to estimate the value of `2.0`, which is used by the equation as a slope of the line.

```
LEARNING_RATE = 0.03

for _ in range(25):
    mse_loss = forward(X)                    ❶ Empty (zero) the
    w.grad = None           ◁─┘                gradient of w.
    mse_loss.backward()
    w.data -= LEARNING_RATE * w.grad

print("MSE ", mse_loss.data, " W ", w.data)
```

You should expect the code to print out numbers close to the following:

```
MSE  tensor(0.7207)  W  tensor([1.9876])
```

In the implementation of gradient descent, the learning rate is set arbitrarily to 0.03 and the number of gradient descent iterations to 25. In upcoming chapters, you will learn more about hyperparameter tuning and more rigorous approaches for choosing the values for learning rate, and number of gradient descent iterations, as well as values for other machine learning hyperparameters.

As you already know from section 6.1, when using autodiff it is critical to zero out gradients before using the `backward` function to accumulate updated gradient values. Note that in the case of PyTorch tensors, the `grad` attribute is zeroed out by setting it to None ❶ rather than to the value of 0. Once the `mse_loss` tensor is returned by the forward method, the gradients are updated by invoking the backward function. The gradient descent step amounts to the update of the w parameter data using the negative product of the learning rate and the updated gradient w.data -= LEARNING_RATE * w.grad.

Note that due to the noise in the values of y, you should not expect the gradient descent nor the analytical solution to linear regression to recover the exact value of 2.0 used for generating the data. To confirm this, you can use the PyTorch tensor APIs to calculate the analytical ordinary least squares solution based on the formula $(X^T X)^{-1} X^T y$,

```
pt.pow(X.T @ X, -1) * (X.T @ y)
```

which should return a value of roughly tensor(1.9876).

## 6.3 *Transitioning to PyTorch optimizers for gradient descent*

This section covers the PyTorch torch.optim package and the Optimizer classes, including Adam and SGD (*stochastic gradient descent*), which you can re-use in your PyTorch-based machine learning models to improve how you train the model parameters.

In addition to the torch.autograd automated differentiation framework, PyTorch also includes the torch.optim package with a collection of optimizers, which are algorithms that implement alternative optimization heuristics for updating the machine learning model parameters based on the loss function's gradients. The details of the optimizer algorithms' implementation are outside the scope of this book, but you should know that the PyTorch development team has been working diligently to maintain links in the PyTorch torch.optim package documentation to the relevant research papers that contain descriptions of the corresponding algorithm implementations.[3]

The optimizer classes have been designed to be easily swappable, ensuring that you can experiment with alternative optimizers without having to change the rest of your machine learning model training code. Recall that in listing 6.3 you implemented a trivial version of linear regression using your own simple rule for updating the model parameter values based on the gradient and the learning rate:

```
w.data -= LEARNING_RATE * w.grad
```

Instead of hardcoding this rule yourself, you can re-use the equivalent update rule in the torch.optim.SGD optimizer by re-implementing the following code.

---

[3]  For example, the documentation for SGD is available from http://mng.bz/zEpB and includes a link to both the relevant research paper and to the details of the SGD implementation.

**Listing 6.4  Linear regression using `torch.optim` optimizers**

```
import torch as pt
pt.manual_seed(0)

X = pt.linspace(-5, 5, 100)
y = 2 * X + pt.randn(len(X))

w = pt.randn(1, requires_grad = True)

def forward(X):
  y_pred = X * w
  return y_pred

def loss(y_pred, y):
  mse_loss = pt.mean((y_pred - y) ** 2)
  return mse_loss

LEARNING_RATE = 0.03
optimizer = pt.optim.SGD([w], lr = LEARNING_RATE)          ◁──

EPOCHS = 25                                        ◁──┐
for _ in range(EPOCHS):                            ❷
  y_pred = forward(X)
  mse = loss(y_pred, y)
  mse.backward()                                   ❸

  optimizer.step()                                 ◁──┘
  optimizer.zero_grad()                            ◁──┐

print(w.item())                                    ❹
```

❶ **Instantiate SGD optimizer using an iterable of model parameter(s) [w].**

❷ **Assume 25 epochs of gradient descent.**

❸ **Perform a gradient update step using gradients computed by backward.**

❹ **Zero out the gradients of the model parameter(s) for the next iteration.**

This should output the model's estimate of the slope of the line `w` as roughly `2.0812765834924307`. The changes needed to use the PyTorch optimizer are highlighted ❶, ❸, and ❹. Notice that when instantiating the optimizer ❶, you are providing the optimizer with a Python iterable (in this case a Python list) over the model parameters. After gradient descent computes the gradients (i.e., after the `backward()` method returns), the call to the optimizer's `step()` method ❸ updates the model parameters based on the gradients. The call to the `zero_grad()` method of the optimizer ❹ clears (empties) the gradients to prepare the call to the `backward()` method in the next iteration of the for-loop.

You may have encountered the `Adam` optimizer if you have prior experience training machine learning models. With the PyTorch library of optimizers, swapping the SGD optimizer ❶ for `Adam` is easy:

```
optimizer = pt.optim.Adam([w], lr = LEARNING_RATE)
```

In general, to use any PyTorch optimizer from the `torch.optim` package, you need to first instantiate one using the constructor,

```
torch.optim.Optimizer(params, defaults)
```

where the params is an iterable of model parameters and defaults are the named arguments specific to an optimizer.[4]

Both SGD and Adam optimizers can be instantiated with additional configuration settings beyond the model parameters and the learning rate. However, these settings will be covered in more detail in chapter 11 on hyperparameter tuning. Until then, the examples will use the SGD optimizer since it is easier to both understand and to explain.

As you progress to more complex training scenarios using gradient descent, it is useful to have clear and comprehensive terminology. As you can see from listing 6.4, training of a machine learning model by gradient descent consists of multiple iterations, where each iteration consists of actions that include the following:

- *Forward* pass, where you use the feature values and the model parameters to return the predicted outputs, for example y_pred = forward(X) from listing 6.4.
- *Loss* calculation, where the predicted outputs and the actual outputs are used to determine the value of the loss function, for example mse = loss(y_pred, y) from listing 6.4.
- *Backward* pass, where the reverse mode autodiff algorithm computes the gradients of the model parameters based on the calculations of the loss function, for example mse.backward() from listing 6.4.
- *Parameter* or *weight updates*, where the model parameters are updated using the values of the gradients computed from the backward pass, which should be optimizer.step() if you are using the optimizers from the torch.optim package.
- *Clearing gradients*, where the gradient values in the model parameter PyTorch tensors are set to None to prevent automatic differentiation from accumulating gradient values across multiple iterations of gradient descent; if you are using the optimizers from the torch.optim package, this should be done using optimizer.zero_grad().

In the industry, the terms *iteration* and *step of gradient descent* are often used interchangeably. Confusingly, the word "step" is also sometimes used to describe the specific action performed as part of gradient descent, for example a *backward step* or a *forward step*. Since PyTorch uses *step* to refer specifically to the action of updating the model parameters by the optimizer based on the gradients of the loss function, this book is going to stick with the PyTorch terminology. Keep in mind that some PyTorch frameworks, such as PyTorch Lightning, use *step* to mean *iteration*.

Before transitioning to the use of batches for model training with gradient descent, it is also useful to clarify the definition of the term *epoch*. In machine learning, an epoch describes one or more iterations of gradient descent needed to train (update) machine learning model parameters using every example in a data set exactly once. For example, listing 6.4 ❷ specifies that gradient descent should be performed for 25 epochs. The use of the word "epoch" also corresponds to *iterations*, for

---

[4]  The base Optimizer class and its constructor are documented here: https://pytorch.org/docs/stable/optim .html#torch.optim.Optimizer.

the simple reason that for every iteration of gradient descent all of the examples from the data set are used to calculate the gradients and update the weights of the model. However, as you will learn in the upcoming section on batches, performing an epoch of training may require multiple iterations of gradient descent.

## 6.4 Getting started with data set batches for gradient descent

This section teaches you about data set batches so that you can prepare for using data set batches for gradient descent with PyTorch. The concept of a data set batch for gradient descent is deceptively simple. A *batch* is just a non-empty collection (or, in mathematical terminology, a *multiset*) of examples randomly sampled[5] from a data set. Nevertheless, gradient descent using batches is nuanced and complex: mathematicians have even dedicated an area of research, known as *stochastic optimization*, to the topic. A training data set batch is more than just a sample of a training data set: in a single iteration of gradient descent, all the data examples from the training data set batch are used to update the gradients of a model.

While you don't need a PhD in mathematical optimization to use gradient descent with batches in PyTorch, it is worthwhile to have precise terminology related to batches and gradient descent to better navigate the complexity of the topic.

The *batch size* is a positive (greater than zero) integer specifying the number of examples in a batch. Many machine learning research papers and online courses use the phrase *mini-batch gradient descent* to describe gradient descent with batch sizes greater than one. However, in PyTorch, the SGD (torch.optim.SGD) optimizer, as well as other optimizers in the torch.optim package, can be used with batch sizes ranging anywhere from 1 to the number of examples in the entire data set. Keep this in mind because often in machine learning literature the phrase *stochastic gradient descent* is used to describe gradient descent with a batch size of exactly one.

The choice of a batch size has as much to do with having enough memory in your machine learning compute nodes as with the machine learning performance of the gradient descent algorithm. This means that the upper bound on the batch size should take into account the amount of the available memory per node of your machine learning platform. The selection of the exact value for the batch size is covered in more detail in chapter 11 on hyperparameter tuning, but first you should know the maximum batch size that you can fit in the memory of your machine learning platform nodes.

Much confusion about application of batches in PyTorch stems from lack of recognition that a batch should be treated as a fraction of data set size, which is the number of examples in a data set. A batch interpreted as a fraction is simply $\frac{batch\_size}{dataset\_size}$ so it is possible to categorize the choice of a batch size as producing either complete or

---

[5] More precisely, by using random sampling without replacement, or equivalently by randomly shuffling the order of examples in a data set.

incomplete batches, where a *complete batch* has a batch size that is an integer factor of the data set size, or more precisely

$$\frac{batch\_size}{dataset\_size} = \frac{batch\_size}{batch\_count * batch\_size}$$

for some positive integer batch_count representing the number of batches in a data set.

## 6.5    *Data set batches with PyTorch Dataset and DataLoader*

This section teaches you how to get started with using data set batches in PyTorch and how to use PyTorch utility classes that can help you manage and load your data sets as batches.

The PyTorch framework provides a collection of data utility classes organized in the torch.utils.data package and implemented to support the use of data batches with gradient descent. The classes in the package, including DataLoader, Dataset, IterableDataset, and TensorDataset, are designed to work together to simplify the development of scalable machine learning model training processes, including scenarios where a data set does not fit in memory of a single node, and where a data set is used by multiple nodes in a distributed computing cluster. While the classes provide scalable implementations, that does not mean they are useful only for large data sets or with large computing clusters. As you will see in this section, the classes work fine (aside from a negligible overhead) with small, in-memory data sets.

Dataset is a highly reusable class and can support a variety of machine learning use cases based on map-style and iterable-style subclasses of the Dataset. The map-style Dataset is the original data set class from the PyTorch framework and is best suited for in-memory, index-addressable data sets. For example, if you were to implement your own map-style Dataset by subclassing PyTorch's Dataset as a MapStyleDataset, you would have to implement the required __getitem__ and __len__ methods.

Listing 6.5    PyTorch map-style Dataset designed to be subclassed

```
import torch.utils.data.Dataset

class MapStyleDataset(Dataset):
    def __getitem__(self, index):
        ...
    def __len__(self):
        ...
```

❶ Map style interface methods to retrieve a specific item from the data set . . .

❷ . . . and to return the total number of items in the entire data set.

Note that the map-style data set makes two assumptions as part of the interface: each example (item) from a data set is expected to be addressable by an index value ❶, and the size of the data set is expected to be known and available at any time ❷.

In most cases, if you are working with an in-memory data set, you can avoid having to implement your own map-style data set subclass, and instead re-use the TensorDataset class. The `TensorDataset` is also a part of the `torch.utils.data` package and implements the required `Dataset` methods by wrapping tensors or NumPy n-dimensional arrays. For example, to create a map-style training `Dataset` for the sample data values in tensors X and y, you can pass the data tensors directly to `TensorDataset` ❶.

**Listing 6.6** `TensorDataset` simplifying batching of PyTorch tensors

```
import torch as pt
from torch.utils.data import TensorDataset
pt.manual_seed(0)

X = pt.linspace(-5, 5, 100)
y = 2 * X + pt.randn(len(X))

train_ds = TensorDataset(y, X)      ◁──❶
```

This allows you to fetch an example at index 0 from the data set by using the Python [0] syntax for the `__getitem__` method,

```
print(train_ds[0])
```

which outputs

```
(tensor(-11.1258), tensor(-5.))
```

and allows you to confirm that the data set length is 100 using the `__len__` method on the `train_ds` data set,

```
assert
 len(train_ds) == 100
```

where the Boolean expression in the assertion evaluates to `True`.

When using an instance of a `Dataset`, the PyTorch code that implements the iterations of gradient descent should not access the data set directly but rather use an instance of `DataLoader` as an interface to the data. You will learn more about the rationale for using the `DataLoader` in the upcoming section on using GPUs with PyTorch.

At its core, a `DataLoader` is a wrapper around a `Dataset`, so by wrapping an instance of `train_ds`, described earlier, you can create a `train_dl` using

```
from torch.utils.data import DataLoader
train_dl = DataLoader(train_ds)
```

Note that by default, when a `DataLoader` is used with a map-style `Dataset`, each batch returned by a `DataLoader` instance is of size 1, meaning that the following expression evaluates to `True`:

```
len(next(iter(train_dl))) == 1
```

This default behavior can be easily modified by specifying the `batch_size` named parameter when instantiating the `DataLoader` so that the expression

```
train_dl = DataLoader(train_ds, batch_size = 25)
len(next(iter(train_dl)))
```

evaluates to 25.

Both values of the `batch_size`, 1 and 25, produce complete batches. While all complete batches have an identical `batch_size`, an *incomplete batch* has fewer than `batch_size` examples. Specifically, given a `batch_size` and a data set, an incomplete batch may include as few as

$$dataset\_size \bmod batch\_size$$

examples, or in Python, `dataset_size % batch_size`.

For instance, when using a `batch_size` of 33, the following code produces an incomplete batch with a `batch_size` of 1 during the fourth iteration of the for-loop:

```
train_dl = DataLoader(train_ds, batch_size = 33)
for idx, (y_batch, X_batch) in enumerate(train_dl):
  print(idx, len(X_batch))
```

This prints out the following:

```
0 33
1 33
2 33
3 1
```

There are no universally accepted techniques for dealing with incomplete batches. While it is possible to try to prevent the incomplete batch problem, it may not have much value in practice: since batches are used when working with sufficiently large volumes of data such that the data sets are too large to fit in memory, ignoring or dropping incomplete batches are options if they do not have negative and measurable impact on the overall performance of a machine learning model. For example, the `DataLoader` class provides a `drop_last` option so that you can ignore the smaller, incomplete batches:

```
train_dl = DataLoader(train_ds, batch_size = 33, drop_last=True)
for idx, (y_batch, X_batch) in enumerate(train_dl):
  print(idx, len(X_batch))
```

This outputs the following:

```
0 33
1 33
2 33
```

Nevertheless, the drop_last option for incomplete batches should be used judiciously when specifying a batch size, especially when working with batch sizes that are a large fraction of a data set. For example, consider a situation where the batch size is inadvertently set to be $\frac{dataset\_size}{2} + 1$. Since this selection of the batch size yields two batches, the sole incomplete batch of the two, with a batch size of $\frac{dataset\_size}{2} - 1$, is dropped when using the drop_last=True option, resulting in a waste of almost half of a data set!

It is possible to prevent incomplete batches by training for multiple epochs while concatenating the data set with itself and using the batch_size window as a *rolling window* over the data set. With this technique, the number of training epochs should be based on the least common multiple (lcm) of the batch size and the data set size:

$$epochs = \frac{lcm(batch\_size, dataset\_size)}{dataset\_size}$$

To illustrate this approach, suppose for the sake of the example that you are working with a batch size of 12 and a data set size of 33, then

```
import math

def lcm(a, b):
    return a * b / math.gcd(a, b)

lcm(12, 33) / 33
```

outputs 4.0, indicating that the training data set needs to be concatenated with itself four times to achieve the four training epochs needed to avoid incomplete batches.[6]

How is a batch selected from a data set? Since a batch is intended to be statistically representative of the data set, the examples in the batch should be as independent of each other as possible. This means ensuring that the taxi fare examples within a batch are sampled randomly (without replacement) from the entire data set. In practice, the most straightforward way of achieving such random shuffling of the data set is to use the shuffle() method of the PySpark DataFrame API.

Since batches need to be statistically representative of the data set, you might be tempted to re-use the batch size based on the test data set size you discovered in chapter 4. While the test data set size metric works as a *lower bound* for batch size, re-using its value isn't the right decision since the test data set size was picked to be as small as possible while being statistically representative of the development data set. Chapter 11 describes in detail how to use a principled hyperparameter tuning

---

[6] Increasing the epoch count based on the least common multiple of the batch size and the data set size produces the minimum number of training epochs needed to avoid incomplete batches. It is also possible to train for any multiple of lcm(batch_size, data set_size) and avoid incomplete batches.

approach to choose the right batch size with the lower and upper bound values introduced in this chapter.

## 6.6    Dataset and DataLoader classes for gradient descent with batches

This section illustrates how to apply the `Dataset` and `DataLoader` classes using a minimalistic example to teach the concepts that also apply when using data set batches with more complex and realistic machine learning problems. To perform linear regression using gradient descent with batches using `Dataset` and `DataLoader`, you need to modify the solution from section 6.3.

---

**Listing 6.7    Basic linear regression using gradient data set with batches**

```
import torch as pt
from torch.utils.data import TensorDataset, DataLoader
pt.manual_seed(0)

X = pt.linspace(-5, 5, 100)
y = 2 * X + pt.randn(len(X))

train_ds = TensorDataset(y, X)
train_dl = DataLoader(train_ds, batch_size=1)

w = pt.empty(1, requires_grad = True)

def forward(X):
  y_pred =  X * w
  return y_pred

def loss(y_pred, y):
  mse_loss = pt.mean((y_pred - y) ** 2)
  return mse_loss

LEARNING_RATE = 0.003
optimizer = pt.optim.SGD([w], lr = LEARNING_RATE)

EPOCHS = 25
for _ in range(EPOCHS):
  for y_batch, X_batch in train_dl:
    y_pred = forward(X_batch)
    mse = loss(y_pred, y_batch)
    mse.backward()

    optimizer.step()
    optimizer.zero_grad()

print(w.item())
```

❶ Provide a data set interface to y and X using TensorDataset.

❷ Create a DataLoader for the data set using a batch size of 1 (default).

❸ Unpack each tuple of a batch of data while iterating over the DataLoader.

❹ Perform the forward step over the batch of features to produce predictions.

❺ Calculate the loss using the batch of labels and the predictions.

This should output the estimated w as roughly `2.0812765834924307`. Once the original tensors y and X are packaged into the map-style `TensorDataset` data set ❶, the resulting `train_ds` instance is further wrapped using a `DataLoader` to produce the `train_dl`.

To use the batches with gradient descent, for each epoch, the code performs 100 gradient descent iterations using individual batches returned in the for-loop by in train_dl ❸. The 100 iterations are performed per epoch since the original data set contains 100 examples and the default batch size of DataLoader is equal to 1. Since the batch size of 1 produces complete batches (recall from the definition of a batch as a fraction of the data set),

$$\frac{batch\_count * batch\_size}{batch\_size} = \frac{100 * 1}{1} = \frac{100 \text{ iteration(s)}}{1 \text{ epoch}}$$

or alternatively, if you used batches with a batch size of 25 to

```
train_dl = DataLoader(train_ds, batch_size=25),
```

then

$$\frac{batch\_count * batch\_size}{batch\_size} = \frac{4 * 25}{1} = \frac{4 \text{ iteration(s)}}{1 \text{ epoch}}$$

The changes in listing 6.7 ❹ and ❺ are straightforward: instead of using the original data set, the code uses the batches returned by the train_dl instance.

In case you modified the batch size to a value that produces incomplete batches, for example by specifying batch size of 51,

```
train_dl = DataLoader(train_ds, batch_size=51)
```

the second iteration of the inner for-loop will produce batches with 49 examples since DataLoader permits incomplete batches by default. In this specific case, this is not an issue, since the parameter of the model with the shape of torch.Size([]) can broadcast to the incomplete batch with the shape of torch.Size([49]). However, in general, you must take care to align the shape of the model parameters to the shape of a batch. In chapter 7, you will learn from an example of aligning the model parameters to the batch shape for the DC taxi data set.

## Summary

- Automatic differentiation is a fundamental algorithm for simplifying complex chain rule applications.
- Python-native data structures can be used to demonstrate the basics of how to implement automatic differentiation for tensors.
- PyTorch tensors provide comprehensive support for automatic differentiation of tensor gradients.
- Optimizers from the torch.optim are a range of algorithms for optimizing parameters in machine learning models using gradient descent.

- PyTorch tensor automatic differentiation and optimizer APIs are central to machine learning with PyTorch.
- `Dataset` and `DataLoader` interface classes simplify the use of batches in PyTorch code.
- `TensorDataset` provides a ready-to-use implementation for in-memory data sets.

# Serverless machine learning at scale

## This chapter covers

- Using `IterableDataset` with AWS and other clouds
- Understanding GPUs for PyTorch programming
- Scaling up gradient descent with a GPU core
- Benchmarking the DC taxi data set using linear regression

In chapters 5 and 6, you learned about using PyTorch on a small scale, instantiating tensors consisting of a few hundred data values and training machine learning models with just a few parameters. The scale used in chapter 6 meant that to train a machine learning model, you could perform gradient descent with an assumption that the entire set of model parameters, along with the parameter gradients and the entire training data set, could easily fit in memory of a single node and thus be readily available to the gradient descent algorithm.

This chapter introduces the concepts that you need to significantly scale your machine learning system. You will build on your existing knowledge of gradient descent (for a refresher, refer to appendix A) to learn how to perform gradient descent over data set batches. Next, you are going to use batches to help you scale to data sets that do not fit in the memory of a single node of your machine learning platform. You are also going to learn about scaling up on a single node, or in other words, about taking advantage of multiple processors such as CPUs and GPUs in a node. The concepts from this chapter are also re-used in chapter 8 to explain scaling out, in other words, ensuring that your machine learning system can take advantage of an aggregation of the compute capabilities of a distributed computing cluster consisting of multiple, inter-networked processing nodes.

## 7.1 What if a single node is enough for my machine learning model?

This section teaches you about the factors that should inform your decision on whether the PyTorch capabilities for scaling machine learning systems are relevant to your machine learning project.

If you (a) work with data sets that fit in memory of a single node of your machine learning platform, (b) expect your data sets to continue to fit in memory even after you launch your system, and (c) find the performance of your machine learning code on a CPU or a GPU to be sufficient, then you can forego the scaling techniques described in this and the next chapter.

> **NOTE** As a general rule of thumb, *if your machine learning model and the data set are guaranteed to fit in memory, keep them in memory.*

The machine learning algorithms that work on in-memory data sets provide the best performance both in terms of the computational efficiency and machine learning effectiveness. This means that your machine learning model training and inference are going to take less time when using machine learning on in-memory data, and you are going to be able to reach the best loss and metric performance sooner. Further, with data sets that fit in memory, you can use single node machine learning frameworks like scikit-learn to develop and test a variety of machine learning models before going to production. If your plan is to avoid implementing the code for scaling machine learning, you can consider skipping to chapter 9 to continue with feature selection and engineering.

Before you rush ahead, you should keep in mind that "The Bitter Lesson," an influential 2019 publication by distinguished computer scientist and artificial intelligence researcher Rich Sutton (http://www.incompleteideas.net/IncIdeas/BitterLesson .html) argues that the machine learning systems that take advantage of massive computational capacity have been the most effective, and by a large margin. Sutton's paper describes examples of breakthrough results from such disparate fields of artificial intelligence research as playing the ancient board game of Go, performing speech recognition, and tackling computer vision. If you are working on a machine learning system hosted on a cloud platform, the scale of the information technology capacity available to your system is bounded by your financial budget rather than technical limitations. So, as part of your machine learning system design, you need to make decisions about the scale at which your system is expected to consume information technology resources available in the cloud. If you are building machine learning systems that need to outperform in the marketplace or deliver state-of-the-art results in academia, then you should learn from the "bitter lesson" and design for both scaling up and scaling out.

If you plan on taking the bitter lesson to heart and scaling your machine learning system, you need to put in some work to get a deeper understanding of data set batching, use of GPUs, and distributed processing using PyTorch. Although there are many popular and effective machine learning algorithms, including gradient-boosted decision trees, what makes the gradient descent and deep learning stand out is their ability to take advantage of compute, storage, and networking at the scale described by Rich Sutton.

## 7.2  *Using IterableDataset and ObjectStorageDataset*

This section introduces you to the applications of the `IterableDataset` class that can help you support out-of-memory and streaming data sets with gradient descent. You are also going to learn about `ObjectStorageDataset`, which can help you use data sets residing in AWS object storage or in similar services from other major cloud providers.

In out-of-memory datasets, an example in the data set may reside on disk or in the memory of an arbitrary node of your machine learning platform. The assumption of in-memory, index-based addressing used by map-style data sets (in the `__getitem__` method) does not fit with this out-of-memory model. Also, the map-style data sets (as described in chapter 6) assume that the data set must use a `__len__` method, rendering them unsuitable for the conceptually unbounded, streaming data sets.

The newer, `torch.utils.data.IterableDataset`, introduced to PyTorch in version 1.2, eliminates the requirement to define the `__getitem__` and `__len__` methods and instead requires only the definition of an `__iter__` method, which can be used with Python built-in iterator APIs.

> **Listing 7.1  Sketch of a declaration for an IterableDataset subclass**

```
import torch.utils.data.IterableDataset

class MyIterableDataset(Dataset):
    def __init__(self, ...):
        ...
    def __iter__(self):
        ...
```

For example to retrieve a single batch of examples from a data set and assign it to a `batch` variable, you can use Python next and `iter` functions:

```
batch = next(iter(MyIterableDataset(...)))
```

While the number of the examples in the `batch` is not specified as part of the `Iterable-Dataset` class, the individual implementations and instances of the `IterableDataset` class are responsible for managing the batch size. For example, in the ObjectStorage-Dataset class used in the rest of this book, the batch size is specified as one of the arguments for the __init__ method of the class.

Just like TensorDataset (described in chapter 6) provides support for tensor-based, in-memory data sets for the map-style interface, the ObjectStorageDataset provides support for tensor-based, out-of-memory data sets for the iterable-style interface. The ObjectStorageDataset is not available by default when you install PyTorch, so you need to install it separately from Kaen framework using

```
pip install kaen[osds]
```

Once installed, import the class in your runtime using

```
from kaen.torch import ObjectStorageDataset as osds
```

The ObjectStorageDataset class provides a standard PyTorch interface to data sets stored in the CSV format, regardless of whether they are located in public cloud object storage or on your local filesystem. For every call to the __iter__ method of the class, the result is a PyTorch tensor of the numeric values from the CSV-based data set. In the case of the DC taxi development data set created by the dctaxi_dev_test.py PySpark job from chapter 4, this means that the tensor returned by Object-StorageDataset must be separated into the label (y) and the features (X) needed to perform an iteration of gradient descent. For example, this can be done using Python slicing notation ❶.

### Listing 7.2 Partitioning a batch tensor

```
batch = next(iter(osds(...)))

def batchToXy(batch):
  batch = batch.squeeze_()          ◁──  Eliminate the leading (batch)
  return batch[:, 1:], batch[:, 0]        dimension of the tensor.
                                   ◁──┐
X_batch, y_batch = batchToXy(batch)    │  Slice batch into first
                                    ❶  │  (y_batch) and remaining
                                       └  columns (X_batch).
```

All of the rows in the first column of the batch are assigned to the label tensor y_batch and all the rows of the remaining columns are assigned to the feature tensor X_batch.

To instantiate the ObjectStorageDataset, you must specify a URL-style path (similar to a Unix glob string) that points to the location of your CSV-formatted data set. For example, if you have configured the BUCKET_ID and AWS_DEFAULT_REGION environment variables for the S3 bucket containing your development data set, you can instantiate the class using

```
import os
BUCKET_ID = os.environ['BUCKET_ID']
AWS_DEFAULT_REGION = os.environ['AWS_DEFAULT_REGION']
```

```
BATCH_SIZE = 1_048_576 # = 2 ** 20

train_ds = \
  osds(f"s3://dc-taxi-{BUCKET_ID}-{AWS_DEFAULT_REGION}/csv/dev/part*.csv",
        partitions_glob = f"s3://dc-taxi-{BUCKET_ID}-
            {AWS_DEFAULT_REGION}/csv/dev/.meta/shards/*.csv",
        storage_options = {'anon': False},
        batch_size = BATCH_SIZE)
```

where the train_ds gets assigned an instance of the ObjectStorageDataset. Since the ObjectStorageDataset supports the wildcard character (*), the Python f-string used to create the train_ds instance specifies that the data set should include all of the objects in S3 matching the /csv/dev/part*.csv glob in the dc-taxi-${BUCKET_ID}-${AWS_DEFAULT_REGION} S3 bucket.

The partitions_glob parameter of the ObjectStorageDataset points to the metadata file about the CSV part files that match the /csv/dev/part*.csv glob. Recall that the dctaxi_dev_test.py PySpark job saved the Spark partition (also known as part-file) metadata to the .meta/shards subfolder of your development and test data sets. For the development part of the data set, you can preview this metadata by loading it in memory as a pandas DataFrame,

```
import pandas as pd
partitions_df = pd.read_csv(f"s3://dc-taxi-{BUCKET_ID}-
  {AWS_DEFAULT_REGION}/csv/dev/.meta/shards/*.csv")
print(partitions_df[:5])
```

which should produce an output similar to the following:

```
id    count
77    164315
10    165314
31    165168
 1    165436
65    164777
```

where the id column represents the ID of one of the part files in the .meta/shards subfolder and the count column represents the count of the number of lines (records) in the part file.

The ObjectStorageDataset is designed to instantiate in the shortest amount of time possible to start the iterations of gradient descent. In practice, this translates to Object-StorageDataset caching in memory and on disk only the data set objects needed to return the first batch of examples from the data set, as illustrated in figure 7.1.

In the example in figure 7.1, ObjectStorageDataset is instantiated using a fictional src S3 bucket containing CSV-formatted objects with a complete URL-style path as s3://src/data/part*.csv (right side of figure 7.1). The partitions of the data set (i.e., the CSV-formatted objects with the names matching part*.csv) reside under the data folder in the src bucket. In figure 7.1, part*.csv objects are shown as

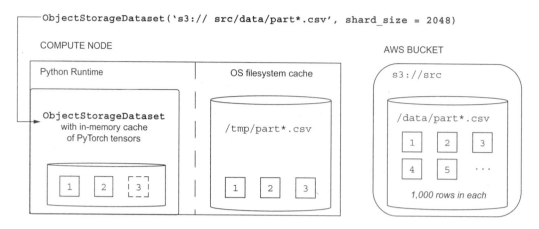

**Figure 7.1  Multilevel cache access to object storage using** `ObjectStorageDataset`

numbered squares in the S3 bucket. For illustration, each one of the `part*.csv` objects in the S3 bucket is assumed to consist of 1,000 examples, which are represented in the CSV format as one line per row.

After `ObjectStorageDataset` is instantiated with a `batch_size` of 2,048 in the Python runtime of a compute node (left side of the figure), the implementation of `ObjectStorageDataset` triggers a network transfer of three data set partitions from the S3 bucket to the filesystem cache of the compute node. Since each object in S3 is 1,000 rows, 3 objects (totaling 3,000 rows) need to be transferred from S3 to the compute node's filesystem for the `ObjectStorageDataset` instance to produce a batch of 2,048 rows. In the figure, the location of the filesystem cache is shown as the /tmp directory; however, a Linux operating system-specific location can vary depending on the operating system defaults. The filesystem cache is needed to minimize the aggregate data transfer over the network in cases where the process for training a machine learning model is repeated for multiple epochs.

Note that the size (number of rows) of the partitions is entirely independent of the `batch_size` used to instantiate `ObjectStorageDataset`, meaning that the `batch_size` can vary while the size of the partitions stays constant. In the DC taxi project used in this book, the number and the size of the partitions are specified in the PySpark jobs that save the cleaned-up data set to object storage. In general, the number and size of the data set partitions vary depending on the specifics of the machine learning project, although it is better to choose partition size in the range of 100–200 MB for efficient transfer over a network connection if you are working with commonly deployed 100 Mbps network interfaces.

**NOTE**  The data set partitions are copied to the filesystem cache unless the URL-style path starts with the file:// protocol handler or the data set originates from the node's filesystem.

When a single batch of training examples fits in memory, after the partitions are cached in the filesystem, partitions 1, 2, and the first 48 lines from partition 3 (shown with a dashed line in figure 7.1) that make up a 2,048-sized shard are cached in memory as PyTorch tensors. Each subsequent call to the __iter__ method of the ObjectStorage-Dataset flushes the in-memory cache, triggers the network transfer of the additional data set partitions needed for the next shard from the bucket to the filesystem cache directory, and loads into memory the next 2,048 examples as PyTorch tensors.

All the capabilities of ObjectStorageDataset described in this section apply to data sets that reside in serverless object storage services from major cloud providers.[1] Although the example in this book focuses on using AWS and S3, you can easily repoint an instance of the ObjectStorageDataset class to a different cloud provider (or a local filesystem) by modifying the protocol specified in the URL-style glob named parameter of the class:

- gcs:// for Google Cloud Storage, for example using

      osds(f"gcs://dc-taxi-${BUCKET_ID}-${AWS_DEFAULT_REGION}/test/part*.csv")

- abfs:// for Azure Blob Storage or Azure Datalake Gen2, for example using

      osds(f"abfs://dc-taxi-${BUCKET_ID}-${AWS_DEFAULT_REGION}/test/part*.csv")

- file:// for the files residing on the local filesystem, for example using

      osds("file://home/user/test/part*.csv")

## 7.3  Gradient descent with out-of-memory data sets

In this section, you are going to extend the basic linear regression example explained in chapter 6 to calculate a weak baseline performance metric for the DC taxi training and test data sets.

So far in this chapter, you have learned about using PyTorch gradient descent based on batches using instances of Dataset and DataLoader classes along with a basic linear regression model with just a single model parameter. Since the DC taxi data set you have prepared for training consists of eight features (latitude and longitude coordinates for pickup and drop-off locations as well as year, month, day of the week, and hour of the trip), to perform linear regression, you need to extend the machine learning model to at least eight parameters, one per feature.

Also, notice that, until now, none of the linear regression examples you have seen used a bias parameter. This was intentional to simplify the sample code: since the previous examples of linear regression relied on data sets with a zero mean, the bias parameter was not necessary. However, the columns of the DC taxi data set do not

---

[1]  The complete list of the storage options supported by ObjectStorageDataset is available from https://filesystem-spec.readthedocs.io/en/latest/.

have a mean of zero in the next example. Hence, you are going to add an extra tensor scalar to represent the bias parameter for linear regression.

Previously, you used the `torch.randn` method to initialize the model parameters by sampling from a normal distribution, but since you are transitioning to more complex models, you can take advantage of better model parameter initialization schemes available from PyTorch.

Kaiming initialization was popularized in a seminal research paper by He and colleagues in 2015 titled "Delving Deep into Rectifiers: Surpassing Human-Level Performance on ImageNet Classification."[2] Kaiming initialization sets the initial model parameter values by taking into account the number of the model parameters that need to be initialized. To use the Kaiming initialization, you simply wrap the calls to `torch.empty` with a call to the `torch.nn.init.kaiming_uniform_` method ❷, ❸.

Listing 7.3   **Using Kaiming initialization for model parameters**

```
pt.set_default_dtype(pt.float64)                    ◁─┐   Use torch.float64 as the dtype
                                                    ❶  for newly created tensors.
FEATURE_COUNT = 8

w = pt.nn.init.kaiming_uniform_(pt.empty(FEATURE_COUNT,
                                1, requires_grad=True))     ◁──❷

b = pt.nn.init.kaiming_uniform_(pt.empty(1,
                                1, requires_grad = True))   ◁──❸
```

Here, the model parameters (also known as coefficients in linear regression) are assigned to the `w` variable and the model bias (intercept) is assigned to `b`.

> **NOTE**   As explained in more detail in chapter 5, the `kaiming_uniform_` method is an example of a PyTorch in-place method, which is indicated by the trailing underscore in the method name. Since the example of the Kaiming initialization in this chapter uses the in-place method, the tensor values returned by the `empty` method are replaced by the initialization.

In section 7.2, you saw that by default `ObjectStorageDataset` returns `float64` as the dtype for the batch tensors. As explained in chapter 5, PyTorch requires that tensors have an identical `dtype` before you can perform operations such as matrix multiplication on the tensors. The `set_default_dtype` method used in listing 7.3 ❶ ensures that the `w` and `b` tensors are created using the `float64` data type to match the `dtype` returned by the `ObjectStorageDataset`.

To take advantage of the modified model parameters, you will have to change the details of the forward step of the gradient descent iteration. At this point, since the feature tensor X for the DC taxi data set has a shape of `torch.Size([DATASET_SIZE,`

---

[2] The abstract of the paper along with a link to the PDF version are available from arXiv: https://arxiv.org/abs/1502.01852.

FEATURE_COUNT]) and the model parameter tensor w has a shape of torch.Size
([FEATURE_COUNT, 1]), their product must have a shape of torch.Size([DATASET_
SIZE, 1]). However, the y_batch tensor created by slicing the batch from the Object-
StorageDataset, as explained in listing 7.2, has a shape of torch.Size([DATASET_
SIZE]). So, before the y_batch and the y_est tensors can be subtracted during the
computation of the loss metric, you should update the y_est tensor using the PyTorch
squeeze method to ensure their shapes are both torch.Size([DATASET_SIZE]):

```
def forward(X):
  y_est = X @ w + b
  return y_est.squeeze_()
```

Given these changes, the baseline linear regression implementation for the DC taxi
data set is ready.

**Listing 7.4  Weak baseline using linear regression**

```
import os
import time
import torch as pt

from torch.utils.data import TensorDataset, DataLoader
from kaen.torch import ObjectStorageDataset as osds

pt.manual_seed(0);
pt.set_default_dtype(pt.float64)

BUCKET_ID = os.environ['BUCKET_ID']
AWS_DEFAULT_REGION = os.environ['AWS_DEFAULT_REGION']

BATCH_SIZE = 2 ** 20 #evaluates to 1_048_576
train_ds = osds(f"s3://dc-taxi-{BUCKET_ID}-
                {AWS_DEFAULT_REGION}/csv/dev/part*.csv",
                storage_options = {'anon': False},
                batch_size = BATCH_SIZE)

train_dl = DataLoader(train_ds, batch_size=None)

FEATURE_COUNT = 8

w = pt.nn.init.kaiming_uniform_(pt.empty(FEATURE_COUNT,
                                1, requires_grad=True))
b = pt.nn.init.kaiming_uniform_(pt.empty(1,
                                1, requires_grad = True))

def batchToXy(batch):
  batch = batch.squeeze_()
  return batch[:, 1:], batch[:, 0]

def forward(X):
  y_est = X @ w + b
  return y_est.squeeze_()
```

```
LEARNING_RATE = 0.03
optimizer = pt.optim.SGD([w, b], lr = LEARNING_RATE)

GRADIENT_NORM = None                    Assume GRADIENT_NORM is not
                                     ❶ initialized by setting it to None.
ITERATION_COUNT = 5

for iter_idx, batch in zip(range(ITERATION_COUNT), train_dl):
  start_ts = time.perf_counter()

  X, y = batchToXy(batch)

  y_est = forward(X)
  mse = pt.nn.functional.mse_loss(y_est, y)
  mse.backward()                              Clip the gradients if the gradients
                                              are above GRADIENT_NORM,
  pt.nn.utils.clip_grad_norm_([w, b],         no-op otherwise.
                       GRADIENT_NORM) if GRADIENT_NORM else None    ◁─❷

  optimizer.step()
  optimizer.zero_grad()

  sec_iter = time.perf_counter() - start_ts

  print(f"Iteration: {iter_idx:03d}, Seconds/Iteration: {sec_iter:.3f}
    MSE: {mse.data.item():.2f}")
```

The `ITERATION_COUNT` in listing 7.4 is intentionally set to a value of 5 because once you execute the code from the listing, you are going to see an output resembling the following:

```
WARNING:root:defaulting to batch_size of 1048576
WARNING:root:stats_glob is not specified at initialization, defaulting to
stats_glob=s3://dc-taxi-c6e91f06095c3d7c61bcc0af33d68382-us-west-
    2/csv/dev/.meta/stats/part-00000-e4fcf448-1123-4bf4-b2bc-9768d30c6dd6-
    c000.csv
Iteration: 000, Seconds/Iteration: 0.020 MSE: 1590566.22
Iteration: 001, Seconds/Iteration: 0.024 MSE: 95402822161212448.00
Iteration: 002, Seconds/Iteration: 0.021 MSE:
  5722549747136962931644694528.00
Iteration: 003, Seconds/Iteration: 0.023 MSE:
  343256645163430856187799115795093520384.00
Iteration: 004, Seconds/Iteration: 0.021 MSE:
  20589650711877918152593680659301796448689601904640.00
```

Notice that unlike the linear regression example from chapter 6, the loss function in this output fails to converge. If you have never seen this behavior from gradient descent before picking up this book, congratulations! You just observed your first exploding gradients!

  If you find this result at all surprising, think back to the synthetic X and y data tensors used in chapter 6: their values had a mean of zero and were relatively small. In contrast, the data in the DC taxi data set consists of the unmodified original values for the locations and the taxi fares, with large values and a non-zero mean. You are going to learn about techniques to properly prepare the data set and prevent the likelihood of exploding (and vanishing) gradients later in this book. For now you should know that exploding gradients can be easily resolved using the built-in PyTorch `torch.nn .utils.clip_grad_norm_` method.

The first two annotations in listing 7.4 ❶ and ❷ illustrate how to include gradient clipping in your gradient descent iteration. When you observed exploding gradients during the execution listing code, the `GRADIENT_NORM` was set to None ❶, which turned off gradient clipping. To enable gradient clipping, the value of `GRADIENT_NORM` should be set to a positive decimal value. The value is used as an upper limit on the maximum gradient value in the model tensors. In other words, gradient clipping amounts to running the Python `min(gradient, GRADIENT_NORM)` function on every gradient value of the tensors passed to the `clip_grad_norm` method. Hence, it is critical to use the `clip_ grad_norm` method after the backward step (which sets the potentially exploding gradient values) but before the optimizer step, which uses the gradient values to update the model parameters.

To obtain the baseline metric for mean squared error over your training data set, modify the `GRADIENT_NORM` to be `0.5` and `ITERATION_COUNT` to be `50`. The values of `GRADIENT_NORM` and `ITERATION_COUNT` are inversely proportional: clipping gradients to smaller values means that gradient descent needs a larger number of iterations to adjust the values of the model parameters. While it is useful to know about gradient clipping when troubleshooting a machine learning model, the better approach is to minimize the risk of having an exploding gradient in the first place.

Assuming that you used the default seed setting of `0` from listing 7.4 and re-executed the code from the listing using `GRADIENT_NORM=0.5` and `ITERATION_COUNT=50`, the training should return the following results for the last 10 iterations of the gradient descent:

```
Iteration: 040, Seconds/Iteration: 0.027 MSE: 2450.01
Iteration: 041, Seconds/Iteration: 0.026 MSE: 416.45
Iteration: 042, Seconds/Iteration: 0.026 MSE: 218.96
Iteration: 043, Seconds/Iteration: 0.026 MSE: 416.74
Iteration: 044, Seconds/Iteration: 0.026 MSE: 214.22
Iteration: 045, Seconds/Iteration: 0.027 MSE: 407.82
Iteration: 046, Seconds/Iteration: 0.029 MSE: 216.30
Iteration: 047, Seconds/Iteration: 0.026 MSE: 415.99
Iteration: 048, Seconds/Iteration: 0.026 MSE: 223.59
Iteration: 049, Seconds/Iteration: 0.026 MSE: 421.73
```

In the last 10 iterations, the value of the MSE loss function is not improving and the range of 200–400 is obviously a weak baseline. However, with gradient clipping enabled the gradients are no longer exploding.

## 7.4    *Faster PyTorch tensor operations with GPUs*

This section describes the graphical processing unit (GPU) support provided by PyTorch tensor APIs and when GPUs can help improve the performance of machine learning algorithms with higher throughput computing. Learning about GPU support in PyTorch is going to prepare you for the next section, where you will modify the weak baseline linear regression implementation for the DC taxi data set to use a GPU instead of a CPU.

Alex Krizhevsky's winning entry at the 2012 ImageNet competition[3] was one of the most visible success stories that helped re-ignite interest in deep learning. While the convolutional neural network, the machine learning model used by Krizhevsky, was well known since the 1990s, it captured the top place in the rankings in large part due to a "very efficient GPU implementation."[4] Since 2012, GPUs and other dedicated processors[5] have been used to efficiently train state-of-the-art machine learning models, in particular for domains with large, unstructured data sets, such as those that contain images, video, audio, or a large quantity of natural language documents.

PyTorch tensors can take advantage of the higher-throughput computation possible with GPUs without changes to the implementation of the machine learning code. However, if you are planning on using GPUs on your machine learning project, you should have a clear understanding of the tensor performance you can get with CPUs, and also be aware of the barriers to entry for using GPUs for PyTorch tensors.

PyTorch relies on Compute Unified Device Architecture (CUDA)-based APIs for interfacing with a GPU. CUDA was introduced in 2007 by nVidia, a major GPU manufacturer, and since then became a de facto standard for software libraries providing applications and frameworks like PyTorch with GPU APIs. CUDA enables PyTorch to perform parallel processing of tensor operations on a GPU regardless of whether the GPU was built by nVidia, Intel, or another processor manufacturer that supports the CUDA standard.

PyTorch can perform a limited degree of parallel processing using CPUs since it is common for modern processors to have anywhere from 2 to 16 cores. To find out the exact number of CPU cores available to PyTorch you can execute the following Python code:

```
import os
os.cpu_count()
```

which in my case returns a 4. In processor terminology, each one of these CPU cores can act as an independent arithmetic logic unit (ALU) that performs the low-level arithmetic computations needed by PyTorch tensor operations. However, as illustrated

---

[3]  The competition website along with the links to the competition results is available here: http://mng.bz/Koqj.

[4]  As described by Alex Krizhevsky's paper: http://www.cs.toronto.edu/~hinton/absps/imagenet.pdf.

[5]  Google has developed a tensor processing unit (TPU) designed to accelerate tensor operations.

in figure 7.2, the number of ALUs on a standard CPU pales in comparison with the number of ALUs on a GPU.

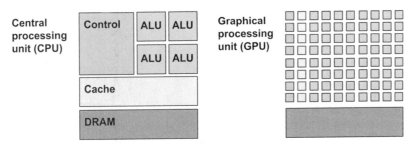

**Figure 7.2 While equipped with a larger cache, a CPU (left) is limited in parallel processing throughput by the number of ALU cores. Smaller cache and control units in a GPU (right) are shared across a larger number of ALU cores having a higher total parallel processing throughput than a CPU.**

PyTorch CUDA APIs can provide you with information about the exact number of ALUs available on your GPU device. In PyTorch, it is customary to initialize the `device` variable before using the GPU.

**Listing 7.5 Checking if GPU and CUDA device drivers are available**

```
device = pt.device("cuda" if pt.cuda.is_available() else "cpu")
```

If you have a CUDA device available on your computer, the `device` variable has the value of `"cuda"`. To find out the number of ALUs you have available, you need to first use the `get_device_capability` method to find out your CUDA compute capability profile:

```
[pt.cuda.get_device_properties(i) for i in range(pt.cuda.device_count())]
```

which in my case reports

```
[_CudaDeviceProperties(name='Tesla P100-PCIE-16GB',
  major=6, minor=0, total_memory=16280MB, multi_processor_count=56)]
```

The values returned by `get_device_capability` are not the actual ALUs counts but rather a generic device profile. To find out the actual number of ALUs for the profile, you need to look up the corresponding entry on the nVidia CUDA website: https://docs.nvidia.com/cuda/cuda-c-programming-guide/index.html. For example, in the case of the 6,0 profile, the specific URL is https://docs.nvidia.com/cuda/cuda-c-programming-guide/index.html#compute-capability-6-x which lists 64 ALUs, matching the number on the right side of figure 7.2.

In section 7.3, you learned about using the `set_default_dtype` method to specify the default `dtype`s for the tensors created in your PyTorch code. For every supported

PyTorch `dtype` (e.g., `torch.float64`), there are two alternative implementations available from the PyTorch library: one for CPU-based and another for GPU-based tensors.[6] PyTorch defaults to using the CPU-based tensors unless you specify the CUDA-based implementation as the default using the `set_default_tensor_type` method. For example,

```
pt.set_default_dtype(pt.float64)

tensor = pt.empty(1)
print(tensor.dtype, tensor.device)
```

outputs

```
torch.float64 cpu
```

where the `device` attribute of the `tensor` instance reports that PyTorch defaulted to a CPU-based implementation. However, you can configure PyTorch to default to a GPU-based implementation (listing 7.6 ❶).

---

**Listing 7.6   Using a GPU tensor as the default tensor type**

```
pt.set_default_tensor_type(pt.cuda.FloatTensor)     ◁┐
pt.set_default_dtype(pt.float64)                      │   Use the
                                                      │   torch.cuda.FloatTensor
tensor = pt.empty(1)                                ❶ │   as default tensor type.
print(tensor.dtype, tensor.device)
```

This code produces

```
torch.float64 cuda:0
```

showing that the tensor is defaulting to the first CUDA GPU device, as indicated by the `cuda` prefix and the 0-based index postfix.

> **NOTE**   In this chapter, you will learn about scaling up PyTorch code to use a single GPU per compute node. Chapter 8 and later chapters explain how to scale out to multiple GPU devices and to multiple compute nodes in a network.

The `set_default_tensor_type` method is a global setting, and as such it may inadvertently impact your entire PyTorch codebase. Even if you specify `set_default_tensor_type` to use a GPU-based implementation for a `FloatTensor` tensor, all tensors created in your code are converted to use GPUs. For example,

---

[6]  For detailed documentation about PyTorch `dtype`s and the corresponding CPU and GPU tensor implementation, refer to http://mng.bz/9an7.

```
pt.set_default_tensor_type(pt.cuda.FloatTensor)
pt.set_default_dtype(pt.float64)

tensor = pt.empty(1, dtype=int)
print(tensor.dtype, tensor.device)
```

prints out

```
torch.int64 cuda:0
```

showing that the `tensor` instance configured as an `int` also defaulted to the GPU-based implementation.

While it is important to be mindful of the global `set_default_tensor_type` setting, a better practice when using a GPU for tensor operations is to create tensors directly on a desired device. Assuming that you initialize the `device` variable as explained in listing 7.5, you can create a tensor on a specific device by setting the `device` named parameter:

```
device = pt.device("cuda" if pt.cuda.is_available() else "cpu")

tensor = pt.empty(1, dtype=int, device=device)
print(tensor.dtype, tensor.device)
```

which outputs

```
torch.int64 cuda:0
```

if a CUDA device is available to PyTorch (i.e., `cuda.is_available` is `True`). When a CUDA device is not available or not configured,[7] the same code outputs

```
torch.int64 cpu
```

In the situations where your PyTorch code processes tensors from external libraries such as NumPy, it can be useful to move the existing tensor to a different device using the `to` method. For example, if your `device` variable is initialized to `cuda`, then to create an array tensor with 100 random elements on a GPU, you can use

```
a = pt.randn(100).to(device)
```

Note that all tensors used by a tensor operation have to reside on the same device for the operation to succeed. This means that

```
b = pt.randn(100).to(device)
a + b
```

---

[7] The `device` parameter is available for all PyTorch tensor creation operations and documented here: http://mng.bz/jj8r.

correctly returns the sum of tensors a and b, while

```
c = pt.randn(100)
a + c
```

fails with a RuntimeError: expected device cuda:0 but got device cpu.

While GPUs offer significant performance improvements for machine learning compared to CPUs, there is a latency overhead involved in moving contents of a tensor from the main computer memory to the memory of the GPU. To quantify the performance advantages of the GPU, you can start with the following benchmark function:

```
import timeit
MAX_SIZE = 28

def benchmark_cpu_gpu(n, sizes):
  for device in ["cpu", "cuda"]:
    for size in sizes:
      a = pt.randn(size).to(device)
      b = pt.randn(size).to(device)
      yield timeit.timeit(lambda: a + b, number = n)

sizes = [2 ** i for i in range(MAX_SIZE)]
measurements = list(benchmark_cpu_gpu(1, sizes))
cpu = measurements[:MAX_SIZE]
gpu = measurements[MAX_SIZE:]
ratios = [cpu[i] / gpu[i] for i in range(len(cpu))]
```

where, after the execution of the benchmark method, the ratio variable contains the performance of the GPU versus CPU (higher is better). For example, in my measurements, a GPU achieved speed-ups of over 1000 times versus the CPU (figure 7.3), especially for larger tensor sizes.

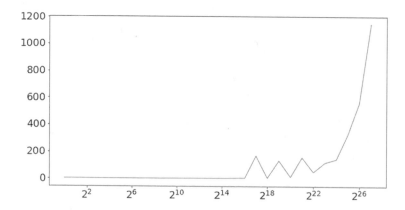

**Figure 7.3   For larger tensor sizes (horizontal axis), a GPU can be up to 150 times faster than a CPU (vertical axis) for tensor addition.**

However, for smaller tensor sizes, those containing 4,096 floating point values or fewer (figure 7.4), the performance of the CPU is either on par or faster than that of the GPU.

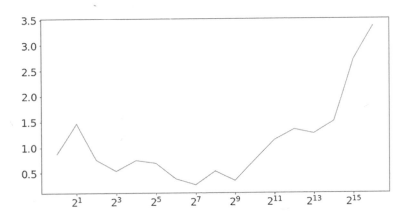

**Figure 7.4   For tensors with fewer than 4K values (horizontal axis), the overhead of data transfer to GPU memory can mean GPU performance at 50% of a CPU (vertical axis).**

## 7.5   Scaling up to use GPU cores

In this section, you will modify the baseline linear regression implementation from listing 7.4 to take advantage of multiple GPU cores of your compute node. As you learned from section 7.4, to adapt your machine learning code to take advantage of GPUs, you need to ensure that the CUDA device and the device drivers are properly configured for PyTorch by invoking the torch.cuda.is_available() method (listing 7.7 ❶), where the available device is assigned to the device variable.

**Listing 7.7   Weak baseline using linear regression**

```
iimport os
import torch as pt
from torch.utils.data import DataLoader
from kaen.torch import ObjectStorageDataset as osds


pt.manual_seed(0);
pt.set_default_dtype(pt.float64)
                                      Use GPU when the
                                      device is available.
device = pt.device("cuda" \
                if pt.cuda.is_available() else "cpu")          ❶


BATCH_SIZE = 1_048_576 # = 2 ** 20


train_ds = osds(f"s3://dc-taxi-{os.environ['BUCKET_ID']}-
                {os.environ['AWS_DEFAULT_REGION']}/csv/dev/part*.csv",
```

```
                      storage_options = {'anon': False},
                      batch_size = BATCH_SIZE)

      train_dl = DataLoader(train_ds,
                            pin_memory = True)

      FEATURE_COUNT = 8
      w = \
        pt.nn.init.kaiming_uniform_(pt.empty(FEATURE_COUNT, 1,
                                    requires_grad=True, device=device))
      b = \
        pt.nn.init.kaiming_uniform_(pt.empty(1, 1,
                                    requires_grad = True, device=device))

      def batchToXy(batch):
        batch = batch.squeeze_().to(device)
        return batch[:, 1:], batch[:, 0]

      def forward(X):
        y_pred = X @ w + b
        return y_pred.squeeze_()

      def loss(y_est, y):
        mse_loss = pt.mean((y_est - y) ** 2)
        return mse_loss

      LEARNING_RATE = 0.03
      optimizer = pt.optim.SGD([w, b], lr = LEARNING_RATE)

      GRADIENT_NORM = 0.5

      ITERATION_COUNT = 50

      for iter_idx, batch in zip(range(ITERATION_COUNT), train_dl):
        start_ts = time.perf_counter()

        X, y = batchToXy(batch)

        y_est = forward(X)
        mse = loss(y_est, y)
        mse.backward()

        pt.nn.utils.clip_grad_norm_([w, b],
                                    GRADIENT_NORM) if GRADIENT_NORM else None

        optimizer.step()
        optimizer.zero_grad()

        sec_iter = time.perf_counter() - start_ts

        print(f"Iteration: {iter_idx:03d}, Seconds/Iteration: {sec_iter:.3f}
          MSE: {mse.data.item():.2f}")
```

**2** Customize the DataLoader to pin the data in memory for accelerated transfer.

Initialize the model parameters . . .

**3**

. . . and the model bias to use the GPU device when available and CPU otherwise.

**4**

Transfer the batch data to the GPU device when available, no-op otherwise.

**5**

The remaining changes are highlighted in listing 7.7 **2**–**5**. Notice that the Data-Loader instantiation is changed to take advantage of the pin_memory parameter **2**. This parameter helps accelerate the transfer of large tensors from CPU memory to GPU by "pinning" virtual memory pages of the operating system to prevent the pages from swapping from physical memory to storage, and vice versa. The remaining changes ❸–❺ are simply to specify the correct device to use with the PyTorch tensors: cuda, if the GPU is available to the PyTorch runtime, and cpu otherwise.

Running the code from listing 7.7 should demonstrate a weak baseline as measured by MSE loss:

```
Iteration: 040, Seconds/Iteration: 0.009 MSE: 865.98
Iteration: 041, Seconds/Iteration: 0.009 MSE: 36.48
Iteration: 042, Seconds/Iteration: 0.009 MSE: 857.78
Iteration: 043, Seconds/Iteration: 0.009 MSE: 39.33
Iteration: 044, Seconds/Iteration: 0.009 MSE: 868.70
Iteration: 045, Seconds/Iteration: 0.009 MSE: 37.57
Iteration: 046, Seconds/Iteration: 0.009 MSE: 870.87
Iteration: 047, Seconds/Iteration: 0.009 MSE: 36.42
Iteration: 048, Seconds/Iteration: 0.009 MSE: 852.75
Iteration: 049, Seconds/Iteration: 0.009 MSE: 36.37
```

## Summary

- While using in-memory approaches is faster and more effective for smaller machine learning problems, using out-of-memory techniques enables scalability to larger data sets and larger pools of information technology resources: compute, storage, networking.
- Using data set batches with gradient descent enables your PyTorch code to scale up to take advantage of the compute resources within a single node and scale out to take advantage of multiple nodes in a compute cluster.
- PyTorch IterableDataset simplifies the use of batches for out-of-memory and streaming data sets in PyTorch code, while the ObjectStorageDataset utility class provides ready-to-use implementations for out-of-memory data sets.
- PyTorch support for GPUs is enabled by CUDA device drivers, providing PyTorch developers with the option to easily scale existing PyTorch code to take advantage of the higher throughput and more parallel compute capabilities of GPUs.
- A basic linear regression implementation in PyTorch can provide a weak baseline for the expected training mean squared error on the DC taxi data set.

# Scaling out with distributed training

In chapter 7, you learned about scaling up your machine learning implementation to make the most of the compute resources available in a single compute node. For example, you saw examples for taking advantage of the more powerful processors in GPU devices. However, as you will discover by launching a machine learning system in production, the rate of growth in the number of training examples and the size of the training data sets can outpace the compute capacity of even the most capable servers and workstations. Although with contemporary public cloud infrastructure scaling up by upgrading to a more powerful processor or by adding more memory or more GPU devices can get you far, you should have a better plan for the long run.

*Distributed data parallel* (DDP) training is a category of machine learning model training that relies on scaling out rather than scaling up. With scaling out, as the training data set size grows, you scale by partitioning and performing the computational workload involved in model training across a cluster of networked compute servers, or nodes. Here, a *node* is a virtual or physical server on a network connecting the nodes into a cluster. Instead of upgrading to the more capable (and often more expensive) compute nodes to perform machine learning model training (the scale-up approach), with scale out you can network a cluster of less powerful, even commodity compute nodes, and open the possibility of finishing training sooner by distributing and doing work across the nodes in parallel. In effect, scaling out to larger training data sets means adding more nodes to a cluster.

DDP model training is more than just scaling out by adding nodes to a cluster. The "data parallel" aspect of DDP describes that, in the cluster, every node computes gradients using only independent and mutually exclusive partitions (also known as *shards*) of the training data set. Typically, the number of training examples in a shard is selected to ensure that the shard can fit in the memory of each of the nodes in the cluster. Although in a DDP approach every training node in the cluster uses a distinct shard of the data set for every iteration of gradient descent, within the scope of the iteration, all nodes must use an identical copy of the model in training to compute the model parameter gradients. Hence, after the nodes compute the gradients based on the training data set (or a batch of training examples), the nodes must all synchronize to an updated version of the model parameters using the computed gradients.

In this chapter, you will learn about alternative approaches to distributed gradient descent and how DDP gradient descent implementations can help you efficiently scale out training across an arbitrary number of nodes while using practical nodes with limited compute, memory, storage, and bandwidth resources.

## 8.1 What if the training data set does not fit in memory?

This section and its subsections provide a step-by-step introduction to gradient accumulation and the role that gradient accumulation plays in gradient descent to enable support for out-of-memory training data sets.

### 8.1.1 Illustrating gradient accumulation

This section demonstrates gradient accumulation using the autograd library of PyTorch. While the example in this section is based on using autograd with a trivial function, later sections apply gradient accumulation to more realistic examples.

When using gradient descent with reverse mode accumulating autodiff it is necessary to clear out the values of the tensor's gradients after performing an optimization step of gradient descent.[1] In PyTorch, this is done by setting the tensor's gradients to `None` or using a `torch.optim.Optimizer` helper method, `zero_grad`. Unless the gradients are zeroed (cleared) out, calls to the `backward` method of the tensor produced by the loss function can result in accumulation of the gradient values in the model's tensors. This behavior is shown in the following listing.

---

**Listing 8.1    Illustration of gradient accumulation for repeated calls to `backward`**

```
import torch as pt
x = pt.tensor(3., requires_grad=True)          ◁───  Use requires_grad=True to
y = x ** 2                                            enable differentiation of y
for _ in range(5):                                    with respect to x.
    y.backward(retain_graph=True)      ◁───  Set retain_graph=True
    print(x.grad)                            to prevent PyTorch from
                                             de-allocating memory.
```

This outputs

```
tensor(6.)
tensor(12.)
tensor(18.)
tensor(24.)
tensor(30.)
```

Based on five repeated calls to `backward` accumulates the value for $\frac{\delta y}{\delta x}$ of $y = x^2$ at 3, which is 6. As the result of accumulation, the output of `x.grad` skips counts by 6 for each of the 5 iterations of the for-loop. Although gradient accumulation may seem like an inconvenient side effect of autodiff, it can serve a useful purpose when scaling gradient descent to out-of-memory data sets and distributed clusters.

### 8.1.2   *Preparing a sample model and data set*

This section describes how to prepare a sample model and a training data set to illustrate the role that gradient accumulation plays in scaling to out-of-memory data sets. In the next section, you will learn how the model and the data set can be used in gradient descent.

Suppose you are working with a training data set of 1,000 structured records and the compute node executing your gradient descent algorithm has just enough memory to hold 250 examples at a time. Of course, modern compute environments can scale to much larger data sets; however, this choice of numbers will prove useful as an illustration. Let's look at a gradient accumulation with a made-up data set that does fit in memory before jumping directly into the complexity of a real-world out-of-memory data set.

---

[1]   This feature of autodiff is covered in detail in chapter 5.

**Listing 8.2 Preparing a sample multivariate linear regression data set**

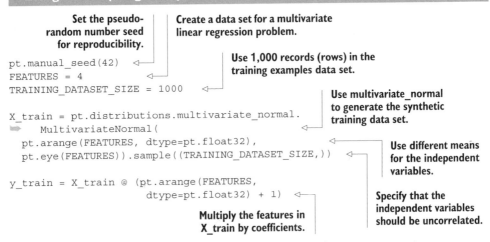

Set the pseudo-random number seed for reproducibility.

Create a data set for a multivariate linear regression problem.

Use 1,000 records (rows) in the training examples data set.

Use multivariate_normal to generate the synthetic training data set.

Use different means for the independent variables.

Specify that the independent variables should be uncorrelated.

Multiply the features in X_train by coefficients.

```
pt.manual_seed(42)
FEATURES = 4
TRAINING_DATASET_SIZE = 1000

X_train = pt.distributions.multivariate_normal.
    MultivariateNormal(
  pt.arange(FEATURES, dtype=pt.float32),
  pt.eye(FEATURES)).sample((TRAINING_DATASET_SIZE,))

y_train = X_train @ (pt.arange(FEATURES,
                    dtype=pt.float32) + 1)
```

The listing created a training data set with four features (independent variables) and a dependent variable (label) based on four coefficients, 1, 2, 3, 4, for each of the four features. For example, assuming that you used seed value 42 when generating the X_train values, the value of the y_train[0] is computed from X_train[0, :]:

```
print(X_train[0, :] @ pt.tensor([1, 2, 3, 4], dtype = pt.float32))
```

which should output

```
tensor(19.1816)
```

You can also confirm the expected shapes of the training data set tensors X_train and y_train by printing

```
print(X_train.shape, y_train.shape)
```

which should output the following based on the values of 1,000 and 4 for the TRAINING_DATASET_SIZE and FEATURES, respectively:

```
(torch.Size([1000, 4]), torch.Size([1000]))
```

With the training data set tensors in place, you can prepare a linear regression model and the supporting methods to train the model using gradient descent. The model w is initialized with random values sampled from a standard normal distribution. Also, since the w model parameter tensor is created with requires_grad=True, the tensor has the initial gradient values set to None.

**Listing 8.3 Defining a model w and utility methods for gradient descent**

Create the model for the multivariate linear regression problem.

```
pt.manual_seed(42)
w = pt.randn(FEATURES, requires_grad = True)
```

```
def forward(w, X):
    return X @ w
```
◁—— **Implement the forward step of gradient descent based on the model w.**

```
def mse(y_est, y):
    err = y_est - y
    return (err ** 2).mean()
```
◁—— **Compute the errors (residuals) of the target (y).**

◁—— **Return the value of the mean squared error.**

Although you could have initialized w using a more sophisticated technique,[2] in this case the multivariate linear regression problem is simple enough that the added complexity is not warranted.

### 8.1.3   *Understanding gradient descent using out-of-memory data shards*

In this section, the model and the data set prepared in section 8.1.2 are used with gradient descent to use the gradient accumulation feature of autodiff to scale to out-of-memory data sets.

By relying on gradient accumulation, gradient descent can compute the gradients based on the entire training data set (i.e., an epoch of gradient descent) using the approach illustrated in figure 8.1. Be careful not to confuse the shards shown in figure 8.1 with batches as used in mini-batch gradient descent; the difference is clarified in the following paragraphs.

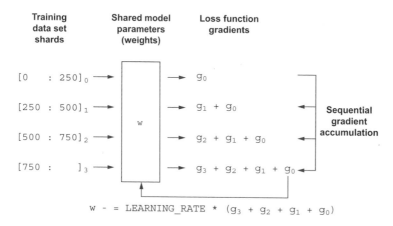

**Figure 8.1   Gradient accumulation re-uses shard memory to enable scaling to out-of-memory data sets.**

---

[2]  For example, many deep learning models are initialized using Kaiming initialization: http://mng.bz/5K47.

The left side of figure 8.1 shows the shards of the training dataset using $[0:250]_0$ to represent the first shard of 250 examples (records) out of the 1,000 in the training data set, $[0:250]_1$, for the second shard of records 250 up to 500, and so on. Here, the Python slicing notation (e.g., [0:250]) is used to specify which of the 1,000 examples in the training data set are included in a shard.

Notice that in figure 8.1 each shard is processed (in the forward and backward steps of gradient descent) using the same model w, or, more precisely, using identical values of the w model parameters. Although the model parameter values are identical in the four sequential steps of gradient accumulation in figure 8.1, since each shard contains a distinct collection of the training examples, the gradients computed for each shard are also distinct and are shard-specific. In the figure, this relationship between the shard and its corresponding gradient is denoted using the subscript so that the shard $[0:250]_0$ produces the gradient $g_0$, and so on.

Once the gradients are computed per shard's worth of training examples (listing 8.4), the shard gradients are not used to update the model parameters. Instead, the gradients are left to accumulate in the model's tensors. Thus, after the second shard of the training examples is processed by the forward method and then the backward method computes the corresponding gradient $g_1$, the model's tensor w.grad contains the sum (accumulation) of the gradients $g_0 + g_1$.

Note that computation with shards is different from computation with batches in mini-batch gradient descent, where the gradients computed from each batch are used to update the model parameters and are subsequently cleared out. It is useful to distinguish batches from shards because both can be used with gradient descent; for example, a shard can be a partition of a batch in cases where a batch of data does not fit into node memory. A shard can also consist of multiple batches so that gradient descent can be sped up by processing multiple batches stored in a memory of a node. Although shards can be used with mini-batch gradient descent, this section focuses on explaining a more basic example of using shards with ordinary gradient descent, where the gradients are computed based on an entire set of training examples.

Only after processing the entire training data set, one shard at a time, does the algorithm illustrated in figure 8.1 perform an optimization step of gradient descent based on the accumulated gradient $g_0 + g_1 + g_2 + g_3$.

**Listing 8.4  Gradient descent using IN_MEMORY_SHARD_SIZE examples**

```
EPOCHS = 500
LEARNING_RATE = 0.01
IN_MEMORY_SHARD_SIZE = 250

for epoch in range(EPOCHS):
  for i in range(0, \
    TRAINING_DATASET_SIZE // IN_MEMORY_SHARD_SIZE):     ◁── ❶

    start_idx = i * IN_MEMORY_SHARD_SIZE
    end_idx = start_idx + IN_MEMORY_SHARD_SIZE
```

❶ Perform **TRAINING_DATASET_SIZE // IN_MEMORY_SHARD_SIZE** iterations per epoch.

**Assign** ②     `y_shard = y_train[start_idx : end_idx]`   ③ **Perform the forward step**
**training**         `X_shard = X_train[start_idx : end_idx]`      **of gradient descent.**
**examples**
**to y_shard**       `y_est = forward(w, X_shard)`     ④ **Compute the shard-size**
**and**         `loss = \`                         **adjusted training loss.**
**X_shard.**           `(IN_MEMORY_SHARD_SIZE / TRAINING_DATASET_SIZE) * mse(y_est, y_shard)`

        `loss.backward()`             ⑤ **Perform back prop and**
                                        **accumulation of the gradients.**

        `#notice that the following is`
        `#in scope of the outer for loop`    ⑥ **Perform the gradient**
        `w.data -= LEARNING_RATE * w.grad`   **descent optimization step.**
        `w.grad = None`              **Clear out the gradients**
                              ⑦ **of the model's tensors.**

Once the code is executed, the print statement

`print(w)`

should output

`tensor([1.0000, 2.0000, 3.0000, 4.0000], requires_grad=True)`

which confirms that the gradient descent correctly recovered the coefficients `[1.0000, 2.0000, 3.0000, 4.0000]` used in listing 8.2 to create the training data set made up of `y_train` and `X_train`.

The fraction (`IN_MEMORY_SHARD_SIZE / TRAINING_DATASET_SIZE`) used in the calculation of the loss in listing 8.4 is subtle but important. Recall that the listing is intended to compute the gradient for the entire epoch of training examples, or, more precisely, `TRAINING_DATASET_SIZE` examples. The default implementation of the `mse` method, which computes the mean squared error of the model's estimates `y_est`, assumes `IN_MEMORY_SHARD_SIZE` of examples during the computation. In other words, every iteration of the inner for-loop in the listing computes `mse` by calculating $\frac{1}{IN\_MEMORY\_SHARD\_SIZE} * \sum (y\_est - y\_shard)^2$, or equivalently in PyTorch using

`(1 / IN_MEMORY_SHARD_SIZE) * ((y_est - y_shard) ** 2).sum()`

which returns the mean squared error per `IN_MEMORY_DATASET_SIZE` examples. The (`IN_MEMORY_SHARD_SIZE / TRAINING_DATASET_SIZE`) fraction used in ④ rescales the mean squared error to the `TRAINING_DATASET_SIZE` examples.

With this multiplication, expressed in terms of an equation, notice that rescaling amounts to `IN_MEMORY_DATASET_SIZE`, which cancels out in the numerator and denominator of

$$\frac{\cancel{IN\_MEMORY\_SHARD\_SIZE}}{TRAINING\_DATASET\_SIZE} * \frac{1}{\cancel{IN\_MEMORY\_SHARD\_SIZE}} * \sum (y\_est - y\_shard)^2.$$

When the inner for-loop finishes, the `w.grad` contains the sum of the training example gradients, so the code `w.data -= LEARNING_RATE * w.grad` computes the optimization step for the entire epoch of shards. In other words, in the gradient descent implementation in listing 8.4, the gradient optimization step is performed once per every epoch of a training example. This confirms that the implementation in listing 8.4 is not a mini-batch gradient descent.

Although the approach illustrated in figure 8.1 enables scaling to out-of-memory data sets while using arbitrary shard sizes, it suffers from a significant algorithm complexity problem: the inner for-loop is sequential, which changes the big-zero performance of the gradient descent implementation from $O(EPOCHS)$ to $O(EPOCHS * SHARDS)$.

Distributing the inner for-loop from listing 8.4 across a cluster of parallel worker nodes can return the implementation to the original $O(EPOCHS)$ worst-case performance. But how can this be implemented efficiently?

## 8.2 *Parameter server approach to gradient accumulation*

This section introduces parameter server-based implementation of distributed gradient descent and explains the role that gradient accumulation plays in the implementation. This section clarifies the limitations of the parameter server-based approach and motivates a more efficient, ring-based implementation.

Legacy machine learning frameworks like TensorFlow 1.x popularized the parameter server-based approach to distributing gradient descent across multiple nodes in a cluster. The parameter server approach illustrated in figure 8.2 is straightforward to understand and implement.

In the figure, each of the worker nodes (shown using dashed lines) performs the forward and backward steps of gradient descent (e.g., the steps from the inner for-loop in listing 8.4) based on a single shard of the training data set to compute shard-specific gradients of the loss function. Notice that in figure 8.2, the gradients have a subscript that corresponds to the subscript of the shard used to compute the gradient just as in figure 8.1.

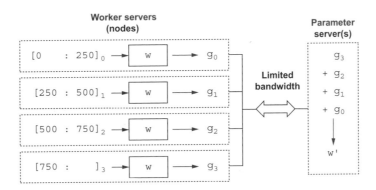

**Figure 8.2   Gradient descent distributed across worker and parameter servers to support scaling out**

Once the worker node computes its gradient, it sends the gradient to a parameter server (or a cluster of parameter servers) for processing. The parameter server(s) (right side of figure 8.2) waits to accumulate the gradients from the worker nodes and uses the accumulated gradients to perform an optimization step of gradient descent, which computes the model parameters for the next iteration of gradient descent. The next version of the model based on the newly computed model parameters (shown as w' in figure 8.2) is then sent to the worker nodes, replacing the previous model parameters (shown as w in figure 8.2) and ensuring that every node computes the next iteration of gradient descent using the identical, updated copy of the model.

The parameter server implementation of distributed gradient descent from figure 8.2 is a kind of distributed data parallel (defined in the introduction to this chapter) approach to gradient descent. In a distributed data parallel approach, the training data set is partitioned (sharded) into independent and mutually exclusive subsets such that there exists a one-to-one relationship between the training data set shard and a worker node. Next, every worker node computes gradients using a shard and an identical copy of the model parameters.

Unlike alternative distributed data parallel approaches (explained in the remainder of the chapter), parameter server implementation of distributed gradient descent suffers from a significant scalability issue: the network connectivity between the worker and parameter servers is a communications bottleneck. Specifically, the limited bandwidth available to communicate between the worker and parameter server nodes is saturated in both communication phases of the implementation: during the many-to-one (or many-to-few) communication of the gradients from the workers to the parameter servers, as well as during the one-to-many (or few-to-many) communication of the updated model parameters from the parameter server(s) to the worker nodes.

## 8.3   *Introducing logical ring-based gradient descent*

This section introduces the fundamental concepts of nodes communicating in a logical ring network. Instead of provisioning actual nodes and having them communicate over a network, this section explains the networking concepts using a simple Python program running in a single-node environment. Once you have a firm grasp of the concepts, you will apply them to the more complex, distributed, multi-node environments.

As opposed to relying on a centralized cluster of parameter servers (the approach illustrated in section 8.2), logical ring-based distributed data parallel algorithms (e.g., Horovod; https://github.com/horovod/horovod) avoid one-to-many and many-to-one communications bottlenecks and rely on nodes communicating just with the two logical neighbors in a ring: the predecessor and the successor nodes.

The illustration in figure 8.3 (left side) shows four nodes, each shown using dashed lines and denoted as nodes $n_0$ through $n_3$ that are organized in a logical ring. Note that with contemporary virtual networks in public cloud environments the nodes do not have to be physically connected to each other in a ring: standard ethernet

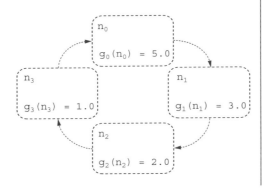

| Node ID | Gradient ID | Example gradient value |
|---|---|---|
| $n_0$ | $g_0(n_0)$ | 5.0 |
| $n_1$ | $g_1(n_1)$ | 3.0 |
| $n_2$ | $g_2(n_2)$ | 2.0 |
| $n_3$ | $g_3(n_2)$ | 1.0 |

**Figure 8.3  A logical networking ring (left) explained using sample values (right)**

networking is sufficient. However, in the logical ring network shown in the figure, every node is constrained such that it communicates only with its predecessor and successor nodes. As you will learn in section 8.4, this helps limit the networking bandwidth needed per iteration of the distributed gradient descent.

For a node with an identifier $n_i$, the identifier of the successor node is defined as $n_{(i+1)}$ % *NODES*, where NODES is the total number of nodes in the logical ring. The modulo operation ensures that the communication pattern forms a ring by having the node with the highest identifier (which is always $n_{NODES-1}$) communicate with the node with the identifier 0, and vice versa. In ring networking, as described in this chapter, every node *sends* data only to the successor node.

Using similar logic, the identifier of the predecessor node is defined as $n_{(i-1)}$ % *NODES* for the ring-based networking so that node 0 can communicate with both node 1 and the node with the highest identifier value, (NODES - 1). Every node in the ring network used in this chapter *receives* data only from the predecessor node.

As with the parameter server-based approach explained in section 8.2, the nodes in figure 8.3 process independent shards of the training data set such that $g_0(n_0)$ represents the gradient values computed from a shard having an index of 0 by the node $n_0$. Continuing with the example from section 8.2, if $[0:250]_0$ is the first of four shards, then $g_0(n_0)$ denotes the gradient values from the first shard computed by the node $n_0$, using model parameter values w. Hence, just like with the parameter server-based approach, the ring-based approach is data-parallel distributed.

In the ring-based distributed data parallel implementation, the dedicated parameter servers do not exist. Instead, after every node in the cluster completes the forward and backward steps of an iteration of gradient descent, the nodes communicate in the logical ring network so that the gradients from all the shards are accumulated on every node in the ring.

What kind of information needs to be communicated between the nodes to ensure that model parameter values and the accumulated gradient values are perfectly synchronized and identical? In the logical ring, since every node can send data only to the successor node, a node can receive accumulated gradients only from a series of iterations of gradient send/receive operations from the predecessor nodes. For instance, in order for the node $n_0$ to accumulate gradients from nodes $n_1$ through $n_3$ (right-most side of figure 8.4), three iterations of the send/receive operations are required. These three iterations are shown in sequence from the left side to the right side of figure 8.4. As you will observe throughout this chapter, it takes (NODES - 1) iterations of send/receive communication in a multi-node cluster consisting of NODES number of nodes.

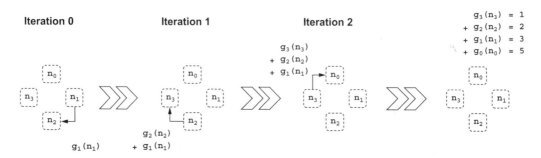

**Figure 8.4   Reduce (sum) gradients to node 0 in a ring of four nodes, a reduce-all algorithm to distribute gradients across nodes**

The source code from listing 8.5 provides the Python pseudocode implementation of the logic described by figure 8.4. In the implementation, the variable NODES is defined using the relationship between the number of the training examples in the training data set (the value of the constant TRAINING_DATASET_SIZE) floor divided by the number of training examples that fit in memory of a node in the multi-node cluster (the value of IN_MEMORY_SHARD_SIZE). The floor division operation // is used to ensure that the value of the NODES constant is set to be an integer value since it is later used as an argument to the Python range operation.

**Listing 8.5   Python pseudocode to illustrate reduction of the gradient to node 0**

```
NODES = \
    TRAINING_DATASET_SIZE // IN_MEMORY_SHARD_SIZE        ◁── Calculate the number of the NODES needed for the training data set.

GRADIENTS = [5., 3., 2., 1.]        ◁── Assign arbitrary GRADIENT values, one per node for an illustration.

node_to_gradients = \
 ▷  dict(zip(range(NODES), GRADIENTS))        Perform NODES - 1 iterations of communication.

for iter in range(NODES - 1):        ◁── Start with node iter+1 so that after NODES-1 . . .
    node = (iter + 1) % NODES        ◁──
    grad = node_to_gradients[node]        ◁── . . . iterations, node 0 accumulates the gradients.
```

Create a dictionary to track the gradient computed by a node.

```
next_node = (node + 1) % NODES          ◁────────   The identifier of the next
                                                      node closes the ring.
# simulate "sending" of the gradient value
# over the network to the next node in the ring
node_to_gradients[next_node] += grad    ◁───┤  Accumulate the gradient
                                                in node_to_gradient.
```

Once the code is done executing, printing the value of the node_to_gradients dictionary

```
print(node_to_gradients)
```

outputs the result:

```
{0: 11.0, 1: 3.0, 2: 5.0, 3: 6.0}
```

where the entry for the key 0 corresponds to the expected gradient computed for $n_0$, with the value of 11 based on the accumulated gradient $5 + 3 + 2 + 1$. Also, notice that since figure 8.4 does not include accumulation of gradients to any nodes other than $n_0$, the gradients for nodes $n_1$ through $n_3$ remain unchanged. Upcoming sections explain how to ensure that identical gradients are accumulated on all nodes in the ring.

During the first (shown with a zero-based index in figure 8.4 as Iteration 0) of the three (NODES - 1) iterations, node $n_1$ sends and node $n_2$ receives the gradient values $g_1(n_1)$ computed by node $n_1$ prior to the start of the iteration 0. Since the purpose of the communication in the ring is to arrive to the accumulated gradient, upon receiving the $g_1(n_1)$ gradient values, the node $n_2$ can accumulate (add to) the gradient values directly to the memory occupied by the gradient $g_2(n_2)$, which ensures the re-use of memory to store the accumulated gradient values: $g_1(n_1) + g_2(n_2)$. For example, if each of the gradient tensors on each of the nodes is 400 MB, then 400 MB' worth of data is communicated between the nodes in the ring, and 400 MB' worth of memory is consumed by each of the nodes to store the accumulated gradient values. By the conclusion of the iteration 0, node $n_2$ accumulates the added (i.e., reduced using a sum operation) gradients.

Hence, during the second iteration (labeled as Iteration 1 in figure 8.4), the accumulated gradient values are sent from node $n_2$ to node $n_3$, resulting in the gradient values $g_1(n_1) + g_2(n_2) + g_3(n_3)$ accumulating on node $n_3$ at the end of the second iteration.

The last and final iteration in this example (labeled Iteration 2 in figure 8.4) completes the accumulation of the gradients on the node $n_0$, adding the gradient computed on the node $g_0(n_0)$ to the accumulated gradient received from $n_3$ during this iteration. The resulting gradient, consisting of $g_0(n_0) + g_1(n_1) + g_2(n_2) + g_3(n_3)$, is sufficient for $n_0$ to compute the model parameter values for the next optimization step of gradient descent to be performed by every node in the cluster.

While the three iterations illustrated in figure 8.4 and listing 8.5 achieved accumulation (reduce step) of the gradients to a single node, for the distributed data parallel gradient descent to work, every node in the ring must have access to the entire accumulated gradient: $g_0(n_0) + g_1(n_1) + g_2(n_2) + g_3(n_3)$. Unless the accumulated gradient is available for every node, the nodes are unable to perform the gradient descent step of changing the values of the model parameters using the accumulated gradient. The upcoming sections build on the reduce steps from listing 8.5 to explain the reduce-all phase of the entire distributed gradient descent algorithm.

## 8.4   *Understanding ring-based distributed gradient descent*

While the naive ring-based reduce operation described in section 8.3 can eliminate the need for parameter servers and ensure that the values of the gradients are reduced (accumulated) on the individual compute nodes in the ring-based multi-node cluster, it suffers from several disadvantages. As the training data set size grows (which is to be expected), the number of the nodes in the cluster must grow to keep up. This also means that the total bandwidth the cluster needs must grow along with the number of the nodes since each node must send the entire gradient to the next node in the ring during each iteration. In this section, you will learn about how ring-based distributed data parallel algorithms (e.g., the well-known Horovod algorithm) help with an efficient use of bandwidth in scale-out situations where both the number of training nodes and the training examples grow.

The Horovod algorithm can support the growth in the training data set (and the number of the nodes in the cluster) while keeping the bandwidth demands constant or even lowering the bandwidth requirements. To support this, Horovod relies on two separate and district phases of ring-based communication: (1) reduce-scatter and (2) all-gather. In both phases, instead of sending/receiving the entire gradient's worth of data between the nodes, Horovod communicates just a single segment of the gradient such that by default the size of the segment is the size of the gradient times $\frac{1}{NODES}$, where *NODES* is the number of the worker nodes in the ring cluster. Hence, increasing the number of the worker nodes to scale with the training data set size reduces the bandwidth requirements in node-to-node communication.

So what is a *segment* of the gradient? You can consider each segment a logical partition of the gradient, as illustrated in figure 8.5. In the figure, the gradient $g_0$ computed by node $n_0$, based on the training data set shard $[0:250]_0$ (where $[0:250]$ is the Python slicing notation), is in turn partitioned into NODES segments, such that by default, a roughly equivalent number of the gradient values exists per segment. Continuing with an earlier example where the gradient occupied 400 MB' worth of data (for example 4 bytes per 100,000,000 of 32-bit floating point gradient values of the model parameters), each segment is 100 MB of the mutually exclusive logical partitions of the segment. Note that in this case, since the shard is computed by the node $n_0$, each $i$ of the four segments is annotated using $s_i(n_0)$.

Also notice that while the segments cannot be accumulated (added) along the horizontal axis of the frame in figure 8.5, it is possible to accumulate the segments along

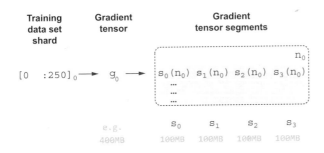

**Figure 8.5  Gradient segments used by Horovod for node-to-node communication**

the vertical axis. Further, the segments $s_i$ shown below the segment frame in figure 8.5 correspond to the accumulation of the corresponding segments computed by each node. For example, $s_0$ is equal to $s_0(n_0) + s_1(n_1) + s_2(n_2) + s_3(n_3)$. Hence, the segments $s_0 s_1 s_2 s_3$ shown below the frame in figure 8.5 are equivalent to a logical partition into segments of the accumulated gradient $g_0 + g_1 + g_2 + g_3$ needed to perform the optimization step of gradient descent.

As with an introduction to the ring-based reduce steps in listing 8.5, the rest of this chapter uses Python pseudocode to explain the Horovod algorithm. Recall that for a distributed data parallel algorithm (such as Horovod) to work correctly, every node in the ring cluster must be initialized with an identical copy of the model parameters. In listing 8.6, the Python list of tensors W is used to represent the identical models. Notice that every tensor in W is initialized using the values from w_src, a tensor of pseudorandom values sampled from a standard normal distribution.

**Listing 8.6   W storing the identical copies of the model tensor**

```
pt.manual_seed(42)
w_src = pt.randn((4,))
W = [pt.tensor(w_src.detach().numpy(),
                requires_grad=True) for _ in range(NODES)]
```

In order to re-use the training data set tensors X_train and y_train from listing 8.4, the following explanation of the Horovod algorithm creates a PyTorch DataLoader, which partitions the training data set into shards of IN_MEMORY_SHARD_SIZE records each. Do not be confused by the batch_size argument to the DataLoader in listing 8.7; although this argument is used to shard the source TensorDataset, the individual shards are not used as batches to update the parameters of the model.

**Listing 8.7   A step of gradient descent using PyTorch DataLoader for sharding**

```
from torch.utils.data import TensorDataset, DataLoader
train_dl = DataLoader(TensorDataset(y_train, X_train), \
                batch_size = IN_MEMORY_SHARD_SIZE,
                shuffle = False)

for node, (y_shard, X_shard) in zip(range(NODES), train_dl):
  y_est = forward(W[node], X_shard)
```

```
loss = \
  (IN_MEMORY_SHARD_SIZE / TRAINING_DATASET_SIZE) * mse(y_shard, y_est)
loss.backward()
```

Once the code is done executing, the expression

```
[W[node].grad for node in range(NODES)]
```

should output

```
[tensor([ -0.1776, -10.4762, -19.9037, -31.2003]),
 tensor([  0.0823, -10.3284, -20.6617, -30.2549]),
 tensor([ -0.1322, -10.9773, -20.4698, -30.2835]),
 tensor([  0.1597, -10.4902, -19.8841, -29.5041])]
```

representing the tensors of the model gradients, one per node in the ring cluster.

Note that after the forward and backward steps of gradient descent are performed on each node using the code in the for-loop in listing 8.7, the Horovod algorithm must perform two phases of ring-based networks in order to communicate the accumulated gradient to every node in the ring. The first phase, known as *reduce-scatter*, is explained in section 8.5, and the second phase, known as *all-gather*, is explained in section 8.6.

## 8.5   Phase 1: Reduce-scatter

This section explains the reduce-scatter phase of Horovod, under the assumption that every node in the ring-based cluster is initialized with an identical copy of the model parameters. The section continues with the example from listing 8.7, where the identical copies of the model parameters are stored in W[node] and every node completed the forward and backward steps of gradient descent, with the resulting gradient values saved in W[node].grad. By the end of this section, you will learn how the reduce-scatter phase of Horovod ensures that every node in the ring ends up with a distinct segment of the accumulated gradient $g_0 + g_1 + g_2 + g_3$.

The first phase of Horovod, known as reduce-scatter, starts after each of the nodes is done computing a gradient based on the node-specific shard of the data set. As explained in the previous section, each node logically partitions the computed gradient into NODES segments. The first iteration (of a total of three iterations) of this phase is shown in figure 8.6, where the top side of the figure illustrates that, at the start of the phase, each node $n_i$ stores the shard-specific segments, $s_0(n_i)$ through $s_{NODES-1}(n_i)$.

Since reduce-scatter sends just a segment's worth of data to the successor node at every iteration, during the first iteration (shown using arrows on the bottom side of figure 8.6), a node $n_i$ forwards a segment $s_{(i-1)\ \%\ NODES}(n_i)$ to the successor node. By the conclusion of the first iteration (bottom side of figure 8.6), each node $n_i$ accumulates a segment $s_{(i-t-1)\ \%\ NODES}(n_{(i-1)\ \%\ NODES}) + s_{(i-t-1)\ \%\ NODES}(n_i)$, where t=1 represents the first iteration.

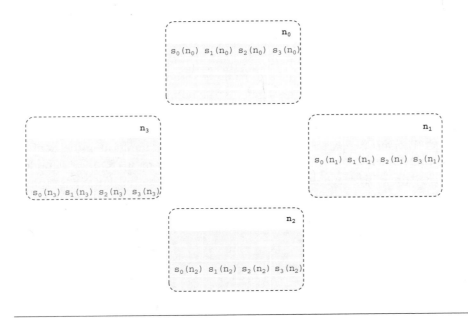

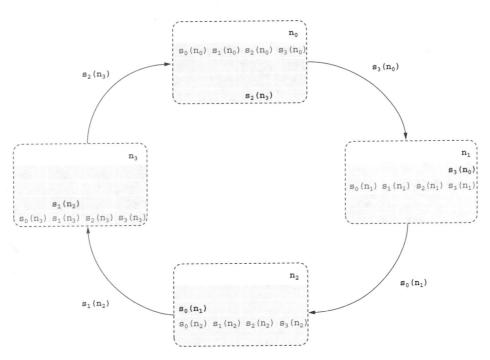

**Figure 8.6** The first iteration of the reduce-scatter phase initiates gradient segment transfer across nodes.

In subsequent iterations, each node sends the segment that was accumulated in the previous iteration to the successor node. For example, in the second iteration (shown in figure 8.7), node $n_1$ sends the segment $s_3(n_0 + n_1)$, node $n_2$ sends the segment $s_0(n_1 + n_2)$, and in general, for iteration t, node $n_i$ sends the accumulated segment $s_{(i - t) \% \text{NODES}}(n_i)$. Since in the example with four nodes only three iterations are needed to reduce-scatter the segments, the bottom side of figure 8.7 shows that, by the conclusion of the second iteration, only one part of each segment is missing on each of the nodes: the segment specified by $s_{(i + 1) \% \text{NODES}}(n_i)$.

This missing part is filled in the third and final iteration of the example, whereby at the conclusion of the iteration (bottom side of figure 8.8), every node $n_i$ accumulates the entire segment $s_i$. For example, notice that in figure 8.8, $n_0$ concludes the final iteration of this phase with $s_0$, node $n_1$ with $s_1$, and so forth.

**Listing 8.8    Python pseudocode for the reduce-scatter phase**

```
for iter in range(NODES - 1):              The first segment is
  for node in range(NODES):                 accumulated on the
    seg = (node - iter - 1) % NODES ◁       first node.
    grad = W[node].grad[seg] ◁
                                            Retrieve the gradient
    next_node = (node + 1) % NODES          values corresponding to
    W[next_node].grad[seg] += grad ◁        node and segment seg.

        Accumulate gradient segment
      value on the next_node in the ring.
```

After the code from listing 8.8 finishes executing, you can output the resulting gradients using

```
print([f"{W[node].grad}" for node in range(NODES)])
```

which should print out

```
['tensor([ -0.0679, -31.9437, -39.7879, -31.2003])',
 'tensor([  0.0823, -42.2722, -60.4496, -61.4552])',
 'tensor([-4.9943e-02, -1.0977e+01, -8.0919e+01, -9.1739e+01])',
 'tensor([ 1.0978e-01, -2.1468e+01, -1.9884e+01, -1.2124e+02])'].
```

Notice that, as expected, the gradient values are scattered across the nodes such that $n_0$ stores the segment $s_0$ of the accumulated gradient, $n_1$ stores the segment $s_1$, and so on. In general, the accumulated segments of the gradient after reduce-scatter can be printed out using

```
print([f"{W[node].grad[node]}" for node in range(NODES)]),
```

which outputs the values of accumulated segment on each node:

```
['-0.06785149872303009', '-42.27215576171875', '-80.91938018798828',
    '-121.24281311035156']
```

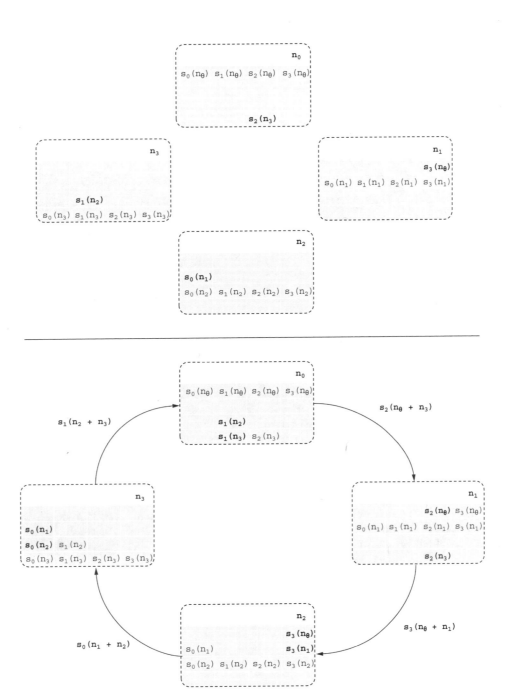

**Figure 8.7** **The second reduce-scatter iteration propagates accumulated gradients.**

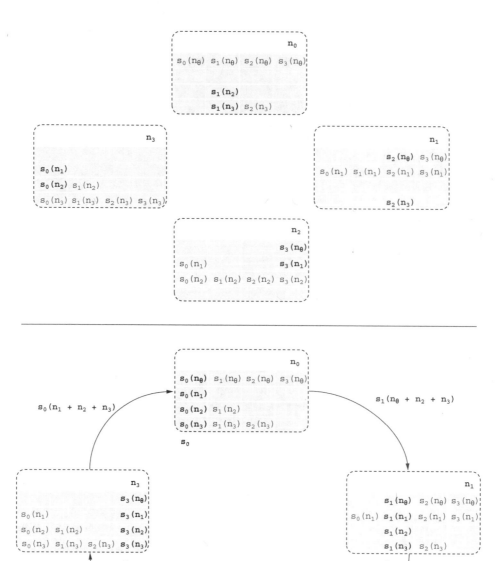

Figure 8.8    The third reduce-scatter iteration finishes gradient accumulation for a four-node ring.

The illustration in figure 8.9 summarizes the code from listing 8.8 for the case when the reduce-scatter ring consists of four nodes.

## 8.6 Phase 2: All-gather

This section explains the second and the final phase of the Horovod algorithm: all-gather. In this section, you can observe how the scattered segments of the accumulated gradient from the reduce-scatter phase are gathered, or sent around the ring, so that by the conclusion of the phase, every node stores the entire accumulated gradient $g_0 + g_1 + g_2 + g_3$. This means that at the conclusion of this phase, every node in the logical ring can perform the optimization step of gradient descent and compute the next iteration of the model parameters for further training.

Given that the reduce-scatter phase performs the nuanced steps of selectively accumulating (reducing) the gradient segment values, the implementation of all-gather, the second and the last phase, is easier to follow. Using an approach introduced with the reduce-all algorithm, this phase involves simply sending the accumulated segments from one node to the next. As with the reduce-scatter phase of the Horovod algorithm, the all-gather phase takes NODES - 1 iterations of node-to-node communication in the logical ring network of the cluster.

The three iterations for the four nodes in figure 8.10 are shown as the upper-left, upper-right, and lower-right quadrants of the figure. The lower-left corner of the figure shows the final state of the nodes in the cluster after the nodes have completed all the steps of the Horovod algorithm. Note that the gradient segments on each node (shown as $s_0$ through $s_3$) store the entire accumulated gradient (shown as $g_0 + g_1 + g_2 + g_3$) computed from the corresponding shards of the training data set.

The upper-left quadrant of the figure indicates that at the beginning of the first iteration the state of the four nodes in the example is such that $n_0$ stores segment $s_0$ of the accumulated gradient, and so forth. During the first iteration of the phase (upper-left quadrant), each node sends only the accumulated segment that it stores to the successor node in the ring, overwriting and replacing any previous segment values stored in the successor node.

### Listing 8.9 Python pseudocode for the all-gather phase

```
for iter in range(NODES - 1):
  for node in range(NODES):
    seg = (node - iter) % NODES          ◁─┐ Start with the first
    grad = W[node].grad[seg]               │ node on the first
                                           │ iteration.

    next_node = (node + 1) % NODES       ◁─┐ Store the gradient values
    W[next_node].grad[seg] = grad          │ of the segment on the next
                                           │ node in the ring.
```

At the beginning of the second iteration (upper-right quadrant in figure 8.10), every node stores exactly two complete segments of the accumulated gradient. During this and the remaining iterations, every node sends the segment received during the

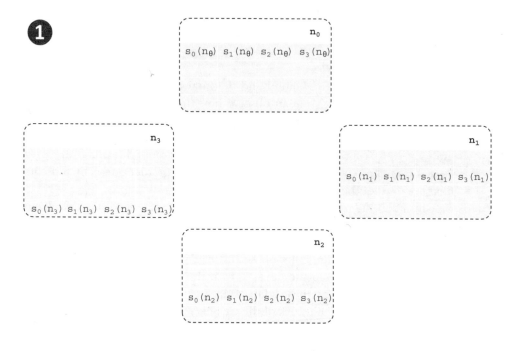

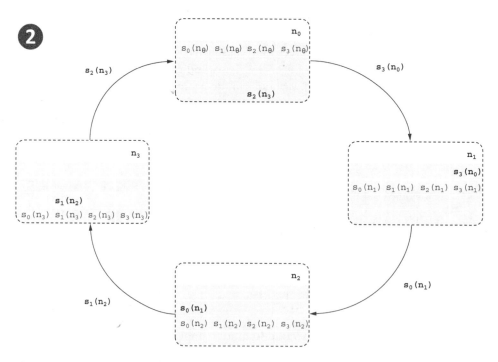

**Figure 8.9a    Iterations of reduce-scatter**

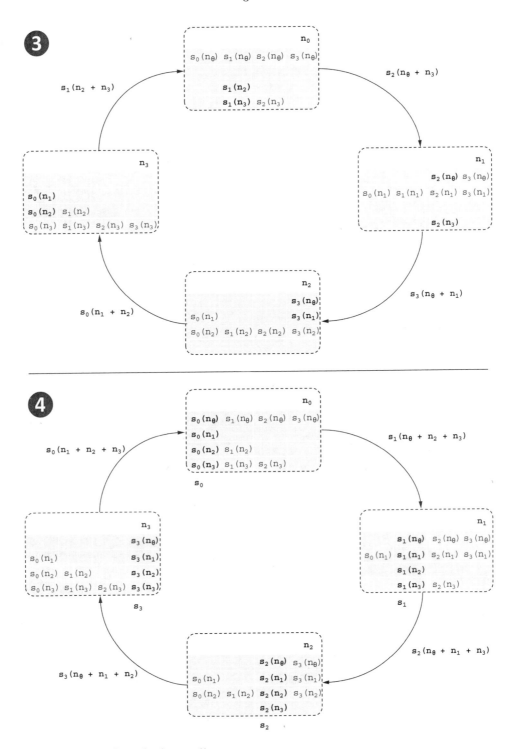

**Figure 8.9b    Iterations of reduce-scatter**

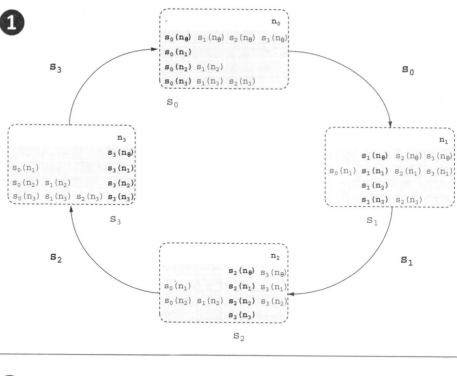

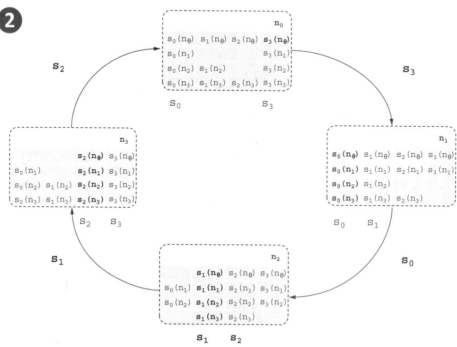

Figure 8.10a    Iterations of all-gather

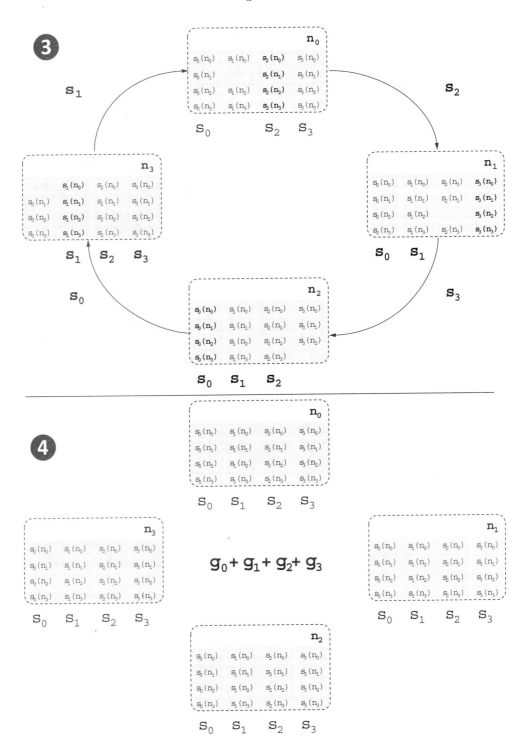

**Figure 8.10b  Iterations of all-gather**

previous iteration (e.g., $s_3$ in case of $n_0$ during the second iteration) to the successor node in the ring. The last iteration (lower-right quadrant) completes the transfer of the remaining segments of the gradient to the nodes in the cluster. At the conclusion of this phase (lower-left quadrant) the accumulated gradient $g_0 + g_1 + g_2 + g_3$ is available on every node in the ring cluster.

At this point, printing the gradients of the model on each node,

```
print([f"{W[node].grad}" for node in range(NODES)]),
```

outputs four identical gradient values for every node in the ring:

```
['tensor([-6.7851e-02, -4.2272e+01, -8.0919e+01, -1.2124e+02])',
 'tensor([-6.7851e-02, -4.2272e+01, -8.0919e+01, -1.2124e+02])',
 'tensor([-6.7851e-02, -4.2272e+01, -8.0919e+01, -1.2124e+02])',
 'tensor([-6.7851e-02, -4.2272e+01, -8.0919e+01, -1.2124e+02])']
```

**Listing 8.10   Horovod ring-based distributed gradient descent algorithm**

```python
import torch as pt
from torch.utils.data import TensorDataset, DataLoader

IN_MEMORY_SHARD_SIZE = 250
TRAINING_DATASET_SIZE = 1000
NODES = TRAINING_DATASET_SIZE // IN_MEMORY_SHARD_SIZE

FEATURES = 4
pt.manual_seed(42)
w_src = pt.randn((FEATURES,))
W = [pt.tensor(w_src.detach().numpy(),
                requires_grad=True) for _ in range(NODES)]

def forward(w, X):
  return X @ w

def mse(y_est, y):
  err = y_est - y
  return (err ** 2).mean()

X_train = pt.distributions.multivariate_normal.MultivariateNormal(
    pt.arange(FEATURES, dtype=pt.float32),
    pt.eye(FEATURES)).sample((TRAINING_DATASET_SIZE,))
y_train = X_train @ (pt.arange(FEATURES, dtype=pt.float32) + 1)
train_dl = DataLoader(TensorDataset(y_train, X_train), \
                    batch_size = IN_MEMORY_SHARD_SIZE,
                    shuffle = False)

EPOCHS = 1000
LEARNING_RATE = 0.01
for epoch in range(EPOCHS):
```

```
#compute per shard gradients on each node
for node, (y_shard, X_shard) in zip(range(NODES), train_dl):
  y_est = forward(W[node], X_shard)
  loss = \
    (IN_MEMORY_SHARD_SIZE / TRAINING_DATASET_SIZE) * mse(y_shard, y_est)
  loss.backward()

#horovod phase 1: reduce-scatter
for iter in range(NODES - 1):
  for node in range(NODES):
    seg = (node - iter - 1) % NODES
    grad = W[node].grad[seg]

    next_node = (node + 1) % NODES
    W[next_node].grad[seg] += grad

#horovod phase 2: all-gather
for iter in range(NODES - 1):
  for node in range(NODES):
    seg = (node - iter) % NODES
    grad = W[node].grad[seg]

    next_node = (node + 1) % NODES
    W[next_node].grad[seg] = grad

#perform a step of gradient descent
for node in range(NODES):
  W[node].data -= LEARNING_RATE * W[node].grad
  W[node].grad = None

print([f"{W[node].data}" for node in range(NODES)])
```

This should output the recovered multivariable linear regression coefficients:

```
['tensor([1.0000, 2.0000, 3.0000, 4.0000])',
 'tensor([1.0000, 2.0000, 3.0000, 4.0000])',
 'tensor([1.0000, 2.0000, 3.0000, 4.0000])',
 'tensor([1.0000, 2.0000, 3.0000, 4.0000])']
```

## Summary

- Distributed data parallel training is an approach to distributed gradient descent where each node in a scale-out cluster uses an identical copy of the trained model but a dedicated shard of the training data set.
- The gradient accumulation feature of the reverse-mode accumulating autodiff enables gradient descent to scale down to limited memory nodes or scale up to out-of-memory data sets.

- Legacy parameter server-based approaches to distributed data parallel gradient descent require expensive, broadcast-style networking operations and do not scale well under bandwidth constraints.
- Horovod is a scalable and bandwidth-efficient algorithm for distributed data parallel gradient descent based on two phases of ring-based networking operations: reduce-scatter and all-gather.

# Part 3

## Serverless machine learning pipeline

A machine learning system is more than just a model and a data set. In this part, you will walk through the steps of engineering an entire machine learning pipeline, starting from the steps involved in automation of feature engineering to hyperparameter optimization and experiment management.

- In chapter 9, you will explore the use cases around feature selection and feature engineering, learning from case studies to understand the kinds of features that can be created for the DC taxi data set.
- In chapter 10, you will adopt a PyTorch framework called PyTorch Lightning to minimize the amount of boilerplate engineering code in your implementation. In addition, you will ensure that you can train, validate, and test your PyTorch Lightning-based machine learning model.
- In chapter 11, you will integrate your machine learning model with the Optuna hyperparameter framework, training alternative models based on Optuna-suggested hyperparameter values and ranking the models according to their loss and metric performance.
- In chapter 12, you will package your machine learning model implementation into a Docker container in order to run the container through the various stages of the entire machine learning pipeline, starting from the development data set all the way to a trained model ready for production deployment.

# *Feature selection*

**This chapter covers**

- Understanding principles for feature selection and feature engineering
- Applying feature selection principles to case studies
- Sharpening feature selection skills based on case study analysis

Thus far, you have been using the original (raw) data values from the DC taxi data set as the features for your machine learning models. A *feature* is a value or a collection of values used as an input to a machine learning model during both the training and inference phases of machine learning (see appendix A). *Feature engineering*, the process of selecting, designing, and implementing synthetic (made-up) features using raw data values, can significantly improve the machine learning performance of your models. Some examples of feature engineering are simple, formulaic transformations of the original data values, for instance rescaling arbitrary numeric values to a range from −1 to 1. *Feature selection* (also known as *feature design*), the initial phase of feature engineering, is the more creative part of the effort and involves specification of features that capture human knowledge or intuition about the data set, such as choosing a feature that measures the distance between pickup and drop-off locations for each ride in the taxi trips data set.

Indiscriminately adding a large number of features to your project data set can be a costly mistake (see the "curse of dimensionality" problem). Feature "over-engineering" may result in overfitting as well as in an overall decline of your machine learning model performance. Which begs the question: what guiding principles can apply to select the right features so that you can avoid the dreaded feature over-engineering? This chapter uses case studies to introduce you to these principles and illustrates how you can apply them in practice.

This chapter covers three case studies that span the financial, advertising, and mobile gaming industries. For each case study, you are given a description of a machine learning project for the industry as well as a high-level specification of the machine learning model you are expected to train for the project. Then, you are given descriptions of candidate features for the project. Finally, a discussion section for each case study describes how to apply the five guiding principles to help you decide whether you should select the candidate feature.

## 9.1    *Guiding principles for feature selection*

This section introduces the five guiding principles to help you choose the right features for your machine learning project. While I have not seen these principles codified as an industry standard, they condense over a decade of my experience in selecting features for data science, machine learning, and deep learning projects. The remainder of this section explains these guiding principles in more detail so that in section 9.2, you can apply them to the case studies and to the concrete examples of candidate features. According to these principles, a candidate feature should be:

- Related to the label
- Recorded before inference time
- Supported by abundant examples
- Expressed as a number with a meaningful scale
- Based on expert insights about the project

### 9.1.1    *Related to the label*

This section teaches you what to consider when evaluating a relationship between a feature (or a potential feature) and a label so that you can select and prioritize features for your feature engineering efforts. Before you decide to include a potential feature in a machine learning model training experiment, make sure you can articulate a rationale (a justification) explaining why the feature is related to the label value. Articulating the rationale can help you convince yourself (and in an ideal case, an impartial observer) that the feature is in fact relevant to the problem you are attempting to solve using machine learning. Of course, some rationales are better than others: "why not?" does not make for a strong rationale for a feature. In general, weak rationales translate to an excessive quantity of potential features with varying strengths of relatedness to the label.

Note that having a rationale for a feature is also important because the relationship between the candidate feature and the label can change depending on your problem. In practice, changing the question you are answering using a data set can change whether a relationship exists between the candidate feature and the label. For example, when estimating the taxi fare for a trip across DC, a feature value of a distance between the pickup and drop-off locations is related to the taxi fare estimate. However, if instead of estimating the taxi fare, you decide to use the distance feature to estimate the number of taxi pickups at a given location in DC at a given time, then the feature loses the relatedness to the label. While it may seem obvious that a feature selected for a different project may become useless when changing the label, in practice, training data sets and feature stores are re-used across machine learning projects, leading to inadvertent re-use of irrelevant and potentially harmful (as illustrated in the rest of this chapter) features.

The meaning of the word *related* when used in this section translates to a variety of possibilities; for instance, *statistical correlation* is one kind of relatedness. As you know, statistical correlation means that causation may or may not play a role in the relationship between a feature and a label.

Consider a well-known example: according to the standard Pearson measure of statistical correlation, reading ability in children is correlated with their shoe size. In other words, according to classical statistics, if you wish to estimate a child's shoe size, you can use the score from the child's latest reading test. Of course, there is no causation in the relationship between the shoe size and the reading ability variables; the correlation exists due to the underlying (confounding) variable of the child's age.

The shoe size estimate example is illustrated in figure 9.1. Notice that the causal relationship between the child's age and shoe size, as well as the child's age and the reading score, also translate to statistical correlation between these pairs of variables. So, while a statistical correlation between a candidate feature and the label can serve as a baseline rationale for the feature, a stronger justification can be based on a causal relationship between the feature and the label.

Is it possible to tell correlation apart from causation? It depends on your definition of causality. Most contemporary machine learning and data science practitioners in the industry and in academia use a kind of causality known as *counterfactual causality*.[1] You can decide whether a counterfactual causal relationship exists between the candidate cause and effect variables by answering a hypothetical question: all other things being equal, if an omnipotent actor were to intervene to change only the cause, would the effect inevitably change? Notice that this kind of causality does not exist for the relationship between the reading test scores and the shoe sizes: had someone intervened

---

[1] Counterfactual causality is closely related to the potential outcomes definition of causality. Judea Pearl et al.'s book, *Causal Inference in Statistics: A Primer* (Wiley, 2016), is a great resource with a more formal treatment of causality.

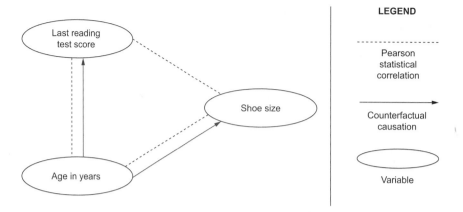

**Figure 9.1**   **A feature can be based on a child's reading test score or age variables, but the age-based feature is more strongly related to the shoe size due to a counterfactual causal relationship between the age and the shoe size.**

and changed the average test scores for kids of a certain age, their shoe size would not change. In contrast, substituting a cohort of younger kids with a cohort of older kids translates to both higher average reading test scores (assuming the tests are not age-adjusted) and larger average shoe sizes.

When articulating the relatedness between a candidate feature and a label, it is useful to identify and prioritize features that have counterfactual causal relationships to the label over the features that demonstrate a correlation or an unclear relationship to the label.

### 9.1.2   *Recorded before inference time*

This section teaches you how to navigate around a common pitfall in feature selection: using features that are known at training time but are unavailable or difficult to obtain once a trained model is deployed to production.

The feature value you are considering must be available at inference time, once your machine learning model is processing data beyond the training and test data sets used to create the model. This is an important but often overlooked aspect of feature selection, particularly since training data sets are retrospective and usually do not contain information about the order in which data values become available. For example, a training data set describing the history of a company's sales deals often does not capture the fact that the customer's name and contact information are available to the company prior to the dollar amount of a closed sales deal.

What makes this issue subtle is that retroactively looking at data from past events, as recorded in the training data set, the sequencing of the events may not be immediately obvious, and you may inadvertently use future information at inference time. For example, suppose you are attempting to estimate the weight of a newborn baby and one of the candidate features is the duration of pregnancy.

**NOTE** Pre-mature newborns have lower-than-average weights while babies born after 42 weeks of pregnancy are heavier on average, so the duration of pregnancy in terms of the number of the weeks seems to be a useful feature to select.

You should not be surprised to find the duration of pregnancy (in terms of weeks) in the training data set since it is a historical measure that makes sense to record at the time of the birth. However, if you are creating a model to estimate the expected weight of the newborn during a routine doctor's visit halfway through the pregnancy, the number of the weeks of pregnancy at birth is unknown.

The example with the estimation of the newborn weight is just one instance of an issue known as *data leakage*. Other examples of data leakage include duplication of observations across training, validation, and test data sets. In general, data leakage occurs when the information about the label value is inadvertently included or "leaked" into the training data set. Symptoms of data leakage include inflated machine learning model performance on the training data set and even complete failures of the model once it is deployed to production. For instance, this issue can arise when working with features from the well-known Titanic data set,[2] as illustrated in figure 9.2.

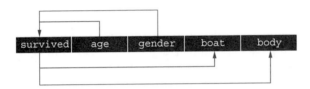

**Figure 9.2  In the subset of features from the Titanic data set, age and gender are known before the survival outcome for the passengers. The values for the boat and body features are recorded for a passenger depending on whether the passenger survived or perished. Hence, boat and body features "leak" data about the survival label.**

It is counterintuitive to reason about prediction of past events; however, the Titanic data set invites you to do exactly that. You can train a machine learning model to predict a binary survival outcome (whether a person survived or perished) for passengers on the Titanic during the fateful crossing of the Atlantic in April of 1912. While the entire data set contains 13 features and a label, figure 9.2 shows just the 4 features that are relevant to this example along with the label (survival). The survival label in the data set uses a value of 1 to indicate that a passenger survived while the value of 0 represents that a passenger perished. The age feature is numeric with the age of the passengers at the time when they boarded the ship, while the gender feature is limited to male and female values represented using 1 and 0, respectively. The boat and body

---

[2]  The Titanic data set, along with documentation, is available from https://www.openml.org/d/40945.

features are both categorical and encoded as strings. The boat feature stores the identifier of the boat (for example "11") on which a passenger was rescued. The morbid body feature stores values like "328" that specify the identifiers assigned to passengers who perished.

To avoid the counterintuitive implication of using the word *predict*, it is helpful to think about inferring the survival outcome for each passenger when considering candidate features for training the machine learning model. From the standpoint of time sequencing, it is reasonable to infer survival based on the features age and gender because both existed for each passenger prior to their survival outcome. This is shown in figure 9.2 using arrows pointing from age and gender features to the survived label. Hence, a machine learning model can be trained to use age and gender features since both should be available at inference time.

In contrast, once a passenger on the Titanic survived or perished, that passenger survived on a rescue boat or ended up with a body tag. This is shown using the arrows pointing from the survival label to body and boat features in figure 9.2. Both body and boat feature values should not be used to train a machine learning model to infer the survival outcome for passengers on the Titanic. Of course, we don't expect more events like this to occur, and hence such a model will never be used to infer survival outcomes for any passengers other than those who traveled on the Titanic. The goal of this example is to introduce you to the importance of understanding the features in your data set and the time sequencing relationship across the features.

In other cases, the feature value may not be available at inference time for legal or ethical reasons. For example, for a European Union (EU)-based company it is perfectly legal to record the birth date of job applicants. If you are using this type of human resources information in the EU to estimate the likelihood that an applicant accepts the job offer, the age of the applicant is a reasonable feature to select. However, as soon as you attempt to apply the same feature in the United States, access to an applicant's birth date might be against the law because, in the US, it is illegal to discriminate on the basis of age when making a hiring decision. Moreover, features that leak information about the birth date, such as the year of high school or college graduation, can also cause legal concerns for the business. So, if you are attempting to adapt a machine learning system built in the EU to the United States, you should re-evaluate whether the features in the training data set are permitted by your organization. As you can imagine, human resources data sets can be full of information (e.g., race or health records) but are illegal or unethical as features for training a machine learning model.

### 9.1.3  *Supported by abundant examples*

This section explores what can go wrong when selecting features that have too many missing values or features that have too few distinct values.

It is embarrassingly simple to introduce a feature to a training data set by simply adding a column of NaN or NULL values. While such a feature is obviously useless, this example serves as a reminder that more does not mean better when it comes to increasing the number of features in a training data set. The other extreme involves adding features that in combination serve as a unique identifier for a label. As a worst-case example for feature engineering, consider a training data set for a classification problem where the categorical label takes on 2^N distinct values. Since N binary features can encode 2^N possibilities, each of the label values might be uniquely identified by the binary values of the N feature columns.

Of course such extreme scenarios of feature over-engineering rarely, if ever, occur in practice, but they make convenient reference points for comparison again your own feature engineering efforts. For example, if you are selecting a feature, do you expect to have a significant fraction (greater than 5%) of the feature values in the training data set to have values other than NaN? If you are selecting multiple features, would the feature values taken together result in a unique identifier for the label value in the training data set but not in the test data set?

To answer these questions, you need to ensure that as you are considering candidate features you are also maintaining statistics on the missing values of the features along with counts of the cross product of the sets of feature values for each of the label values.

### 9.1.4 Expressed as a number with a meaningful scale

This section teaches a convenient rule of thumb you can use to check for whether a feature can be correctly expressed as a number for using with machine learning algorithms.

As you know from chapter 1, this book focuses on supervised machine learning from structured data sets. For the purposes of feature engineering, this means that if the raw data you are planning to use for training machine learning models contains unstructured content such as video, images, audio, or natural language text, then before you can start with the feature engineering steps described in this book, you must convert the corresponding unstructured data values to a numeric representation. Specific techniques for these conversions, such as word embeddings for natural language text or image classifications for photographic data, are outside the scope of this book.

Having a project data set that consists of numeric values is a prerequisite to feature engineering since supervised machine learning models amount to sequences of arithmetic operations on numeric (either continuous or categorical per the the definition in appendix A) feature values to estimate label values. However, even if your raw data values are numeric (i.e., expressed using a number) that does not mean that the corresponding features that you use to train a machine learning model have meaningful numeric scales and magnitudes. If you are not convinced, consider that letters A and B are represented as numbers 65 and 66, respectively, by the ASCII encoding standard. The sum of the encoding, 131 (65 + 66) corresponds to the character â (letter a with a circumflex accent), which is not a meaningful result.

If you are comfortable applying the formal definitions from figure A.9 in appendix A to this example, you should recognize that ASCII encodes a categorical variable that describes the finite dictionary of the ASCII characters. As a general rule of thumb, you can check whether a numeric value can be treated as a continuous variable by performing basic arithmetic operations on the values to confirm whether you can obtain meaningful results.

### 9.1.5   *Based on expert insights about the project*

This section describes the most important guiding principle for feature design, selection, and engineering—the one that can have the most positive impact on the performance of your machine learning model.

When working on machine learning projects with subject matter experts (SMEs) who have deep domain expertise in their respective industries, I find that the most productive way to encourage the SMEs to propose useful features is to ask them, "What information would you share with your team to help them better estimate the label value?" This style of conversation motivates the SMEs to take their mind away from the complexity of machine learning system design and instead think about the problem in natural, human-centric terms. Next, I ask, "How can this information be gleaned from the existing data in the project data set?"

Taken together, answers to these questions provide a pathway to generate candidate features from the project data set. For example, suppose you are working on the problem of classifying photos of cars taken in cities around the world to estimate whether a photo contains or does not contain a taxi from the respective city. While it is possible to set out on a complex engineering exercise, extracting text of medallion number, license plates, or other unique taxi identifiers to join this information with a municipal data set of taxis, there is an easier path forward. Human SMEs who know the city can immediately spot a taxi by color, such as yellow in New York City or black in London. This rule of thumb is something an SME can easily share with someone who never traveled to the city and help them identify a taxi from a sea of cars in a street.

Successful feature selection is more than just algorithmic data processing; it is a creative process based on applying human common sense about the world and insights about the problem domain to the machine learning project. Keep in mind that the case study approach in this section can introduce you to the basics of ideation and design for feature selection. However, it is not a replacement for the real-world experience of putting a machine learning system in production.

## 9.2   *Feature selection case studies*

This section introduces applications of supervised machine learning across three different case studies spanning the financial, advertising, and mobile gaming industries. In each case study, you will learn about an industry-specific machine learning project so that you can learn how to apply feature selection principles to other projects.

- *Financial: Credit card fraud classification.* You are working with a financial industry company that issues credit cards to its customers and monitors customer credit card transactions for signs of fraud. The purpose of your supervised machine learning classification model is to estimate whether a given transaction is fraudulent or non-fraudulent. To keep the feature engineering exercise simple, assume that you are working with a balanced data set (which isn't true in production) of fraudulent versus non-fraudulent examples, so the accuracy of your classifier is a meaningful machine learning model performance metric.

- *Advertising: Online banner advertisement clicks estimation.* You are working with an advertising industry company that manages online ad banners for its customers and charges them whenever a viewer clicks on the banner. Since the company has a tool that designs the banner ads for the customers (for an example of a banner ad designer, look at https://github.com/osipov/banner-designer), it has a data set of the banner ad designs and the corresponding number of clicks that the ad received during the campaign. The purpose of your supervised machine learning regression model is to estimate the total number of clicks an ad should receive based on the banner design. The features for the model should be selected based on the ad content and design settings.

- *Mobile gaming: Churn prediction.* You are working with a rapidly growing mobile gaming startup to help them improve customer satisfaction with upgrades to their top-selling Shoot'em Up Clash Legends game. The purpose of your supervised machine learning regression model is to estimate the total number of customers (game players) expected to uninstall the game from their mobile device (i.e., churn) in the next week.

## 9.3    Feature selection using guiding principles

In this section, for each case study from section 9.2, there are several proposed features along with a discussion about whether they should be selected for the application. Notice that for every case study, using domain knowledge and some common sense helps with the decision about whether to choose the feature.

### 9.3.1    Related to the label

This section teaches the concepts needed to assess candidate features based on how strongly they are related to the label so that you can prioritize and select more effective features.

**Case study: Credit card fraud classification**

**Feature:** The number of times the credit card in the transaction was used to purchase from the same vendor

**Discussion:** A fraudulent credit card transaction is likely to involve a purchase that was not authorized. For example, a fraudster may use the stolen credit card to purchase from a fake online store that belongs to the fraudster or from a physical vendor that operates without video security or keeps poor records. Conversely, if the card was used for many purchases from a vendor in the transaction without fraud reports, then the association is less likely. For this feature, the association should be clear, and the feature should be selected for the model.

**Feature:** The number of milliseconds that the credit card was inserted into the credit card reader during the transaction

**Discussion:** This is an example of a technical piece of information that is often available to a machine learning practitioner but does not translate to a valuable feature for the model. Notice that during physical transactions with credit cards, sometimes the card is taken out of the reader quickly; other times it remains in the reader longer. As long as the transaction completes successfully, there is no association between this feature and whether a given transaction is fraudulent. Even though you might argue that a fraudster is likely to have stolen a batch of cards and cycles though them quickly when making fraudulent transactions, recall that the purpose of the model does not classify a batch of transactions and instead must classify any single arbitrary transaction. Most transactions are non-fraudulent and involve a variety of credit card readers and many users who may leave the cards in the reader for arbitrary periods of time. There is no clear association in this case to select this feature.

**Feature:** Vendor's business category in the transaction

**Discussion:** It is well known that in the United States it is common for a stolen credit card to be used for a small purchase at a gas station so that the fraudster can confirm that the card is working as expected. Although other associations may not be known at the time of feature selection, it is possible that the application of machine learning can uncover associations between specific business categories of the vendors and fraudulent transactions.

**Feature:** Expiration date of the credit card

**Discussion:** If this candidate feature simply captures the expiration month of the card, and the cards have approximately a uniform chance of having expiration months, then there is no reason to believe that an association exists between the feature and fraud. Also, capturing just the expiration month and year does not indicate whether fraud occurred with an expired card: when a card is expired a transaction cannot happen, so it does not need to be classified as fraudulent or non-fraudulent. In other words, there is no reason to believe that fraudsters somehow target cards expiring in December versus January. However, in the United States, there is a potential for fraudulent transactions with credit cards stolen out of mailboxes. This means that you can select a more sophisticated feature that captures the difference between the date of the transaction and the expiration date of the card so that you can detect when fraudulent transactions happen close to the date of the card issuance, for example two to five years before the card expiry.

**Case study: Online banner advertisement clicks estimation**

**Feature:** The price of the item in the banner ad

**Discussion:** This is one of the most obvious features that can be selected from the ad. The price of the item is likely to be the single most important factor in whether an ad viewer has interest in the ad and clicks on the banner. Given the strength of the association, this should be a priority feature for your regression model.

**Feature:** The category of the font for the text in the banner ad

**Discussion:** In this case, the feature is based on the named category of the font used in the advertisement, such as Times New Roman or Comic Sans. To describe the association of this candidate feature with the label, keep in mind that design elements such as fonts elicit an emotional response from viewers. Since some fonts can be more or less engaging, a categorical feature capturing the type of the font used in the ad can model the nuanced association between the engagement generated by the font and the total number of clicks on the ad. Of course, this feature should be used in conjunction with the other design elements of the ad, including content. For instance, choosing Comic Sans to advertise clown apparel is likely to generate more clicks than using that font for a wealth management ad.

**Feature:** The number of items left in stock as shown on the banner ad

**Discussion:** You must have shopped on one of the online retail websites and seen a message like "only three left" next to the item you wanted to buy. So, would it be appropriate to select a feature indicating the number of items shown as left in the inventory on the banner ad? Since you must have seen this message on real banner ads, you are probably tempted to pick this feature, but what is the association between this feature and the label? The association in this case is related to a greater sense of urgency the ad viewer might have after seeing the limited stock of the advertised item. The sense of urgency may translate to a higher click rate, which is what you are attempting to capture.

**Feature:** The number of advertised items as reported by the inventory system

**Discussion**: Although you might try to make the case that low inventory levels for an item are a proxy for popularity, indicating an in-demand item, you should think about this feature in terms of many ad campaigns across many different banner ads. For example, toy cars are stocked at different quantities than actual cars and in different quantities than sheets of paper. Further, the ad viewer has no knowledge of the actual number of items stocked for item advertised, so there is no association between the decision to click on the ad and the actual number of items in stock.

**Case study: Churn prediction**

**Feature:** ZIP code of the customer

**Discussion:** The geographical location of the players can be associated with their potential to churn in the next quarter for a variety of reasons. Some reasons are technical: perhaps the networking infrastructure used by the gaming server infrastructure results in higher latencies (and hence a poor experience) for ZIP codes in the southeast of the United States compared to the customers in California's Bay Area. Other reasons could originate from demographics: some ZIP codes have older or younger populations compared to the "sweet spot" for the game.

**Feature:** USD amount spent on the service per month

**Discussion:** Since it is common for mobile games to include both a recurring monthly subscription price as well as various options, such as the ability to spend money to purchase power-ups, player character decorations, and other options to stand out from other players, the amount of money a player spends on the game is a proxy for their level of engagement and a measure of how invested they are. So, there is a possibility for a complex relationship between the amount of money spent and the likelihood of churning in the next quarter. For example, spending no money on the game can mean that the player lost interest and is more likely to uninstall the game. On the other hand, if the player is overly engaged, spending an excessive amount of money (e.g., in the top 0.1% percentile), they are also likely to burn out from the game or blame it for consuming too much of their time, also leading to uninstalling the game from their device.

**Feature:** Number of days until the next tax filing date for the gaming company

**Discussion:** Companies in the United States are required to file quarterly and annual tax returns with the Internal Revenue Service, the United States' tax authority. Surprisingly, many companies noticed a correlation between the tax filing dates and the changes in the customer churn. Although an internal analyst in the company may notice and report this correlation, you should be skeptical about this association: do the players even know these dates when making a decision to uninstall the date? More likely if the correlation exists, it is about the end of the month, when many individuals review their monthly spending and make a decision to cut down on nonessential items. Since the IRS tax filing dates coincide with the time many individuals re-evaluate their spending, this can show up as a spurious correlation between the IRS schedule and the customer churn.

**Feature:** Number of weeks subscribed to the game

**Discussion:** Many uninstalls of a game happen shortly after the player installs it for the first time and decides against keeping it.

### 9.3.2  *Recorded before inference time*

This section explains the concept of data leakage, how it may subtly disrupt the performance of your machine learning models, and illustrates how effective feature selection can help you avoid problems from this.

**Case study: Credit card fraud classification**

**Feature:** The card was used at the store before

**Discussion:** This information should be available at inference time as physical card transactions made with the physical card readers are classified differently, with the appropriate information recorded for each transaction.

**Feature:** The store item sold in the transaction is a newly stocked item

**Discussion:** If you have made credit card purchases, you know that, at the transaction level, the details of the purchase are not available to the credit card-issuing company. For example, if you are making a purchase at a grocery store and are buying a new flavor of CocaCola, the credit card company can't distinguish this information from other purchases at the store; all the items are simply aggregated into a single charge, so this would not make a good feature for your machine learning model.

**Feature:** Category of the item sold in the transaction

**Discussion:** This may or not be available at inference time. For example, if the transaction is for a gas (petrol) purchase, then the category is obvious. In other cases, when the purchase is at a general retailer such as Target or Walmart, where there are thousands of different item categories, the information it not available at inference time.

**Feature:** The card was used at a physical (versus online) location

**Discussion:** This information should be available at inference time as physical card transactions made with the physical card readers are classified differently, with the appropriate information recorded for each transaction.

**Case study: Online banner advertisement clicks estimation**

**Feature:** Total number of items purchased using the discount code

**Discussion:** Although this information should be available in the data warehouse of the company running the campaign after the campaign has concluded, this information cannot be available at inference time.

**Feature:** Number of items purchased using the discount code over the past 30 days

**Discussion:** If the company running the ad maintains the transaction data about the number of times the discount code was used, then it is possible to maintain the *sliding window* of the 30 days' worth of data and calculate this value for any given transaction. Further, by predicting the number of clicks on the banner ad with the discount code, it is possible to use this daily value to make a better estimate of the total banner ad clicks.

**Feature:** Number of customers who viewed the banner ad about the item

**Discussion:** For an online banner ad, information should be available from a data warehouse or a data analytics source.

**Feature:** The number of items advertised in stock at the manufacturer

**Discussion:** This candidate feature is deliberately chosen to spark a thought-provoking discussion about the potential features and the ad engagement. Recall that training data sets are historical, based on the data from the past advertising campaigns and the actual numbers of banner ad clicks. While you may have historical inventory data about the items used in the advertising campaigns at the time of the ad impression (when the ad was viewed), should this data be used for a feature in your machine learning model? Although you may make the case that low inventory levels indicate a popular or in-demand item, you should think about the feature in terms of many ad campaigns across many different banner ads. There is no reasonable association that you can establish for this feature. Further, obtaining the value for this feature at run-time (when performing the inference or producing the estimate), can be a technical challenge that outweighs the value from experimenting with this association.

**Case study: Churn prediction**

**Feature:** Total minutes spent playing the game

**Discussion:** Note that using the word *total* in the description of this feature can lead to confusion. For someone who uninstalled the game, the total refers to the number of minutes spent playing the game over the entire period of having it installed. In contrast, the total for someone who did not uninstall the game describes the number of minutes up to the point that their data was recorded in the training data set. Once the possibility of the dual interpretation is clear, it should also be clear that this feature should not be used, since at inference time it is impossible to tell the total number of minutes spent with the game for a player who never unsubscribed or uninstalled the game.

**Feature:** Total number of minutes spent playing the game in the past 28 days

**Discussion:** With a minor change to restrict the measurement of the number of minutes spent with the game to the past 28 days, it is possible to use the key idea from the previous feature. Regardless of whether a player churns in the next month, it is possible to measure their previous 28 days' worth of game activity and use that as a feature for both training and inference.

**Feature:** Uninstall reason provided by the customer

**Discussion:** When the player uninstalls the game, they can specify the feedback with a reason as to why they decided to uninstall. Clearly this information is available only for the players who have uninstalled the game and only after they have uninstalled it. Hence, it is not available at inference time and should not be used for training the machine learning model.

**Feature:** Customer satisfaction score in three months prior to churn

**Discussion:** If customer satisfaction is gathered randomly across players, including those who uninstalled the game as well as those who kept on playing, this is a useful feature to include for inference.

### 9.3.3 *Supported by abundant examples*

This section provides examples of candidate features that may or may not have enough values to train a machine learning model to guide you on the use of this principle in real-world examples.

#### Case Study: Credit card fraud classification

**Feature:** Distance between the cardholder address and the merchant address

**Discussion:** Having information about the distance between the address of the cardholder and the location the transaction took place can be useful when classifying fraud. However, to use this feature, a practitioner needs to evaluate whether it is feasible to have examples for this feature in practice. Unless the customer has been proactive at geocoding the distances at the time of the transaction, you should not expect to have enough examples for this feature.

**Feature:** Whether the ZIP codes of the cardholder address and the merchant address are the same

**Discussion:** Notice that unlike the feature that attempts to use geocoding to estimate the distances between the cardholder and the merchant locations, a feature that checks whether the ZIP codes of the merchant and the cardholder match can be supported by the customer's historical transactions data. Since every financial transaction should have this feature there should be an abundant number of examples for this feature.

**Feature:** The card was used at the merchant before

**Discussion:** The financial company maintains a history of transactions for a given card, so it is possible to check the previous transactions for whether the card was used at a given merchant. An absence of transactions with a merchant indicates that the card was not used at the merchant, so for every transaction in the data set it is possible to assign either a true or a false value to this feature.

**Feature:** Category of item being purchased

**Discussion:** Although for some merchants such as gas stations, it is possible to uniquely identify the category of the item or items purchased in a transaction, many companies maintain proprietary item inventory codes. In general, there is no guarantee that a transaction includes information about the items purchased. You should not expect to have a sufficient number of examples of the categories of the item purchased for a general purpose fraud versus non-fraud classifier. However, you may be able to create a more specialized classifier for specific subcategories of merchants such as gas stations.

### Case study: Online banner advertisement clicks estimation

**Feature:** The day of the year the advertising campaign started

**Discussion:** As long as the company managing the banner ad campaigns maintains the start and end for the campaign, this date should be available for every training example.

**Feature:** The person viewing the banner ad already purchased the item in the ad

**Discussion:** Most of the time, the number of purchases of an item shown in a banner ad is less than 0.1% compared to the number of the banner ad views. You should not expect to have a significant number of examples where you know whether the ad viewer purchased the item.

**Feature:** The discount percentage offered in the banner ad

**Discussion:** Most discount percentages offered in ads are based on a small collection of well-known values, such as 10%, 20%, 25%, 50%, 75%, or 90% off. You should not expect to see discounts of 27.54% off shown on the banner ad. As long as the number of the distinct discount amounts offered across marketing campaigns is a small fraction of the training data set, you should have a sufficient number of examples for this feature.

### Case study: Churn prediction

**Feature:** Latitude and longitude of the player's billing address location

**Discussion:** Since both latitude and longitude of the billing address location are unique per the customer billing location, using these values to estimate whether the player is going to uninstall the game is a mistake. Unless used with caution, the specific coordinate values may produce a model that overfits the training data set. The raw latitude and longitude values of the billing address location should not be used to predict customer churn.

**Feature:** The number of times the player previously uninstalled the game

**Discussion:** If a player uninstalled the game in the past, it likely that they will again. Notice that an absence of a record of the game uninstall can mean that the player never uninstalled it, as long as the gaming platform accurately reports uninstall events to the gaming company. Hence, it should be possible to select this feature with a value for every training example.

**Feature:** The USD amount the player intends to spend next month on gaming

**Discussion:** Although knowing how much a given player has in their budget to pay for a mobile game in the next month can be exceptionally useful to estimate whether they will churn, it is also highly unlikely that the company will have this information for any or any meaningful fraction of the total players.

### 9.3.4 *Numeric with meaningful magnitude*

This section compares alternative feature representations to help you chose between continuous and categorical features.

**Case study: Credit card fraud classification**

**Feature:** ZIP code of vendor in the transaction

**Discussion:** Although the ZIP code in the transaction is an integer number, it should be clear that it is not a continuous value to be used as is in the machine learning model. If you are not convinced, you can apply the rule of thumb about the arithmetic values: adding 10001, a ZIP code for New York City, to 20002, a ZIP code for Washington DC, yields a ZIP code of 30003, which is a ZIP code for Norcross, Georgia—clearly a meaningless result. The ZIP code value should be encoded and treated as a categorical variable.

**Feature:** The number of times the credit card in the transaction was used to purchase from the same vendor

**Discussion:** Although it is possible to treat this count as a continuous variable and obtain meaningful results, notice that knowing the actual number of the times the card was used at a vendor is not particularly meaningful.

**Feature:** Expiration date of the credit card

**Discussion:** Month and year of the credit card expiration are not useful as continuous variables. You can re-encode this information to the number of days until expiration, but the raw numeric values for this information are not meaningful.

**Case study: Online banner advertisement clicks estimation**

**Feature:** Percent value of the discount, such as 10%, 25%, or 50% off

**Discussion:** On the surface this appears as a simple numeric feature value. However, what about negative values? Is it possible to get a negative 100% discount? This should be classified as a categorical feature for relisting feature values.

**Feature:** Size of the banner ad

**Discussion:** On the surface, amounts like 400px by 400px or 100px by 400px seem like traditional numeric features. However, as the model attempts to both extrapolate and interpolate from these values, you may find yourself working with unexpected results.

**Feature:** Font used by the banner ad

**Discussion:** Adding or multiplying font values produces meaningless results. This is not a continuous but a categorical feature.

**Feature:** Color used for the banner ad font

**Discussion:** Although it is possible to represent color as a combination of numbers, for example using red-green-blue values, in this value the feature is about predicting the clicks on the ad, so a categorical representation is more appropriate, since the color is uniform across the ad and falls into the human-readable categories such as blue, black, or green.

**Feature:** Item category identifier discounted by the coupon

**Discussion:** Number categories like 1 for dairy, 3 for canned goods, and so on are not meaningful as continuous values and should be re-encoded as categorical variables.

**Case study: Churn prediction**

**Feature:** Customer average minutes played versus average minutes played per user across the user base

**Discussion:** This feature should be encoded as a continuous value. It has a meaningful zero value (i.e., when the average of the customer coincides with the average for the entire user base) and has a meaningful range from negative to positive values.

**Feature:** Number of weeks subscribed to the game

**Discussion:** This feature should be encoded as a continuous value since it can be subdivided into more fine-grained parts.

**Feature:** Mobile operating system used by the customer (e.g., iOS, Android, or other)

**Discussion:** Since there is a finite set of operating systems supported by the mobile gaming application, this feature should be encoded as a categorical variable.

### 9.3.5   *Bring expert insight to the problem*

This section guides you through examples of expert insights about the domains of finance, advertising, and gaming to help you hone your skills on these features for more effective machine learning.

As described in this chapter, although it is technically feasible to select a variety of features, not every potential feature contributes to the success of a machine learning system, and some can result in more harm than benefit to a system. The successful features are those where expert knowledge as well as common sense augments the raw data set and simplifies the task of the machine learning algorithm by making the relationship between the feature and the label values more direct.

## Case study: Credit card fraud classification

**Feature:** A transaction with a suspect vendor in the past month

**Discussion:** According to experts, a significant number of fraudulent transactions are due to a compromised vendor where an employee steals credit card information and later uses the stolen information to commit fraud. Human experts often use graph-based analysis, as shown in figure 9.3, to identify vendors suspected of facilitating fraud. Figure 9.3 shows that three credit cards that went on to report a fraudulent transaction were used in the same suspect vendor, shown on the left in bold.

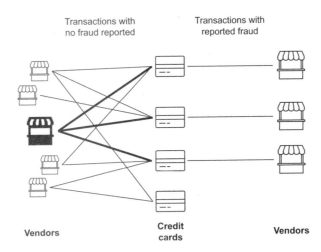

Transactions with no fraud reported

Transactions with reported fraud

Vendors

Credit cards

Vendors

**Figure 9.3 Legitimate credit card transactions with a suspect vendor (on the left in bold) led to transactions that were reported as fraudulent (on the right).**

Based on the expert insight, you can use a numeric feature for each vendor of the total number of credit cards that reported fraud over the past month.

## Case study: Online banner advertisement clicks estimation

**Feature:** A score measuring the relevance of the ad topic to the top trending topics on Twitter

**Discussion:** As you probably expect, the number of clicks on an online banner ad depends not just on the content of the ad itself but also on its relevance to the marketplace. For example, an ad about flashlights is going to generate more clicks on the eve of a hurricane's landfall. Similarly, ads about private tennis lessons generate more clicks during the weekend of the Wimbledon finals. Based on this insight, you can design a numeric feature that captures the similarity between the topic of the words in the online banner ad and the trending topics on Twitter during the ad campaign.

## Case study: Churn prediction

**Feature:** A number of connections on social networks who play the game.

**Discussion:** Video game designers will tell you that peer pressure is one of the strongest predictors of whether a player continues to play the game. That's why so many mobile games try to connect to your Facebook and other social media accounts: if the game developers know that your "friends" play the game, they will know that you are likely to play it too.

## 9.4    *Selecting features for the DC taxi data set*

In this section, you will learn about expert insights that concern the DC taxi fare data set and how to apply these insights to select a set of candidate features to use for your machine learning model.

Recall from chapter 4 that the set of features for the DC taxi data set is quite sparse: the only raw data available at inference time includes the date and timestamp of the start of the trip along with the latitude and longitude coordinates for the pickup and drop-off locations of the taxi ride. What insights can you bring to the taxi fare estimation problem in order to select the right features?

In the case of the DC taxi data set, a key expert insight concerns the GPS used to specify the location coordinates for the trip. The GPS system is precise down to 1 meter (just over 3 feet) from the actual location. However, from the standpoint of taxi fare estimation, GPS precision is excessive: as described in chapter 2, the business rules for the taxi rides use the granularity of 1/8th of a mile for pricing. This corresponds to a roughly 200-meter (or about 660 feet) precision for a location. The pricing precision is about two orders of magnitude more coarse than what's estimated by the GPS coordinates. Hence, features for this data set could include a more coarse representation of the taxi pickup and drop-off coordinates.

The boundaries of the locations for the taxi rides in the DC taxi data set are specified using minimum and maximum values for the latitude and longitude coordinates. How can these minimum and maximum values be used for features? The illustration in figure 9.4 explains the concept behind the coarse-gained representation of the pickup and drop-off coordinates.

For clarity, the actual DC taxi data set's minimum and maximum values for the latitude and longitude coordinates are replaced with a more convenient set of numbers. Although these made-up coordinate numbers are in close proximity to Washington, DC, they were picked to make the explanation easier. Hence, both the left and the right side in figure 9.4 assume that the coordinates for all the trips in the DC taxi data set range from 38.30 to 38.90 along the latitude (north-south) and from −76.48 to −76.12 along the longitude (east-west) coordinates.

In addition to using the raw latitude and longitude values to train the machine learning model, features for a coarse-grained representation of the pickup and drop-off coordinates can use the concept of *binning* (also known as *discretization* or *quantanization*) the GPS coordinate values, as illustrated on the right side of figure 9.4, which

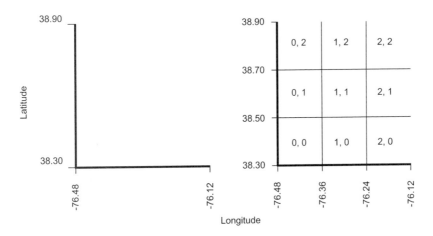

**Figure 9.4  Original minimum and maximum latitude and longitude coordinates (left) can be used to engineer numeric features based on binning of the coordinates (right).**

assumes that both the latitude and the longitude coordinates were "binned" into three bins each, corresponding to three equally sized intervals:

- $(38.30, 38.50)$, $(38.50, 38.70)$, and $(38.70, 38.90)$ for the latitude
- $(-76.48, -76.36)$ $(-76.36, -76.24)$, and $(-76.24, -76.12)$ for the longitude

The diagram on the right side of figure 9.4 indexes each of the three bins using integers 0, 1, and 2. As the result, each of the nine coarse-grained locations can be represented using a pair of integers. For example, a taxi ride from a pickup location $(38.31, -76.47)$ to a drop-off location $(38.61, -76.14)$ can be represented using the locations $(0, 0)$ and $(2, 1)$, respectively. Keep in mind that the selection of nine locations is arbitrary. Since it is unclear how coarse the location boundaries should be, ultimately the selection of the coarseness for the coordinates should be measured by how well the corresponding features help the model to predict the taxi fare.

In the upcoming chapters, you will learn how to apply feature engineering techniques to implement the coarse-grained pickup and drop-off location features described in this section. Note that while the features based on the expert insight about the coarse-grained location representation do not guarantee improved taxi fare estimation, the features can be used during the iterative process of machine learning model development and can be evaluated in terms of their impact on the machine learning model performance metrics.

## Summary

- Effective feature engineering can make the difference between a mediocre and a successful machine learning system.

- Although feature selection is more of an art than a science, a machine learning practitioner can learn the skills needed to identify the right features for a machine learning system by practicing guiding principles to real-world examples.
- Case studies in this chapter help machine learning practitioners learn how to consistently apply the feature selection principles to case studies from diverse industries, including financial, advertising, and mobile gaming.
- Successful feature engineering complements the raw training data with carefully selected and designed features that incorporate commonsense knowledge and expert insights about the machine learning problem.

# Adopting PyTorch Lightning

**This chapter covers**

- Implementing PyTorch Lightning to reduce boilerplate code
- Adding training, validation, and test support for the DC taxi model
- Analyzing DC taxi model training and validation using pandas

Thus far, you have written your own implementation related to training and testing your machine learning model. However, much of the code you wrote was unrelated to your machine learning model architecture and could have applied to a broad range of distinct models. Building on this observation, this chapter introduces you to PyTorch Lightning, a framework that can help you reduce the amount of boilerplate engineering code in your machine learning system, and consequently help you focus on evolving your model design and implementation.

## 10.1 Understanding PyTorch Lightning

This section introduces the PyTorch Lightning framework for your PyTorch DC taxi fare estimation model and teaches you the steps involved in enabling PyTorch Lightning training, validation, and test features.

Thus far, you have implemented a sizable portion of Python and PyTorch boiler-plate code for your machine learning model. This meant that only a few parts of your implementation were model specific, such as the code to

- Package the feature values as tensors
- Configure the neural net layers
- Calculate the tensors for the loss
- Report on the model metrics

Much of the remaining code, such as the code to iterate over the training batches, val-idation batches, and epochs of training, is largely boilerplate, meaning that it can be re-used unmodified across various changes to the model-specific code.

As your machine learning system grows more complex, so does the boilerplate code in your system's implementation. For example, mature machine learning sys-tems require periodic saving (checkpointing) of the model's weight values to stor-age in order to enable reproducibility. Having model checkpoints also enables machine learning training pipelines to resume from a pre-trained model. Other examples include the code involved in integration with hyperparameter optimiza-tion services, metric tracking, and other experiment management tools that control repeated executions of a machine learning pipeline. This should not come as a sur-prise: recall from chapter 1 that over 90% of the components of a production machine learning system are complementary to the core machine learning code.

The PyTorch Lightning framework (https://www.pytorchlightning.ai) aims to make PyTorch developers more productive by helping them focus on developing core machine learning code instead of getting distracted by the boilerplate. In case of the DC taxi model, adopting PyTorch Lightning is straightforward. Before starting, you need to ensure that you have the `pip` package for PyTorch Lightning installed by run-ning the following in your shell environment:

```
pip install pytorch_lightning
```

PyTorch Lightning is a comprehensive framework with a sizable feature set for machine learning model development. This book does not aim to replace existing PyTorch Lightning tutorials or documentation; instead, the upcoming sections focus on the features of the framework you can adopt for the DC taxi model.

### 10.1.1  *Converting PyTorch model training to PyTorch Lightning*

This section teaches you about the PyTorch Lightning `__init__`, `training_step` and `configure_optimizers` methods and then illustrates how to implement these meth-ods for the DC taxi model and how to train the PyTorch Lighting–based DC taxi model using a small, sample training data set.

Assuming that the PyTorch Lighting package is installed correctly in your environ-ment, you can implement a minimal, trainable version of the DC taxi model.

**Listing 10.1   A basic PyTorch Lightning DC taxi model with support**

Use torch.float64 for dtype of the model parameters.

Import the PyTorch Lightning library and alias it as pl.

PyTorch Lightning models must extend from LightningModule.

The **kwargs are used to pass hyperparameters to the model.

The LightningModule subclass must call parent __init__ first.

Save hyperparameters from **kwargs to self.hparams.

Re-use functions from chapter 7 for the batchToXy . . .

. . . and forward implementations.

Use a simple linear regression model for this illustration.

Set the pseudorandom number generator per hyperparameter settings.

Use PyTorch Lightning built-in logging for MSE and RMSE measures.

The training_step method must return the loss tensor.

A LightningModule subclass must have a configure_optimizers method.

Return a configured optimizer instance specified by hyperparameters.

Instantiate a PyTorch Lightning version of the DcTaxiModel as model.

```python
import torch as pt
import pytorch_lightning as pl

pt.set_default_dtype(pt.float64)

class DcTaxiModel(pl.LightningModule):
  def __init__(self, **kwargs):
    super().__init__()
    self.save_hyperparameters()
    pt.manual_seed(int(self.hparams.seed))
    self.layers = pt.nn.Linear(int(self.hparams.num_features), 1)

  def batchToXy(batch):
    batch = batch.squeeze_()
    X, y = batch[:, 1:], batch[:, 0]
    return X, y

  def forward(X):
    y_est = self.model(X)
    return y_est.squeeze_()

  def training_step(self, batch, batch_idx):
    X, y = self.batchToXy(batch)
    y_est = self.forward(X)
    loss = pt.nn.functional.mse_loss(y_est, y)
    for k,v in {
        "train_mse": loss.item(),
        "train_rmse": loss.sqrt().item(),
    }.items():
      self.log(k, v, on_step=True, on_epoch=True, prog_bar=True, logger=True)

    return loss

  def configure_optimizers(self):
    optimizers = {'Adam': pt.optim.AdamW,
                  'SGD': pt.optim.SGD}
    optimizer = optimizers[self.hparams.optimizer]

    return optimizer(self.layers.parameters(),
                     lr = float(self.hparams.lr))

model = DcTaxiModel(**{
    "seed": "1686523060",
    "num_features": "8",
    "optimizer": "Adam",
    "lr": "0.03",
    "max_batches": "100",
    "batch_size": "64",
})
```

Notice that the DcTaxiModel class inherits from the base pl.LightningModule class, which requires a separate initialization in the __init__ method by the super()

.__init__() method call. The rest of the __init__ method of the class is simplified here for illustration and to highlight the following key concepts: storage of a reference to the model's hyperparameters in self.hparams as well as the instantiation of the model parameters in the self.layers instance.

The training_step method is the workhorse of the PyTorch Lightning implementation, performing the forward step through the model layers, computing the loss, and returning the loss value. Notice that it relies on the batchToXy method (introduced in chapter 7) responsible for converting a batch of training examples into the format suitable for model training.

The conversion amounts to eliminating any dimensions that have a shape of 1 using the squeeze_ method. For example, a tensor with a shape of [1, 128, 5, 1] is reshaped to [128, 5] after the application of squeeze_. The use of squeeze_ (with the trailing underscore) instead of the squeeze method is a minor performance optimization. Recall from chapter 5 that the trailing underscore in squeeze_ indicates that this PyTorch method performs the operation in place, mutating the tensor, as opposed to returning a new tensor instance.

The DcTaxiModel implementation assumes that the first column in the tensor is the label with the remaining columns as features, so the concluding portion of the batchToXy code simply aliases the label as y and features as X, returning the result.

The calls to self.log in the training_step method report the training MSE and RMSE values computed by the model. As explained in chapter 5, in the PyTorch tensor API the item method of a PyTorch scalar tensor returns a regular Python value instead of a tensor. Hence, the values that are logged using self.log are Python numerics rather than PyTorch tensors. The self.log method of PyTorch Lightning is a generic API for an extensible logging framework, which will be covered in more detail later in this chapter.

The configure_optimizers method in the example uses a dictionary of optimizers in order to enable the model to switch between different optimization algorithms (Adam versus SGD) based on the value of the optimizer hyperparameter. Although this implementation of model training does not yet use hyperparameter optimization, the dictionary-based lookup approach shown in configure_optimizers ensures that the model code does not need to be changed at the later stages of development when hyperparameter optimization is enabled.

In PyTorch Lightning, training of a model is performed using an instance of a Trainer.

### Listing 10.2   PyTorch Lightning `Trainer` to train a subclass

```
from pytorch_lightning.loggers import CSVLogger
csvLog = \
    CSVLogger(save_dir = "logs",
              name = "dctaxi",
              version = f"seed_{model.hparams.seed}")
```

**CSVLogger is used to illustrate analysis with pandas.**

**The seed hyperparameter is used to uniquely identify the model log.**

```
trainer = \
    pl.Trainer(gpus = pt.cuda.device_count() \
                    if pt.cuda.is_available() else 0,
    max_epochs = 1,
    limit_train_batches = \
        int( model.hparams.max_batches ) \
            if 'max_batches' in model.hparams else 1,
    log_every_n_steps = 1,
    logger = [csvLog])
```

**Use multiple GPUs for training when available.**

**Use 1 since the training duration is controlled by max_batches.**

**Use max_batches to set the number of the training iterations.**

**Ensure that every call to self.log is persisted in the log.**

**Persist the values sent to self.log based on csvLog setup.**

The hyperparameter values can be applied to the machine learning pipeline and not just to the model: for example, the max_batches hyperparameter controls the duration of the model training. As you will see in the remainder of this chapter, hyperparameter values can be used throughout the stages of the machine learning pipeline. The max_epochs settings in the code example is designed to ensure that the training pipeline can support both Iterable as well as Map PyTorch data sets. Recall from chapter 7 that IterableDataset instances have a variable number of examples per training data set; hence, training with this category is controlled by limiting the number of training batches. This number is specified using the limit_train_batches parameter of the Trainer.

The progress_bar_refresh_rate and weight_summary settings in listing 10.2 are reasonable defaults to use with the Trainer to minimize the amount of the logging information reported during training. If you prefer to have a report on the training model parameters, you can change weights_summary to "full" to report all weights, or to "top" to report just the weights of the top (the ones connected to the trunk of the model) layers in the model. Similarly, the progress_bar_refresh_rate can be changed to an integer value representing the frequency (in terms of the number of training steps) for how often to redraw a progress bar showing progress toward training completion.

To provide the model with the training examples, you can use the ObjectStorage-Dataset introduced in chapter 7. Before executing the code snippet in the next example, ensure that you have the Kaen framework installed using

```
pip install kaen[osds]
```

Next, to execute just the training of the model, you can invoke the fit method on the instance of pl.Trainer, passing in a PyTorch DataLoader with the training examples:

```
from torch.utils.data import DataLoader
from kaen.torch import ObjectStorageDataset as osds

train_ds = osds('https://raw.githubusercontent.com/osipov/
                    smlbook/master/train.csv',
                batch_size = int(model.hparams.batch_size) )

train_dl = DataLoader(train_ds,
                    pin_memory = True)
```

```
trainer.fit(model,
            train_dataloaders = train_dl)

trainer.fit(model, train_dl)
```

In the example, the sample of the DC taxi data set available from http://mng.bz/nr9a is used to simply illustrate how to use PyTorch Lightning. In the next chapter, you will see how to scale to larger data sets by simply changing the URL string passed to osds.

Since during training the loss and metric values are logged to a CSV file, once the training is finished, you can load the values into a pandas DataFrame and plot the results using

```
import pandas as pd
metrics_df = pd.read_csv(f'logs/dctaxi/seed_{model.hparams.seed}/
                          metrics.csv')
ax = metrics_df.plot('step', 'train_rmse_step')
```

which should output a graph resembling figure 10.1.

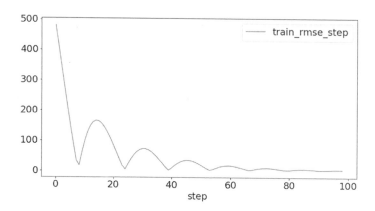

**Figure 10.1   On a small sample, the trivial linear regression model converges as expected.**

According to figure 10.1, the naive linear regression model from listing 10.1 converges to a consistent loss value. To examine the details of the loss value at the trailing 25 steps of the convergence, you can again take advantage of pandas DataFrame APIs,

```
ax = metrics_df.iloc[-25:].plot('step', 'train_rmse_step')
ax.plot(metrics_df.iloc[-25:]['step'],
        pt.full([25], metrics_df[-25:]['train_rmse_step'].mean())),
```

which plots figure 10.2.

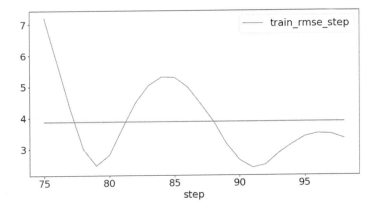

**Figure 10.2   Trailing 25 steps of training converge to a RMSE of roughly 4.0.**

You can confirm that toward the last 25 steps of training, the model converges at an average RMSE of about 4.0. Even with the trivial linear regression model, this should not come as a surprise since this illustration used a tiny training sample.

At this point, it is useful to introduce a `build` function that can be invoked to instantiate, train, and later validate, as well as test the model. For convenience, here's the entire implementation of this version of the model with the training steps encapsulated.

**Listing 10.3   Basic PyTorch Lightning DC taxi model**

```
import torch as pt
import pytorch_lightning as pl
from torch.utils.data import DataLoader
from kaen.torch import ObjectStorageDataset as osds

pt.set_default_dtype(pt.float64)

class DcTaxiModel(pl.LightningModule):
    def __init__(self, **kwargs):
        super().__init__()
        self.save_hyperparameters()

        pt.manual_seed(int(self.hparams.seed))

        self.layers = pt.nn.Linear(int(self.hparams.num_features), 1)

    def batchToXy(self, batch):
      batch = batch.squeeze_()
      X, y = batch[:, 1:], batch[:, 0]
      return X, y

    def forward(self, X):
      y_est = self.layers(X)
      return y_est.squeeze_()
```

```python
    def training_step(self, batch, batch_idx):

        X, y = self.batchToXy(batch) #unpack batch into features and label

        y_est = self.forward(X)

        loss = pt.nn.functional.mse_loss(y_est, y)

        for k,v in {
          "train_mse": loss.item(),
          "train_rmse": loss.sqrt().item(),
        }.items():
          self.log(k, v, on_step=True,
                        on_epoch=True, prog_bar=True, logger=True)

        return loss

    def configure_optimizers(self):
        optimizers = {'Adam': pt.optim.AdamW,
                      'SGD': pt.optim.SGD}
        optimizer = optimizers[self.hparams.optimizer]

        return optimizer(self.layers.parameters(),
                        lr = float(self.hparams.lr))

def build(model):
  csvLog = CSVLogger(save_dir = "logs",
                    name = "dctaxi",
                    version = f"seed_{model.hparams.seed}"
                    )

  trainer = pl.Trainer(gpus = pt.cuda.device_count() \
                            if pt.cuda.is_available() else 0,
    max_epochs = 1,
    limit_train_batches = int( model.hparams.max_batches ) \
                        if 'max_batches' in model.hparams else 1,
    progress_bar_refresh_rate = 20,
    weights_summary = None,
    log_every_n_steps = 1,
    logger = csvLog)

  train_ds = osds('https://raw.githubusercontent.com/osipov/smlbook/
                    master/train.csv',
                  batch_size = int(model.hparams.batch_size) )

  train_dl = DataLoader(train_ds,
                        pin_memory = True)

  trainer.fit(model,
            train_dataloaders = train_dl)

  return model, trainer

model = build(DcTaxiModel(**{
        "seed": "1686523060",
```

```
        "num_features": "8",
        "optimizer": "Adam",
        "lr": "0.03",
        "max_batches": "100",
        "batch_size": "100",
}))
```

## 10.1.2 *Enabling test and reporting **for a trained model***

This section describes the `test_step` method for a PyTorch Lightning model and how
the method can be used to test and report on the metrics of a trained model.

Once the model is trained, the `Trainer` instance can also be used to report on the
model loss and metrics against a test data set. However, in order to support testing in
PyTorch Lightning, a `LightningModule` subclass must be extended with an implementation of a `test_step` method. The following code snippet describes the corresponding implementation for `DcTaxiModel`:

```
def test_step(self, batch, batch_idx):
    X, y = self.batchToXy(batch)                    Ignore the gradient graph during
                                                    testing for better performance.
    with pt.no_grad():
        loss = pt.nn.functional.mse_loss(self.forward(X), y)
                                                    Use test_mse instead
                                                    of train_mse . . .
    for k,v in {
        "test_mse": loss.item(),
        "test_rmse": loss.sqrt().item(),              . . . and test_rmse instead
    }.items():                                        of train_rmse when logging
        self.log(k, v, on_step=True, on_epoch=True,   test measurements.
                    prog_bar=True, logger=True)
```

The PyTorch Lightning `test_step` does not require any return values; instead, the
code is expected to report the metrics computed using a trained model. Recall from
the discussion of autodiff in chapter 6 that maintaining the backward graph of the
gradients carries additional performance overhead. Since the model gradients are not
needed during model testing (or validation), the `forward` and `mse_loss` methods are
invoked in the context of `with pt.no_grad():`, which disables the tracking needed
for gradient calculations of the loss.

Outside of the minor change related to renaming the logged loss and metric measures (e.g., `test_rmse` versus `train_rmse`), the implementation of `test_step` logging
is identical to the one from `training_step` function.

To introduce configuration changes to the `Trainer` instance for testing and to create the `DataLoader` for the test data, the `build` function needs to be modified **❶–❹**:

```
def build(model, train_glob, test_glob):            Pass URL globs to instantiate
    csvLog = CSVLogger(save_dir = "logs",        ❶  DataLoader for training and test data.
                    name = "dctaxi",
                        version = f"seed_{model.hparams.seed}")

    trainer = pl.Trainer(gpus = pt.cuda.device_count() \
                        if pt.cuda.is_available() else 0,
```

```
   max_epochs = 1,
   limit_train_batches = int ( model.hparams.max_batches ) \
                    if 'max_batches' in model.hparams else 1,
   limit_test_batches = 1,
   log_every_n_steps = 1,
   logger = csvLog)

   train_ds = osds(train_glob,
                batch_size = int(model.hparams.batch_size) )

   train_dl = DataLoader(train_ds,
                pin_memory = True)

   trainer.fit(model,
            train_dataloaders = train_dl)

   test_ds = osds(test_glob,
                batch_size = int(model.hparams.batch_size) )

   test_dl = DataLoader(test_ds,
                pin_memory = True)

   trainer.test(model,
            test_dataloaders=test_dl)

   return model, trainer
```

② Use the test data set only once to report on the loss and metric measures.

③ Use test_glob to instantiate the train_ds . . .

④ . . . and train_dl instances.

⑤ Test and report on the model performance using the Trainer.test method.

After executing the training and test using the updated model and `build` implementation using

```
model = build(DcTaxiModel(**{
        "seed": "1686523060",
        "num_features": "8",
        "optimizer": "Adam",
        "lr": "0.03",
        "max_batches": "100",
        "batch_size": "100",}),
   train_glob = 'https://raw.githubusercontent.com/osipov/smlbook/
                master/train.csv',
   test_glob = 'https://raw.githubusercontent.com/osipov/smlbook/
                master/train.csv')
```

you should get test results resembling the following:

```
--------------------------------------------------------------------
DATALOADER:0 TEST RESULTS
{'test_mse': 9.402312278747559,
 'test_mse_epoch': 9.402312278747559,
 'test_rmse': 3.066318988800049,
 'test_rmse_epoch': 3.066318988800049}
--------------------------------------------------------------------
```

### 10.1.3 *Enabling validation during model training*

This section illustrates how to use the `validation_step` method in a `Lightning-Module` subclass to enable support for PyTorch model validation.

The advantages of using PyTorch Lightning become more evident when you modify your implementation to support recurring validation steps during training. For example, to add model validation to the `DcTaxiModel` implementation, you simply introduce the `validation_step` method:

```
def validation_step(self, batch, batch_idx):
    X, y = self.batchToXy(batch)

    with pt.no_grad():
        loss = pt.nn.functional.mse_loss(self.forward(X), y)

    for k,v in {
      "val_mse": loss.item(),
      "val_rmse": loss.sqrt().item(),
      }.items():
        self.log(k, v, on_step=True, on_epoch=True, prog_bar=True, logger=True)

    return loss
```

The following code describes the remaining changes needed to configure the `trainer` instance to perform validation over a fixed-sized data set (as opposed to k-fold cross validation):

```
trainer = pl.Trainer(gpus = pt.cuda.device_count() \
                         if pt.cuda.is_available() else 0,
    max_epochs = 1,
    limit_train_batches = int( model.hparams.max_batches ) \
                         if 'max_batches' in model.hparams else 1,
    limit_val_batches = 1,
    num_sanity_val_steps = 1,
    val_check_interval = min(20,
                         int( model.hparams.max_batches ) ),
    limit_test_batches = 1,
    log_every_n_steps = 1,
    logger = csvLog,
    progress_bar_refresh_rate = 20,
    weights_summary = None,)
```

**Validate just 1 batch of validation DataLoader data.**

**Validate after every 20 training iterations (steps) of gradient descent.**

**Validate before training to ensure the validation data set is available.**

The `limit_val_batches` acts similarly to `limit_train_batches` in specifying the number of batches from the validation `Dataset` to use for validation. The `num_sanity_val_steps` parameter to the `Trainer` controls a feature of PyTorch Lightning that uses the validation data set to ensure that the model, as well as the validation `DataLoader`, are instantiated correctly and are ready for training. In the example, setting the value of `num_sanity_val_steps` to 1 performs a single validation step and reports the corresponding metrics. The val_check_interval parameter specifies that at most after every 20 iterations of training, PyTorch Lightning should perform validation using the number of batches specified by the limit_val_batches parameters. The use of the min function with val_check_interval ensures that if the hyperparameter for max_batches is set to be less than 20, the validation is performed at the conclusion of training.

**Listing 10.4   PyTorch Lightning DC taxi linear regression model**

```
import torch as pt
import pytorch_lightning as pl
from torch.utils.data import DataLoader
from kaen.torch import ObjectStorageDataset as osds

pt.set_default_dtype(pt.float64)

class DcTaxiModel(pl.LightningModule):
    def __init__(self, **kwargs):
        super().__init__()
        self.save_hyperparameters()

        pt.manual_seed(int(self.hparams.seed))

        self.layers = pt.nn.Linear(int(self.hparams.num_features), 1)

    def batchToXy(self, batch):
      batch = batch.squeeze_()
      X, y = batch[:, 1:], batch[:, 0]
      return X, y

    def forward(self, X):
      y_est = self.layers(X)
      return y_est.squeeze_()

    def training_step(self, batch, batch_idx):

        X, y = self.batchToXy(batch)

        y_est = self.forward(X)

        loss = pt.nn.functional.mse_loss(y_est, y)

        for k,v in {
          "train_mse": loss.item(),
          "train_rmse": loss.sqrt().item(),
        }.items():
          self.log(k, v, on_step=True, on_epoch=True,
                      prog_bar=True, logger=True)

        return loss

    def validation_step(self, batch, batch_idx):
      X, y = self.batchToXy(batch)
```

```
    with pt.no_grad():
        loss = pt.nn.functional.mse_loss(self.forward(X), y)

    for k,v in {
      "val_mse": loss.item(),
      "val_rmse": loss.sqrt().item(),
    }.items():
        self.log(k, v, on_step=True, on_epoch=True,
                     prog_bar=True, logger=True)


    return loss

def test_step(self, batch, batch_idx):
    X, y = self.batchToXy(batch)

    with pt.no_grad():
        loss = pt.nn.functional.mse_loss(self.forward(X), y)

    for k,v in {
        "test_mse": loss.item(),
        "test_rmse": loss.sqrt().item(),
    }.items():
        self.log(k, v, on_step=True, on_epoch=True,
                     prog_bar=True, logger=True)


def configure_optimizers(self):
    optimizers = {'Adam': pt.optim.AdamW,
                  'SGD': pt.optim.SGD}
    optimizer = optimizers[self.hparams.optimizer]

    return optimizer(self.layers.parameters(),
                     lr = float(self.hparams.lr))

def build(model, train_glob, val_glob, test_glob):
  csvLog = CSVLogger(save_dir = "logs",
                   name = "dctaxi",
                   version = f"seed_{model.hparams.seed}")

  trainer = pl.Trainer(gpus = pt.cuda.device_count() \
                               if pt.cuda.is_available() else 0,
    max_epochs = 1,
    limit_train_batches = int( model.hparams.max_batches ) \
                          if 'max_batches' in model.hparams else 1,
    limit_val_batches = 1,
    num_sanity_val_steps = 1,
    val_check_interval = min(20, int( model.hparams.max_batches ) ),
    limit_test_batches = 1,
    log_every_n_steps = 1,
    logger = csvLog,
    progress_bar_refresh_rate = 20,
    weights_summary = None,)

  train_dl = \
    DataLoader(osds(train_glob,
```

```
                        batch_size = int(model.hparams.batch_size) ),
                pin_memory = True)

    val_dl = \
      DataLoader(osds(val_glob,
                        batch_size = int(model.hparams.batch_size) ),
                pin_memory = True)

    trainer.fit(model,
                train_dataloaders = train_dl,
                val_dataloaders = val_dl)

    test_dl = \
      DataLoader(osds(test_glob,
                        batch_size = int(model.hparams.batch_size) ),
                pin_memory = True)

    trainer.test(model,
                dataloaders=test_dl)

    return model, trainer
```

You can train, validate, and test the entire model by running

```
model, trainer = build(DcTaxiModel(**{
        "seed": "1686523060",
        "num_features": "8",
        "optimizer": "Adam",
        "lr": "0.03",
        "max_batches": "100",
        "batch_size": "100",}),
    train_glob = 'https://raw.githubusercontent.com/osipov/smlbook/
                  master/train.csv',
    val_glob = 'https://raw.githubusercontent.com/osipov/smlbook/
                  master/valid.csv',
    test_glob = 'https://raw.githubusercontent.com/osipov/smlbook/
                  master/train.csv').
```

If you load the resulting logs from the logs/dctaxi/version_1686523060 folder as a pandas DataFrame and plot the result using

```
import pandas as pd
metrics_df = \
  pd.read_csv(f'logs/dctaxi/seed_{model.hparams.seed}/metrics.csv')

ax = (metrics_df[['step', 'train_rmse_step']][20:]
        .dropna()
        .plot('step', 'train_rmse_step'))

ax = (metrics_df[['step', 'val_rmse_step']][20:]
        .fillna(method='ffill')['val_rmse_step']
        .plot(ax = ax))
```

you should observe a graph resembling figure 10.3. Since the `val_check_interval` parameter was set to 20, most of the values for the `val_rmse_step` column in the data frame are missing. The `fillna(method='ffill')` call fills the missing values forward, for example by setting missing values for steps 81, 82, and so on, based on the validation RMSE from step 80.

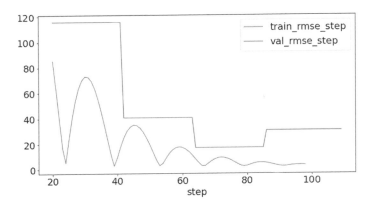

**Figure 10.3**   **Despite reasonable test performance, validation RMSE signals overfitting.**

The lackluster performance against the validation data set, as shown in figure 10.3, points at the likelihood of the model overfitting on the training data set. Before putting the code in production, the model implementation should be refactored to become more generalizable and less reliant on memorization of the training data set. This means that to move forward, you need a model development approach with more comprehensive support for experimentation and hyperparameter optimization.

## Summary

- Adopting the PyTorch Lightning framework can help you refactor your machine learning implementation to reduce the fraction of incidental, boilerplate code and to focus on model-specific development.
- In a PyTorch Lightning-based implementation for a machine learning model, you can incrementally add support for model training, validation, and test support, along with pluggable features such as a logging framework for analysis.
- The `CSVLogger` from PyTorch Lightning saves the results of model training, validation, and test features to CSV files that you analyzed using pandas.

*11*

# *Hyperparameter optimization*

**This chapter covers**

- Understanding machine learning with hyperparameter optimization
- Introducing hyperparameter optimization for the DC taxi model
- Visualizing the outcomes of hyperparameter optimization trials

In chapter 10, you integrated your DC taxi model with the PyTorch Lightning framework, factoring out boilerplate engineering code and paving the way to hyperparameter optimization support. In this chapter, you are going to adopt Optuna, a hyperparameter optimization framework, to progress beyond a trial-and-error approach to selection of your machine learning hyperparameter values. You will train a collection of DC taxi model instances based on the hyperparameter values selected using Optuna's Tree-Structured Parzen Estimator(TPE) that fits a Gaussian mixture model (GMM) to the hyperparameters in your machine learning system. The performance of these model instances is compared using various Optuna visualization plots.

## 11.1  *Hyperparameter optimization with Optuna*

This section teaches about Optuna for hyperparameter optimization (HPO) and how to add support for HPO to the DC taxi fare estimation model.

Optuna is one of many open source HPO frameworks available for PyTorch. Like other HPO frameworks, Optuna includes a collection of gradient-free[1] optimization algorithms that range from random search, and Bayesian optimization, to TPE. Optuna uses the concept of a *trial* to describe an instance of a process to compute the value of a loss function, for example an instance of an experiment on the DcTaxiModel model to compute its test loss based on a set of hyperparameter values.

In Optuna, a trial must produce a value for the loss function that you seek to minimize (or maximize). The implementation of the process to compute the loss value is usually captured in an objective function. Note that the implementation is intentionally incomplete ❸ to explain just the parts relevant to understanding the Optuna API.

---

**Listing 11.1  A starter for DC taxi HPO with `objective` function**

❶ **An objective function is a standard interface to the Optuna trial.**

❷ **suggest_int returns integers chosen by Optuna to optimize the objective function.**

❸ **hparams's implementation is completed later in this chapter.**

❹ **Optuna suggests hyperparameters for each trial to reduce the value of train_val_rmse.**

```
def objective(trial):
  hparams = {
    "seed": trial.suggest_int('seed',
              0,
              pt.iinfo(pt.int32).max - 1),
    "num_features": "8",
    ...
  }
  model, trainer = build(DcTaxiModel(**hparams),
    train_glob = "https://raw.githubusercontent.com/osipov/smlbook/
      master/train.csv",
    val_glob = "https://raw.githubusercontent.com/osipov/smlbook/
      master/valid.csv")

  return (trainer
          .callback_metrics['train_val_rmse']
          .item())
```

---

Notice that, in the `hparams` dictionary, there is a single `int` hyperparameter value requested from Optuna for the seed. The `suggest_int` method is one of several methods available from the Optuna `trial` API to obtain a value for a hyperparameter. (Other methods available from the `trial` interface are described here: http://mng.bz/v4B7.) In the example, the `suggest_int('seed', 0, pt.iinfo(pt.int32).max - 1)` method call specifies that Optuna should recommend values for the pseudorandom number seed generator from 0 up to and excluding the maximum positive 32-bit integer.

Recall that the implementation of the `DcTaxiModel` depends on additional hyperparameter values, including, `optimizer`, `bins`, `lr` (the learning rate), `max_batches`,

---

[1]  Gradient-free algorithms do not require computation of the gradient of a loss (or any objective) function to optimize the function parameters. In other words, gradient-free hyperparameter optimization can optimize an objective function even when the function does not have computable gradients.

and potentially more. To enable support for these hyperparameters in the implementation of the DcTaxiModel, you need to expand the hparams dictionary with Optuna
specification for the other hyperparameter values. Since the strategies for sampling
these hyperparameters are more complex than suggest_int, the next section explains
some foundational concepts.

## 11.1.1 Understanding loguniform hyperparameters

This section puts forward the rationale for using log-uniform hyperameters during
training and proposes the hyperparameters that should be set as log-uniform for the
DC taxi model.

   For many continuous valued hyperparameters such as the learning rate, it is convenient to use the suggest_loguniform method of the Optuna trial API, which is
invoked using the upper and lower boundary values for the hyperparameter. Since in
the Optuna trial API there are several options for continuous hyperparameter values,
it is useful to clarify why the learning rate should use Optuna suggest_loguniform as
opposed to suggest_uniform. In general, loguniform is preferred to search over a
range where the upper bound is more than one order of magnitude larger than the
lower bound. The rationale has to do with how the base-10 numeric system works and
is illustrated in the following example:

```
x = pt.linspace(1, 1_000, 300)
#prints the 1s, 10s, 100s
print(pt.count_nonzero(x[(x > 0) & (x < 10) ]).item(),
    pt.count_nonzero(x[(x > 10) & (x < 100) ]).item(),
    pt.count_nonzero(x[(x > 100) & (x < 1_000) ]).item())
```

which outputs

```
3 27 269
```

Since x is assigned to contain 300 floating point values from 0 to 1,000 (three orders
of magnitude), the print statement outputs the count of values that appears within a
range for each of the orders of magnitude (i.e., 0 to 10, 10 to 100, and 100 to 1,000).
In this example, there is approximately a 100-times difference in the number of values
of x that fall in the 0 to 10 range versus the number of the values in the 100 to 1,000
range, or more precisely 3 versus 269.

   In general, when sampling with uniform likelihood from a linear range that is $10N$
larger, you can expect to obtain on average $10N$ times more samples from the larger
range. Application of the log function eliminates this unintended skew due to the
base-10 numeric system, as evidenced by the following example:

```
y = pt.logspace(pt.log10(pt.tensor(1)),
              pt.log10(pt.tensor(1_000)),  300)

#prints the 1s, 10s, 100s
print(pt.count_nonzero(y[(y > 0) & (y < 10) ]).item(),
```

```
pt.count_nonzero(y[(y > 10) & (y < 100) ]).item(),
pt.count_nonzero(y[(y > 100) & (y < 1_000) ]).item())
```

which outputs

```
100 100 99
```

illustrating a roughly equal distribution of the 300 samples across the entire range from 1 to 1,000 due to the use of the log-base 10 scale as opposed to the regular unit scale.

The concept of using the sampling hyperparameter values over log-scaled ranges applies to discrete integer values as much as to the continuous values. For example, the max_batches hyperparameter can be initialized using log = True in the Optuna Trial API function call suggest_int('max_batches', 40, 4000, log = True) since the lower and upper boundary values in the call span a range greater than an order of magnitude.

### 11.1.2 *Using categorical and log-uniform hyperparameters*

This section builds on what you learned about log-uniform hyperparameters to explain how the optimizer learning rate can be initialized using a hyperparameter sampled from a log-uniform scale by Optuna.

The optimizer and the corresponding learning rate are some of the other hyperparameters you may want to include in the HPO trials. As the optimizer learning rate is best represented with a continuous value over a range that spans several orders of magnitude, it should be optimized in the trial using the suggest_loguniform method. This can be implemented as follows, for values of candidate learning rates in the range [0.001, 0.1]:

```
hparams = {
...
"lr": trial.suggest_loguniform('lr', 0.001, 0.1),     ◁—  Use an optimizer learning
...                                                        rate from the log-uniform
}                                                          range [0.001, 0.1].
```

Since the existing implementation of the configure_optimizers method of the DcTaxiModel already includes support for stochastic gradient descent and Adam, you can have Optuna suggest the choice of these values (SGD or Adam) in the implementation of the objective method. This requires the use of the suggest_categorical method of the trial object as shown:

```
hparams = {
...
"optimizer": \
    trial.suggest_categorical('optimizer',
                              ['Adam', 'SGD']),     ◁—  Use Adam and SGD as
...                                                     optimizer options in
}                                                       each HPO trial.
```

The arguments for the `trial` API are computed at program runtime, which means that you can use standard Python features for a more expressive specification of the hyperparameter values. For example, the `batch_size` hyperparameter can be specified using a list of integers, where the integers are generated dynamically, resolving to powers of two from $2^{16}$ up to and including $2^{21}$—in other words, the values [65536, 131072, 262144, 524288, 1048576, 2097152]:

```
hparams = {                                    Pre-compute a Python list of
    ...                                        hyperparameter values before
    "batch_size": \                            using suggest_categorical.
      trial.suggest_categorical('batch_size',
                [2 ** i for i in range(16, 22)]),     ◁──────────────────┘
    ...
}
```

A more interesting application of `suggest_categorical` is shown, with implementation of the specification for the `num_hidden_neurons` hyperparameter.

**Listing 11.2   Optuna trials to discover the neural net architecture**

```
hparams = {                                         Specify the network architecture
    ...                                             as a hyperparameter (for
    "num_hidden_neurons": \        ◁────────        example, [5, 11, 7]).
      [trial.suggest_categorical(f"num_hidden_layer_{layer}_neurons",
                    [7, 11, 13, 19, 23]) for layer in \
                    range(trial.suggest_categorical('num_layers',
                                    [11, 13, 17, 19]))],
    ...
}
```

The `DcTaxiModel` can use a string representation of the number of neurons in hidden layers to build its model layers. For example, a string representation [3, 5, 7, 8] can represent four hidden `torch.nn.Linear` layers with three neurons in the first layer, five in the second, and so on.

This type of a specification can be implemented as an Optuna hyperparameter using a combination of `suggest_categorical` calls. First, the hyperparameter for the total number of hidden layers (`num_layers`) is assigned a value by Optuna based on a set of possible hidden layer quantities from the list in listing 11.2 with the integer values [11, 13, 17, 19]. Next, depending on the value selected by Optuna for the number of hidden layers (`num_layers`), the next `suggest_categorical` call is invoked multiple times by the `for` operator, once for each hidden layer. Each of the invocations changes the assignment to the `layer` variable and instantiates a new hyperparameter, for example `num_hidden_layer_0_neurons` for the first layer in the architecture, `num_hidden_layer_1_neurons` for the second, and so on, depending on the value of the number of hyperparameter layers (`num_layers`). The value for each of these hyperparameters (each describing the number of neurons per hidden layer) is assigned from a different `suggest_categorical` list, specified as [7, 11, 13, 19, 23].

Ultimately, num_hidden_neurons resolves to a Python list with an Optuna-proposed configuration of hidden layers and neurons.

Combining these hyperparameters with the an entire implementation of the objective function results in the following:

```
def objective(trial):
  hparams = {
    "seed": trial.suggest_int('seed', 0, pt.iinfo(pt.int32).max - 1),
    "num_features": "8",
    "optimizer": trial.suggest_categorical('optimizer', ['Adam', 'SGD']),
    "lr": trial.suggest_loguniform('lr', 0.009, 0.07),
    "num_hidden_neurons": \
      str([trial
              .suggest_categorical(f"num_hidden_layer_{layer}_neurons",
              [7, 11]) for layer in \
                range(trial.suggest_categorical('num_layers', [2, 3]))]),
    "batch_size": trial.suggest_int('batch_size', 30, 50, log = True),
    "max_batches": trial.suggest_int('max_batches', 30, 50, log = True)
    "batch_norm_linear_layers": \
      str(trial.suggest_int('batch_norm_linear_layers', 0, 1)),
  }
  model, trainer = build(DcTaxiModel(**hparams),
    train_glob = 'https://raw.githubusercontent.com/osipov/smlbook/
      master/train.csv',
    val_glob = 'https://raw.githubusercontent.com/osipov/smlbook/
      master/valid.csv')

  return trainer.callback_metrics['train_val_rmse'].item()
```

## 11.2 *Neural network layers configuration as a hyperparameter*

This section teaches how to extend the DC taxi model to enable support for deep learning models, with an arbitrary number of hidden layers and neurons per layer. The section also describes how a hyperparameter value can be used to specify this configuration.

Instead of arbitrarily choosing the configuration of the neural network parameters (e.g., the number of layers or the number of the neurons per layer), it is valuable to treat the configuration as a hyperparameter to be optimized. Although neither PyTorch nor PyTorch Lightning has a straightforward technique for optimizing over your neural net configuration, you can easily implement a utility method to convert a string representation of a network's hidden layers into a collection of nn.Module instances that mirror the string. For example, a string [3, 5, 8] can represent the three hidden layers of a neural network with three neurons in the first layer, five in the second layer, and eight in the third layer. The build_hidden_layers utility method shown in the following code snippet implements this conversion from a string to the torch.nn.Linear instances along with an arbitrary activation function:

```
def build_hidden_layers(self, num_hidden_neurons, activation):
    linear_layers = \
        [ pt.nn.Linear(num_hidden_neurons[i],
          num_hidden_neurons[i+1]) for i in range(len(num_hidden_neurons) - 1) ]

    classes = \
        [activation.__class__] * len(num_hidden_neurons)

    activation_instances = \
        list(map(lambda x: x(), classes))

    hidden_layer_activation_tuples = \
        list(zip(linear_layers, activation_instances))

    hidden_layers = \
        [i for sublist in hidden_layer_activation_tuples for i in sublist]

    return hidden_layers
```

**Create a Python list of the linear (feedforward) layers ...**

**... and create a list of matching length consisting of activation classes.**

**Convert activation classes to activation instances.**

**Zip the linear layers with the activation function instances.**

**Return the result as a flat Python list.**

With the build_hidden_layers utility method added to the implementation of DcTaxiModel, you are ready to modify the __init__ method to use the build_hidden_layers as follows:

```
import json
import torch as pt
import pytorch_lightning as pl
class DcTaxiModel(pl.LightningModule):
    def __init__(self, hparams = None):
        super().__init__()
        self.hparams = hparams

        pt.manual_seed(self.hparams['seed'])

        num_hidden_neurons = \
            json.loads(self.hparams.num_hidden_neurons)

        self.layers = \
            pt.nn.Sequential(
                pt.nn.Linear(int(self.hparams.num_features), num_hidden_neurons[0]),
                pt.nn.ReLU(),
                *self.build_hidden_layers(num_hidden_neurons, pt.nn.ReLU()),
                pt.nn.Linear(num_hidden_neurons[-1], 1)
            )

model = build(DcTaxiModel(**{
        "seed": "1686523060",
        "num_features": "8",
        "num_hidden_neurons": "[3, 5, 8]",
        "optimizer": "Adam",
        "lr": "0.03",
        "max_batches": "100",
        "batch_size": "100",}),
```

**Create a list of hidden layer neurons (for example, [3, 5, 8]).**

**Use sequences of feed-forward hidden layers for the model.**

**Specify the hidden layers using a string format.**

```
train_glob = 'https://raw.githubusercontent.com/osipov/smlbook/
                master/train.csv',
val_glob = 'https://raw.githubusercontent.com/osipov/smlbook/
              master/valid.csv',
test_glob = 'https://raw.githubusercontent.com/osipov/smlbook/
              master/train.csv')
```

In the example, the `json.loads` method is used to convert the hidden layer string representation of a list, for example [3, 5, 8], to a Python list of integer values. Also, while the `self.layers` reference to the neural network model still has four input features and one output value, the hidden values are specified by unrolling the list of the `torch.nn.Linear` instances from the `build_hidden_layers` method as individual objects passed to the `torch.nn.Sequential` initializer.

## 11.3 *Experimenting with the batch normalization hyperparameter*

Batch normalization is a widely used technique to increase the rate of gradient descent convergence.[2] Despite the widespread use of batch normalization, it is useful to collect data that demonstrates it can help create more effective DC taxi models.

Since the batch normalization feature should be enabled or disabled depending on a Boolean HPO flag, it is useful to introduce an automatic way of rewiring the layers of the DC taxi model to take advantage of the feature. The following `batch_norm_linear` method implements an automatic insert of PyTorch `torch.nn.BatchNorm1d` class instances before each `torch.nn.Linear` layer in the model. The following implementation also correctly configures each of the `BatchNorm1d` instances to have the right number of inputs, matching the number of inputs in the corresponding `Linear` layer, which should follow the `BatchNorm1d`:

```
def batch_norm_linear(self, layers):
    idx_linear = \                                    ⟵——————  Build a list with the positional index
        list(filter(lambda x: type(x) is int,                  of the Linear classes in the model.
            [idx if issubclass(layer.__class__, pt.nn.Linear) else None \
            for idx, layer in enumerate(layers)]))
                                                              Use the maximum int value as the
    idx_linear.append(sys.maxsize)        ⟵——————————————      last element of the list to represent
                                                              an infinite value.

    layer_lists = \                                    ⟵————  Create sublists with s as
        [list(iter(layers[s:e])) \                             an index of each Linear
            for s, e in zip(idx_linear[:-1], idx_linear[1:])]  and e as an index before
                                                               each Linear.

    batch_norm_layers = \
        [pt.nn.BatchNorm1d(layer[0].in_features) for layer in layer_lists]
```

Instantiate BatchNorm1d with inputs matching
the inputs of the corresponding Linear.

---

[2] The original, widely cited paper "Batch Normalization: Accelerating Deep Network Training by Reducing Internal Covariate Shift" that introduced batch normalization is available from https://arxiv.org/abs/1502.03167.

```
batch_normed_layer_lists = \                    ◄───
  [ [bn, *layers] for bn, layers in \
    list(zip(batch_norm_layers, layer_lists)) ]
```

**Insert the BatchNormId instances before the corresponding Linear.**

```
result = \                                      ◄───
  pt.nn.Sequential(*[layer for nested_layer in \
    batch_normed_layer_lists for layer in nested_layer ])

return result
```

**Package the entire sequence of BatchNormId and Linear layers into Sequential.**

Once the `batch_norm_linear` method is added to the `DcTaxiModel` class, the `__init__` method of the class should be modified (listing 11.3 ❶) to apply batch normalization depending on the value of the `batch_norm_linear_layers` hyperparameter.

**Listing 11.3   Using optional batch normalization**

```
from distutils.util import strtobool

def __init__(self, **kwargs):
  super().__init_'()
  self.save_hyperparameters()

  self.step = 0
  self.start_ts = time.perf_counter()
  self.train_val_rmse = pt.tensor(0.)

  pt.manual_seed(int(self.hparams.seed))
  #create a list of hidden layer neurons, e.g. [3, 5, 8]
  num_hidden_neurons = json.loads(self.hparams.num_hidden_neurons)

  self.layers = pt.nn.Sequential(
      pt.nn.Linear(int(self.hparams.num_features), num_hidden_neurons[0]),
      pt.nn.ReLU(),
      *self.build_hidden_layers(num_hidden_neurons, pt.nn.ReLU()),
      pt.nn.Linear(num_hidden_neurons[-1], 1)
  )

  if 'batch_norm_linear_layers' in self.hparams \        ◄───
    and strtobool(self.hparams.batch_norm_linear_layers):
      self.layers = self.batch_norm_linear(self.layers)
```

❶ **Batch normalize Linear layers if batch_norm_linear_layers is True.**

With the batch normalization in place, `DcTaxiModel` and the matching `build` method are ready for HPO.

**Listing 11.4   `DcTaxiModel` implementation with HPO support**

```
import sys
import json
import time
import torch as pt
import pytorch_lightning as pl
from distutils.util import strtobool
from torch.utils.data import DataLoader
from kaen.torch import ObjectStorageDataset as osds
```

```
pt.set_default_dtype(pt.float64)

class DcTaxiModel(pl.LightningModule):
    def __init__(self, **kwargs):
        super().__init__()
        self.save_hyperparameters()

        self.step = 0
        self.start_ts = time.perf_counter()
        self.train_val_rmse = pt.tensor(0.)

        pt.manual_seed(int(self.hparams.seed))
        #create a list of hidden layer neurons, e.g. [3, 5, 8]
        num_hidden_neurons = json.loads(self.hparams.num_hidden_neurons)

        self.layers = \
          pt.nn.Sequential(
            pt.nn.Linear(int(self.hparams.num_features),
                            num_hidden_neurons[0]),
            pt.nn.ReLU(),
            *self.build_hidden_layers(num_hidden_neurons, pt.nn.ReLU()),
            pt.nn.Linear(num_hidden_neurons[-1], 1)
          )

        if 'batch_norm_linear_layers' in self.hparams \
          and strtobool(self.hparams.batch_norm_linear_layers):
          self.layers = self.batch_norm_linear(self.layers)

    def build_hidden_layers(self, num_hidden_neurons, activation):
        linear_layers = [ pt.nn.Linear(num_hidden_neurons[i],
            num_hidden_neurons[i+1]) for i in \
              range(len(num_hidden_neurons) - 1) ]

        classes = [activation.__class__] * len(num_hidden_neurons)

        activation_instances = list(map(lambda x: x(), classes))

        hidden_layer_activation_tuples = \
          list(zip(linear_layers, activation_instances))

        hidden_layers = \
          [i for sublist in hidden_layer_activation_tuples for i in sublist]

        return hidden_layers

    def batch_norm_linear(self, layers):
        idx_linear = \
          list(filter(lambda x: type(x) is int,
          [idx if issubclass(layer.__class__, pt.nn.Linear) else None \
            for idx, layer in enumerate(layers)]))

        idx_linear.append(sys.maxsize)
        layer_lists = \
          [list(iter(layers[s:e])) \
            for s, e in zip(idx_linear[:-1], idx_linear[1:])]
```

```
    batch_norm_layers = \
      [pt.nn.BatchNorm1d(layer[0].in_features) for layer in layer_lists]
    batch_normed_layer_lists = \
      [ [bn, *layers] for bn, layers in \
        list(zip(batch_norm_layers, layer_lists)) ]

    return \
      pt.nn.Sequential(*[layer \
        for nested_layer in batch_normed_layer_lists \
        for layer in nested_layer ])

def batchToXy(self, batch):
  batch = batch.squeeze_()
  X, y = batch[:, 1:], batch[:, 0]
  return X, y

def forward(self, X):
  y_est = self.layers(X)
  return y_est.squeeze_()

def training_step(self, batch, batch_idx):
    self.step += 1

    X, y = self.batchToXy(batch) #unpack batch into features and label

    y_est = self.forward(X)

    loss = pt.nn.functional.mse_loss(y_est, y)

    for k,v in {

      "train_mse": loss.item(),
      "train_rmse": loss.sqrt().item(),
      "train_steps_per_sec": \
        self.step / (time.perf_counter() - self.start_ts),

    }.items():
      self.log(k, v, on_step=True, on_epoch=True,
                  prog_bar=True, logger=True)

    self.train_val_rmse = loss.sqrt().item()

    return loss

def validation_step(self, batch, batch_idx):
  X, y = self.batchToXy(batch)

  with pt.no_grad():
      loss = pt.nn.functional.mse_loss(self.forward(X), y)

  for k,v in {
    "val_mse": loss.item(),
    "val_rmse": loss.sqrt().item(),
    "train_val_rmse": self.train_val_rmse + loss.sqrt().item(),
  }.items():
```

```
            self.log(k, v, on_step=True, on_epoch=True,
                            prog_bar=True, logger=True)

    return loss

    def test_step(self, batch, batch_idx):
      X, y = self.batchToXy(batch)

      with pt.no_grad():
          loss = pt.nn.functional.mse_loss(self.forward(X), y)

      for k,v in {
          "test_mse": loss.item(),
          "test_rmse": loss.sqrt().item(),
      }.items():
          self.log(k, v, on_step=True, on_epoch=True,
                          prog_bar=True, logger=True)


    def configure_optimizers(self):
        optimizers = {'Adam': pt.optim.AdamW,
                      'SGD': pt.optim.SGD}
        optimizer = optimizers[self.hparams.optimizer]

        return optimizer(self.layers.parameters(),
                            lr = float(self.hparams.lr))

def build(model, train_glob, val_glob, test_glob = None):
  csvLog = CSVLogger(save_dir = "logs",
                    name = "dctaxi",
                    version = f"seed_{model.hparams.seed}")

  trainer = pl.Trainer(gpus = pt.cuda.device_count() \
                                  if pt.cuda.is_available() else 0,
    max_epochs = 1,
    limit_train_batches = int( model.hparams.max_batches ) \
                                if 'max_batches' in model.hparams else 1,
    limit_val_batches = 1,
    num_sanity_val_steps = 1,
    val_check_interval = min(20, int( model.hparams.max_batches ) ),
    limit_test_batches = 1,
    log_every_n_steps = 1,
    logger = csvLog,
    gradient_clip_val=0.5,
    progress_bar_refresh_rate = 0,
    weights_summary = None,)

  train_dl = \
    DataLoader(osds(train_glob,
                    batch_size = int(model.hparams.batch_size) ),
              pin_memory = True)

  val_dl = \
    DataLoader(osds(val_glob,
                    batch_size = int(model.hparams.batch_size) ),
              pin_memory = True)
```

```
    trainer.fit(model,
                train_dataloaders = train_dl,
                val_dataloaders = val_dl)

    if test_glob is not None:
      test_dl = \
        DataLoader(osds(test_glob,
                        batch_size = int(model.hparams.batch_size) ),
                   pin_memory = True)

      trainer.test(model,
                   dataloaders=test_dl)

    return model, trainer

model, trainer = build(DcTaxiModel(**{
        "seed": "1686523060",
        "num_features": "8",
        "num_hidden_neurons": "[3, 5, 8]",
        "batch_norm_linear_layers": "1",
        "optimizer": "Adam",
        "lr": "0.03",
        "max_batches": "100",
        "batch_size": "100",}),

    train_glob = 'https://raw.githubusercontent.com/osipov/smlbook/
                  master/train.csv',
    val_glob = 'https://raw.githubusercontent.com/osipov/smlbook/
                  master/valid.csv',
    test_glob = 'https://raw.githubusercontent.com/osipov/smlbook/
                  master/train.csv')
```

## 11.3.1 Using Optuna study for hyperparameter optimization

This section introduces the concept of an Optuna study, describes its relationship to
the Optuna trials, and helps you use a study instance to run and analyze a collection of
trials in your HPO implementation.

The `objective` function in Optuna is responsible for the execution of a single
`trial`, including the steps to retrieve the hyperparameter values from Optuna, train a
model, and then evaluate the trained model in terms of the validation loss. Hence,
each trial returns just a single evaluation measure to the Optuna HPO algorithm in
order to make the decision about the next set of hyperparameter values to suggest for
the next trial. A typical HPO process involves tens or hundreds of trials; therefore, it is
important to have the capability to organize the trials, compare their outcomes, and
analyze the hyperparameters involved in the trials. In Optuna, a `study` serves the role
of a container for related trials and provides tabular as well as visual data about the
trial outcomes and associated hyperparameters.

As shown in listing 11.5, with an `objective` function in place, a study is defined by
the direction of optimization (e.g., to minimize or maximize a function) and by a

sampler, which is instantiated based on one of many HPO algorithms and frameworks supported by Optuna. The seed (listing 11.5 ❷) used to initialize a study is different from the seed values used to initialize PyTorch and NumPy. When using HPO, this seed can be used to create the seed values for downstream random number generators, including Python's own random number generator. Although the HPO seed value is useless from the standpoint of the optimization of the DcTaxiModel machine learning performance, it serves the important purpose of ensuring the reproducibility of the HPO trials.

The entire HPO implementation for the DcTaxiModel from listing 11.4 is shown.

---

**Listing 11.5  An Optuna study used to execute HPO**

```
def objective(trial):
  hparams = {
    "seed": trial.suggest_int('seed', 0, pt.iinfo(pt.int32).max - 1),

    "num_features": "8",

    "batch_norm_linear_layers": \
      str(trial.suggest_int('batch_norm_linear_layers', 0, 1)),

    "optimizer": trial.suggest_categorical('optimizer', ['Adam', 'SGD']),

    "lr": trial.suggest_loguniform('lr', 0.009, 0.07),

    "num_hidden_neurons": \
      str([trial.suggest_categorical(f"num_hidden_layer_{layer}_neurons",
           [7, 11]) for layer in \
             range(trial.suggest_categorical('num_layers', [2, 3]))]),

    "batch_size": trial.suggest_int('batch_size', 30, 50, log = True),

    "max_batches": trial.suggest_int('max_batches', 30, 50, log = True)
  }
  model, trainer = build(DcTaxiModel(**hparams),
    train_glob = 'https://raw.githubusercontent.com/osipov/smlbook/
                  master/train.csv',
    val_glob = 'https://raw.githubusercontent.com/osipov/smlbook/
                  master/valid.csv')

    return trainer.callback_metrics['train_val_rmse'].item()

import optuna
from optuna.samplers import TPESampler
study = \
  optuna.create_study(direction = 'minimize',
                sampler = TPESampler( seed = 42 ),)

study.optimize(objective, n_trials = 100)
```

❶ Configure the study to minimize MSE loss of the DcTaxiModel.

❷ Use the TPE algorithm for HPO.

❸ Start the HPO using 100 trials.

After executing the code in listing 11.5, the study.optimize method completes 100 trials of HPO. The details of the individual trials are made available using

```
study_df = study.trials_dataframe().sort_values(by='value',
                                          ascending = True)
study_df[:5][['number', 'value', 'params_seed']],
```

which should return a pandas data frame with the values resembling the following:

| number | value | params_seed |
|--------|----------|-------------|
| 96 | 2.390541 | 1372300804 |
| 56 | 7.403345 | 1017301131 |
| 71 | 9.006614 | 939699871 |
| 74 | 9.139935 | 973536326 |
| 94 | 9.817746 | 1075268021 |

where the number column specifies the index of the trial suggested by Optuna, the value is the corresponding value of the loss function returned by trainer.callback_metrics['train_val_rmse'].item() in the objective method, and the params_seed is the seed value used to initialize the model parameters (weights) of the DcTaxiModel.

## 11.3.2  *Visualizing an HPO study in Optuna*

This section illustrates the HPO study executed in this chapter using three different Optuna visualizations and compares the visualizations in terms of their relevance to HPO.

A completed study instance can also be visualized using the Optuna visualization package. While a comprehensive overview of the various visualizations in Optuna is outside the scope of this book, I found myself reusing just three visualizations consistently across a range of machine learning models. These visualizations are explained in the rest of this section in the order of declining importance.

The hyperparameter importance plot reveals surprising information about the relative influence of the study of hyperparameters on the objective function. It is particularly useful to have the seed hyperparameter included in the list to assess whether some hyperparameters had more or less importance than just a random variable used for model initialization. The hyperparameters that are more important than the random seed deserve further study, while the hyperparameters that are less important than a random variable should be de-prioritized.

To create an importance plot you can use

```
optuna.visualization.plot_param_importances(study)
```

which should render a bar graph resembling the one in figure 11.1.

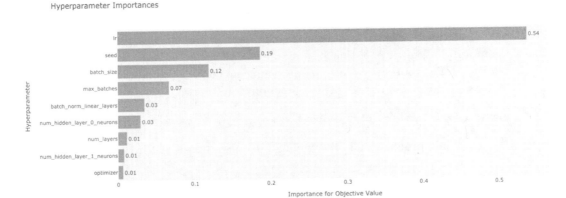

Figure 11.1   **The importances plot assists in guiding later HPO iterations.**

Once you have identified a subset of hyperparameters that you wish to explore in more detail, the next step is to plot them on a parallel coordinates chart. You can instantiate this plot using

```
optuna.visualization.plot_parallel_coordinate(study,
    params=["lr", "batch_size", "num_hidden_layer_0_neurons"])
```

which plots the relationship between the lr (learning rate), batch_size, and num_hidden_layer_0_neurons hyperparameters. Notice that in figure 11.2, the lines represent the individual trial configurations, with those of the darker shade corresponding to the trials with a lower value for the objective function. Hence, a collection of the darker lines that pass though a certain interval for a hyperparameter indicate that the hyperparameter interval deserves closer inspection and may warrant another iteration of HPO.

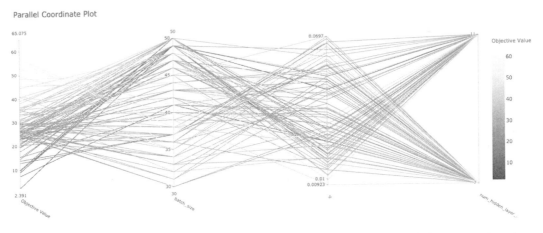

Figure 11.2   **The parallel coordinate plot is useful in pinpointing the impactful intervals for hyperparameter values.**

Out of the plots described so far, the contour plot comes in last in terms of its ability to generate insights about the outcomes in a study. Since the contour plot is limited to visualization of pairs of hyperparameter values, you will find yourself generating multiple contour plots, often based on hyperparameters selected from either the importance or the parallel coordinate plots. As an example, to contour plot the relationship among batch_size, lr, and the objective function, you can run

```
optuna.visualization.plot_contour(study, params=["batch_size", "lr"])
```

which should produce a plot resembling the one in figure 11.3.

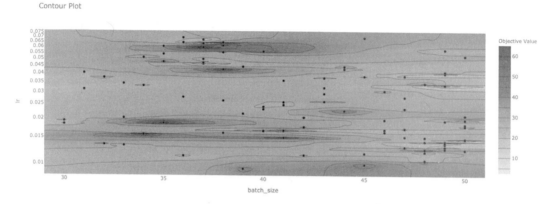

**Figure 11.3   The contour plot helps in the analysis of hyperparameter pairs relative to the loss function.**

## Summary

- Optuna is a hyperparameter optimization framework with the native Python integration to support nontrivial hyperparameter configurations for your machine learning model experiments.
- When using HPO for hyperparameters with ranges that span orders of magnitude, it is useful to adopt log-uniform sampling to ensure even (not skewed) distribution of samples over the range.
- After the execution of HPO trials, Optuna visualization features help with the analysis of the trial outcomes and the associated hyperparameters.

# 12

# *Machine learning pipeline*

## This chapter covers

- Understanding machine learning pipelines with experiment management and hyperparameter optimization
- Implementing Docker containers for the DC taxi model to reduce boilerplate code
- Deploying a machine learning pipeline to train the model

Thus far, you have learned about the individual stages or steps of machine learning in isolation. Focusing on one step of machine learning at a time helped to concentrate your effort on a more manageable scope of work. However, to deploy a production machine learning system it is necessary to integrate these steps into a single pipeline: the outputs of a step flowing into the inputs of the subsequent steps of the pipeline. Further, the pipeline should be flexible enough to enable the hyperparameter optimization (HPO) process to manage and to experiment with the specific tasks executed across the stages of the pipeline.

In this chapter, you will learn about the concepts and the tools you can use to integrate the machine learning pipeline, deploy it to AWS, and train a DC Taxi fare estimation machine learning model using experiment management and hyperparameter optimization.

## 12.1  Describing the machine learning pipeline

This section introduces the core concepts needed to explain the machine learning pipeline implementation described in this chapter.

To clarify the scope of the machine learning pipeline described in this chapter, it is helpful to start with the description of the inputs and outputs of the entire pipeline. On the input side, the pipeline expects a data set produced from exploratory data analysis (EDA) and data quality (data cleanup) processes. The output of the machine learning pipeline is one or more trained machine learning model(s), meaning that the scope of the pipeline excludes the steps from the deployment of the model to production. Since the inputs and the outputs of the pipeline require either human-computer interaction (EDA and data quality) or repeatable automation (model deployment), they are both out of scope for HPO.

For an illustration of the desired features of a machine learning pipeline look at figure 12.1.

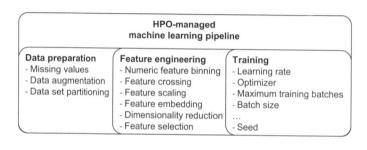

Figure 12.1  A unified machine learning pipeline enables hyperparameter optimization at every stage.

In the diagram, the data preparation, feature engineering, and machine learning model training stages are managed by HPO. Using HPO-managed stages may result in experiments about whether

- During the data preparation stage, the training examples with missing numeric features are dropped from the training data set or are updated to replace missing values with the expected (mean) values for the features
- During the feature engineering stage, numeric location features (such as latitude or longitude coordinates) are converted into categorical features using binning into categories with 64 or 128 distinct values
- During the machine learning training stage, the model is trained using stochastic gradient descent (SGD) or the Adam optimizer

Although it may appear that implementing the pipeline in figure 12.1 should be complex, by using a collection of PyTorch and complementary frameworks you will be able to deploy it by the conclusion of this section. The implementation of the pipeline in this section relies on the following technologies:

- *MLFlow*—For open source experiment management
- *Optuna*—For hyperparameter optimization
- *Docker*—For pipeline component packaging and reproducible execution
- *PyTorch Lighting*—For PyTorch machine learning model training and validation
- *Kaen*—For provisioning and management of the pipeline across AWS and other public cloud providers

Before proceeding, it is helpful to summarize the key concepts that are going to describe the HPO aspects of the pipeline in more detail. The diagram in figure 12.2 clarifies the relationship across the pipeline, HPO, and associated concepts. Experiment management platforms such as MLFlow (other examples include Weights & Biases, Comet.ML, and Neptune.AI) store and manage experiment instances such that each instance corresponds to a different machine learning pipeline. For example, an experiment management platform may store an experiment instance for a machine learning pipeline implemented to train DC Taxi fare estimation models and a different experiment instance for a machine learning pipeline that trains natural language processing models for online chatbots. The experiment instances are isolated from each other but are managed by a single experiment management platform.

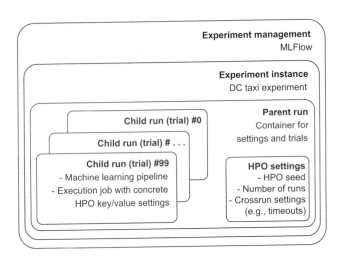

**Figure 12.2** An experiment manager controls the execution of pipeline execution (job) instances according to HPO settings.

Each experiment instance uses a *parent run* as a collection of one or more machine learning pipeline executions (*child runs*). The parent run is configured with the settings that apply across multiple pipeline executions, for instance the value of the pseudorandom number seed used by an HPO engine such as Optuna. The parent run also specifies the total number of child runs (machine learning pipeline executions) that should be executed to complete the parent run. Since each machine learning pipeline execution also corresponds to a unique combination of hyperparameter key/value pairs, the number of the child runs specified by the parent run also specifies the total number of HPO trials (sets of values) that should be produced by the HPO engine to complete the parent run.

The machine learning pipeline code along with the services for experiment management, hyperparameter optimization, and machine learning model training are deployed as Docker containers interconnected by a virtual private cloud (VPC) network in a cloud provider. This deployment is illustrated in figure 12.3.

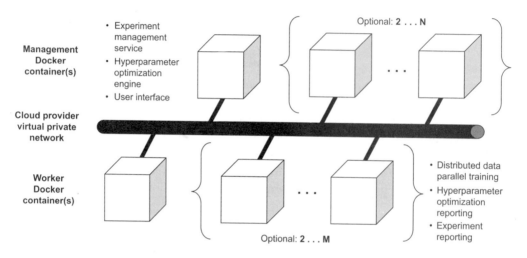

**Figure 12.3** A machine learning pipeline with HPO is deployed as a collection of Docker containers with at least one management and one worker node as well as optional management and worker nodes.

As shown in the figure, in order to deploy a machine learning pipeline with HPO, at least two Docker containers are connected on a virtual private cloud's network, with at least one manager and at least one worker node in the deployment. The manager node(s) host container(s) with the

- Experiment management service (e.g., MLFlow)
- HPO engine (e.g., Optuna) running as a service integrated with experiment management (e.g., Kaen's `BaseOptunaService`)
- Experiment management user interface
- Worker management service for scheduling and orchestration of the machine learning pipeline child runs across the worker nodes

The worker node(s) host the Docker containers with the machine learning model (e.g., PyTorch code) along with the code describing how to train, validate, and test the machine learning model based on the hyperparameters (e.g., PyTorch Lightning code).

Note that the life cycle of the manager and worker nodes is different from the life cycle of the Docker container execution on the nodes. This means that the same nodes can host the execution of multiple container instances and multiple machine learning pipeline runs without having to be provisioned or de-provisioned. Also, while the containers on the management nodes are long running, for example to provide the experiment service user interface and hyperparameter optimization engine services across multiple machine learning pipeline executions, the containers on the worker nodes stay running only for the duration of the machine learning pipeline execution.

Although the deployment configuration described in this section may appear complex, provisioning of the nodes, machine learning middleware (experiment management, hyperparameter optimization, and so on), as well as the orchestration of the machine learning pipeline execution across the worker nodes, are handled entirely by the Kaen framework and associated Docker containers. You are going to learn more about the framework and how to build your machine learning pipeline on top of existing Kaen containers later in this chapter.

## 12.2 *Enabling PyTorch-distributed training support with Kaen*

This section illustrates how to add PyTorch-distributed training support using the PyTorch `DistributedDataParallel` class. By the conclusion of this section, the `train` method for the DC taxi fare model will be extended to integrate with the Kaen framework for distributed training in a cloud environment.

Unlike the code and Jupyter notebook instructions from the previous chapters of this book, the code in the remainder of this chapter requires that your environment has Docker and Kaen installed. You can find more about installing and getting started with Docker in appendix B. To install Kaen to an environment with an existing Docker installation, execute

```
pip install kaen[cli,docker]
```

which will download and install the kaen command line interface (CLI) in your shell environment. For example, if Kaen is installed correctly, you can get help about the Kaen commands using

```
kaen --help
```

which should produce an output resembling the following:

```
Usage: kaen [OPTIONS] COMMAND [ARGS]...

Options:
  --help  Show this message and exit.

Commands:
  dojo     Manage a dojo training environment.
  hpo      Manage hyperparameter optimization.
  init     Initialize a training dojo in a specified infrastructure...
  job      Manage jobs in a specific dojo training environment.
  jupyter  Work with a Jupyter notebook environment.
```

To execute the instructions in the remainder of this book, launch a Kaen Jupyter environment using

```
kaen jupyter
```

from your shell environment, which should launch a specialized Jupyter notebook environment as a new Docker container in your local Docker host. The kaen jupyter command should also navigate your default browser to the Jupyter home page and output text in the shell that resembles the following:

```
Started Jupyter. Attempting to navigate to Jupyter in your browser using
➡ http://127.0.0.1:8888/?token=...
```

which specifies the URL that you can use in your browser to open the newly launched Jupyter instance.

In the Jupyter environment, create and open a new notebook. For example, you can name the notebook ch12.ipynb. As the first step in the notebook, you should execute the shell command

```
!mkdir -p src
```

to create an src director for your code in this environment. Recall that when you use the exclamation sign ! in a Python code cell in Jupyter, the command that follows it is executed in the underlying bash shell. So, the result of running the code is to create an src directory in the filesystem.

Next, save the latest version of the DC taxi model (as described in the chapter 11) to a model_v1.py file in the src directory using the %%writefile magic.

**Listing 12.1   Saving the implementation to `model_v1.py`**

```
%%writefile src/model_v1.py
import sys
import json
import time
import torch as pt
import pytorch_lightning as pl
from distutils.util import strtobool

pt.set_default_dtype(pt.float64)
class DcTaxiModel(pl.LightningModule):
    def __init__(self, **kwargs):
        super().__init__()
        self.save_hyperparameters()
        pt.manual_seed(int(self.hparams.seed))

        self.step = 0
        self.start_ts = time.perf_counter()
        self.train_val_rmse = pt.tensor(0.)
```

```
#create a list of hidden layer neurons, e.g. [3, 5, 8]
num_hidden_neurons = json.loads(self.hparams.num_hidden_neurons)

self.layers = \
  pt.nn.Sequential(
    pt.nn.Linear(int(self.hparams.num_features),
                 num_hidden_neurons[0]),
    pt.nn.ReLU(),
    *self.build_hidden_layers(num_hidden_neurons, pt.nn.ReLU()),
    pt.nn.Linear(num_hidden_neurons[-1], 1)
)

if 'batch_norm_linear_layers' in self.hparams \
  and strtobool(self.hparams.batch_norm_linear_layers):
  self.layers = self.batch_norm_linear(self.layers)

def build_hidden_layers(self, num_hidden_neurons, activation):
  linear_layers = [ pt.nn.Linear(num_hidden_neurons[i],
    num_hidden_neurons[i+1]) \
      for i in range(len(num_hidden_neurons) - 1) ]

  classes = [activation.__class__] * len(num_hidden_neurons)

  activation_instances = list(map(lambda x: x(), classes))

  hidden_layer_activation_tuples = \
    list(zip(linear_layers, activation_instances))

  hidden_layers = [i for sublist in \
    hidden_layer_activation_tuples for i in sublist]

  return hidden_layers

def batch_norm_linear(self, layers):
  idx_linear = \
    list(filter(lambda x: type(x) is int,
        [idx if issubclass(layer.__class__, pt.nn.Linear) else None \
          for idx, layer in enumerate(layers)]))
  idx_linear.append(sys.maxsize)
  layer_lists = [list(iter(layers[s:e])) \
    for s, e in zip(idx_linear[:-1], idx_linear[1:])]
  batch_norm_layers = [pt.nn.BatchNorm1d(layer[0].in_features) \
    for layer in layer_lists]
  batch_normed_layer_lists = [ [bn, *layers] \
    for bn, layers in list(zip(batch_norm_layers, layer_lists)) ]
  return pt.nn.Sequential(*[layer \
    for nested_layer in batch_normed_layer_lists \
    for layer in nested_layer ])

def batchToXy(self, batch):
  batch = batch.squeeze_()
  X, y = batch[:, 1:], batch[:, 0]
  return X, y
```

```python
def forward(self, X):
  y_est = self.layers(X)
  return y_est.squeeze_()

def log(self, k, v, **kwargs):
    super().log(k, v,
            on_step = kwargs['on_step'],
            on_epoch = kwargs['on_epoch'],
            prog_bar = kwargs['prog_bar'],
            logger = kwargs['logger'],)


def training_step(self, batch, batch_idx):
    self.step += 1

    X, y = self.batchToXy(batch) #unpack batch into features and label

    y_est = self.forward(X)

    loss = pt.nn.functional.mse_loss(y_est, y)

    for k,v in {
      "train_step": self.step,
      "train_mse": loss.item(),
      "train_rmse": loss.sqrt().item(),
      "train_steps_per_sec": \
        self.step / (time.perf_counter() - self.start_ts),
    }.items():
      self.log(k, v, step = self.step, on_step=True, on_epoch=True,
                                    prog_bar=True, logger=True)

    self.train_val_rmse = loss.sqrt()

    return loss

def validation_step(self, batch, batch_idx):
  X, y = self.batchToXy(batch)

  with pt.no_grad():
      loss = pt.nn.functional.mse_loss(self.forward(X), y)

  for k,v in {
    "val_mse": loss.item(),
    "val_rmse": loss.sqrt().item(),
    "train_val_rmse": (self.train_val_rmse + loss.sqrt()).item(),
  }.items():
    self.log(k, v, step = self.step, on_step=True, on_epoch=True,
                                  prog_bar=True, logger=True)

  return loss

def test_step(self, batch, batch_idx):
  X, y = self.batchToXy(batch)
```

```
with pt.no_grad():
    loss = pt.nn.functional.mse_loss(self.forward(X), y)

for k,v in {
    "test_mse": loss.item(),
    "test_rmse": loss.sqrt().item(),
}.items():
    self.log(k, v, step = self.step, on_step=True, on_epoch=True,
                                prog_bar=True, logger=True)


def configure_optimizers(self):
    optimizers = {'Adam': pt.optim.AdamW,
                  'SGD': pt.optim.SGD}
    optimizer = optimizers[self.hparams.optimizer]

    return optimizer(self.layers.parameters(),
                     lr = float(self.hparams.lr))
```

Since the code in listing 12.1 saved version 1 of the DC taxi model to a file named model_v1.py, the entry point (in a trainer.py file of the src directory) to the process of building and testing this version of the model starts by loading the DC taxi model instance from the model_v1 package:

```
%%writefile src/trainer.py
from model_v1 import DcTaxiModel

import os
import time
import kaen
import torch as pt
import numpy as np
import pytorch_lightning as pl
import torch.distributed as dist
from torch.utils.data import DataLoader
from torch.nn.parallel import DistributedDataParallel

from kaen.torch import ObjectStorageDataset as osds

def train(model, train_glob, val_glob, test_glob = None):
    #set the pseudorandom number generator seed
    seed = int(model.hparams['seed']) \
                if 'seed' in model.hparams \
                else int( datetime.now().microsecond )      ◄─── Initialize the pseudorandom number seed using the hyperparameters or a current timestamp.

    np.random.seed(seed)
    pt.manual_seed(seed)

    kaen.torch.init_process_group(model.layers)      ◄─── Automatically update the DC taxi model to take advantage of multiple trainer nodes if available.

    trainer = pl.Trainer(gpus = pt.cuda.device_count() \
                             if pt.cuda.is_available() else 0,
        max_epochs = 1,
```

```
                limit_train_batches = int( model.hparams.max_batches ) \
                                      if 'max_batches' in model.hparams else 1,
                limit_val_batches = 1,
                num_sanity_val_steps = 1,
                val_check_interval = min(20, int( model.hparams.max_batches ) ),
                limit_test_batches = 1,
                log_every_n_steps = 1,
                gradient_clip_val=0.5,
                progress_bar_refresh_rate = 0,
                weights_summary = None,)

        train_dl = \
        DataLoader(osds(train_glob,
                        worker = kaen.torch.get_worker_rank(),
                        replicas = kaen.torch.get_num_replicas(),
                        shard_size = \
                          int(model.hparams.batch_size),
                        batch_size = \
                          int(model.hparams.batch_size),
                        storage_options = {'anon': False},
                        ),
                    pin_memory = True)


        val_dl = \
        DataLoader(osds(val_glob,
                        batch_size = int(model.hparams.batch_size),
                        storage_options = {'anon': False},
                        ),
                    pin_memory = True)


        trainer.fit(model,
                    train_dataloaders = train_dl,
                    val_dataloaders = val_dl)
        if test_glob is not None:
            test_dl = \
              DataLoader(osds(test_glob,
                            batch_size = int(model.hparams.batch_size),
                            storage_options = {'anon': False},
                            ),
                        pin_memory = True)


            trainer.test(model,
                        dataloaders=test_dl)


        return model, trainer


if __name__ == "__main__":
    model, trainer = train(DcTaxiModel(**{
            "seed": "1686523060",
            "num_features": "8",
            "num_hidden_neurons": "[3, 5, 8]",
            "batch_norm_linear_layers": "1",
            "optimizer": "Adam",
            "lr": "0.03",
```

**As described in chapter 8, in a distributed cluster the shard_size is often distinct from . . .**

**. . . the batch_size used to compute the gradients.**

```
            "max_batches": "1",
            "batch_size": str(2 ** 18),}),

      train_glob = \
        os.environ['KAEN_OSDS_TRAIN_GLOB'] \
          if 'KAEN_OSDS_TRAIN_GLOB' in os.environ \
          else 'https://raw.githubusercontent.com/osipov/smlbook/
                  master/train.csv',

      val_glob = \
        os.environ['KAEN_OSDS_VAL_GLOB'] \
          if 'KAEN_OSDS_VAL_GLOB' in os.environ \
          else 'https://raw.githubusercontent.com/osipov/smlbook/
                  master/valid.csv',

      test_glob = \
        os.environ['KAEN_OSDS_TEST_GLOB'] \
          if 'KAEN_OSDS_TEST_GLOB' in os.environ \
          else 'https://raw.githubusercontent.com/osipov/smlbook/
                  master/valid.csv')

    print(trainer.callback_metrics)
```

At this point you can unit test `trainer.py` by running the following from your shell environment.

**Listing 12.2  Run a simple test to confirm that the implementation works as expected.**

```
%%bash
python3 src/trainer.py
```

This should train, test, and report on the metrics of your model using a small sample of the DC taxi data.

### 12.2.1  Understanding PyTorch-distributed training settings

This section illustrates the configuration of the environment variables and related settings expected by PyTorch models when performing distributed training.

The distributed training approach for PyTorch models is surprisingly straightforward to enable. Although native PyTorch does not provide integration with cloud providers such as AWS, Azure, or GCP, the code in listing 12.3 illustrates how to use the Kaen framework (http://kaen.ai) to bridge PyTorch and PyTorch Lightning with distributed training in cloud providers.

The PyTorch-specific implementation used by the `kaen.torch.init_process_group` method enables distributed training for the DC taxi model, as specified by the model PyTorch Lightning module, where the PyTorch `torch.nn.Sequential` layers are stored in the `model.layers` attribute.

**Listing 12.3   Kaen framework configuring PyTorch model**

**Set PyTorch MASTER_ADDR to localhost address unless otherwise specified by Kaen.**

```
#pytorch distributed training requires MASTER_ADDR and MASTER_PORT to be set
os.environ['MASTER_ADDR'] = \
   os.environ['KAEN_JOB_MANAGER_IP'] \
    if 'KAEN_JOB_MANAGER_IP' in os.environ else "127.0.0.1"

MASTER_ADDR = os.environ['MASTER_ADDR']
os.environ['MASTER_PORT'] = \
   os.environ['MASTER_PORT'] if 'MASTER_PORT' in os.environ else "12355"
MASTER_PORT = os.environ['MASTER_PORT']

BACKEND = os.environ['KAEN_BACKEND'] \
                    if 'KAEN_BACKEND' in os.environ else "gloo"
RANK = int(os.environ['KAEN_RANK'])
WORLD_SIZE = int(os.environ['KAEN_WORLD_SIZE'])

if not dist.is_initialized():
    dist.init_process_group(init_method = "env://",
                            backend = BACKEND,
                            rank = RANK,
                            world_size = WORLD_SIZE)
     model.layers = \
        DistributedDataParallel(model.layers, device_ids=[])
```

**Set PyTorch MASTER_PORT to 12355 unless otherwise specified in the MASTER_PORT variable.**

**Initialize the distributed data parallel training rank . . .**

**. . . and the count of training nodes based on KAEN_RANK and KAEN_WORLD_SIZE variables.**

**Ensure that the distributed training process group is ready to train.**

**Use the CPU-based gloo backend unless otherwise specified by KAEN_BACKEND.**

**Enable distributed training for the model using DistributedDataParallel.**

When training a PyTorch model using the DistributedDataParallel implementation, there are several prerequisites that must be met before the training can start. First, the distributed training library must be configured with the MASTER_ADDR and MASTER_PORT environment variables for the model training manager node on the network. These values must be specified even when DistributedDataParallel is used in a scenario with a single node. In a single-node scenario, MASTER_ADDR and MASTER_PORT are initialized to the values 127.0.0.1 and 12355, respectively. When the distributed training cluster consists of more than a single node, MASTER_ADDR must correspond to the IP address of the manager node (node rank 0, per the description in chapter 11) in the distributed node in the cluster.

The Kaen framework can initialize the runtime environment of your model training environment with the runtime IP address for the manager node used for PyTorch training. Hence, in the example, MASTER_ADDR is initialized to the value of KAEN_JOB_MANAGER_IP if the latter environment variable is set by the Kaen framework and to 127.0.0.1 (for single-node training) otherwise. In the example, MASTER_PORT is initialized to 12355 by default unless a different value is preset before starting the training runtime.

Notice that the init_method parameter to the init_process_group method is hardcoded to env:// to ensure that the distributed training initialization happens according to the values of the MASTER_ADDR and MASTER_PORT environment variables described earlier. Although it is possible to use a file or a key/value store for initialization, the environment-based approach is demonstrated in this example because it is natively supported by the Kaen framework.

In addition to the initialization method, notice that init_process_group is invoked with the values for the BACKEND, WORKER, and REPLICAS settings. The BACKEND setting corresponds to the name of one of several distributed communication backend libraries supported by PyTorch. (The details of the features supported by the libraries are available here: https://pytorch.org/docs/stable/distributed.html.) gloo is used to enable distributed training over CPUs while nccl is used for GPU-based distributed training. Since CPU-based distributed training is easier, cheaper, and often faster to provision in cloud providers like AWS, this chapter focuses on CPU-based training first and then on how to introduce the changes needed to support GPU-based training.

The values for RANK and WORLD_SIZE needed to initialize distributed training are also provided by the Kaen framework. The WORLD_SIZE value corresponds to a natural count (i.e., starting with one) of the integer count of the nodes used in distributed training, while the RANK value corresponds to a zero-based integer index of the node executing the Python runtime training in the PyTorch model. Note that both RANK and WORLD_SIZE are initialized based on the Kaen's framework's environment variable settings. For example, if you instantiate a Kaen training environment with only a single training node, then KAEN_WORLD_SIZE is set to 1 while the RANK value of the single training node is set to 0. In contrast, for a distributed Kaen training environment consisting of 16 nodes, KAEN_WORLD_SIZE is initialized to 16 and each of the training nodes is assigned a RANK value in the range from [0, 15], in other words inclusive of both the start (0) index and the end (15) index.

Lastly, notice that the DistributedDataParallel training is initialized only once, after checking the is_initialized status. The initialization involves executing init_process_group using the backend, rank, and world_size settings described earlier in this section. Once the initialization completes (in other words, the init_process_group returns), the DistributedDataParallel instance is wrapped around the PyTorch nn.Module-based model instance, which is assigned to model.nn in the example. At this point, the model is ready to be trained by a distributed cluster.

## 12.3 *Unit testing model training in a local Kaen container*

This section describes how to unit test the model implementation in a local Kaen container prior to deploying the code to a cloud environment like AWS.

Although the code implementation supports distributed training, it can be tested without having to provision (and pay for) a distributed training environment in a cloud provider. You will start the unit test by downloading a Kaen-provided base container image provided for PyTorch models targeted at AWS.

Ensure that you can authenticate with DockerHub where you can download the base container image. Once you execute the following code snippet in your Kaen

Jupyter environment, you will be prompted to enter your DockerHub username, which is then stored in the DOCKER_HUB_USER Python variable:

```
DOCKER_HUB_USER = input()
DOCKER_HUB_USER
```

Next, enter the DockerHub password for your username when prompted. Notice that the password is cleared out from the DOCKER_HUB_PASSWORD variable after the authentication is finished:

```
import getpass
DOCKER_HUB_PASSWORD = getpass.getpass()

!echo "{DOCKER_HUB_PASSWORD}" | \
docker login --username {DOCKER_HUB_USER} --password-stdin

DOCKER_HUB_PASSWORD = None
```

You should see an output with the message Login Succeeded if you specified valid DockerHub credentials.

The base PyTorch Docker image is quite large, about 1.9 GB. The Kaen-based PyTorch image (kaenai/pytorch-mlflow-aws-base:latest), which adds binaries with support for AWS and MLFlow, is roughly 2 GB in size, so be prepared that the following download will take a few minutes, depending on the speed of your internet connection.

To execute the download, run

```
!docker pull kaenai/pytorch-mlflow-aws-base:latest
```

Once the download completes, you can package your source code to an image derived from kaenai/pytorch-mlflow-aws-base:latest using the following Docker-file. Notice that the file simply copies the Python source code to the /workspace directory of the image filesystem:

```
%%writefile Dockerfile
FROM kaenai/pytorch-mlflow-aws-base:latest
COPY *.py /workspace/
```

Since the source code files model_v1.py and trainer.py described earlier in this chapter were saved to an src directory, notice that the following command to build your Docker image uses the src/ directory as the root of the Docker image build process. To ensure that the image you build can be uploaded to DockerHub, the image is tagged using {DOCKER_HUB_USER} as a prefix:

```
!docker build -t {DOCKER_HUB_USER}/dctaxi:latest -f Dockerfile src/
```

After the `docker build` command is finished, you can run you newly created Docker container using

```
!docker run -it {DOCKER_HUB_USER}/dctaxi:latest \
"python /workspace/trainer.py"
```

which should produce an output identical to the output of listing 12.2. Why should you bother creating the Docker image? Recall that having the Docker image will simplify deployment and training of your model in the cloud provider environment such as AWS. How will the image be shared from your local environment to the cloud provider environment? In general, Docker images are shared using Docker Registry instances such as DockerHub.

To push (upload) your newly built image to DockerHub, execute

```
!docker push {DOCKER_HUB_USER}/dctaxi:latest
```

which should complete in just a few seconds since the `docker push` operation will need to push only the content of the source code (Python files) to DockerHub. The rest of your `dctaxi` image is mounted from the base `kaenai/pytorch-mlflow-aws-base:latest` image.

## 12.4 *Hyperparameter optimization with Optuna*

This section teaches about Optuna for HPO and how to use the Kaen framework to add support for HPO to the DC taxi fare estimation model.

Thus far, you have been unit testing your implementation using a static set of hyperparameter values for model training. Recall from chapter 11 that you can use Optuna to perform hyperparameter optimization (HPO) for your code.

Optuna is one of several HPO frameworks supported by Kaen. To incorporate support for HPO in distributed training, you need to use one of the Kaen-based Docker images that expose Optuna as a service to your code and implement a sub-classable Python class named `BaseOptunaService`. Recall from chapter 11 that hyperparameters in Optuna are specified using the trial API. The `BaseOptunaService` in Kaen provides access to the Optuna `trial` instance to subclasses of `BaseOptunaService`. For example:

```
import optuna
import numpy as np
from kaen.hpo.optuna import BaseOptunaService
class DcTaxiHpoService(BaseOptunaService):
  def hparams(self):
    trial = self._trial                          ◁──── The _trial attribute
                                                        references an Optuna
                                                        trial instance.
    #define hyperparameter
    return {                                      ◁──── The trial instance supports
        "seed": \                                        Optuna trial API methods
          trial.suggest_int('seed', 0, np.iinfo(np.int32).max)   such as suggest_int.
    }
```

Notice that there is a single hyperparameter requested from Optuna in the dictionary instance returned by the `hparams` method. The `suggest_int` method is one of several methods available from the Optuna trial API to obtain a value for a hyperparameter. (Other methods available from the trial interface are described here: https://optuna .readthedocs.io/en/stable/reference/generated/optuna.trial.Trial.html#.) In the example, the `suggest_int('seed', 0, np.iinfo(np.int32).max)` method specifies that Optuna should recommend values for the pseudorandom number seed generator from 0 up to and including the maximum positive 32-bit integer.

Recall that the training of the `DcTaxiModel` depends on additional hyperparameter values, including `optimizer`, `bins`, `lr` (the learning rate), `num_hidden_neurons`, `batch_size`, and `max_batches`. The implementation of these hyperparameters using the Optuna trial API was covered in chapter 11. To enable support for these hyperparameters in the implementation of the `DcTaxiHpoService` class, you need to expand the dictionary returned by the `hparams` method with the Optuna specification for the hyperparameter values that should be tried during HPO:

```
def hparams(self):
  trial = self._trial

  return {
    "seed": \
        trial.suggest_int('seed', 0, np.iinfo(np.int32).max - 1),

    "optimizer": \
        trial.suggest_categorical('optimizer', ['Adam']),

    "lr": \
        trial.suggest_loguniform('lr', 0.001, 0.1),

    "num_hidden_neurons": \
        [trial.suggest_categorical(f"num_hidden_layer_{layer}_neurons", \
            [7, 11, 13, 19, 23]) for layer in \
            range(trial.suggest_categorical('num_layers',
                                            [11, 13, 17, 19]))],

    "batch_size": \
        trial.suggest_categorical('batch_size',
                                    [2 ** i for i in range(16, 22)]),

    "max_batches": \
        trial.suggest_int('max_batches', 40, 400, log = True)
  }
```

In addition to a trial, Optuna uses a concept of a *study* (corresponding to an MLFlow parent run), which is a collection of trials. In the Kaen framework, Optuna studies are used to generate reports about the summary statistics of the trials and to generate reports in the form of custom visualizations of the completed trials.

To persist the summary statistics about the trials, you can use the `trials_dataframe` method of the Optuna study API, which returns a pandas DataFrame describing the completed trials along with summary statistics of the associated hyperparameter values. Notice that in the following example the data frame is persisted to an html file based on the name of the experiment:

```
def on_experiment_end(self, experiment, parent_run):
    study = self._study
    try:
      for key, fig in {
        "plot_param_importances": \
            optuna.visualization.plot_param_importances(study),

        "plot_parallel_coordinate_all": \
            optuna.visualization.plot_parallel_coordinate(study, \
                params=["max_batches",
                        "lr",
                        "num_hidden_layer_0_neurons",
                        "num_hidden_layer_1_neurons",
                        "num_hidden_layer_2_neurons"]),

        "plot_parallel_coordinate_l0_l1_l2": \
            optuna.visualization.plot_parallel_coordinate(study, \
                params=["num_hidden_layer_0_neurons",
                        "num_hidden_layer_1_neurons",
                        "num_hidden_layer_2_neurons"]),

        "plot_contour_max_batches_lr": \
            optuna.visualization.plot_contour(study, \
                params=["max_batches", "lr"]),
      }.items():
        fig.write_image(key + ".png")
        self.mlflow_client.log_artifact(run_id = parent_run.info.run_id,
                          local_path = key + ".png")

    except:
      print(f"Failed to correctly persist experiment
              visualization artifacts")
      import traceback
      traceback.print_exc()

    #log the dataframe with the study summary
    study.trials_dataframe().describe().to_html(experiment.name + ".html")
    self.mlflow_client.log_artifact(run_id = parent_run.info.run_id,
                      local_path = experiment.name + ".html")

    #log the best hyperparameters in the parent run
    self.mlflow_client.log_metric(parent_run.info.run_id,
                        "loss", study.best_value)
    for k, v in study.best_params.items():
      self.mlflow_client.log_param(parent_run.info.run_id, k, v)
```

In the example, the calls to the Optuna APIs are executed in the content of the on_experiment_end method, which is, unsurprisingly, invoked by the BaseOptunaService base class after the conclusion of the experiment. After persisting the html file with the summary statistics of the experiment, the remainder of the method's implementation generates and persists visualizations of the study using the Optuna visualization package (http://mng.bz/4Kxw). Notice that for each visualization the corresponding image is persisted to a png file.

The `mlflow_client` in the code acts as a generic reference to the MLFlow Client API (http://mng.bz/QqjG), enabling reads from and writes to MLFlow as well as to monitoring the progress of the experiment. The `parent_run` variable is a reference to the "parent" run, or, in other words, a collection of trials or executions of the experiment with specific configuration of hyperparameter values suggested by the Optuna HPO service.

The entire HPO implementation described in this chapter is shown in the following code snippet. Notice that the snippet saves the implementation source code as an hpo.py file in your `src` folder:

```
%%writefile src/hpo.py
import optuna
import numpy as np
from kaen.hpo.optuna import BaseOptunaService

class DcTaxiHpoService(BaseOptunaService):
  def hparams(self):
    trial = self._trial

    #define hyperparameters
    return {
      "seed": trial.suggest_int('seed', 0, np.iinfo(np.int32).max - 1),
      "optimizer": trial.suggest_categorical('optimizer', ['Adam']),
      "lr": trial.suggest_loguniform('lr', 0.001, 0.1),
      "num_hidden_neurons": \
        [trial.suggest_categorical(f"num_hidden_layer_{layer}_neurons",
          [7, 11, 13, 19, 23]) for layer in \
            range(trial.suggest_categorical('num_layers',
                                        [11, 13, 17, 19]))],

      "batch_size": \
        trial.suggest_categorical('batch_size', \
                              [2 ** i for i in range(16, 22)]),

      "max_batches": trial.suggest_int('max_batches', 40, 400, log = True)
    }

  def on_experiment_end(self, experiment, parent_run):
    study = self._study
    try:
      for key, fig in {
        "plot_param_importances": \
          optuna.visualization.plot_param_importances(study),
        "plot_parallel_coordinate_all": \
          optuna.visualization.plot_parallel_coordinate(study,
            params=["max_batches",
                    "lr",
                    "num_hidden_layer_0_neurons",
```

```
                "num_hidden_layer_1_neurons",
                "num_hidden_layer_2_neurons"]),
        "plot_parallel_coordinate_10_11_12": \
          optuna.visualization.plot_parallel_coordinate(study,
            params=["num_hidden_layer_0_neurons",
            "num_hidden_layer_1_neurons",
            "num_hidden_layer_2_neurons"]),

        "plot_contour_max_batches_lr": \
          optuna.visualization.plot_contour(study,
            params=["max_batches", "lr"]),
      }.items():
        fig.write_image(key + ".png")
        self.mlflow_client.log_artifact(run_id = parent_run.info.run_id,
                          local_path = key + ".png")

    except:
      print(f"Failed to correctly persist experiment
              visualization artifacts")
      import traceback
      traceback.print_exc()

    #log the dataframe with the study summary
    study.trials_dataframe().describe().to_html(experiment.name + ".html")
    self.mlflow_client.log_artifact(run_id = parent_run.info.run_id,
                      local_path = experiment.name + ".html")

    #log the best hyperparameters in the parent run
    self.mlflow_client.log_metric(parent_run.info.run_id,
                                "loss", study.best_value)
    for k, v in study.best_params.items():
      self.mlflow_client.log_param(parent_run.info.run_id, k, v)
```

With the source code in place, you are ready to package it as a Docker container. Start by pulling a base Kaen container for Optuna and MLFlow:

```
!docker pull kaenai/optuna-mlflow-hpo-base:latest
```

Once that's finished, create a Dockerfile for a derived image using

```
%%writefile Dockerfile
FROM kaenai/optuna-mlflow-hpo-base:latest
ENV KAEN_HPO_SERVICE_PREFIX=hpo \
    KAEN_HPO_SERVICE_NAME=DcTaxiHpoService

COPY hpo.py /workspace/.
```

Notice that the package prefix for your DcTaxiHpoService implementation corresponds to the filename hpo.py, as specified by the KAEN_HPO_SERVICE_NAME and the KAEN_HPO_SERVICE_PREFIX environment variables, respectively. Once the Dockerfile is saved, build the image by running

```
!docker build -t {DOCKER_HUB_USER}/dctaxi-hpo:latest -f Dockerfile src/
```

and push it to DockerHub using

```
!docker push {DOCKER_HUB_USER}/dctaxi-hpo:latest.
```

### 12.4.1 Enabling MLFlow support

This section describes how to add integration between your DcTaxiModel and the MLFlow framework in order to manage and track HPO experiments.

Although the base kaenai/pytorch-mlflow-aws-base:latest image includes support for MLFlow, the implementation of training in trainer.py does not take advantage of MLFlow experiment management and tracking. Since MLFlow uses the concept of an experiment to organize a collection of HPO trials and run, Kaen provides a BaseMLFlowClient class, which can be used to implement an MLFlow-managed experiment for DcTaxiModel. The subclasses of BaseMLFlowClient are responsible for instantiating the untrained PyTorch model instances using the hyperparameter values that BaseMLFlowClient fetches from MLFlow and Optuna.

Start by saving an instance of your BaseMLFlowClient subclass named DcTaxi-Experiment by running the following in your Kaen Jupyter environment:

```
%%writefile src/experiment.py
import os
from model_v1 import DcTaxiModel
from trainer import train
from kaen.hpo.client import BaseMLFlowClient

class DcTaxiExperiment(BaseMLFlowClient):

    def on_run_start(self, run_idx, run):
        print(f"{run}({run.info.status}): starting...")

        #create a set of default hyperparameters
        default_hparams = {"seed": "1686523060",
                        "num_features": "8",
                        "num_hidden_neurons": "[3, 5, 8]",
                        "batch_norm_linear_layers": "1",
                        "optimizer": "Adam",
                        "lr": "0.03",
                        "max_batches": "1",
                        "batch_size": str(2 ** 18),}

        #fetch the MLFlow hyperparameters if available
        hparams = run.data.params if run is not None \
                and run.data is not None else \
                default_hparams

        #override the defaults with the MLFlow hyperparameters
        hparams = {**default_hparams, **hparams}

        untrained_model = DcTaxiModel(**hparams)
        def log(self, k, v, **kwargs):
            if self.mlflow_client and 0 == int(os.environ['KAEN_RANK']):
```

```
          if 'step' in kwargs and kwargs['step'] is not None:
              self.mlflow_client.log_metric(run.info.run_id,
                  k, v, step = kwargs['step'])
          else:
              self.mlflow_client.log_metric(run.info.run_id,
                  k, v)

      import types
      untrained_model.log = types.MethodType(log, self)

      model, trainer = \
        train(untrained_model,
              train_glob = os.environ['KAEN_OSDS_TRAIN_GLOB'],
              val_glob = os.environ['KAEN_OSDS_VAL_GLOB'],
              test_glob = os.environ['KAEN_OSDS_TEST_GLOB'])

      print(trainer.callback_metrics)
```

This saves the code to train your model to the src/experiment.py file.

With the experiment support in place, you are ready to build the updated dctaxi image using

```
%%writefile Dockerfile
FROM kaenai/pytorch-mlflow-aws-base:latest
COPY * /workspace/
ENV KAEN_HPO_CLIENT_PREFIX=experiment \
    KAEN_HPO_CLIENT_NAME=DcTaxiExperiment
```

which specifies a new entry point into the image using experiment.DcTaxiExperiment from experiment.py by changing the default values of the KAEN_HPO_CLIENT_PREFIX and the KAEN_HPO_CLIENT_NAME environment variables.

As previously, build your dctaxi image using

```
!docker build -t {DOCKER_HUB_USER}/dctaxi:latest -f Dockerfile src/
```

and push it to DockerHub using

```
!docker push {DOCKER_HUB_USER}/dctaxi:latest.
```

### 12.4.2 *Using HPO for DcTaxiModel in a local Kaen provider*

At this point, you are prepared to build a Docker container capable of suggesting hyperparameter optimization trials and managing the associated experimental runs of the trials. In the container, the hyperparameter values are suggested by Optuna, and the experiments based on the values are managed by MLFlow.

Before provisioning the more expensive cloud provider, it is a good idea to start by provisioning a local Kaen provider so that you can unit test your HPO and model training code. You can create a Kaen training *dojo* by executing

```
!kaen dojo init --provider local
```

which should return an alphanumeric identifier for the newly created Kaen dojo.

You can list available Kaen dojos in your workspace using

```
!kaen dojo ls
```

which should print out the ID of the dojo you just created.

You will want the identifier of the dojo saved as a Python variable for future use, and you can do so using the Jupyter syntax for assignment of bash scripts to Python variables as follows:

```
[MOST_RECENT_DOJO] = !kaen dojo ls | head -n 1
MOST_RECENT_DOJO
```

Before a Kaen dojo can be used for training, it should be activated. Activate the dojo specified by the identifier in the MOST_RECENT_DOJO variable by running

```
!kaen dojo activate {MOST_RECENT_DOJO}
```

Since the Jupyter ! shell shortcut provides access to Python variables, in the previous code snippet the {MOST_RECENT_DOJO} syntax is replaced with the value of the corresponding Python variable. You can confirm that the dojo is active by inspecting it using

```
!kaen dojo inspect {MOST_RECENT_DOJO}
```

which should include an output line with KAEN_DOJO_STATUS=active.

Before you can start a training job in the dojo, you need to create one specifying both the dojo and the Kaen image for training.

To create a job to train the DcTaxiModel, execute

```
!kaen job create --dojo {MOST_RECENT_DOJO} \
--image {DOCKER_HUB_USER}/dctaxi:latest
```

which will attempt to pull the specified image from DockerHub and if successful will return the alphanumeric identifier for the job.

Just as with the dojo, you can save the identifier of the job to a Python variable using

```
[MOST_RECENT_JOB] = !kaen job ls | head -n 1
MOST_RECENT_JOB
```

which should print out the identifier of the job you created.

Every job in Kaen is configured with dedicated networking settings you can inspect by running

```
!kaen job inspect {MOST_RECENT_JOB}
```

Since you have not yet enabled HPO for this job, the inspected job settings do not include the information about the HPO image used to serve MLFlow experiment management and Optuna hyperparameter values. You can configure the job with a single run of HPO by executing

```
!kaen hpo enable \
--image {DOCKER_HUB_USER}/dctaxi-hpo:latest \
--num-runs 1 \
--service-prefix hpo \
--service-name DcTaxiHpoService \
--port 5001 5001 \
{MOST_RECENT_JOB}
```

which overrides the default settings of your `dctaxi-hpo` image to specify that the `hpo.DcTaxiHpoService` class should be used to start the HPO service. The executed statement also configures the MLFlow UI port `5001` using the `--port` setting.

Assuming the `hpo enable` command completes successfully, you can inspect the job again to observe the HPO-specific settings:

```
!kaen job inspect {MOST_RECENT_JOB}
```

Notice that at this time the output includes the `KAEN_HPO_MANAGER_IP` for the IP address of the internal Docker network (specified by `KAEN_JOB_SUBNET`) that handles the communication across your container instances.

At this time, the HPO service should be up and running, so you should be able to access the MLFlow user interface by navigating your browser to http://127.0.0.1:5001, which should show a screen similar to the one in figure 12.4. Note that you need to

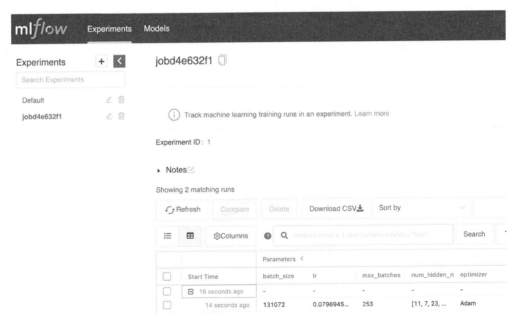

**Figure 12.4** Screen capture of the MLFlow browser-based interface illustrating the parent run and the sole child run for the experiment instance

open the MLFlow experiment that starts with a `job` prefix on the left-side bar of the MLFlow interface before you can explore the details of the HPO experiment.

Since at this point you have just started the HPO service, your experiment consists of just a single parent run with a single child run. The parent or main run has a one-to-one relationship with the MLFlow experiment and contains the individual child runs that define specific hyperparameter configurations that should be used by the machine learning pipeline execution instances. If you navigate to the child run in the MLFlow user interface, you should see a screen resembling the screenshot in figure 12.5.

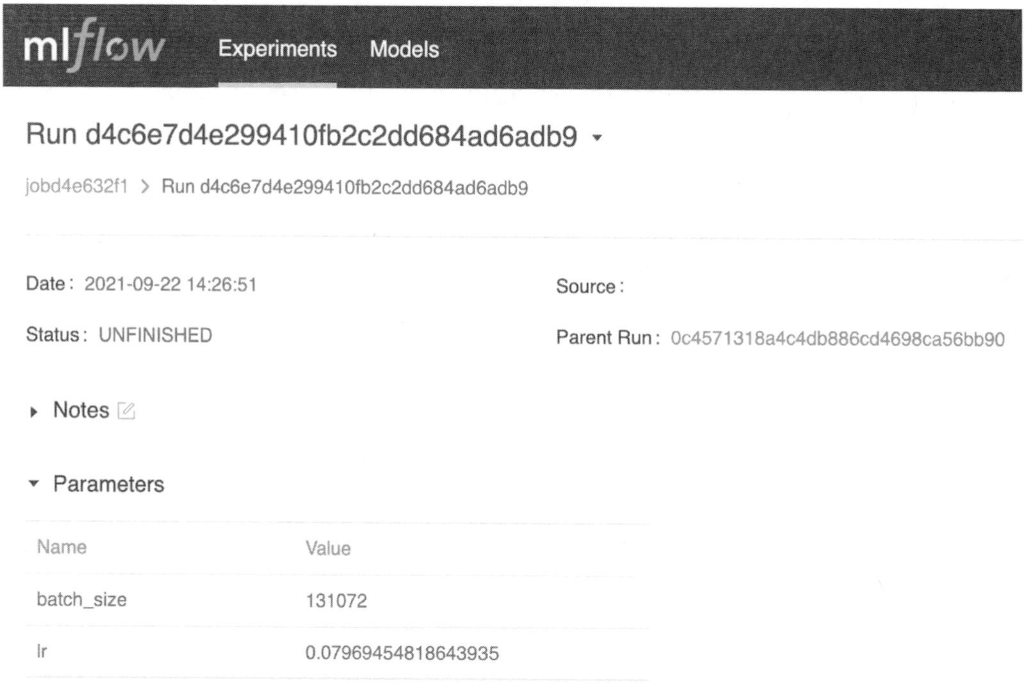

**mlflow**    Experiments    Models

## Run d4c6e7d4e299410fb2c2dd684ad6adb9 ▾

jobd4e632f1  >  Run d4c6e7d4e299410fb2c2dd684ad6adb9

Date : 2021-09-22 14:26:51

Status : UNFINISHED

Source :

Parent Run : 0c4571318a4c4db886cd4698ca56bb90

▸ Notes ☑

▾ Parameters

| Name | Value |
| --- | --- |
| batch_size | 131072 |
| lr | 0.07969454818643935 |

**Figure 12.5   MLFlow screen capture of the settings suggested by Optuna HPO for the child run**

To start training your model in the local provider using the data available in your AWS bucket, you need to configure environment variables with your AWS credentials. In the following code snippet, replace the Python `None` with your matching AWS credentials for `AWS_ACCESS_KEY_ID`, `AWS_SECRET_ACCESS_KEY`, and `AWS_DEFAULT_REGION`. Also, perform the same replacement for your `BUCKET_ID` value and execute the code to configure the corresponding environment variables in your Kaen Jupyter environment:

```
import os
os.environ['MOST_RECENT_JOB'] = MOST_RECENT_JOB
```

```
os.environ['BUCKET_ID'] = None
os.environ['AWS_ACCESS_KEY_ID'] = None
os.environ['AWS_SECRET_ACCESS_KEY'] = None
os.environ['AWS_DEFAULT_REGION'] = None
```

I recommend that you execute the following sequence of echo commands from your bash shell to ensure that all of the environment variables are configured as expected:

```
%%bash
echo $BUCKET_ID
echo $AWS_ACCESS_KEY_ID
echo $AWS_SECRET_ACCESS_KEY
echo $AWS_DEFAULT_REGION
echo $MOST_RECENT_JOB
```

Now you are ready to start training your model by running kaen job start. For simplicity, start by training with a single training worker (as specified by --replicas 1). Notice that the KAEN_OSDS environment variables in the command are pointing to your data CSV files in the AWS bucket:

```
!kaen job start \
--replicas 1 \
-e KAEN_HPO_JOB_RUNS 1 \
-e AWS_DEFAULT_REGION $AWS_DEFAULT_REGION \
-e AWS_ACCESS_KEY_ID $AWS_ACCESS_KEY_ID \
-e AWS_SECRET_ACCESS_KEY $AWS_SECRET_ACCESS_KEY \
-e KAEN_OSDS_TRAIN_GLOB "s3://dc-taxi-$BUCKET_ID-
➥ $AWS_DEFAULT_REGION/csv/dev/part*.csv" \
-e KAEN_OSDS_VAL_GLOB "s3://dc-taxi-$BUCKET_ID-
➥ $AWS_DEFAULT_REGION/csv/test/part*.csv" \
-e KAEN_OSDS_TEST_GLOB "s3://dc-taxi-$BUCKET_ID-
➥ $AWS_DEFAULT_REGION/csv/test/part*.csv" \
$MOST_RECENT_JOB
```

While the training job is running, you should be able to navigate to the details of the child run in the MLFlow user interface, and assuming that your training process ran for at least 25 training steps, the resulting graph for the train_rmse metric should resemble the one in figure 12.6.

### 12.4.3  *Training with the Kaen AWS provider*

This section illustrates how to use the Kaen framework to train your containers in an AWS virtual private cloud environment instead of your local provider so you can take advantage of the elastic, horizontal scaling available in AWS.

To create a Kaen dojo in AWS, you need to use the --provider aws setting when running kaen init. By default, when using the AWS provider, Kaen provisions t3.micro instances as both worker and manager nodes in AWS. Although the t3.micro instances

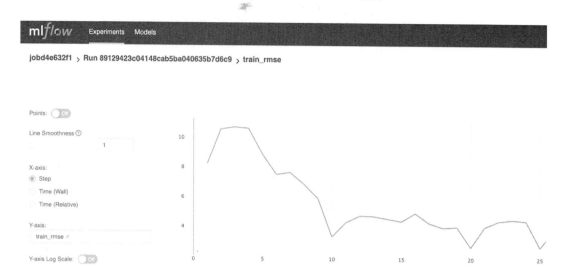

**Figure 12.6  MLFlow screen capture of the graph for the `train_rmse` metric**

are low-cost defaults suitable for simple demos, for the DcTaxiModel, I recommend provisioning t3.large instances as follows:

```
!kaen dojo init --provider aws \
--worker-instance-type t3.xlarge --manager-instance-type t3.xlarge
```

This, upon a successful provisioning, should report the dojo ID.

To configure the MOST_RECENT_DOJO Python variable, you should execute

```
[MOST_RECENT_DOJO] = !kaen dojo ls | head -n 1
MOST_RECENT_DOJO
```

and then activate the dojo using

```
!kaen dojo activate {MOST_RECENT_DOJO}
```

Notice that if you provision underpowered AWS node instances (such as t3.micro), the activation process could take a while. Once the activation is finished correctly, you should be able to inspect the Dojo using

```
!kaen dojo inspect {MOST_RECENT_DOJO}
```

and the output should include a line that starts with KAEN_DOJO_STATUS=active and the timestamp of when the activation completed.

Just as with a local provider, to perform training in AWS, you should start by creating a job:

```
!kaen job create --dojo {MOST_RECENT_DOJO} \
--image {DOCKER_HUB_USER}/dctaxi:latest
```

Unlike the case of the local provider, running `kaen job create` in the AWS provider may take a while. This is caused by the fact that the `dctaxi` image that you pushed to DockerHub needs to be downloaded to the AWS node in your dojo. After the job is created, you should save the ID of the job to the `MOST_RECENT_JOB` Python variable using

```
[MOST_RECENT_JOB] = !kaen job ls | head -n 1
os.environ['MOST_RECENT_JOB'] = MOST_RECENT_JOB
MOST_RECENT_JOB
```

which also sets the `MOST_RECENT_JOB` environment variable to the value matching the corresponding Python variable.

Next, enable HPO for the job using the following:

```
!kaen hpo enable \
--num-runs 1 \
--image {DOCKER_HUB_USER}/dctaxi-hpo:latest \
--service-prefix hpo \
--service-name DcTaxiHpoService \
--port 5001 5001 \
{MOST_RECENT_JOB}
```

Once the `kaen hpo enable` operation is finished, you can open the MLFlow user interface by constructing the URL in your notebook using

```
!echo "http://$(kaen dojo inspect {MOST_RECENT_DOJO} \
| grep KAEN_DOJO_MANAGER_IP | cut -d '=' -f 2):5001"
```

and navigating to the URL in your browser. Since it may take a few seconds for the MLFlow UI to become available (depending on the performance of your AWS management node instances), you may need to refresh your browser to get access to this interface.

To start the training, the `kaen job start` command is identical to the one you used before:

```
!kaen job start \
--replicas 1 \
-e AWS_DEFAULT_REGION $AWS_DEFAULT_REGION \
-e AWS_ACCESS_KEY_ID $AWS_ACCESS_KEY_ID \
-e AWS_SECRET_ACCESS_KEY $AWS_SECRET_ACCESS_KEY \
-e KAEN_OSDS_TRAIN_GLOB "s3://dc-taxi-$BUCKET_ID-
⇒ $AWS_DEFAULT_REGION/csv/dev/part*.csv" \
-e KAEN_OSDS_VAL_GLOB "s3://dc-taxi-$BUCKET_ID-
⇒ $AWS_DEFAULT_REGION/csv/test/part*.csv" \
-e KAEN_OSDS_TEST_GLOB "s3://dc-taxi-$BUCKET_ID-
⇒ $AWS_DEFAULT_REGION/csv/test/part*.csv" \
$MOST_RECENT_JOB
```

As in the case with the local provider, you can navigate your browser to the MLFlow UI and monitor the metrics as the model trains.

When you are done, do not forget to remove the AWS training dojo using

```
!kaen dojo rm {MOST_RECENT_DOJO}.
```

## Summary

- Experiment management and hyperparameter optimization are integral phases of a machine learning pipeline.
- Docker containers facilitate packaging, deployment, and integration of machine learning code with the machine learning pipeline services.
- Training a machine learning model translates to numerous experiments executed as instances of machine learning pipeline runs.

# *appendix A*
# *Introduction to*
# *machine learning*

When discussing machine learning with newcomers to the field, I find that many have picked up on the basics but found the quantity of information about the topic and the depth of the mathematics intimidating. I remember that when I was just starting out with machine learning, I had a similar experience: it felt like there was just too much to learn. This appendix is designed for those who may have attempted to understand machine learning from a patchwork of tutorials or a few online courses. In the appendix, I organize basic machine learning concepts into a big picture and explain how the concepts fit together so that you have enough of a review of the basics to attempt the project in this book. Whenever possible I am going to present machine learning concepts intuitively, keeping mathematical notation to a minimum. My goal is not to replace comprehensive coursework on machine learning or deep-dive blog posts; instead, I'd like to show you the most important, most salient parts of machine learning needed for practical applications.

Novice students of machine learning often start their educational journey with in-depth study of machine learning algorithms. This is a mistake. Machine learning algorithms enable solutions to problems, and the full understanding of the problems that are suitable for machine learning should come first. As a machine learning practitioner (e.g., as a machine learning engineer or a data scientist), you are going to be expected to understand your customer's business problem and decide whether it can be recast as a machine learning problem. So, section A.1 through section A.3 introduce you to the fundamentals of machine learning and cover the most common machine learning use cases for structured data sets. Starting with section A.4 and through the conclusion of this appendix, I introduce you to the machine learning algorithms that can be used to solve machine learning problems as well as to the details about how to apply the algorithms.

## A.1    *Why machine learning?*

If you are reading this book, chances are that you are at least willing to consider machine learning as a topic of study or perhaps even as a solution to your problem. However, is machine learning the right technology for you to study or to use? When does applying machine learning make sense? Even if you are interested in machine learning you may find the barrier to entry (which is substantial) intimidating and decide against putting in the effort needed to understand machine learning in enough depth to apply the technology. In the past, numerous technologies came to market claiming to "change everything" but failed to deliver on the promise. Is machine learning destined to capture the headlines for a few years and then fade away into obscurity? Or is there something different about machine learning?

On the surface, machine learning can appear quite ordinary to the users of contemporary computer software and hardware. Machine learning depends on human beings who write code, and the code in turn depends on information technology resources such as compute, storage, networking, as well as the input and output interfaces. However, to gain a perspective on the magnitude of the change brought by machine learning to the field of computing, it is useful to revisit the time computing went through a transformation at a similar scale.

You may find it surprising to read in a machine learning book about a 1940s "computer" for mathematical computations. That is, if you don't know that prior to the invention and a broad adoption of electronic and digital computers in the 1950s, the term *computer* was used to describe a human being who performed mathematical computations, often in concert with a group of other "computers." A photograph of a computer team from 1949 is shown in figure A.1.

At its core, computing is about programs (algorithms) that use data to answer questions. Prior to the broad deployment of digital computers in the 1950–60s, computers (the human beings) played key roles in answering computational questions. For assistance in this job, the human computers often relied on external computing tools that ranged from pen and paper to early calculators or punch card-based tabulating machines. In this paradigm of computing, the computing instructions, the program describing how to compute, remained in the human computers' minds (left side of figure A.2).

The modern computers transformed this computing paradigm by changing the role of the human beings in relation to the computing devices. Instead of storing the program with the computing instructions in the human mind, human programmers took on the job of entering the programs into the memory of the computing devices in the form of code, or machine-readable instructions for how to compute (right side of figure A.2).

**Figure A.1** An office of human computers at work in the Dryden Flight Research Center Facilities during the summer of 1949. (This photograph is in the public domain; more information is available from http://mng.bz/XrBv.)

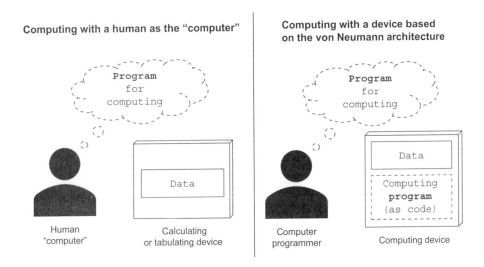

**Figure A.2** Human computers relied on devices to store the data used in computing. The devices ranged from pen and paper to electro-mechanical calculators and even punch card–based tabulating machines. However, none of these had an internal memory, which was used for the storage and execution of computing instructions, in other words, the program code (left side of the figure). In contrast, the von Neumann architecture for computing, which used computer device memory for both the data and the computer instructions, created a transformative practice of computer programming: the transfer of instructions for how to compute (the program) to the memory of the computing device for storage and execution (right side of the figure).

The von Neumann architecture changed the global economy at a scale comparable to the transformations brought about by the Industrial Revolution. Nearly every contemporary computing device on the planet, from pocket-sized mobile phones to massive servers powering cloud-computing data centers, uses the von Neumann architecture. The field of artificial intelligence became possible once computation transitioned away from the paradigm, where instructions for computing were stored in the biological minds of human computers.

The von Neumann computing paradigm also produced notable breakthroughs for the field of artificial intelligence; for example, DeepBlue, the first chess program to defeat the human chess champion Garry Kasparov, was built by IBM based on the paradigm. Despite this and many other successes, the hard-crafted programs produced by human programmers proved too simplistic for many subfields of artificial intelligence, including computer vision, speech recognition, natural language understanding, and many others. The code programmed by humans to perform tasks such as classifying objects in digital images or recognizing speech ended up too inaccurate and too brittle for broad adoption.

Contemporary machine learning is changing the relationship of the programmer to the modern computing devices at a level that is as fundamental as the transformation that happened with computing in the 1950s. Instead of programming a computer, a machine learning practitioner trains a machine learning system (using a machine learning algorithm) with bespoke data sets to produce a machine learning model (figure A.3). Since a machine learning model is just computer code, a machine learning algorithm can empower a machine learning practitioner with the ability to produce code capable of computing answers to questions that are beyond the capacity of human-generated programs. For instance, in the 2010s machine learning models were used to classify images with superhuman performance, recognize human speech so effectively that many households installed speech-recognizing digital assistants (such

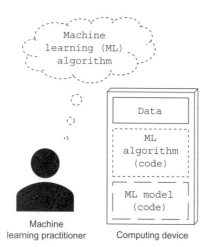

Machine learning practitioner    Computing device

Figure A.3  Machine learning relies on a machine learning practitioner who uses a machine learning algorithm to "train" a machine learning model based on a bespoke data set. Although a trained machine learning model is just code created by the machine learning algorithm, the model can answer questions that are too complex for a human to manually program as code. For example, machine learning models can classify objects in digital images or recognize human speech in digital audio better than handcrafted code developed by human programmers.

as Amazon Alexa and Google Home), and defeat Lee Sedol, the human champion at the ancient board game of Go.

This appendix introduces machine learning as a subfield of computer science focused on using computers to learn from data. Although this definition is accurate, it does not fully communicate the importance and the lasting effect of machine learning on transforming the field of computing. At the other end of the spectrum, marketing slogans about machine learning as "the new electricity" or the enabler of artificial general intelligence sensationalize and obfuscate the field. It is clear that machine learning is changing the parts of the computing architecture that remained fundamentally static from the 1950s to 2010s. The extent to which machine learning will transform computing is unclear. I hope you find the uncertainty and the potential role that you can play in this transformation as exciting as I do!

## A.2 *Machine learning at first glance*

This section introduces you to the changes brought to traditional computer science by the machine learning algorithms, illustrates machine learning with an easy-to-understand example, and describes how to implement the machine learning example using the Python programming language and the pandas, Numpy, and scikit-learn libraries. By the conclusion of this section you should be prepared to explain basic machine learning concepts and use the concepts with simple machine learning examples.

Before the advent of machine learning, the traditional computer science algorithms[1] had focused on computing answers on the basis of what is known: the data. Machine learning expanded the field of computer science with algorithms that use data to compute answers to questions on the basis of what is possible but is not known: the uncertain.

To illustrate the essence of the change machine learning brought to computer science, suppose you are working with the following easy-to-understand data set describing Ford Mustangs manufactured from 1971 through 1982 and their fuel efficiency[2] in terms of miles per gallon (mpg) fuel consumption. With the Python programming language and the pandas library for structured data,[3] you can prepare this data set for analysis by instantiating it in the computer memory as a pandas data structure called a DataFrame.

---

[1] A comprehensive review of the traditional computer science algorithms is available from Donald E. Knuth in his seminal work *The Art of Computer Programming* (Addison-Wesley Professional, 2011).

[2] The values are based on a data set from the publicly available University of California Irvine Machine Learning Repository https://archive.ics.uci.edu/ml/datasets/Auto+MPG

[3] Also known as panel or tabular data, structured data sets are based on values organized into rows and columns

Listing A.1  Creating a data set in memory as a pandas DataFrame to be ready for analysis

**Import the pandas library**
**and give it the alias pd.**

```
import pandas as pd        ◁            Import the NumPy library
import numpy as np         ◁            and give it the alias np.
df = \
        pd.DataFrame([{"mpg": 18, "model year": 1971, "weight": 3139},
                      {"mpg": 13, "model year": 1975, "weight": 3169},
                      {"mpg": 25.5, "model year": 1977, "weight": 2755},
                      {"mpg": 23.6, "model year": 1980, "weight": 2905},
                      {"mpg": 27, "model year": 1982, "weight": 2790}])
print(df.to_string(index=False))     ◁
```

**The pandas DataFrame for storing and managing**
**structured data can be constructed from a list of**
**Python dictionaries such that each row is specified**
**using a dictionary instance with the data frame**
**column names as the keys and the rows'**
**contents as the dictionary values.**

**To avoid printing the default,**
**zero-based index for each row,**
**df.to_string(index=False) is**
**used instead of print(df).**

This produces the output, shown as a table on the left side of figure A.4.

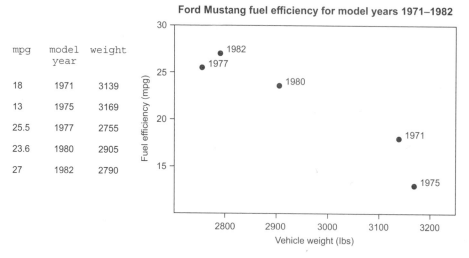

| mpg | model year | weight |
|-----|------------|--------|
| 18 | 1971 | 3139 |
| 13 | 1975 | 3169 |
| 25.5 | 1977 | 2755 |
| 23.6 | 1980 | 2905 |
| 27 | 1982 | 2790 |

Figure A.4  Ford Mustang fuel efficiency data set (left) and the corresponding scatter plot (right) based on the same data set. (This publicly available data set is sourced from University of California Irvine Machine Learning Repository: https://archive.ics.uci.edu/ml/datasets/Auto+MPG.)

It should come as no surprise that well-known computer science algorithms and data structures (e.g., a hash table) can be used to answer questions about what is known from this data set, such as the mpg efficiency of a Ford Mustang with a weight of 2,905 pounds. With pandas this question can be answered using

```
df[ df['weight'] == 2905 ]['mpg'].values
```

which outputs a NumPy[4] array with a single element corresponding to the value of the mpg column and the fourth row of the data set from listing A.1:

```
array([23.6])
```

### pandas DataFrame

pandas is used throughout this appendix to illustrate common operations on machine learning data sets. While a pandas DataFrame is an easy-to-learn and easy-to-use data structure, it does not scale to data sets that do not fit into the memory of a single node (a computer on a network). Further, pandas was not designed for data analysis with distributed computing clusters like those that are available in cloud computing environments from major cloud providers. This appendix will continue using pandas DataFrames to introduce machine learning; however, the rest of the book focuses on SQL tables and PySpark DataFrames that scale to much larger data sets than pandas. Many concepts about pandas DataFrames apply directly to PySpark and SQL. For example, the descriptions of structured data sets and supervised machine learning in section A.3 apply to data sets regardless of whether they are managed using pandas, PySpark, or SQL.

What about the fuel efficiency of a 3,000-pound Ford Mustang? Answering this question was outside the scope of the traditional computer science algorithms prior to the advent of machine learning.

Nonetheless, as a human being, you can observe the data set (the right side of figure A.4) and notice a *pattern* (a recurring rule) across the related Ford Mustangs described by the data set: as the weight of the vehicles increases, their fuel efficiency decreases. If asked to estimate fuel effiency of a 3,000-pound Ford Mustang (which is not specified by the data set), you can apply your mental model of the pattern to estimate an answer of roughly 20 miles per gallon.

Given the right machine learning algorithm, a computer can learn a software-based model (known as a machine learning model, to be defined more precisely in section A.3) of the data set, such that the learned (also known as trained) model can output estimates much like the mental model you intuited to estimate the fuel efficiency of the 3,000-pound Ford Mustang.

scikit-learn, a popular machine learning library,[5] includes a variety of ready-to-use machine learning algorithms, including several that can construct a machine learning model of the pattern you have observed in the data set. The steps to create the model

---

[4] NumPy is a Python library for high-performance numerical computing. pandas wraps the NumPy library and uses it for high-performance data analysis.

[5] scikit-learn (scikit-learn.org) was designed for machine learning with in-memory data sets as is used here to illustrate machine learning with a simple example. Machine learning with out-of-memory data sets using cloud computing requires other frameworks.

using a machine learning algorithm known as *linear regression* based on the values just from the weight column are shown.[6]

**Create an instance of a linear regression machine learning model.**

**Import the linear regression implementation from the scikit-learn library.**

```
from sklearn.linear_model import LinearRegression
model = LinearRegression()
model = \
        model.fit(df['weight'].values.reshape(len(df), 1), df['mpg'].values)
```

**Train (fit) the linear regression model using the weight column from the Ford Mustang data set as the model input and the mpg values as the model output. The reshape function reshapes the NumPy array returned by df['weight'].values to a matrix consisting of a single column. The reshape is needed here due to the scikit-learn requirement for the model input to be structured as a matrix.**

The linear regression algorithm, widely considered one of the fundamental algorithms in machine learning,[7] *trains* (i.e., "fits") the machine learning model instance based on the data set passed to the fit method of the LinearRegression class. Once trained by the fit method, the model instance can answer questions such as "What is the estimated fuel efficiency of a 3,000-pound Ford Mustang?"

```
model.predict( np.array(3_000).reshape(1, 1) )[0]
```

**Reshape an array containing a single value of 3,000 (representing a 3,000-pound Ford Mustang) into a matrix with one row and one column and ask the model to estimate the output value using the predict method. Since the output of the predict method is returned as a NumPy array, retrieve the first element from the array of the estimated values using a [0] index.**

This outputs

```
20.03370792
```

which represents the estimate of roughly 20.03 miles per gallon (MPG). The machine learning model can also produce estimates for other values of the vehicle weight. Note that the code that follows is more straightforward and thus easier to understand for existing Python developers who are new to machine learning.[8]

---

[6] Although it is commonly associated with modern statistics, linear regression originates from the early 19th-century work by Gauss and Lagendere on predictions of planetary movement.

[7] As well as in many other scientific fields, including statistics, econometrics, astronomy, and more.

[8] It is possible to implement this code more concisely at the expense of having to explain additional NumPy and pandas concepts, including multidimensional arrays. If you are interested in learning more about this topic and a more general topic of tensors, check out chapter 5.

**Listing A.4   Estimating MPG for vehicles weighing 2,500, 3,000, and 3,500 pounds**

The Python for expression iterates over weight values from the [2_500, 3_000, 3_500] list. For each weight in the list, the expression returns a row of a matrix consisting of two columns: the left column with the value of mpg predicted by the model for the weight, and the right column with the value of the weight itself. The resulting matrix is stored in the ds variable.

```
ds = \
   np.array([[ model.predict(np.array(weight).reshape(1, 1))[0], weight] \
        for weight in [2_500, 3_000, 3_500] ])

df = \
      pd.DataFrame(data=ds, columns=['mpg_est', 'weight'])

print(df.to_string(index=False))
```

The pandas DataFrame is instantiated using the ds matrix and annotated with column names mpg_est and weight for the left and right columns, respectively.

To avoid printing the default, zero-based index for each row, df.to_string(index=False) is used instead of print(df).

This outputs the results shown as a pandas DataFrame on the left side of figure A.5. The right side of figure A.5 shows that the model learned by LinearRegression from the original data set has a dashed line and can be used to estimate mpg values for arbitrary values of weight.

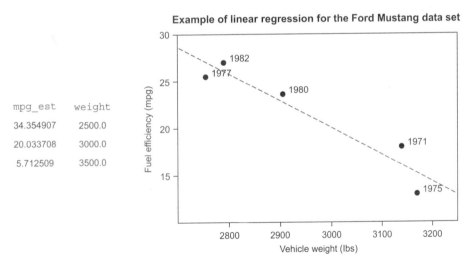

| mpg_est   | weight  |
|-----------|---------|
| 34.354907 | 2500.0  |
| 20.033708 | 3000.0  |
| 5.712509  | 3500.0  |

**Figure A.5**   A table of the estimated fuel efficiency mpg for hypothetical Ford Mustangs with the weight values given by the weight column (left) and the corresponding linear model (right) plotted by connecting the data points from the table

In this section, you learned from an example where the machine learning problem, the data set, and the machine learning algorithm were prepared for you in advance. This meant that you did not have to fully understand the nuances of the problem, how to prepare the data set for the problem, or how to choose the right machine learning algorithm to solve the problem. In the rest of the appendix, you will explore these dimensions of working with machine learning in greater depth and prepare to apply your understanding to the machine learning project in this book.

## A.3   *Machine learning with structured data sets*

In the previous section, you were introduced to an application of machine learning using an example data set describing the fuel efficiency of Ford Mustangs. This section teaches the concepts needed to apply machine learning across arbitrary structured data sets.

For the purposes of this appendix, a *structured data set* stores observations[9] about

- Related objects, for example cars of different makes and models, publicly traded companies in the S&P 500 index, iris flowers of different sub-species, or
- Recurring events, such as won or lost sales opportunities, on-time or late meal deliveries, or button clicks on a website

as records (usually rows) in a table, where each *record* consists of numeric values organized as at least two but typically three or more columns of the table. Note that figure A.6 illustrates a structured data set with N observations (records in rows) and M columns, as well as the related terminology explained later in this section.

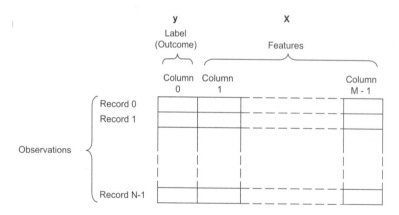

Figure A.6   **A conceptual representation of a structured data set for machine learning. The data set is organized into N rows of observations such that each row has an observation label column along with M - 1 (the remaining) columns of features. By convention, the first column is often the observation label. In cases when observations are about events (e.g., labeling whether a sales opportunity was won or lost), the label is sometimes called the *outcome* of the event. When using the data set for machine learning, the label is often described as the *truth*, *target*, or *actual* value. Variables y and X are commonly used in machine learning to denote the label and the features, respectively.**

---

[9]   To be mathematically precise, the observations are expected to be statistically independent and identically distributed, though most real-world data sets exist in the gray area of this definition.

A *supervised machine learning algorithm* (e.g., the linear regression algorithm used in section A.2) for a structured data set trains (outputs) a machine learning model, which can estimate the value for one of the columns in a record (the label) using the values from the other columns in the record (the features).

In supervised machine learning, a *label* is the numeric value used as the target[10] for the estimates produced by a machine learning model during training. By convention, machine learning practitioners often use the first column of a structured machine learning data set to store the values for the label (often designating it using the variable y) and the remaining columns (using variable X) to store the features. The *features* are the numeric values used by a supervised machine learning model to estimate the label value. When a collection of records consisting of labels and features is used to train a machine learning model, the records are described as a *training data set*.

## The term *label* is ambiguous in machine learning

Unfortunately, the use of the word *label* isn't consistent in the machine learning community, leading to much confusion for newcomers to machine learning. While the use of the word is frequent when the observations in a structured data set describe related objects (e.g., Ford Mustangs), the word *outcome* is used synonymously with label when the observations in the data set describe events (e.g., sales opportunities). Machine learning practitioners with a statistics background often resort to describing the label as the *dependent variable* and the features as the *independent variables*. Others use *target value* or *actual value* synonymously with *label*. This book aims to simplify the terminology and uses the word *label* whenever possible.

The field of machine learning is much broader than supervised machine learning and includes topics like unsupervised machine learning (where the label is not used or not available), reinforcement learning (where algorithms seek to maximize a reward), generative adversarial networks (where neural nets compete to generate and classify data), and more. However, even at Google, arguably a leader in adopting machine learning, more than 80% of the machine learning models that are put into production are based on supervised machine learning algorithms using structured data. Hence, this book focuses entirely on this important area of machine learning.[11]

---

[10] Hence, you should not be surprised when you hear the label described as a "target value."

[11] If you are interested in broadening your knowledge of machine learning beyond supervised machine learning and are willing to read more math-heavy books, check out *Artificial Intelligence: A Modern Approach* by Stuart Russell and Peter Norvig (Pearson, 2020); *Pattern Recognition and Machine Learning* by Christopher Bishop (Springer, 2006); *Deep Learning* by Ian Goodfellow, Yoshua Bengio, and Aaron Courville (The MIT Press, 2016); and *The Elements of Statistical Learning* by Trevor Hastie, Robert Tibshirani, and Jerome Friedman (Springer, 2016).

## Mathematical definition of supervised machine learning

Although it is not required for this book, here's a more formal definition of supervised machine learning: if $y_i$ is the value to be estimated from a record with an index $i$, then a supervised machine learning model can be described as a function F that outputs the estimate $F(X_i)$ based on values $X_i$ of the remaining (i.e., other than $y_i$) columns in the record. The training process for a supervised machine learning model describes construction of the function F based on a training data set $y, X$. The training algorithm is often iterative using $y, X, F(X)$, where the base $F(X)$ is produced from some random initialization of F.

For an illustration of supervised machine learning, recall that in section A.2 you learned about a structured data set describing the fuel efficiency of Ford Mustangs. The training data set consisted of just two columns: a label with the mpg values, and a single feature with the value of the vehicle weight. This data set is also shown as an example in figure A.7. The corresponding supervised machine learning model based on the data set can estimate the average fuel efficiency in miles per gallon (mpg column) for 1971 to 1982 models of Ford Mustangs, based on the values from the weight column.

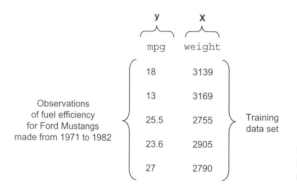

Figure A.7  A sample data set of Ford Mustang fuel efficiency in terms of miles per gallon.

With most machine learning algorithms, training is an iterative process (illustrated in figure A.8) that starts with a machine learning algorithm producing the first iteration of a machine learning model. Some algorithms use the training data set to create the first iteration of the model, but this is not required: most neural network-based deep learning models are initialized according to a simple random scheme.

Once the first iteration of the model is ready, it is used to output the first iteration of the estimates (predictions) based on the features from the training data set. Next, the quality of the estimates is evaluated by the machine learning algorithm by comparing how close the estimates are to the labels from the training data set. This quantifiable measure used to evaluate the quality (i.e., the performance) of the machine learning model is known as *loss* (also known as the *cost* or *objective function*) and is covered in

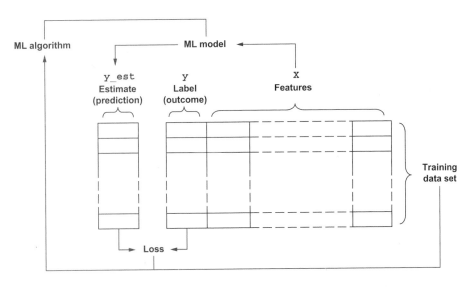

**Figure A.8**  The initial machine learning model produced by the machine learning algorithm is used to output estimated label values (`y_est`), estimates per record based on the records' feature values. The machine learning model is then improved iteratively by changing the model (specifically the model parameters) to improve the model performance score (loss), which is based on the comparison of the estimated and label values.

more detail in section A.4. For the next iteration of the process, the loss along with the training data set are used by the algorithm to produce the next iteration of the model. The non-iterative machine learning algorithms can output a machine learning model after a single iteration of the process shown in figure A.8.

Iterative machine learning algorithms vary in how they approach the decision to stop the training process; some have built-in criteria used to stop iterating, while others require the machine learning practitioner to provide explicit stopping criteria, or to provide a schedule or a function for deciding when to stop. Additional details on how to approach the stopping criteria when covering different machine learning algorithms starts in section A.4.

So far, this appendix has used the phrase *numeric values* intuitively, without providing a clear definition of the numeric values suitable for machine learning. As mentioned in section A.1, machine learning algorithms require a custom prepared data set and may fail when used with arbitrary data values. Hence, it is imperative for a machine learning practitioner to have a clear understanding of the numeric values present in a structured data set. Illustrated in figure A.9 is a detailed taxonomy (originating from a similar taxonomy in statistics) for classifying numeric variables based on their values.

This appendix and the rest of the book focus on machine learning with continuous and categorical variables, specifically using interval, ratio, and nominal data. Whenever possible, the book provides hints and tips for working with ordinal values; however, the

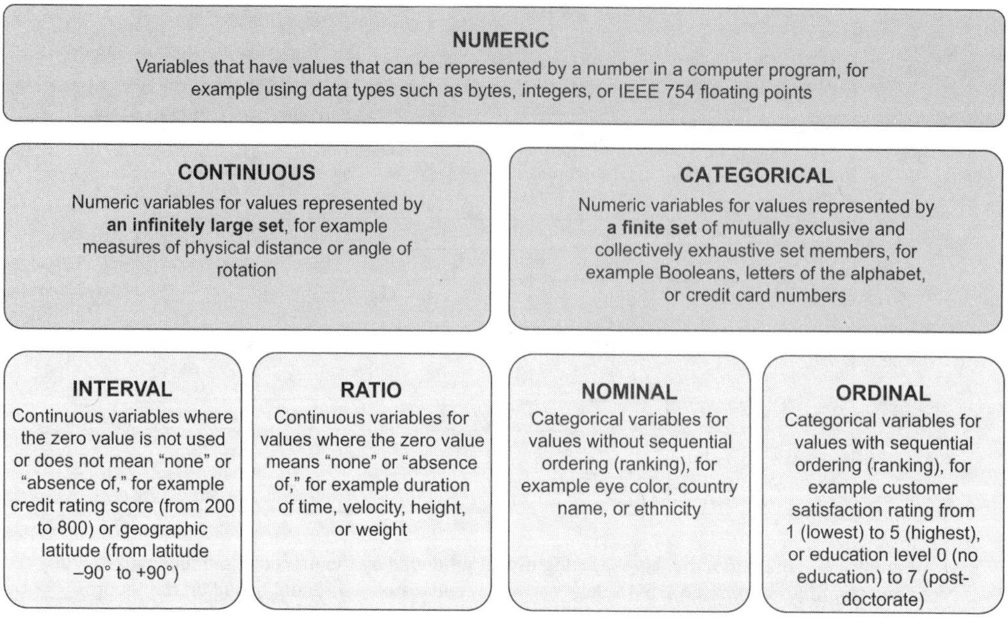

**NUMERIC**
Variables that have values that can be represented by a number in a computer program, for example using data types such as bytes, integers, or IEEE 754 floating points

**CONTINUOUS**
Numeric variables for values represented by **an infinitely large set**, for example measures of physical distance or angle of rotation

**CATEGORICAL**
Numeric variables for values represented by **a finite set** of mutually exclusive and collectively exhaustive set members, for example Booleans, letters of the alphabet, or credit card numbers

**INTERVAL**
Continuous variables where the zero value is not used or does not mean "none" or "absence of," for example credit rating score (from 200 to 800) or geographic latitude (from latitude −90° to +90°)

**RATIO**
Continuous variables for values where the zero value means "none" or "absence of," for example duration of time, velocity, height, or weight

**NOMINAL**
Categorical variables for values without sequential ordering (ranking), for example eye color, country name, or ethnicity

**ORDINAL**
Categorical variables for values with sequential ordering (ranking), for example customer satisfaction rating from 1 (lowest) to 5 (highest), or education level 0 (no education) to 7 (post-doctorate)

Figure A.9   The categories of numeric values for supervised machine learning are adapted from a well-known framework for classifying statistical variables by Stanley Smith Stevens (http://mng.bz/0w4z). Numeric values can be classified into mutually exclusive subsets of continuous and categorical values. Continuous values can be further classified as interval or ratio, while categorical can be either nominal or ordinal.

project in the book does not cover any specific use cases for these two types of values. As a machine learning practitioner, you are expected to prepare and convert the messy, real-world data sets to the numeric values that can be correctly used by machine learning. Much of part 1 is dedicated to sharpening your skills in this domain.

In this section, you learned about training, the sequence of steps performed by a machine learning algorithm to produce a machine learning model. During training, a subset of the structured data set (known as the *training data set*) is used by the algorithm to produce the model, which can then be used to output the estimates (also known as *predictions*), given the feature values from a record.

## A.4    *Regression with structured data sets*

In this section, you will learn about the two commonly used categories of supervised machine learning problems: regression and classification. The section introduces a definition of loss (also known as the cost or the objective function), a quantitative and technical measure of the performance of a machine learning model on a data set of labels and features. By the conclusion of the section, you will be familiar with the terminology related to the problems and review applications of regression.

*Regression* for structured data sets is a supervised machine learning problem where the label is a continuous (as defined in figure A.9) variable. For example, when estimating

Ford Mustang fuel efficiency in section A.2, you worked on an instance of a regression problem since mpg is a continuous (more precisely an interval) value. In section A.5, you will learn more about classification for structured data sets, a supervised machine learning problem where the label is a categorical variable. Comprehensive understanding of these machine learning problems is critical to a machine learning practitioner, since, as explained in section A.3, regression and classification make up over 80% of production machine learning models at top information technology companies like Google.

An example of a regression problem and the related loss calculations based on the Ford Mustang data set is shown in figure A.10. Recall that in section A.2 you played the role of the machine learning algorithm and intuited a mental model for estimating the mpg value. Suppose that you reprise the same role in this section, but here you estimate the mpg value by taking the value of the weight and multiplying it by 0.005. Since the training process is iterative, the value of 0.005 is just an initial (perhaps a lucky) but a reasonable guess. Better approaches for making the guesses will be introduced shortly. In the meantime, the values of the estimates based on this calculation are shown in the Estimate column of figure A.10.

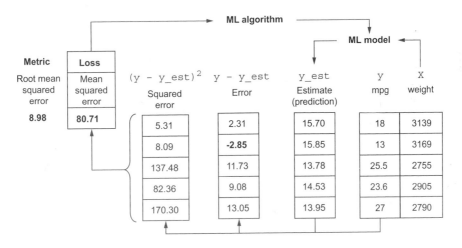

**Figure A.10   In regression problems, many machine learning practitioners start with an application of the mean squared error loss function to establish a baseline before moving on to more complex machine learning approaches and experimenting with more complex loss functions.**

Recall from the process explained in figure A.8 that the next step is to evaluate the loss, a quantifiable measure of the quality of the estimates produced by the machine learning model. The choice of the loss function depends on the machine learning problem and more precisely on the numeric type of both the label and estimated values in the problem.

In the regression problem, one of the most frequently used loss functions is the *mean squared error* (MSE), defined as the arithmetic mean of the individual squared error (also known as *residual* or *difference*) values, as illustrated in the Squared Error column of figure A.10.

The Python code to derive the values shown in the columns of figure A.10 is provided.

Listing A.5   The squared errors for the calculation of the model loss

Instantiate the Ford Mustang data set as a pandas DataFrame. For brevity and following an accepted practice, this example uses y for the label and X for the feature(s). A more detailed explanation is available in listing A.1.

The variable name W is often used to represent the values for the machine learning model parameters. Notice that the NumPy slicing notation [:, None] is equivalent to using reshape(1,1) to reshape W to a matrix needed in the next step.

```
df = pd.DataFrame([{"y": 18,   "X": 3139},
                   {"y": 13,  "X": 3169},
                   {"y": 25.5, "X": 2755},
                   {"y": 23.6, "X": 2905},
                   {"y": 27,  "X": 2790}])

W = np.array([0.007])[:, None]

df['y_est'] = df[['X']] @ W

df['error'] = df['y'] - df['y_est']
df['squared_error'] = df['error'] ** 2

df[['squared_error', 'error', 'y_est', 'y', 'X']]
```

The error is just the difference between the label and the estimated values.

The squared_error is calculated using Python ** exponentiation notation.

The list of the column names is specified to ensure that the order of the columns in the output corresponds to the order shown in figure A.10.

The double-squared bracket notation used by the expression df[['X']] returns a matrix of feature values and the matrix product (using the @ operation), with the matrix containing the model parameter value producing the resulting matrix with a single column containing the weights multiplied by 0.005. Matrix multiplication is used here since it easily scales to many features and model parameter values without having to change the implementation.

Assuming the values for the squared error are stored in a pandas DataFrame column named squared_error, the corresponding value for MSE can be computed using simply

```
df['squared_error'].mean()
```

which in the case of the values from figure A.10 outputs a number that is approximately equal to

```
80.71
```

As you should expect, since the value of W was picked randomly, the value of the mean squared error is nowhere near zero. In figure A.11, you can explore the results of various random choices for W (subplot (a) corresponds to using 0.005 as W) as well as the relationship between the random values of W and the corresponding mean squared error.

**Exploring the relationship between random values for W versus mean squared error (MSE) based on the data set of Ford Mustang fuel efficiency for model years 1971–1982**

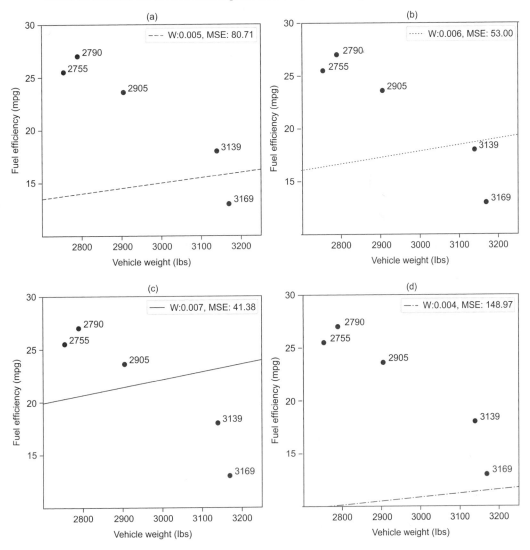

Figure A.11 Subplots a–d illustrate the impact of choosing alternative, randomly selected values of W on the mean squared error. Notice that in all cases, the value of W corresponds to the slope of the line that passes through the points specified by the pair of the feature and label values. Unlike the linear regression model used in figure A.5, the lines on this figure pass through the origin and hence do not capture the pattern of lower weight corresponding to higher miles per gallon in fuel efficiency.

Since the line-based (linear) model based on W is so simple, instead of randomly guessing the value of W, you can rely on an analytical solution for the problem of estimating W that minimizes the mean squared error for the data set. The analytical solution known as the *ordinary least squares* (OLS) *formula* $((X^T X)^{-1} X^T y)$ can be implemented using Python code.

**Listing A.6   Ordinary least squares solution for linear regression**

```
X = df.X.values        ◁─── Assign X as a NumPy array
y = df.y.values             of the feature values.

W = \                  ◁─── Assign y as a NumPy array
  np.linalg.inv( np.array(X.T @ X,      of the label values.
                    dtype = np.float,
                    ndmin = 2) )
              @ np.array( X.T @ y,
                    dtype = np.float,
                    ndmin = 2)
W
```

Assign X as a NumPy array of the feature values.

Assign y as a NumPy array of the label values.

Compute the expression X.T @ X from the OLS formula, convert it to a NumPy matrix (using ndmin=2), and invert the resulting matrix using np.linalg.inv.

Multiply the inverted matrix by X.T @ y from the OLS formula.

This returns a $1 \times 1$ matrix:

```
array([[0.00713444]])
```

You can confirm, using the sample code from listing A.5, that when using the optimal value of W based on the OLS formula produces MSE of 40.88. What does this mean? Note that unlike the LinearRegression model shown in figure A.5, the model based only on W is not complex enough to capture the underlying pattern in the data: the heavier weight leads to lower fuel efficiency. Of course, just by visual examination of the subplots in figure A.11 the reason is obvious: a line based on a single W parameter must pass though the origin (i.e., the y intercept is zero); hence, it is impossible to use it to model the inverse relationship between the greater-than-zero values in the mpg and weight data columns.

However, when working with more complex data sets, where the data has too many dimensions to be easily visualized, a visualization does not help with the decision about whether the model is sufficiently flexible to capture the desired patterns in the data set. Instead of relying on a visualization, you can perform additional tests to evaluate the flexibility of the model. In a regression problem, you can compare your model to the mean squared error of estimating the label values using the mean label value from the training data set. For example, using the DataFrame with the training data set, this can be done by evaluating

```
np.mean((df['y'] - df['y'].mean()) ** 2)
```

which should output approximately

```
27.03
```

The difference between the optimal model MSE of 40.88 and the naive MSE (using the average) of 27.03 shows that the model is not sufficiently complex (has too few parameters) to capture the desired pattern in the data.

## A.5  *Classification with structured data sets*

This section introduces you to and illustrates the cross-entropy loss function used by many machine learning algorithms to train classification models. With the understanding of cross-entropy in place, the section walks you through the steps needed to implement the one-hot encoding of labels and how to use the encoded labels to compute values of cross-entropy loss. Before concluding, the section teaches you the best practices for using NumPy, pandas, and scikit-learn so that you can train and evaluate a baseline `LogisticRegression` classification model.

Recall from section A.4 that classification for structured data sets is a machine learning problem of estimating the value of a categorical label from the feature(s). For example, the Ford Mustang data set shown in figure A.12 can be used to train a classification model (also known as a *classifier*) to estimate the decade of the model year, 1970s versus 1980s, using the `mpg` (fuel efficiency) and `weight` features.

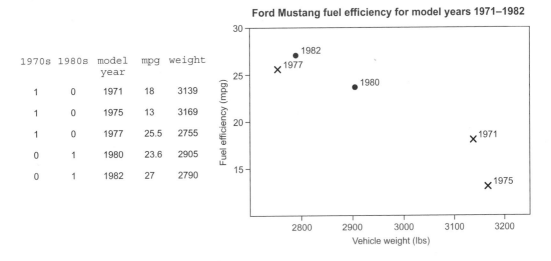

Figure A.12  The one-hot encoding of the `model year` label using columns named 1970s and 1980s representing the Ford Mustang decade of the car's make (left). The one-hot nature of the encoding refers to a single `1` value across every row in the columns used for the encoding; the remainder of the values are `0`. A scatter plot (right) for the data set illustrates the vehicles from 1970s and 1980s using "x" and "•" markers, respectively. Given any location on the grid (not limited to the locations shown using the markers), a trained classification model must be able to estimate whether the vehicle was manufactured in the 1970s or 1980s.

Although the mean squared error loss function can be used for some classification problems,[12] many baseline classifiers use the *cross-entropy loss*. Machine learning algorithms designed to optimize the cross-entropy loss include logistic regression (which is

---

[12] It is possible to use mean squared error for classification problems if the label is binary and is encoded as either −1 or 1.

a machine learning algorithm for classification and should not be confused with the regression machine learning problem) and neural networks, among others. A closely related loss function known as *Gini impurity* is used by the popular decision tree and random forest algorithms. This section explains classification using the cross-entropy loss first, to prepare you to understand the variations on cross-entropy used by the more advanced classification machine learning algorithms.

Unlike the mean squared loss, which expects the output of a regression model to be a single numeric value, cross-entropy loss expects the classification model to output a probability for each possible value of the categorical label. Continuing with the working data set for estimation of the decade of Ford Mustang models, figure A.13 illustrates four informative examples of the outputs for a hypothetical classification model based on the data set.

In example 1 shown on the upper left of figure A.13, the classification model assigns a 0.6 probability to the estimate of 1970s as the decade of the model year. Since probabilities must add up to 1, the estimate of 1980s is 0.4. In this example, the corresponding loss value (shown in the title of the example) of approximately 0.51 is significantly greater than zero since the classification model estimates the correct value (1970s) but lacks confidence in the estimate. Observe from example 2 on the upper right of figure A.13 that when the model is completely uncertain of the correct value, lacking confidence or preference to estimate either 1970s or 1980s (due to 0.5 probability for both),[13] the loss increases further, reaching approximately 0.6931.[14] In a nutshell, the cross-entropy loss function decreases toward zero when the classification model outputs a high probability (effectively a high confidence) value for the correct label estimate and increases otherwise.

The loss function increases even further, beyond the loss number reported in case of the complete uncertainty, if the classification model is incorrect in the estimation of the label value, as shown in example 3 on the lower left of figure A.13. In this example, the correct label value is 1980s while the model is slightly more confident in the estimate of 1970s than 1980s with probabilities of 0.6 and 0.4, respectively. Note that the loss value increases further, from 0.9163 in example (3) to 4.6052 in example 4, on lower right of figure A.13, where the classification model is highly confident about the wrong estimate.

Since the output of a classification model consists of probabilities (a probability distribution) for label values, the original labels in the working data set must be encoded (converted) into the same format before training or testing the machine learning model. The result of the encoding is shown in columns 1970s and 1980s on the left side of figure A.12. The process of this conversion is known as *one-hot encoding*, referring to the fact that just a single value is set to be one (1) across the entire row in the columns encoding the label.

---

[13]  This state of a uniform probability distribution is also known as *maximum entropy*.

[14]  You may have noticed that this is approximately the value of the e constant since the cross-entropy calculations here use natural logarithms.

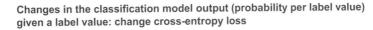

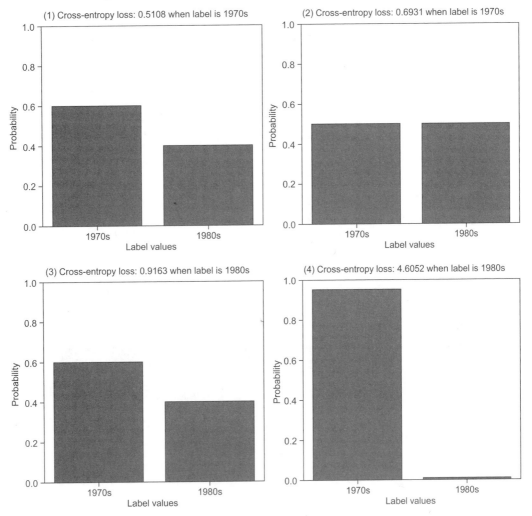

**Figure A.13** **(1) The model is slightly more confident in the correct value. (2) The model is entirely uncertain about which of the two values to choose. (3) The model is slightly more confident in the incorrect value. (4) The model is highly confident in the incorrect value.**

The cross-entropy loss function can be defined in terms of NumPy operations. The xe_loss function definition implements the calculation for cross-entropy loss given an array of the classification model output y_est and the corresponding one-hot encoded array of the label values y. Note that with the implementation you need to take care not to confuse the label and the model output array parameters because the np.log function outputs -Inf and 0.0 for the values of 0 and 1, respectively.

**Listing A.7  `xe_loss` computing and returning the cross-entropy loss**

```
def xe_loss(y, y_est):
  return -np.sum( y * np.log( y_est ) )

print( xe_loss ( np.array([1., 0.]),
                 np.array([.6, .4]) ) )
print( xe_loss ( np.array([1., 0.]),
                 np.array([.5, .5]) ) )
print( xe_loss ( np.array([0., 1.]),
                 np.array([.6, .4]) ) )
print( xe_loss ( np.array([0., 1.]),
                 np.array([.99, .01]) ))
```

Compute the loss value of 0.5108 based on example 1 in figure A.13.

Compute the loss value of 0.6931 based on example 2 of figure A.13.

Compute the loss value of 0.9163 based on example 3 of figure A.13.

Compute the loss value of 4.6052 based on example 4 of figure A.13.

Running the code from listing A.7 outputs the following cross-entropy loss values corresponding to examples 1–4 from figure A.13:

```
0.5108256237659907
0.6931471805599453
0.916290731874155
4.605170185988091
```

**Mathematical definition of cross-entropy loss.**

Here's a mathematical description of cross-entropy loss: given a single training example y, X of a label and features, respectively, the function is defined as

$$-\sum_{k=1}^{K} y_k * log(\hat{y}_k),$$ where $K$ is the number of the values of the categorical label variable, $y_k$ is the probability of a specific label value in a one-hot encoded label y, and $\hat{y}_k$ is the probability estimate of a specific label value for the estimate $\hat{y}$ produced by a classification model.

The examples used so far in this section relied on label values that have already been one-hot encoded for you. In practice, you must implement the label encoding before training a classification model. Although it is possible to use a comprehensive set of scikit-learn classes to one-hot encode the model year column label,[15] since in this appendix the data set is instantiated as a pandas DataFrame it is easier to use a generic pandas get_dummies method for label encoding. The whimsical get_dummies naming

[15] scikit-learn provides a comprehensive set of classes, including LabelEncoder and LabelBinarizer, designed to help with label encoding, as well as OneHotEncoder and OrdinalEncoder for feature encoding; these classes are best suited to the development scenarios that do not use pandas to store and manage data sets. For example, if your entire data set is stored as NumPy arrays, these scikit-learn classes are a good option. However, if your data set is a pandas DataFrame or a pandas Series, it is more straightforward to apply pandas's own get_dummies method for both label and feature encoding.

of the method stems from *dummy variables*, a term used in statistics to describe binary indicator variables that are either 1 to indicate a presence or 0 to indicate absence of a value.

Given the label and the features for the data set as a pandas DataFrame, a direct application of the get_dummies method to the model year label is shown.

**Listing A.8   Using `get_dummies` on a categorical label**

```
import pandas as pd                    Instantiate the data set as a pandas DataFrame.
                                       Since this instantiation uses model year as the
df = \                                 label, it is placed in the leading column.
    pd.DataFrame([{"model year": 1971, "mpg": 18,   "weight": 3139},
                  {"model year": 1975, "mpg": 13, "weight": 3169},
                  {"model year": 1977, "mpg": 25.5,  "weight": 2755},
                  { "model year": 1980, "mpg": 23.6, "weight": 2905},
                  {"model year": 1982, "mpg": 27,   "weight": 2790}])

enc_df = \
        pd.get_dummies(df['model year'], prefix='le', sparse=False)
print(enc_df.to_string(index=False))              Print the resulting enc_df
                                                  DataFrame without the
                                                  zero-based index.
```

Using get_dummies with a pandas Series identifies the set of unique values in a series and creates a new column for each value in the set. The prefix parameter ensures that each new column is named using the specified prefix. Setting sparse to True may result in, but does not guarantee, reduced memory utilization by the resulting DataFrame. Labels with a larger number of distinct values and correspondingly more columns in a one-hot encoded format benefit from sparse array representations enabled by sparse set to True.

This produces

```
le_1971  le_1975  le_1977  le_1980  le_1982
   1        0        0        0        0
   0        1        0        0        0
   0        0        1        0        0
   0        0        0        1        0
   0        0        0        0        1
```

which is not the desired encoding. Although you can easily implement the code to convert the exact model year of the vehicle from the column name to the desired encoding of the model decade, *binning* is an alternative and a more flexible approach to perform label encoding for this use case. Using the pandas cut method, you can "bin" the label values into a range:

```
pd.cut(df['model year'], bins=[1969, 1979, 1989])
```

which outputs a pandas.Series of range intervals:

```
0    (1969, 1979]
1    (1969, 1979]
2    (1969, 1979]
```

```
3     (1979, 1989]
4     (1979, 1989]
Name: model year, dtype: category
Categories (2, interval[int64]): [(1969, 1979] < (1979, 1989]]
```

Notice that the first three vehicles were correctly placed in the 1970s (1969 is excluded, as indicated by the open parenthesis) while the remaining vehicles are placed in the 1980s.

Combining the label binning with get_dummies for one-hot encoding,

```
enc_df = pd.get_dummies(pd.cut(df['model year'], bins=[1969, 1979, 1989]),
             prefix='le', sparse=False)
print(enc_df.to_string(index = False))
```

outputs the desired encoding from figure A.12:

```
le_(1969, 1979]  le_(1979, 1989]
          1                0
          1                0
          1                0
          0                1
          0                1
```

Prior to evaluating the cross-entropy loss function with the encoded values, it is convenient to join the columns of the label encoding with the original data set, replacing the original label values with the encoded ones:

```
enc_df = pd.get_dummies(pd.cut(df['model year'], bins=[1969, 1979, 1989]),
             prefix='le', sparse=False)
         .join(df[df.columns[1:]])

print(enc_df.to_string(index = False))
```

which results in

```
le_(1969, 1979]  le_(1979, 1989]    mpg  weight
          1                0   18.0    3139
          1                0   13.0    3169
          1                0   25.5    2755
          0                1   23.6    2905
          0                1   27.0    2790
```

At this point the data set is prepared to be partitioned into the label and the features used for training and then converted to NumPy arrays. Starting with the label values,

```
y_train = df[ df.columns [df.columns.str.startswith('le_') == True] ].values
print(y_train)
```

outputs

```
array([[1, 0],
       [1, 0],
       [1, 0],
       [0, 1],
       [0, 1]], dtype=uint8)
```

To place the feature values into the NumPy X_train array, use

```
X_train = df [['mpg', 'weight']].values
print(X_train)
```

which prints out

```
array([[  18. , 3139. ],
       [  13. , 3169. ],
       [  25.5, 2755. ],
       [  23.6, 2905. ],
       [  27. , 2790. ]])
```

At this point you are ready to train a LogisticRegression classifier model,

```
from sklearn.linear_model import LogisticRegression
model = LogisticRegression(solver='liblinear')
model.fit(X_train, y_train.argmax(axis = 1))
```

and compute the cross-entropy loss,

```
def cross_entropy_loss(y, y_est):
  xe = -np.sum(y * np.log (y_est))
  return xe

cross_entropy_loss(y_train, model.predict_proba(X_train))
```

which outputs

```
2.314862688295351
```

## A.6   *Training a supervised machine learning model*

When training a machine learning model, you will virtually never use your entire structured data set as the training data set. Instead, the pattern followed by most machine learning practitioners is to partition the initial data set into two mutually exclusive subsets:[16] a development (dev) data set and a test (also known as a held-out) data set.

Many newcomers to the machine learning field are not familiar with the concept of the dev data set. While it is possible to use it directly as the training data set (and many online courses and tutorials use this simplified approach), training machine

---

[16] Here "mutually exclusive" means that duplicate records are removed prior to partitioning, and following the de-duplication any given record exists either in one or the other subsets.

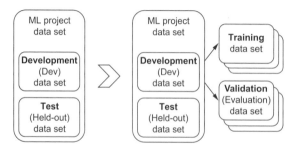

**Figure A.14**   Once the machine learning project data set is partitioned to extract the held-out, test data set, it is common to start exploratory data analysis and machine learning model training directly with the dev data set, in other words to use the dev data set as the training data set (left). A more mature machine learning training workflow that can help detect overfitting early and optimize the hyperparameters includes further partitioning of the dev data set into training and validation data sets, as well using cross-validation with the dev data set.

learning for production requires a more robust approach. The distinction between the two approaches is illustrated in figure A.14. As shown on the right-hand side of figure A.14, the dev data set is further split into the training and validation data sets. As before, the purpose of the training data set is to train the machine learning model; however, the purpose of the validation (or evaluation) data set is to estimate the expected performance of the trained machine learning model on the held-out (test) data set. For example, in the Ford Mustang fuel efficiency data set, one record can be chosen randomly to be in the test data set, and four records in the dev data set. Next, one record chosen randomly from the dev data set can again be placed in the validation data set, and the remaining three records placed in the training data set to train a machine learning model.

Since the purpose of the validation data set is to estimate the performance of the training machine learning model on the test data set, having just one record in the validation data set is an issue. However, it is also valuable to use as many observations from the dev data set for training as possible. One solution to this dilemma is to use a technique known as *K-fold cross-validation*, illustrated in figure A.15. The key idea behind using K-fold cross-validation is to train K different machine learning models by reusing the dev data set K times, each time partitioning the dev data set into K folds where K-1 folds are used as the training data set and the remaining K-th fold is used as the validation data set. The example in figure A.15 uses three partitions, or three-fold cross-validation. When the number of observations in the data set does not divide without a remainder into K-folds, the partition with the smallest number of observations is designated as the validation data set. Otherwise, all the partitions have the same size in terms of the number of the observations.

Next, K separate machine learning models are trained using the K-1 training data set partitions and are validated using the remaining K-th validation partition. Hence,

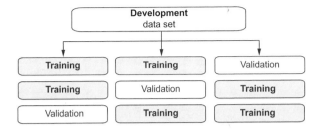

**Figure A.15**   **The K-fold cross-validation technique includes training K different machine learning models and reporting the training as well as the validation loss (and metric) based on the average of the training and validation values obtained from each of the K independent models. Note that each of the K models is validated using a different validation partition of the dev data set, using the remainder of the dev data set for training.**

in the example in figure A.15, three separate machine learning models are trained using the two training folds in each of the three different partitions.

The dev data set may be used as-is to train a machine learning model, in other words, as a training data set. However, this is rarely the case for production machine learning models.

Instead, the dev data set is split further into training and validation data sets. Chapter 4 explains and illustrates this process in more detail, but for the purposes of this appendix, you can expect that the validation data set is used to estimate the performance of the machine learning model on the held-out (test) data set, which is not used for training.

# appendix B
# Getting started
# with Docker

If you have ever used public clouds to enable your applications with autoscaling, the feature where you can easily add or remove compute nodes for your application cluster, you have already used virtual service instances. You may have even used programs like ssh to log in to your instances and then managed them remotely via this ssh session. At first glance, it may appear that a Docker container instance is no different from a virtual server. If you ssh into a Docker container, you may not even notice a difference compared to a session in a virtual server hosted by a public cloud service like AWS EC2. However, while traditional virtual servers from public cloud services like EC2 are related to Docker, there are important features Docker provides that are important to know.

An approachable way to understanding Docker is in terms of lightweight (compared to virtual servers) virtualization. This refers to dimensions like the following:

- Storage, where Docker image snapshots take up less disk space than traditional virtual server/machine images
- Memory, since Docker container instances consume less memory than guest instances (virtual servers)
- Latency, as Docker containers start up faster than their virtual server counterparts
- Performance, as programs running in Docker containers have near-zero CPU overhead compared to programs running in virtual guest instances

Yet the differences between Docker containers and virtual servers are much more fundamental at the core hardware/software level. The traditional virtualization technology (e.g., VMWare, Xen) virtualizes the host computer hardware, or creates software-based proxies for the underlying hardware components, including central processing units, storage, network devices, and more, instantiating guest environments with their own copies of the operating system on disk and in memory along with device drivers and other supporting software. In contrast, Docker containers virtualize the operating system such that each guest container instance shares the same operating system but operates as if it has isolated access to the entire operating system.

## B.1 Getting started with Docker

If you don't have Docker installed in your environment, you can get access to a lab environment with Docker by visiting https://labs.play-with-docker.com/.

Docker is an overloaded term, and it describes a variety of Docker technology components (e.g., Docker Engine, Docker Swarm, and so on), the Docker company itself, as well as the Docker container image registry maintained on hub.docker.com. When you install the Docker engine, you do not have any Docker images installed in your environment.

Assuming that you have your Docker Engine, your Docker host software, configured correctly, it is traditional to start using Docker with a variant of the `hello-world` program by running the following command in your shell environment:

```
docker run hello-world
```

Assuming you do not already have a `hello-world` Docker image downloaded (pulled), this should output the following:

```
Unable to find image 'hello-world:latest' locally
latest: Pulling from library/hello-world
0e03bdcc26d7: Pull complete
Digest: sha256:7f0a9f93b4aa3022c3a4c147a449bf11e094
➥ 1a1fd0bf4a8e6c9408b2600777c5
Status: Downloaded newer image for hello-world:latest

Hello from Docker!
```

It is important to understand that `run` is a composite Docker command that performs multiple operations behind the scenes. The following breaks down the commands performed by `run` to help you understand what it does.

Since you have already done the basic `hello-world`-style example using Docker, let's try a slightly more complex example using the popular `nginx` webserver. To download a Docker image from hub.docker.com (also known as Docker Hub) to your local Docker host, you can perform a `pull` command as shown here:

```
docker pull nginx
```

This should output the following:

```
docker pull nginx
Using default tag: latest
```

```
latest: Pulling from library/nginx
bf5952930446: Pull complete
cb9a6de05e5a: Pull complete
9513ea0afb93: Pull complete
b49ea07d2e93: Pull complete
a5e4a503d449: Pull complete
Digest: sha256:b0ad43f7ee5edbc0effbc14645ae7055e21b
➥ c1973aee5150745632a24a752661
Status: Downloaded newer image for nginx:latest
docker.io/library/nginx:latest
```

> **NOTE**  Because it's possible that the nginx image may have changed since the time this book was created, your hash codes in the message may not correspond to those in the examples, but the concepts in this appendix apply regardless of the specific values of the hash codes in the examples.

The message produced by the pull command indicates that Docker defaulted to using the tag with the value latest for the nginx image. Since it is also possible to specify the fully qualified domain name from where Docker can pull an image, Docker also defaulted to using the Docker Hub FQN docker.io/library as the prefix uniquely identifying the nginx image.

Notice the mention of the various hash codes in the message returned by the pull command, for example

```
bf5952930446: Pull complete.
```

Each of the hash code values preceding the Pull complete message (as well as the download progress messages that you observed while running the pull command) is a unique identifier or a *fingerprint* of a layer in union, also known as a layered filesystem used by Docker container images. In contrast, the hash code that follows the Digest: sha256: message is the unique fingerprint for the entire nginx Docker image.

Once the image is on your Docker host server, you can use it to create an instance of a Docker container. The container is the lightweight virtual machine described earlier, or a virtual guest operating system environment running in a near isolation from the rest of your Docker host server operating system.

To create the container you can execute

```
docker create  nginx
```

which should return a unique container ID resembling the following:

```
cf33323ab079979200429323c2a6043935399653b4bc7a5c86
➥ 553220451cfdb1
```

Instead of using the full, lengthy container ID in your command, Docker allows you to specify the first few characters of the container ID, as long as it is unambiguous in your Docker host environment. To confirm that the container was created in your environment, you can use the `docker ls -a | grep <CONTAINER_ID>` command, where `docker ls -a` lists all the containers in your environment and the piped `grep` command filters just the containers that you need. For instance, since the container I created had an ID starting with `cf33`, I can execute

```
docker ps -a | grep cf33
```

which in my case outputs

```
cf33323ab079        nginx
➥ "/docker-entrypoint.…"
➥ 5 minutes ago
➥    Created                                 ecstatic_gagarin
```

Notice that Docker automatically created a human-readable Docker container ID `ecstatic_gagarin` for the container so that it is easier to remember and specify in the command line compared to the hash code. Also, the container has a state of `Created` since the container was just created from the image and never started. To start the container you can execute

```
docker start -p 8080:80 CONTAINER_ID
```

replacing `CONTAINER_ID` with you container ID value or prefix. The output simply echoes the container ID, but you can confirm that the container changed state by rerunning

```
docker ps -a | grep CONTAINER_ID
```

which should report the uptime for the container, similar to the following:

```
cf33323ab079        nginx
➥ "/docker-entrypoint.…"    11 minutes ago
➥ Up 2 minutes              80/tcp
➥ ecstatic_gagarin
```

Although you may expect that you should be able to access the NGINX web server since you started an `nginx` container, that's incorrect. Simply starting the container does not include the step of mapping (exposing) the ports opened in the guest container environment to the host environment. To resolve this problem, you can shut down the running container using

```
docker stop CONTAINER_ID
```

which should echo your `CONTAINER_ID` value.

Next, rerun the container with the port 80 (the web server HTTP port) exposed as port 8080 of your host Docker environment. This can be performed using

```
docker run -p 8080:80 nginx
```

which invokes a new instance of a new Docker container, returning the log messages from the NGINX service in your terminal. At this point, if you open your web browser and navigate to the port 8080 of your Docker host server IP address, for example by navigating to 127.0.0.1:8080, you should see the HTML page with the message:

```
Welcome to nginx!
```

At this point, the behavior of the container instance created by Docker is different from what you observed earlier when you executed docker start. In this case, if you press Ctrl-C in the terminal session, the container instance will terminate, which you can easily confirm by rerunning docker ps. This time, docker ps should not show any running container instances since you just shut it down by pressing Ctrl-C.

To prevent the Docker container instance from taking over your terminal session, you can rerun it in a detached mode by specifying the -d parameter:

```
docker run -d -p 8080:80 nginx
```

This should return the container ID for the instance you just started.

Of course, it is not interesting to have a web server that only shows a Welcome to nginx! message. What would it take to change the contents of the HTML file used to serve the welcome web page?

You can start by confirming the location of the index.html file with the welcome message. The exec command allows you to use the host shell docker CLI to execute arbitrary Linux commands in a running guest container instance. For example, to output the contents of the /usr/share/nginx/html/index.html file in your nginx instance, run

```
docker exec CONTAINER_ID /bin/bash -c
    'head /usr/share/nginx/html/index.html'
```

which, if you use the correct CONTAINER_ID value for your nginx container instance, should output

```
<!DOCTYPE html>
<html>
<head>
<title>Welcome to nginx!</title>
<style>
```

Note that in the exec command, you specified that you wish to execute the Bash shell using /bin/bash, and the specific shell command is specified as the command-line argument to /bin/bash using the -c flag and the head /usr/share/nginx/html/index.html as the actual command. Recall that the head command can be used to echo the first five lines of a file.

Similarly, you can easily modify the contents of the index.html file by changing its contents in the guest container instance. If you execute

```
docker exec CONTAINER_ID /bin/bash
 ⇒ -c 'echo "Hello from my Docker tutorial" >
 ⇒ /usr/share/nginx/html/index.html'
```

and refresh your localhost:8080 page in your browser, you should receive the "Hello from my Docker tutorial" message.

It is critical that you realize the change to the index.html file happened in the container instance and *not* in the container image used to start the instance. If you are ever unsure about what changes you made to the container image to start the container instance, you can find out the details using the `diff` command:

```
docker diff CONTAINER_ID
```

This should output the following given the changes made to the index.html file and files changed (`C`) or added (`A`) by the NGINX web server:

```
C /usr
C /usr/share
C /usr/share/nginx
C /usr/share/nginx/html
C /usr/share/nginx/html/index.html
C /var
C /var/cache
C /var/cache/nginx
A /var/cache/nginx/client_temp
A /var/cache/nginx/fastcgi_temp
A /var/cache/nginx/proxy_temp
A /var/cache/nginx/scgi_temp
A /var/cache/nginx/uwsgi_temp
C /etc
C /etc/nginx
C /etc/nginx/conf.d
C /etc/nginx/conf.d/default.conf
C /run
A /run/nginx.pid
```

In section B.2, you will learn about creating your own custom Docker image so you can persist your desired changes and re-use them across many Docker container instances.

When you frequently start and stop multiple container instances in your Docker host environment, it is convenient to manage them as a batch. You can list all the container instance IDs using

```
docker ps -aq
```

which should return a list resembling the following:

```
c32eaafa76c1
078c98061959
...
a74e24994390
6da8b3d1f0e1
```

where the ellipsis illustrates that you may have an arbitrary number of container IDs returned by the command. To stop all of the container instances in your environment, you can use the xargs command

```
docker ps -aq | xargs docker stop
```

which stops any and all container instances. Next, you can repeat the process to remove any remaining container instances using docker rm combined with xargs:

```
docker ps -aq | xargs docker rm
```

After stopping and removing the docker container instance, if you rerun

```
docker ps -aq
```

you should see an empty response, meaning that your Docker host environment is free of any container instances.

## B.2   *Building a custom image*

It is remarkably simple to create your own Docker image and then share it with the world. It starts with a Dockerfile, a declarative specification for how to take an existing (base) container image and extend it (think layer on top) with your own changes.

You should start the process of building your own Docker image by creating and navigating to an empty directory, tmp:

```
mkdir tmp
```

It is good practice to have an empty directory ready because Docker makes a copy of the contents of the directory (known as the context directory) used during the build process, so if you accidentally launch the build process from a directory that contains gigabytes' worth of unrelated content, you are going to end up waiting for Docker to unnecessarily copy that unrelated content instead of promptly returning with the resulting image.

Since every Docker image starts with a base image, the Dockerfile must specify a FROM statement with the identifier of the base image to use during the build process. This example continues using the NGINX web server:

```
echo "FROM nginx:latest" > Dockerfile
```

Here, the echo command does not produce an output but creates a new Dockerfile in the current directory with a single line containing the FROM statement specifying nginx:latest as the base image. Now you are ready to build your first custom NGINX image using the following build command:

```
docker build -t just-nginx:latest -f Dockerfile tmp/
```

which should output

```
docker build -t just-nginx:latest -f Dockerfile tmp/
Sending build context to Docker daemon  1.583kB
Step 1/1 : FROM nginx:latest
 ---> 4bb46517cac3
Successfully built 4bb46517cac3
Successfully tagged just-nginx:latest
```

At this point, you can confirm that you have a new Docker image in your Docker host environment with

```
docker image ls | grep nginx
```

which produces an output that may surprise you with an odd creation date timestamp. In my case, for the image ID `4bb46517cac3` the timestamp reported a creation date of `3 weeks ago`

```
just-nginx       latest
 4bb46517cac3        3 weeks ago         133MB
```

Recall that Docker relies on hash code–based fingerprints for the image layers and the entire container image. Since your Dockerfile did not introduce any changes to the image, the hash code stayed the same despite the change to the metadata values like the image name (just-nginx).

What about an example that actually changes the base Docker image? You can start by creating your own custom index.html file that you would like to see rendered when you access the NGINX web server. Note that this file is created in the `tmp` subdirectory using

```
echo
 '<html><body>Welcome to my custom nginx message!
 </body></html>' > tmp/index.html
```

After the index.html file is prepared, you modify the Dockerfile with a command to copy the file into the image during the build process,

```
echo 'COPY index.html
 /usr/share/nginx/html/index.html' >> Dockerfile
```

so that the entire `Dockerfile` should consist of the following:

```
FROM nginx:latest
COPY index.html /usr/share/nginx/html/index.html
```

At this point you are ready to build another image with your customized welcome message. Run

```
docker build -t custom-nginx:latest -f Dockerfile tmp/
```

which should output

```
Sending build context to Docker daemon  2.607kB
Step 1/2 : FROM nginx:latest
 ---> 4bb46517cac3
Step 2/2 : COPY index.html
 /usr/share/nginx/html/index.html
 ---> c0a21724aa7a
Successfully built c0a21724aa7a
Successfully tagged custom-nginx:latest
```

where the hash codes may not match with yours.

Notice that the Docker COPY command finished successfully because you used tmp as the build context directory and the index.html resided in tmp. In general, any file you wish to copy into the Docker image during the build process must reside in the build context directory.

Now you are ready to start the newly built image,

```
docker run -d -p 8080:80 custom-nginx:latest
```

and confirm that if you visit localhost:8080 NGINX responds with

```
Welcome to my custom nginx message!
```

## B.3    *Sharing your custom image with the world*

Before you can take you Docker image and upload it to the Docker image registry, you must create your personal account on hub.docker.com Assuming you have created your account and have your username and password for Docker Hub, you can login using these credentials from the command line:

```
docker login
```

Upon successful login, you should observe output similar to the following:

```
docker login
Login with your Docker ID to push and pull images
 from Docker Hub. If you don't have a Docker ID,
 head over to https://hub.docker.com to create one.
Username: YOUR_USER_NAME
Password: YOUR_PASSWORD
Login Succeeded
```

For a Docker image to be ready for an upload, it must be tagged with your Docker username as a prefix. To assign this prefix to your custom-nginx image, you can use the tag command

```
docker tag custom-nginx:latest
 YOUR_USER_NAME/custom-nginx:latest
```

replacing `YOUR_USER_NAME` with your Docker Hub username. To upload (push) your image to Docker Hub you can execute

```
docker push YOUR_USER_NAME/custom-nginx:latest
```

which should produce an output similar to the following:

```
The push refers to repository
➥ [docker.io/YOUR_USER_NAME/custom-nginx]
088b6bf061ef: Pushed
550333325e31: Pushed
22ea89b1a816: Pushed
a4d893caa5c9: Pushed
0338db614b95: Pushed
d0f104dc0a1f: Pushed
latest: digest: sha256:9d12a3fc5cbb0a20e9be7afca476
➥ a0603a38fcee6ccfedf698300c6023c4b444 size: 1569
```

This indicates that you can log back into your Docker registry dashboard on hub.docker.com and confirms that the `custom-nginx:latest` image is available in your registry.

# *index*

**Symbols**

// operation  172

**A**

Adam optimizer  132–134, 231
__add__ method  126–127
add_ method  113
all-gather phase, gradient accumulation  181–187
alpha variable  106
ALU (arithmetic logic unit)  154
arange method  111
arrays  104
arr tensor  107
*Artificial Intelligence* (Norvig)  283
AS keyword  48
Athena interactive query
    overview  40–42
    using from browser  43–44
athena_query_to_pandas function  48
athena_query_to_table function  46
autodiff functionality, PyTorch  121–129
    linear regression using PyTorch automatic
        differentiation  129–132
    transitioning to PyTorch optimizers for gradient
        descent  132–135
AVG function  40
AWS_ACCESS_KEY_ID environment variable
    23–24
AWS (Amazon Web Services)
    Athena
        overview  40–42
        using from browser  43–44
    authenticating object storage with  22–23
    Glue data catalog  26–27

awscli_to_df() method  48
AWS_DEFAULT_REGION environment
    variable  24–25, 43
aws glue create-database command  29
aws glue get-crawler command  30
aws glue get-table command  30, 37
aws glue start-crawler command  30
aws iam attach-role-policy command  28
aws iam create-role command  27
aws iam get-role command  30
aws iam put-role-policy command  28
aws s3api command  24
aws s3api create-bucket command  24
aws s3 command  24
aws s3 ls command  25
aws s3 sync command  25
AWS_SECRET_ACCESS_KEY environment
    variable  23–24

**B**

BACKEND setting  257
backward method  124–130, 164, 167
backward pass  124, 134
BaseMLFlowClient class  264
BaseOptunaService class  259, 261
batch normalization hyperparameter
    using Optuna study for  240–242
    visualizing an HPO study in Optuna
        242–244
batch_norm_linear_layers hyperparameter
    236
batch_norm_linear method  235–236
batch size  135
batch_size hyperparameter  232, 244
batchToXy method  216

binning 210, 295
Bishop, Christopher 283
BLOBs (binary large objects) 26, 118
BOOLEAN data type 53
broadcasting, PyTorch tensors 112–115
browser, using Athena interactive query from
    43–44
BUCKET_DST_PATH parameter 76–77
BUCKET_ID variable 24–25, 146, 268
buckets (containers) 21
build command 306
build_hidden_layers method 233–235
build method 219, 221, 236
business rules, DC taxi rides data set 16
business service, DC taxi rides data set
    data assets 19
    implementing 18
    schema for 17

## C

categorical hyperparameters 231–233
child runs (pipeline executions) 247
clip_grad_norm method 153
columnar storage 31–37
    migrating to 33–37
    overview 31–33
comma-separated values (CSVs) 20
configure_optimizers method 214, 216,
    231
containers (buckets) 21
COPY command 308
COUNT(*) function 60
counterfactual causality 193
COUNT function 40, 61
crawler 27
    authorizing to access objects 27–28
    using to discover data set 28–31
createOrReplaceTempView method 33
creation operations, PyTorch tensors
    108–109
cross-entropy loss 291
CSVs (comma-separated values) 20
custom images
    building with Docker 306–308
    sharing with Docker 308–309
custom-nginx:latest image 309
custom-nginx image 308
cut method 295

## D

DataFrame createOrReplaceTempView
    method 75
data leakage 195

DataLoader class 136–138, 149
    data set batches with 136–140
    for gradient descent with data set batches
        140–141
DataLoader instance 137, 160
data quality 49–58
    "garbage in, garbage out" 50
    preparing to work on 51–52
    VACUUM model 52–58
        accuracy 55–56
        consistency 56–57
        uniformity 57
        unity 57–58
        valid data 52–55
data sampling 82–100
    choosing right sample size 86–88
    statistics of alternative sample sizes
        88–92
    summary statistics 82–85
    using PySpark for 92–100
data set batches
    DataLoader class for gradient descent
        with
        140–141
    Dataset class for gradient descent with
        140–141
    for gradient descent 135–136
    with DataLoader class 136–140
    with Dataset class 136–140
Dataset class 136–137, 149
    data set batches with 136–140
    for gradient descent with data set batches
        140–141
data set. See DC taxi rides data set
DATE_PARSE function 60–61
DC taxi rides data set
    business rules 16
    business service
        data assets 19
        implementing 18
        schema for 17
    business use case 16
    columnar storage 31–37
        migrating to 33–37
        overview 31–33
    data quality 49–58
        "garbage in, garbage out" 50
        preparing to work on 51–52
        VACUUM model 52–58
    data set 16–20
    discovering schema for 26–31
        authorizing crawler to access objects
            27–28
        AWS Glue data catalog 26–27
        using crawler to discover 28–31

DC taxi rides data set *(continued)*
  downloading and unzipping 19–20
  interactive querying 39–49
    AWS Athena 40–44
    choosing right use case for 39–40
    DC taxi data set 49
    preparing sample data set 42–43
    using sample data set 44–48
  object storage 20–26
    authenticating with AWS 22–23
    creating serverless object storage bucket 23–26
    filesystems vs. 21–22
  VACUUM model 58–74
    cleaning up invalid fare amounts 63–66
    ensuring valid values 59–63
    improving accuracy 66–74
    in PySpark job 74–79
DDP (distributed data parallel) 163–169
*Deep Learning* (Goodfellow) 283
describe method 83
device attribute 156
device named parameter 157
device variable 155, 157, 159
df instance 93
diff command 305
difference 288
dimension 105
diminishing returns 89
discretization 210
DistributedDataParallel class 249, 256
Docker 247
  building custom images 306–308
  overview 301–306
  sharing custom images 308–309
docker build command 259
DOCKER_HUB_PASSWORD variable 258
DOCKER_HUB_USER Python variable 258
docker ls -a | grep <CONTAINER_ID> command 303
docker push operation 259
docker rm container instance 306
DOUBLE data type 33, 42, 52–54, 63, 67
DOUBLE value 57, 64
downloading data set 19–20
drop_last option 138–139
ds_size variable 85
dtype attribute 107, 109, 150, 155–156
du command 20
dummy variables 295

**E**

echo command 269, 306
EDA (exploratory data analysis) 246
*Elements of Statistical Learning, The* (Hastie) 283
enumeration constraint 53
epochs 134
ETL (extract, transform, and load) 33, 41
exec command 304

**F**

features 283
feature selection 192–198
  availability at inference time 194–196, 203–205
  basing on expert insights 198, 208–210
  case studies 198–199
  DC taxi data set 210–211
  expressed as a number with meaningful scale 207–208
  expressed as number with meaningful scale 197–198
  features with missing values 196–197, 205–207
  relating feature to label 192–194, 199–202
filesystems, object storage vs. 21–22
fingerprints 302
fit method 217, 280
FloatTensor tensor 156
for operator 232
forward method 123, 130–132, 167, 221
forward pass 134
FROM statement 306

**G**

"garbage in, garbage out" 50
get_device_capability method 155
get_dummies method 294–296
__getitem__ method 136–137, 145
Gini impurity 292
Glue data catalog 26–27
GPUs (graphical processing units)
  effect on PyTorch tensor operations 154–159
  scaling up to use 159–161
grad attribute 130–131
gradient accumulation
  all-gather phase 181–187
  gradient descent using out-of-memory data shards 166–169
  overview 163–164
  parameter server approach to 169–170
  preparing sample model and data set 164–166
  reduce-scatter phase 176–181

gradient descent
    DataLoader class for  140–141
    data set batches for  135–136
    Dataset class for  140–141
    ring-based  170–174
    ring-based distributed  174–176
    using out-of-memory data shards  166–169
    with out-of-memory data sets  149–153
GROUP BY clause  40, 69
GROUP BY MOD(CAST(objectid AS INTEGER),
        1000) clause  69

**H**

head command  304
hello-world Docker image  301
hello-world program  301
hparams dictionary  229–230
hparams method  260
hpo enable command  267
HPO (hyperparameter optimization)  229, 245,
        259
    batch normalization hyperparameter
        using Optuna study for  240–242
        visualizing an HPO study in Optuna
            242–244
    categorical hyperparameters  231–233
    log-uniform hyperparameters  230–233
    neural network layers configuration
        233–235
    with Optuna  229–233, 259–272
        enabling MLFlow support  264–265
        training with Kaen AWS provider  269–272
        using for DC Taxi Model in local Kaen
            provider  265–269

**I**

IaaS model, serverless machine learning vs.
        10–11
__init__ method  124, 146, 214–216, 234, 236
init_method parameter  83, 256
init_process_group method  256–257
INTEGER data type  53
interactive querying  39–49
    AWS Athena
        overview  40–42
        using from browser  43–44
    choosing right use case for  39–40
    DC taxi data set  49
    preparing sample data set  42–43
    using sample data set  44–48
interval constraint  53
item method  107–108, 216
Iterable data set  217

IterableDataset class  136, 145–149, 217
iterations  134
__iter__ method  145–146

**J**

json.loads method  235

**K**

Kaen  247
    enabling PyTorch-distributed training
        support with  249–257
    training with Kaen AWS provider
        269–272
    unit testing model training in local
        container  257–259
kaen CLI (command line interface)  249
KAEN_HPO_CLIENT_NAME environment
        variable  265
KAEN_HPO_CLIENT_PREFIX environment
        variable  265
kaen hpo enable operation  271
KAEN_HPO_SERVICE_NAME environment
        variable  263
KAEN_HPO_SERVICE_PREFIX environment
        variable  263
kaen init function  269
kaen job create function  271
kaen job start command  271
kaen job start function  269
KAEN_OSDS environment variable  269
KAEN_RANK variable  256
kaen.torch.init_process_group method  255
KAEN_WORLD_SIZE variable  256
kaiming_uniform_ method  150
K-fold cross-validation  298

**L**

labels  283
lambda: None function  126
layer variable  232
learning rate (lr)  229, 243–244, 260
__len__ method  136–137, 145
Lightning framework. *See* PyTorch Lightning
LightningModule subclass  221, 223
limit_train_batches parameter  217
limit_val_batches parameter  224
Linear layer  235
linear regression  280
LinearRegression class  280–281, 290
linspace method  111–112
list-buckets command  25
Login Succeeded message  258

LogisticRegression classification model 291
log-uniform hyperparameters 230–233
loss (cost/objective function) 284
loss function 134
lr (learning rate) 229, 243–244, 260
ls command 26

## M

machine learning
    classification with structured data sets
        291–297
    overview 277–282
    reasons for using 274–277
    regression with structured data sets 286–290
    training machine learning model 297–299
    with structured data sets 282–286
machine learning pipeline
    enabling PyTorch-distributed training support
        with Kaen 249–257
    hyperparameter optimization with
        Optuna 259–272
        enabling MLFlow support 264–265
        training with Kaen AWS provider 269–272
        using for DC Taxi Model in local Kaen
            provider 265–269
    overview 246–249
    unit testing model training in local Kaen
        container 257–259
machine learning platform
    defined 5
    design challenges 5–7
    public clouds for 7
manual_seed method 110
MapStyleDataset class 136, 217
marginal function 91–92
MASTER_ADDR environment variable 256–257
MASTER_PORT environment variable 256–257
matplotlib library 89
max_batches hyperparameter 217, 229, 231, 260
max_epochs settings 217
max method 85
mean function 131
mean squared error (MSE) 288
min function 224
min(gradient, GRADIENT_NORM) function
    153
mini-batch gradient descent 135
MLFlow support 264–265
model.layers attribute 255
model PyTorch Lightning module 255
model training
    enabling test and reporting for trained
        model 221–222
    enabling validation during 223–227

unit testing model training in local Kaen
    container 257–259
model_v1 package 253
mse.backward() function 134
mse_loss method 221
mse_loss tensor 131
MSE (mean squared error) 288
mtx[0][0].item() function 108
mtx tensor 108
multisets 135

## N

NaN values 85, 196
native Python lists, PyTorch tensors vs.
    116–119
NestedTensor class 108
NestedTensor package 108
neural network layers configuration, as
    hyperparameter 233–235
nginx container 303–304
nginx image 302
nginx webserver 301
ni identifier 171
nn.Module-based model instance 257
nn.Module instances 233
NODES constant 172
NODES segments 174, 176
node_to_gradients dictionary 173
None values 49, 85
non-leaf tensor 130
non-NULL values 60–61, 63
normal method 110–111
Norvig, Peter 6, 283
np.log function 293
nullability 51, 53
NULL values 53, 59–61, 63–64, 66, 75–76,
    85, 196
numeric values 285
num_hidden_layer_0_neurons
    hyperparameter 243
num_hidden_neurons hyperparameter 232
num_layers (hidden layers) 232
num_sanity_val_steps parameter 223

## O

objective function 229, 233, 240, 243–244
objective method 231, 242
object storage
    authenticating with AWS 22–23
    creating serverless object storage bucket
        23–26
    filesystems vs. 21–22
    Washington, DC, taxi rides data set 20–26

ObjectStorageDataset class 145–151, 217
OLS (ordinary least squares) formula 290
one-hot encoding 291–292
ones method 109
one-to-many relationship 40
on_experiment_end method 261
operations, PyTorch tensors 112–115
Optimizer class 132
optimizer hyperparameter 216
optimizer.step() function 134
optimizer.zero_grad() 134
Optuna
    batch normalization hyperparameter
        240–242
    categorical hyperparameters 231–233
    hyperparameter optimization with 229–233,
        259–272
        enabling MLFlow support 264–265
        training with Kaen AWS provider
            269–272
        using for DC Taxi Model in local Kaen
            provider 265–269
    log-uniform hyperparameters 230–233
    visualizing an HPO study in 242–244
ordinary least squares (OLS) formula 290
or keyword 54
out-of-memory data shards, gradient descent
    using 166–169

**P**

PaaS model, serverless machine learning vs.
    10–11
Parameters.classification key 37
parameter server approach to, gradient
    accumulation 169–170
parent run 247
parent_run variable 262
part*.csv objects 147–148
partitions_glob parameter 147
*Pattern Recognition and Machine Learning*
    (Bishop) 283
pin_memory parameter 160
pip package 214
pl.LightningModule class 215
predictions 286
progress_bar_refresh_rate setting 217
–provider aws setting 269
pseudorandom values, PyTorch tensors
    110–112
pt.no_grad(): function 221
pull command 301–302
Pull complete message 302
PyObject_HEAD metadata descriptor 117
PyObjects (Python objects) 117

PySpark
    implementing VACUUM model in 74–79
    using to sample test set 92–100
PyTorch
    autodiff functionality 121–129
        linear regression using PyTorch automatic
            differentiation 129–132
        transitioning to PyTorch optimizers for
            gradient descent 132–135
    converting PyTorch model training to
        PyTorch Lightning 214–219
    data set batches
        DataLoader class for gradient descent
            with 140–141
        Dataset class for gradient descent with
            140–141
        for gradient descent 135–136
        with DataLoader class 136–140
        with Dataset class 136–140
    effect of GPUs on tensor operations
        154–159
    PyTorch-distributed training 249–257
    tensors
        creation operations 108–109
        interval values 110–112
        native Python lists vs. 116–119
        operations and broadcasting 112–115
        overview 104–108
PyTorch Lightning 213–227
    converting PyTorch model training to
        214–219
    enabling test and reporting for trained
        model 221–222
    enabling validation during model training
        223–227

**Q**

quantization 210

**R**

randint method 111
randn method 110, 129–130
$RANDOM environment variable 24
randomSplit method 93
range constraint 53
range operation 172
range operator 111
rank setting 257
ratio variable 158
README prefix 30
READY state 29–30
reduce-scatter phase, gradient accumulation
    176–181

reference data 51
regular expression constraint 54
replace method 75
REPLICAS setting 257
__repr__ method 122–123
requires_grad attribute 131
reverse-mode accumulation automatic
    differentiation 121
ring-based distributed gradient descent
    174–176
ring-based gradient descent 170–174
roles 27
rolling window 139
rule constraint 54
RUNNING state 29

**S**

s3fs library 83
SAMPLE_COUNT environment variable 97
SAMPLE_SIZE environment variable 97
save_stats_metadata function 76, 82
Scalar class 122, 124, 127–128
scaling techniques
    distributed data parallel 163–169
    GPUs
        effect on PyTorch tensor operations
            154–159
        scaling up to use 159–161
    gradient accumulation
        all-gather phase 181–187
        gradient descent using out-of-memory
            data shards 166–169
        overview 163–164
        parameter server approach to
            169–170
        preparing sample model and data
            set 164–166
        reduce-scatter phase 176–181
    gradient descent
        ring-based 170–174
        ring-based distributed gradient descent
            174–176
    gradient descent with out-of-memory data
        sets 149–153
    IterableDataset class 145–149
    ObjectStorageDataset class 145–149
    single node 144–145
schema-on-read approach 39, 41
SDK (Software Development Kit), AWS 22
segments of gradients 174
self.backward() function 126
self.hparams 216
self.log method 216
sem_df.cumsum() function 90

sem_over_range function 89
SEM (standard error of the mean) 88–89
serverless machine learning
    defined 8
    IaaS and PaaS models vs. 10–11
    life cycle 11
    machine learning platform
        defined 5
        design challenges 5–7
        public clouds for 7
    overview 8–10
    scaling techniques
        Faster PyTorch tensor operations with
            GPUs 154–159
        gradient descent with out-of-memory data
            sets 149–153
        IterableDataset class 145–149
        ObjectStorageDataset class 145–149
        Scaling up to use GPU cores 159–161
        single node 144–145
    software engineering approach to 12
    target audience 11–12
    when not to use 13–14
serverless object storage bucket 23–26
set_default_dtype method 150, 155
set_default_tensor_type method 156–157
SGD (stochastic gradient descent) optimizer
    134–135, 246
shape attribute 107
shards 163
shuffle() method 139
single node 13, 144–145
SMEs (subject matter experts) 198
software engineering approach, serverless
    machine learning 12
source utils.sh command 46
spark_df_to_stats_pandas_df function 93
squeeze method 151, 216
squeeze_ method 216
src bucket 147
src S3 bucket 147
standard deviation (sigma) statistics 85
standard error of the mean (SEM) 88–89
stats subquery 64
step of gradient descent 134
stochastic gradient descent 135
stochastic gradient descent (SGD) optimizer
    134–135, 246
stochastic optimization 135
STOPPING state 29
STRING data type 33, 42, 45–47
structured data sets
    classification with 291–297
    overview 282–286
    regression with 286–290

sts:AssumeRole permission  27
studies  260
study.optimize method  242
suggest_categorical function  232
suggest_categorical method  231
suggest_int method  229–230, 260
suggest_loguniform method  230–231
SUM function  40
summary statistics, of cleaned-up data set
    82–85
super().__init__() method  215
supervised machine learning algorithm
    283
survival label  195–196
survived label  196
sync command  25

**T**

t3.large instances  270
t3.micro instances  269–270
tag command  308
TensorDataset class  136–137, 140, 146,
    175
tensor rank  105
tensors, PyTorch
    creation operations  108–109
    effect of GPUs on  154–159
    interval values  110–112
    native Python lists vs.  116–119
    operations and broadcasting  112–115
    overview  104–108
    pseudorandom values  110–112
test_step logging  221
test_step method  221
timeit library  118
TIMESTAMP data type  53–54
torch.autograd automated differentiation
    framework  132
torch.cuda.is_available() method  159
torch.LongTensor class  106
torch.nn.BatchNorm1d class instances  235
torch.nn.init.kaiming_uniform_ method
    150
torch.nn.Linear instances  233, 235
torch.nn.Linear layer  232, 235
torch.nn.Sequential initializer  235
torch.nn.Sequential layers  255
torch.nn.utils.clip_grad_norm_ method
    153
torch.optim.Optimizer method  164
torch.optim package  132, 134–135
torch.optim.SGD optimizer  132, 135
torch.randn method  150
torch.Size class  107

torch.utils.data package  136–137
TPE (Tree-Structured Parzen Estimator)
    228
train_dl instance  137, 141
train_ds data set  137
train_ds instance  140, 147
Trainer instance  221, 223
training data set  283, 286
training_step method  214, 216, 221
train method  249
train_rmse metric  269–270
trial API  229, 232
trial interface  229
trial method  231
trial object  231
trials  229
trials_dataframe method  260
twob tensor  114
type coercion  112
type method  106–107

**U**

unicorns  4
unit testing model training, in local Kaen
    container  257–259
*Unreasonable Effectiveness of Data, The* (Norvig)  6
unzipping data set  19–20
usingdc_taxi_csv_sample_strings table  46

**V**

VACUUM model  52
    accuracy  55–56
    applying to data set  58–74
        cleaning up invalid fare amounts  63–66
        ensuring valid values  59–63
        improving accuracy  66–74
    consistency  56–57
    implementing in PySpark job  74–79
    uniformity  57
    unity  57–58
    valid data  52–55
val_check_interval parameter  224, 227
validation_step method  223

**W**

Washington, DC taxi rides data set. *See* DC taxi
    rides data set
watch command  36
w.grad tensor  167, 169
WITH clause  64
WORKER setting  257
W parameter  290

w parameter  130
wscli_to_df() function  49
WS_DEFAULT_REGION environment
      variable  146
w_src tensor  175
ws s3api create-bucket command  25

## X

xargs command  306
xargs container instance  306
xe_loss function  293

## Y

y_batch tensor  151
y_est classification model output  293
y_est tensor  151
y_pred - y tensor  130

## Z

zero_grad() method  133
zero_grad function  129
zeros factory method  108–109

# Hands-on projects for learning your way

liveProjects are an exciting way to develop your skills that's just like learning on-the-job.

In a Manning liveProject you tackle a real-world IT challenge and work out your own solutions. To make sure you succeed, you'll get 90 days full and unlimited access to a hand-picked list of Manning book and video resources.

Here's how liveProject works:

- **Achievable milestones.** Each project is broken down into steps and sections so you can keep track of your progress.

- **Collaboration and advice.** Work with other liveProject participants through chat, working groups, and peer project reviews.

- **Compare your results.** See how your work shapes up against an expert implementation by the liveProject's creator.

- **Everything you need to succeed.** Datasets and carefully selected learning resources come bundled with every liveProject.

- **Build your portfolio.** All liveProjects teach skills that are in-demand from industry. When you're finished, you'll have the satisfaction that comes with success and a real project to add to your portfolio.

**Explore dozens of data, development, and cloud engineering liveProjects at www.manning.com!**